The Politics of Authenticity
in Presidential Campaigns, 1976–2008

The Politics of Authenticity in Presidential Campaigns, 1976–2008

ERICA J. SEIFERT

McFarland & Company, Inc., Publishers
Jefferson, North Carolina, and London

LIBRARY OF CONGRESS CATALOGUING-IN-PUBLICATION DATA

Seifert, Erica J., 1979–
   The politics of authenticity in presidential campaigns,
1976–2008 / Erica J. Seifert.
      p.   cm.
   Includes bibliographical references and index.

   ISBN 978-0-7864-6996-3
   softcover : acid free paper ∞

   1. Presidents — United States — Election — History.
2. Political campaigns — United States — History.   I. Title.
JK524.S43 2012
324.973'092 — dc23   2012016590

BRITISH LIBRARY CATALOGUING DATA ARE AVAILABLE

On the cover: The official White House photographs of
Jimmy Carter, Ronald Reagan, George H. W. Bush,
Bill Clinton, George W. Bush and Barack Obama.
Front cover design by David Landis (Shake It Loose Graphics)

Manufactured in the United States of America

*McFarland & Company, Inc., Publishers
   Box 611, Jefferson, North Carolina 28640*

Table of Contents

For my parents

Acknowledgments

This book would not have happened without the dedication, humor, patience, and support of many advisors, friends, colleagues, and family.

I am especially grateful to the University of New Hampshire Department of History, which funded this research. UNH gave me far more than fellowships, funding, employment, and the opportunity to spend a few years in my home state. I was fortunate to find a team of unrivaled mentors. Bill Harris, Ellen Fitzpatrick, and Andy Smith weeded through multiple drafts of this book and offered invaluable counsel and cogent criticism. Cynthia Van Zandt and Jeff Bolster made herculean efforts to push me in the right direction. They both failed miserably, but I appreciated their effort, patience, and humor along the way. Lucy Salyer and Kurk Dorsey offered more time, advice, and support than I probably deserved. Kurk and Molly Dorsey gave me unparalleled mentorship, kindness, and friendship. My tenure at UNH would have been lonelier and less successful without them.

A small forest of drafts were edited with the help of many patient, bored, and eagle-eyed readers: Diana Seifert, Gretchen Seifert, Charles Seifert, Nathan Olson, and Aaron Shaw. Luke and Nick Dorsey marked up early drafts in mixed media, mostly crayon. I thank their parents for using red pen and track changes.

I am particularly grateful to Greg Pfitzer and Mary Lynn at Skidmore College. Thanks also to Stan Greenberg and my colleagues at Greenberg Quinlan Rosner for teaching me a great deal about numbers and politics and nothing at all about work–life balance. They are the smartest, sharpest, hardest working people in politics.

I am most grateful to the people who make life interesting: the members of the Wednesday Club, without whom I would have written a joyless tome. I am also grateful to the Nokomis and Skidmore girls for reminding me to get out of my own way.

Finally, I have racked up a substantial debt with those who never let me let myself down. Mum, Mommy, Gretchen, KP, Meg, Charlie, and Nathan spent too many hours listening to me talk about authenticity. My husband, Nathan Olson, makes my life wonderful every day. My father was in my head throughout this process and inspired much of what made it to page. My mother supplied me with wise counsel, editing services, Diet Coke, and so much more.

In the time it took to write this book, the country elected its first black president. The economy crashed. Natural disasters changed the face of the planet. Populist uprisings changed the face of geopolitics. I got a PhD, got married, moved to Washington, became a pollster, and learned to use public transportation. And despite these changes, one thing remained constant. At least once a week my mother still calls to say, "You'll never guess what I heard on NPR. It was all about authenticity." Thanks, Mommy.

Preface

Real America

In August 2008, Americans were introduced to Sarah Palin, John McCain's often hapless (but always charismatic) gun-toting, moose-hunting, flag-waving, snowmobile-riding "rogue" of a running mate. She came to define "authenticity" in g-droppin' vernacular and populist anti-Washington, anti-east, anti-elite rhetoric. "We believe that the best of America is not all in Washington, DC.... We believe that the best of America is in these small towns ... of what I call the *real* America." To Palin, the election was not merely a contest for the presidency, but a great battle between representations of "real America" and its elitist enemies in Boston, New York, San Francisco, and Washington, DC. Whether she was praised for her small-town credentials or mocked for her big-ticket shopping sprees, authenticity provided the framework through which Americans assimilated images of the previously unknown Alaskan governor.

Although she became the most notable "authentic" national candidate, Sarah Palin was only the last in a long line of just-like-you narratives in 2008. Each candidate peddled authenticity at one point or another during the 2008 election cycle. Mike Huckabee gained national legitimacy after a meteoric rise in Iowa on the coattails of a Southern accent and a holy-rolling, family values personal narrative. Hillary Clinton reemerged after a New Hampshire sobfest suddenly humanized and personalized her campaign struggle, which had been deemed "robotic" by her critics. By his own admission, John McCain meant to capitalize on the "straight talk" brand he had created during his 2000 bid for the presidency. When Barack Obama announced his choice for vice president, Joe Biden immediately branded himself as one of us: "Ladies and gentlemen, your kitchen table is like mine. You sit there at night.... You talk about how much you are worried about being able to pay the bills."[1] Biden did not merely look out for the average guy's interests, he *was* the average guy. Although a long-serving senator, Biden emphasized the fact that

1

he had never lived in Washington, packaging himself instead as a blue-collar, working-class kid from Scranton. Where Biden might have highlighted his many legislative accomplishments, he chose instead to share heartwarming stories about hard knocks and kitchen tables. Biden, like Palin, not only attempted to define himself, but also to define himself within the boundaries of "real America."[2]

This brand of authentic campaigning was not unique to the 2008 election cycle. Its symbolic impulse can be located in the founding debates over democracy versus republicanism and in the "Man from Libertyville"–style campaign commercials of the 1950s.[3] However, it would be a mistake to assume that the brand of American authenticity that propelled Sarah Palin in 2008 would have had currency in 1776, 1876, or even 1956. While not new, as the dominant framework in American elections, authenticity is not old either; it is a frame that largely originated in the 1970s.[4] As Kathleen Hall Jamieson and Paul Waldman noted in *The Press Effect*, "Before the latter half of the twentieth century, the question of whether a candidate was 'authentic' was rarely raised."[5] By 2008, it was a dominant theme in political television and print media.

This book illustrates the ways in which this dominant cultural value, authenticity, became central to presidential campaign discourse in the late twentieth century. Beginning in 1976, Americans elected a series of presidents whose campaigns represented evolving standards of authenticity. In reciprocal discourse with the media and their publics, these successful presidential candidates structured their campaigns and images around projecting authenticity. This book is predicated on the assumption that it is worth knowing why.

This is neither a series of presidential biographies nor a definitive history of American presidents; it is not even a comprehensive history of their campaigns. Instead, this is a cultural history of the evolution of authenticity as a unique value in recent American presidential campaign discourse. This book tells eight stories about the ways in which candidates, campaigns, and American voters constructed, evaluated, and promoted authenticity.

The central focus of this book is general election campaigns for president. It does not closely examine campaigns for party nominations because primaries, caucuses, and intra-party elections are very different kinds of contests. Voters in these elections are a highly self-selected group with a subset of motives not conducive to the study: they tend to be party loyalists whose objective is to nominate the most "electable" candidate to represent their party. As a result, primary campaigns attempt to reach entirely different audiences than general election campaigns. Therefore, I cover primary campaigns only to the extent that they became operative during general elections.

While readers will not find detailed timelines examining every major campaign event since 1976, this book is full of rich stories — some well-worn, others previously unexamined. It offers original cultural analysis of political products and close reading of candidate images. This book is not ideological. All along, the intent was to make this book primarily a cultural history. The result is a sometimes fresh and unique history that occasionally caught me off-guard as I wrote it. While I knew that this perspective would present unusual interpretations of well-known events, I was surprised to see what happened when I removed partisanship and ideology from politics — strange parallels between political enemies and competitors began to emerge. For example, I was more than a little amused to learn that the 1980 Reagan campaign took many of its cues from the 1976 Carter campaign. This book is full of these strange anecdotes, held together by even stranger threads.

While this book is neither partisan nor ideological, I certainly am. I am a Democratic political consultant and pollster with a professional stake in the country's election outcomes. However, readers will have a difficult time locating partisan bias in the pages that follow. Indeed, one of the major early criticisms of this book was that I seemed to celebrate, rather than condemn, Ronald Reagan. If you find this book wanting an exegesis on burgeoning inequality during the Reagan years, or a diatribe about a conservative orthodoxy that marginalizes women, labor, minorities, and the poor, you need to read a different book. This book is about politics, not policy. It is about campaigns, not cabinets. Most importantly, it is about presidentiality, not presidents.

Nonetheless, I tried to be cautious in my approach to the material. I am progressive, and, more to the point, this book details a recent history, most of which I witnessed and about which I had (and have) strong opinions. As a result, I have tried to remain true to my sources. What follows (I believe) reflects years of extensive research, not a lifetime of personal judgment.

Methods, Theory and Approach

This book begins with the assumption that authenticity has been the dominant cultural terrain on which modern campaigns are waged. However, until now, new "authentic" patterns in public speech have been intensely examined only by journalists, linguists, sociologists, neuroscientists, and communication scholars. Political scientists and historians have been reluctant to break with existing orthodoxies in order to understand cultural political phenomena that have made public space increasingly more personal and campaign media more intensely focused on "authenticity." As Drew Westen has argued, no five-point plan or well-reasoned position paper can trump a candidate who makes voters think, "This guy's like me."[6]

In recent years, scholars like Drew Westen, Geoffrey Nunberg, and George Lakoff have made headlines (and caused a few headaches) as their work in neurolinguistics and political psychology entered the fringes of political studies. While it is easy enough to dismiss this extra-disciplinary work, it would be a mistake to ignore the very real contributions that linguists, neuroscientists, and political psychologists have made to the study of political history. Neuroscientists and psycholinguists have not reduced the study of political participation to the examination of subliminality and political phraseology. Instead, neuroscientists, political psychologists, and cognitive linguists have created space for historians to study political cultures in new ways, given what we now know about political psychology. However, there is a major lacuna in the current discourse — these new psycholinguistic studies of political participation and engagement exist without cultural textures and historical contexts. Historians of political culture must begin to engage these contributions in order to add that cultural texture and historical context. This book is one attempt to do just that.

Why Candidate Image Matters

In the late 1970s, several political scientists, cognitive psychologists, cultural scholars, and sociologists formed a new field of inquiry, candidate image studies. Although the field of candidate image has grown and developed substantially over the last three decades, it is still loosely organized and underdeveloped. As Arthur Miller, Martin Wattenberg, and Oksana Malanchuk noted in their 1986 study, candidate image is "one of the most important but least understood facets of American politics."[7] Some twenty years later, Kenneth Hacker, one of the leading scholars in the field, noted that "there is a long way to go in order for there to be more theoretical development of the construct of presidential candidate image. We still need theories and models of image formation."[8] Accepting Hacker's challenge, this book is an examination of candidate image through the medium of one relatively unexplored theme in the literature, authenticity. More importantly, by offering historical context, this study brings a disciplinary focus that is absent in the current literature on candidate image.

It is clear to scholars in the field that candidate image plays an important role in American elections. Although party affiliation, ideology, current events, and economic conditions are all important factors in determining vote outcomes, scholars have persuasively argued that candidate image is an essential factor in determining the ways in which voters measure potential election outcomes.[9] Although the field is still emergent and evolving, more than three decades of research have shown that candidate image is an important, if not the most important, variable in understanding American political behavior.

Early work in candidate image attempted to define image in a limited way. The goal was to prove the importance of candidate image in determining election outcomes. In his study of voter defection published in 1969, Richard Boyd discovered that candidate image was an elusive yet important factor in determining voting behavior. Studying three variables in partisan defection over three election cycles, Boyd found that voters' perceptions of candidates were the most frequent cause for party defection.[10] In their seminal work in the field, *Candidates and Their Images*, published in 1976, Dan Nimmo and Robert Savage argued that candidate image was the single most important factor in predicting voting behavior and analyzing election outcomes.[11] Since that pioneering study was published, researchers have examined the influence of candidate image in determining voting behavior and election outcomes and have found that it is at least a major factor, if not the most important factor, in analyzing American elections.[12]

Definitions and Directions

Since those early publications, the field has grown in disciplinary scope and complexity. Taking new research into consideration, recent work has examined the increasing influence of image in candidate elections. In 1995, Kathleen Kendall and Scott Paine noted that "researchers have consistently confirmed that voters are far more interested in candidate characteristics than in party identification or specific issues and are more likely to vote on the basis of the candidate's image."[13] More recently, William L. Benoit and John P. McHale located the growing consequence of image. Not only do a "substantial number of voters indicate that ... personal character" is "the most important determinant of their presidential vote" but also, candidates themselves have increasingly emphasized personal traits in their campaign messages.[14] In a series of election studies, Benoit and McHale found that the largest portion of campaign messages addressed "personal qualities."[15] This assertion should not be taken lightly. If for no other reason than this, we must gain a better understanding of candidate image in order to understand and interpret election year national discourse.

Focusing on developing research models to uncover the variables responsible for constructing candidate image, recent work has both broadened and narrowed the range of questions relevant to the field. Scholars of candidate image have focused their attention across disciplines in order to better understand the cultural, political, and cognitive processes at work in the construction of candidate image. In the 1990s, researchers working on candidate image turned to cognitive psychology to understand the processes through which voters receive, process, and interpret information. This crossover with political psychology resulted in a number of studies about decision making and cognition. In 1995, for example, Kathleen Kendall and Scott Paine argued that candidate choice must be examined as one of many daily choices relevant to voters' lives.[16] In the same year, Dan Nimmo sought to uncover the cognitive processes through which voters perceive candidate images. He argued that voters interpret new speech and action through familiar and known narratives derived from voters' daily lives and previous experiences.[17]

The psychology of decision making has helped researchers to understand the process of image formation. The research in this book is driven by an understanding that image is reciprocally constructed between actors and audience. As far back as 1976, Dan Nimmo and Robert Savage employed psychological models to understand the reciprocal process of image formation. "Candidates formulate and project not only images of themselves and each other but also imagine what voters think of them as office-seekers. Voters construct and project self-images and images of the candidates — the qualities they perceive in each candidate and how they think the candidates" reflect their lives and interests.[18] Taking his cues from Nimmo and Savage, in 1981, Dwight Davis put forward a slightly more modern and only slightly less narcissistic theory on reciprocity in image formation: "Images result from the interaction of candidate messages received by voters and voters' subjective processing of the messages."[19]

Moving away from that overwhelmingly psychological formulation, other recent studies have pushed the scholarship in different directions. In 1992, Allan Louden examined the two-way discourse between candidates and voters, noting that image construction is a reciprocal process. He argued that "image ... is ... an evaluation negotiated and constructed by candidates and voters in a cooperative venture."[20] Other scholars have argued that image is not merely a negotiation between candidates and voters, but a multi-level and protean process of discourse among multiple actors: in other words, image must be understood as a dialogue among candidates, their publics, and influential message mediators (the press). In his 2004 re-evaluation, for example, Alan Louden (with Kristen McAuliffe) argued that candidate image is "an evaluation negotiated and constructed by candidates, voters, and the media in a cooperative venture."[21]

Most important to the field of candidate image today is that it must grow and mature. As it comes of age, the field requires substance. For the most part, scholars in candidate image have devoted their work to endless hand-wringing over theory and definition. This study is one of the first book-length substantive examinations of candidate images; it is the first written from the perspective of a historian. Because the scholarship in candidate image has largely been written without regard for historical contexts, this study fills a major lacuna in the literature.

Note on Sources

In my endeavor to provide depth and texture, the sources I chose vary widely from candidate to candidate and election to election. Nonetheless, readers will find that some kinds sources are emphasized more heavily throughout than others. I was originally trained in the discipline of American Studies where I learned to critically interpret nontraditional cultural texts, including film, popular magazines, and commercial material. The impulse to emphasize audience over author, and popular over elite, is reflected in my selection of sources.[1] Moreover, because I examine the construction of presidentiality and "authenticity" as a reciprocal dialogue between candidates and the voting public, I tend to emphasize those sources that were most widely available and most widely appropriated by the public — these were the speeches, newspaper articles, campaign commercials, and television programs that most broadly shaped and influenced the national discourse during the election seasons. These media not only branded candidates, but also served to create a national conversation about the choices available in the political storefront window.

Throughout the chapters, I give close textual and contextual reading to paid campaign media. Close textual reading of these messages illustrates, first, the dominance of authenticity as a theme, and, second, the ways in which campaigns attempted to frame candidates' authenticities and opponents' inauthenticities. The television spots, speeches, print advertisements, and circulars promoted by campaigns were instructive to voters' opinion formation and to overall campaign narratives.[2] The textual interpretation of these sources is bolstered by information gathered from internal campaign documents, including memoranda and oral history interviews with campaign strategists.

While I do examine internal campaign documents, for the most part these are less relevant than the messages they produced and the ones that voters received. For example, while it is important to know that campaigns intended to showcase candidates' personal lives, it is more essential to understand how voters assimilated those messages and how they felt about the candidates associated with those messages. This is reflected in the selection of sources in which public documents overwhelmingly outweigh the private and internal campaign documents.

Thus sources have not been limited to images created by the campaigns themselves. Equally important to this study was the news media's interpretation of candidate images. Candidates were not merely packaged and sold by campaigns. Journalists mediated candidate images and voters turned to these opinion makers for information and interpretation. Most Americans did not see or hear every stump speech, television advertisement, or debate. Instead, voters saw, read, or heard about these events on the television news, on late night comedy programs, or in popular magazines. Viewers turned to these sources for (albeit often oversimplified) analyses and interpretations of candidates. While voters did not completely absorb the messages they received from the news media (and while media backlash became an increasingly important political message over this period) voters relied on these sources to interpret issues and messages. This second layer of primary sources focuses on messages from both major and minor news sources, and also popular periodical literature and television transcripts. With this in mind, this set of primary sources covers a broad range of media. While the *New York Times, Time* magazine, and the three television networks provided a bulk of information, I give equal billing to satirical caricature on *Saturday Night Live,* widely circulated political cartoons, and stories printed in popular magazines, including *People, Playboy,* and *Rolling Stone.*

In order to emphasize audience response and voting behavior, my source base also includes citizens' responses to narratives constructed by campaigns and the press.[3] While these responses are more difficult to parse, this project includes a breadth of sources that, taken together, give some insight into how candidate images were received and interpreted by citizens. These sources include polling data, focus group transcripts, letters to the editors, and man-on-the-street interviews conducted by a range of media outlets.[4] While there is no specific polling data on which candidate was more "authentic" in any given election cycle, a number of questions, taken together, give some insight into this elusive quality. Focus group transcripts provide a more accurate and robust, if not statistically significant, account of how voters interpreted candidate images. Letters to the editors of media publications have been included, but they have been examined with caution, understanding that individuals who compose such letters are typically a self-selected category of engaged voter. Man-on-the-street interviews conducted for television and print news are not wholly reliable, but do give a glimpse into how voters felt about par-

ticular candidates. To be sure, these sources are not understood to be con-
clusive, nonetheless, they are included because voters tend to repeat words,
phrases, and opinions that are widely circulated in their communities and by
respected sources of authority and influence (e.g., neighbors, religious leaders,
and local broadcasters).

I was also forced to work with the selection of sources currently available.
The campaign documents of sitting presidents are considered to be "personal"
records, and presidential archives are not required to make them available for
public use. For example, the Michael Deaver files for the 1984 campaign (Reagan
Library: OA 9980-OA 13381) are closed to researchers.[5] Similarly, access to the
1980 Carter files, the 1992 Bush files, and the 1996 Clinton campaign files is
limited under this restriction. Equally, non-elected challengers maintain complete control over their own campaign records. While the Bob Dole and Michael
Dukakis archives were generous with both time and resources, non-elected candidates' archives suffer a paucity of records, funding, and information.

The larger discrepancy among available sources, however, is merely a
matter of time. One major difference in sources results from the availability
of records due to FOIA restrictions. For the 1976 through 1988 campaigns,
primary sources from the campaigns themselves were available for my use
through the presidential libraries and individual candidates' archives. For the
1996, 2000, and 2004 elections, and to some extent for the 1992 election,
sources close to the candidates are yet unavailable. The 1992 chapter, "The
Man From Hope," is something of a bridge chapter, resembling the sources
used in both the earlier and later chapters.

Another major difference in the use of sources resulted from the onset
of digital media. The source advantage in the later chapters is obvious. Most
of these digitally archived sources are external to the campaigns themselves —
they include television transcripts, third party political advertisements, and
newspaper articles. Some digitally preserved materials include those produced
by the campaigns — websites, blogs, and campaign commercials.

As we are only now beginning to understand the full impact of electronic
media on political discourse, the final chapter, on 2004, explores the influence
of evolving media. This evolution toward electronic media began in 1996.
Between 1992 and 2008, the American media landscape changed dramatically.
Voters increasingly accessed information from nontraditional sources, largely
Internet-based media.[6] A 2000 Pew Research Center survey found that 9 percent of respondents regularly accessed information about the presidential campaign from the Internet.[7] By 2008, nearly a quarter of respondents reported
learning about presidential candidates primarily from Internet-based sources.[8]
Although the numbers were relatively small in proportion to traditional news

sources, such as evening news programs and Sunday morning talk shows, the shifting source of origin for campaign news, from traditional media to the Internet, had a yet untold impact on American politics.[9] The advent of the Internet fundamentally altered voters' expectations of their political candidates. I turn to this matter in the conclusion. For the most part, however, this is an examination of the evolving construction of presidentiality and American authenticity in the television age. In order to make best use of the available sources, and in order to provide a broad range of approaches for tackling this topic in the future, each chapter emphasizes a different approach to uncovering the role of authenticity in the development of candidate images.

Chapter 1 (on the 1976 campaign) begins by contextualizing authenticity and locating the theme within the historical framework of post-Watergate elections. Jimmy Carter began as a dark horse candidate for his party's nomination. Although he was not the insiders' choice, new rules governing the nomination made his candidacy viable. He traveled all over the country, mounting a grassroots campaign for the nomination — and won. His campaign carried this approach into the general election season, providing voters with a stark contrast between the grassroots peanut-farmer outsider and the president, who was running his campaign from inside the White House. Carter's strategy was so successful that President Ford's campaign eventually adopted a similar approach — bringing the race to a very close finish in the fall of 1976. In this chapter, I analyze internal campaign documents, which illustrate campaign managers' participation in the new culture of authenticity. The chapter also makes heavy use of textual interpretation of campaign media, particularly campaign commercials. These interpretations are contextualized by journalists' firsthand accounts of candidate authenticity. Finally, I analyze polling data to show how voters responded to candidate images in 1976.

Chapter 2 (on the 1980 campaign) details Carter's difficulty campaigning as the establishment. Due to the Iranian hostage crisis, the energy crisis, and intractable stagflation, the Carter team bet on a Rose Garden strategy, to position the president as a strong and in-control leader. By contrast, the challenger, Ronald Reagan, ran as a Washington outsider — a neighbor and a citizen to whom voters could relate. As a result, Carter became symbolic of the mess in Washington, while Reagan was perceived as an authentic outsider. My analysis relies heavily on internal campaign strategy documents. These sources illustrate the ways in which the Reagan and Carter campaigns interpreted their publics' responses to authentic campaign imagery. They provide insight into voters' responses to the candidates (through focus groups and internal polling) and illustrate the ways in which campaign managers responded to voters' demands for increasingly authentic candidate images.

Chapter 3 (on the 1984 campaign) explores how Reagan was able to define his candidacy in terms of American authenticity by combining patriotism, nostalgia, and Main Street values. Unlike Ford in 1976 and Carter in 1980, Reagan was able to invent himself as the anti-Washington establishment candidate, even while serving as the incumbent. By contrast, his opponent, Walter Mondale, was circumscribed by his credentials as a long-serving senator and a Beltway insider. This chapter focuses on textual analysis of campaign media, contextualized by journalists' reactions to (and interpretations of) candidate authenticity.

Chapter 4 illustrates what happens when Americans must choose between two decidedly inauthentic candidates (George H.W. Bush and Michael Dukakis). Although each was perceived as inauthentic for different reasons, neither had a natural claim to authenticity. As a result, 1988 was arguably the most negative campaign in recent history. Nineteen ninety-eight was also the first year in which the political backstage became a consistently front page story. As a result, this chapter focuses on extra-campaign media sources (largely newspapers) to show the extent to which the political backstage (particularly campaign management) entered the public discourse. These sources also illustrate the ways in which journalists helped to construct a national discourse about the available candidate images.

Chapter 5 covers the 1992 election between sitting president George H.W. Bush and his challenger(s), Arkansas governor Bill Clinton and intermittent third party candidate, Texas businessman Ross Perot. Bill Clinton introduced new symbols of authenticity in 1992, centered on comfortable and easy style of dress and diction, southern regional identity, and youth (Clinton was the first babyboomer president). This chapter focuses as much on the media environment as it does on the three candidates. Because this chapter introduces talk shows as a new landscape on which political topics were negotiated, I emphasize textual analysis of these media.

Chapter 6 (on the 1996 campaign) examines the ways in which Bill Clinton, like Reagan before him, was able to cast himself as the outsider, while circumscribing his challenger, another long-serving senator, to the role of Washington establishment candidate. Clinton maintained his easy and casual style while serving in the White House, and was able to remain in touch by appearing on popular television talk shows, by highlighting (and mocking) his low-rent gastronomical exploits, and by using roadside diners, rather than the Rose Garden, as a backdrop for his candidacy. This chapter also emphasizes discourse around the new media; that is, while the 1996 chapter includes textual analysis of talk shows, it contextualizes these interpretations using journalists' and pundits' responses to candidates' attempts to be "real" in new media formats.

Chapter 7, on the 2000 election, takes on the challenge of examining a campaign that resulted in conflicting popular and electoral vote outcomes. Al Gore spent most of the campaign season well ahead in the polls. Absent other factors — the economy was strong, the country was at peace, and the candidate was scandal-free — 2000 was Al Gore's election to lose. And he sort of did. On Election Day, half of the country opted to vote for his authentic opponent, George W. Bush. This chapter is grounded in public opinion polling in large part because the campaigns closely watched the polls throughout the course of the tight election season. In several places, the analysis opens up into textual and contextual interpretation of campaign media in order to explore the ways in which the two campaigns reacted to public opinion polls. Finally this chapter also makes use of nontraditional media (*Saturday Night Live* transcripts, for example) to showcase the ways in which political historians can explore cultural formats to understand political topics.

More than the other chapters, the final chapter (on 2004) examines the role of inauthenticity in voters' evaluations of candidates. While voters had already begun to turn against George Bush's foreign and domestic policies in 2004, a majority balloted for the sitting president. His challenger, John Kerry, was branded a "flip-flopper" during the summer of 2004, and the moniker stuck. Kerry's speeches, biography, advertisements, campaign events, hairstyles, clothes, and vacations were thoroughly scrutinized by the opposing campaign, the media, and new media for inconsistencies. The new viral media turned small missteps into big stories. As a result, this chapter is grounded in interpretation of new media, and in voters' responses to the candidates, which are examined through focus group transcripts and polling.

In every chapter, I use quotes from newspapers, popular magazines, television news programs, and popular television shows in a variety of ways. First, I use these sources to illustrate the extent to which the vocabulary of authenticity framed public discourse about candidate images. Second, these sources provide valuable contemporary information. On the one hand, these stories often reflected the ways in which many Americans interpreted and understood candidate images. On the other hand, these stories also served to inform readers' and viewers' opinions, shaping the ways in which they assimilated candidate images. I have attempted to use these sources carefully, but with the understanding that they offer the best possible insight into the ways in which campaign texts framed national discourse during election years.

Introduction

In January 2008, Democratic primary candidate Hillary Clinton broke down at a café in Portsmouth, New Hampshire. Clinton's emotional moment came in response to a sincere question from an undecided voter: "My question is very personal. How do you do it?" In response, Clinton discussed the challenges of the campaign and, with her voice breaking, explained why she put herself through such a harrowing fight. The media's response was entirely framed by authenticity. Many praised her for finally revealing that there was a human being behind her otherwise steely exterior. Others questioned the authenticity of Clinton's moment. In her *New York Times* column, Maureen Dowd wrote that a reporter in her office jokingly responded,

> "That crying really seemed genuine. I'll bet she spent hours thinking about it beforehand."[1]

Authenticity is an evasive, nuanced, and complicated political brand. Candidates alone do not set the terms on which their images are negotiated; their awkward attempts to be "just plain folk" are not passively absorbed by viewers and voters, who are equal participants in establishing a candidate's authenticity. Instead, audiences interrogate the sincerity and quality of images, rejecting Faux Joes as inauthentic political fabrications.

There is no single operative authenticity in American politics. Since 1976, three distinct authenticities have defined the "real" in candidate image making — personal authenticity, American authenticity, and human authenticity. First, personal sincerity, the kind of authenticity defined by Heidegger, Trilling, and more recent scholars like Charles Lindholm and Miles Orvell, reflect the importance of a candidate's ability to remain true to his genuine self. Second, Americans value candidates who reflect "American" authenticity — the stuff of traditional narrative and American mythotype. Finally, Americans value emotional authenticity — the stuff that makes politicians appear almost human.

Personal Authenticity

In an age of Tele PrompTed made-for-TV candidates, it is not surprising that voters search for sincerity in their candidates for president. As a result, they privilege candidates who seem to be true to their real selves. These are candidates who do not appear to act according to a consultant's campaign plan, reading from an expertly scripted speech. Voters search for the spaces between the script — often in a candidate's nonverbal expression — that allow them to see "inside" candidates' characters.

Honesty and consistency are essential expressions of personal authenticity. While honesty was always valued in electoral politics, the relative premium on this value evolved in the late twentieth century. As Kathleen Hall Jamieson noted of the 2000 campaign, "Reporters and citizens were willing to entertain the possibility that a high I.Q. and experience were not necessary qualities in a president, but no one was willing to suggest it was acceptable to be less than totally trustworthy and honest."[2]

Voters know and understand that candidates often switch positions in order to win votes. Voters prefer candidates who express deeply held beliefs, rather than those who change with the whims of political circumstance. In evaluating a candidate's authenticity, voters look to a candidate's consistency in appearance, ability to maintain dialectical integrity, and remain true to original positions on issues. These qualities are not mere appurtenances for presidential candidates — this kind of authenticity is a powerful predictor of vote outcomes.[3]

As neuroscientist Drew Westen has shown, "The first two questions voters ask in every election are, 'Does this person embody my values?' and 'Is this person genuine, trustworthy, and enough like me that I can feel comfortable with him or her as my representative?'"[4] This should not suggest that voters are somehow duped by campaigns. Because campaign promises tend to be poor indicators of a candidate's future performance, voters search for deeply held values in order to predict how a candidate will perform once in office.

American Authenticity

Despite the obvious importance of authenticity as a matter of personal sincerity, this narrow definition falls short of its linguistic and cultural evolution. We run into trouble, for example, trying to explain the success of authentic candidate folk heroes like Ronald Reagan and Bill Clinton. Indisputably authentic in their own ways, an actor and an accused liar nonetheless fail to meet a narrowly constructed definition of authenticity. If for no other reason than these giants, the definition of authenticity requires expansion.

To be sure, voters search for candidates who are comfortable in themselves — who are honest, sincere, believable, and truthful. However, voters also privilege candidates who are both personally authentic and also authentically *American* — candidates who embody the American traditions and myths with which voters are already familiar. In the same way that an ethnic restaurant or foreign costume can be praised for authentically representing a particular locale, American authenticity is based on a national understanding of what it means to be American.[5] Americans want the president to embody their deeply embedded ideas about American identity and tradition. As Richard Joslyn found, "As candidates project emotional images and attempt to construct symbolic connections with voters, 'cultural icons and values' become more important to voter preferences 'than ... an appreciation of policy alternatives.'"[6]

The obvious public preference for American authenticity is at least partially derived from a psychological proclivity for comfortable and known narratives. In large part, however, it is also driven by the media and by campaigns themselves. In order to simplify images into easily condensed, easily understood tropes, journalists and television hosts rely on mythotypes and American symbols in order to establish boxed narratives for candidates.

This broad definition, however, is complicated by the fact that different Americans understand "America" differently. Recently, authenticity has been defined in regional ways — New England has become symbolic of an un-American, over-educated effete liberal elite. Those with ties to the South and Midwest, by contrast, have an automatic purchase on Sarah Palin's "Real America." Authenticity has also been defined racially, as when African Americans identified with Barack Obama, or when Toni Morrison claimed Bill Clinton as one of her own: "Clinton displays almost every trope of blackness: single-parent household, born poor, working-class, saxophone-playing, McDonald's-and-junk-food-loving boy from Arkansas."[7]

Similarly, for strong partisans, American authenticity might include a candidate's party identification, particularly if he or she lives in an area dominated by a single political party.[8] Because American authenticity is so particularized, candidates must embody a range of values, traditions, and mythotypes depending on the publics to whom they were speaking, thus creating a tug-of-war between competing local, regional, and ethnic ideas about Americanness.

Human Authenticity

One of the ways in which successful candidates negotiate these competing demands is by connecting personally and emotionally to voters as human beings. A candidate can narrate an honest story line, but if it is not a narrative that voters understand — if it is not a story to which voters can relate — it is not authentic. In assessing a candidate's authenticity, therefore, voters look for candidates who are personally revealing, preferring the candidate who is unchanged by money, power, education, or status. Most often this results in a clear preference for the candidate who most reminds voters of themselves.[9] As Christopher Lehmann-Haupt observed in 1977, "Public life and its figures only interest us to the extent that they reflect our private selves. We are tyrannized by our quest for intimacy."[10]

There is an important political-psychological reason for the dominance of human authenticity in recent campaign communication. Researchers have found that when voters connect emotionally to candidates, they perceive that their preferred candidates' politics align with their own. Thus emotional and human connections are integral to garnering popular support. In modern campaigning, "what matters most is that isolated individuals sense that a candidate understands" them. To that end, the best campaigns understand that nothing is more "important than the psychological experience of fragmented individuals feeling somehow connected on a daily basis to a highly personalized (if distant) political figure."[11]

Voters, however, do not blindly purchase stories to which they can relate. In order to believably connect with voters, candidates must convey a set of human emotions that are common to ordinary voters. Most people do not live in a White House or make decisions according to a five- or ten-point plan. In order to reach voters, candidates must be personable and self-disclosive. Indeed, personal narratives and images are so potent that "candidates known personally ... come to appear more attractive than candidates" who have not connected with voters on a personal or emotional level.[12]

Inauthenticity

To be clear, authenticity is not just about saying the right things. Words and gestures must appear natural and sincere in order to have a positive effect. Voters are not passive spectators. When candidates project images and repeat the same stump speech ad nauseam, voters interrogate that information: Does this image seem true to me? Does it conflict with existing images of this candidate? Does this message conflict with what I already believe about this candidate?

Inauthenticity is as potent as authenticity and has been the source of the most cringe-inducing moments in recent American politics. The chapters that follow offer examples aplenty. For now, I offer only three examples for illustration, in chronologically descending order. In an attempt to display his American authenticity at a particularly patriotically charged moment in 2004, John Kerry arrived on stage at the Democratic National Convention in Boston and announced, "I'm John Kerry and I'm reporting for duty!" The script was right. Kerry was a bona fide Vietnam War hero running against a draft-dodging wartime president. However, as Kerry stood up on stage and delivered his opening punch, the line seemed so scripted, stilted, stiff, and pandering that it had the opposite of its intended effect. Kerry not only undermined the American authenticity he was reaching for, but killed further attempts at displaying his human and personal authenticity.

Sixteen years earlier, another Democrat from Massachusetts made a different attempt to portray his American authenticity. In 1988, Michael Dukakis, who had been accused of being soft on defense, visited a defense contractor plant in Michigan to bolster his commander in chief image. Cameramen followed him outside to get footage of the Democrat riding in an M1Abrams tank, manufactured at the plant. In the resulting video footage, Dukakis appeared to be a faux GI Joe, riding around in circles and waving to the distance like a small child on an amusement park ride. The image was so damaging that his opponent, George H.W. Bush, used it in his own campaign ads.

Twelve years prior, while attempting to prove his human and American authenticity to Hispanic voters in Texas, Gerald Ford made a famously misguided attempt to eat an un-shucked tamale. Anyone who has eaten a tamale would have known to shuck it. And to those tamale-eating voters, "he betrayed an unfamiliarity with their food which suggested a lack of familiarity with their whole culture ... assuming that personal familiarity with a culture and the acceptability of a candidate's policies to a group were linked."[13] That he tried was not the problem — that he tried to fake it was. Each of these anecdotes shows that, while it is essential for candidates to connect personally and culturally to constituents, their ability to do so successfully also depends on their ability to do so authentically.

The Real Thing

These brands of authenticity have not always been so constitutive to American campaign politics, or even to American culture. The latter predates the former, but even in American culture, authenticity is a relatively recent obsession.

Of the countless theories, ideas, and priorities kindled by babyboomer radicals in the 1960s, perhaps the most influential and enduring was their renewed emphasis on the value of authenticity. Authenticity remained at the periphery of American thought through much of the 20th century. It was only as post-war babyboomers came of age that authenticity "became a widespread preoccupation."[14]

According to historian Doug Rossinow, the New Left vanguard of the 1960s was on a quest to become "less inhuman humans."[15] Feelings of alienation and cultural bankruptcy were widespread among young people who felt estranged "from their own real selves."[16] Inspired by C. Wright Mills and others, members of the New Left began to formulate a critique of post-war American values, which they believed had deprived them of genuine feelings, personal introspection, and meaningful participation in both public and private life. Their quest for authenticity was driven by an impulse to mitigate the ennui of affluence that had created interpersonal alienation, suburban sameness, and estrangement from selfhood. To be sure, Rossinow's subjects (members of the New Left at the University of Texas) were not representative of the country at large. Nonetheless, the theories of social alienation fomented in radical groups in the 1960s came to define broader evaluations of American life.

As New Left movements imploded in the late 1960s and early 1970s, creating offshoots, sub-groups, and counter-movements, the underlying value of authenticity was not only carried forth, but also honed and focused. It was constitutive to the sociopolitical critique that emerged on both the left and the right in the 1970s — particularly among radical feminists and black nationalists. "The ... challenge was to find one's authentic self rather than to ... slavishly bow to social conventions. In a sense the individual became the site of political activity in the '60s. In the black movement, the task was to discover the black inside the negro, and in the women's movement this took the form of challenging" social and political norms that had been established by, and enforced to maintain, white male dominance.[19]

The dialectic of authenticity was central to black nationalist groups in the late 1960s and early 1970s. Black nationalism promoted authenticity to the point where "'Black authenticity' ... became the hallmark of Black Power-era cultural expression."[20] Leaders emphasized a "lower-class urban vernacular culture as the expression of 'authentic' Blackness" but also African cultures and "back to Africa" blackness.[21] But black authenticity in the 1970s was not purely cultural. Its political impulses were also rooted in authenticity, insofar as adherents believed integrationist efforts were not only dangerous but also contrived. In more mainstream ways, this black nationalist critique was expressed through the revival of ethnic nationalism, the emphasis on roots quests and genealogy, and the development of regional heritage societies.

Radical feminists also participated in the dialectic of authenticity in the late 1960s and early 1970s, and probably did more to both promote and redefine authenticity than any other single group. Radical feminists were on their own quest for authenticity as they sought to re-draw the terrain of public space and create more intimate forms of public engagement. Breaking down the artifice of male-dominated power structures and modes of social interaction, these feminists did not achieve all of their goals, but they did collapse the boundaries between public and private space — they made the personal political, but more importantly for the purposes of this book, they made the political much more personal.

In the the 1970s, authenticity gained currency beyond the New Left. Twentieth-century historian Bruce Schulman argued that in the 1970s "the search for authenticity ... [became] detached from the radical politics of the 1960s" and "Americans' obsession with self-exploration" became a national phenomenon, engrossing old and young, rich and poor, black and white.[17] As the quest for authenticity became mainstream, many Americans began to think more introspectively about themselves and more seriously about "getting real." As Rossinow argued, the "search for authenticity ... acquired a popular basis ... appear[ing] among much broader strata of American society and [leading] to a widespread yearning for authenticity."[18]

The renewed value of authenticity gained widespread traction and currency in the 1970s because of the experiences, events, and ideas that defined that moment in history. As Bruce Schulman and others have argued, the 1970s marked a great turning point in American politics, culture, and society. This has been well documented elsewhere, and for our purposes here, the important outcomes of these social, political, and cultural changes was the expectation that public life would become more personal, that speech patterns would become less formal and artificial, that the structures of public debate would be re-shaped to upend the traditional relationship between authority and audience, and that political discourse would reflect the growing currency of authenticity.

The renewed value of authenticity in the 1970s became apparent in many ways: in the currency of psychoanalysis, the movies of Francis Ford Coppola and Woody Allen, and in *People,* which debuted in 1974 to fulfill *Time* magazine readers' new demand for stories about individuals rather than current events.[22] There was also an introspective, naval-gazing side to the quest for authenticity in the 1970s. As Tom Wolfe chided in his 1976 essay, or "The Me Decade and the Third Great Awakening," in the 1970s, Americans' "analysis of the self" and others "was unceasing." Through hours of self-scrutiny Americans attempted to "strip away all the shams and excess baggage of society ... in order to find the Real Me."[23]

By 1976, what had emerged was a country more deeply "in touch" with its "real" self, and more determined to break down and mock artifice. As the debut of *People* shows, Americans in the 1970s were not content to deal on the surface, but rather more determined to dig beneath in order to locate the authentic. In its first issue, *People*'s editors wrote, "As we say, we will concentrate on individuals rather than issues, on the force of personality, on what's happening to human beings and how those human beings react.... Our attitude toward our subjects is amiable and perhaps a little skeptical.... This attitude, we think, is peculiarly American.... We aim to be the indispensable guide to those millions of aware Americans who cheerfully acknowledge that what interests them most is other people." To that end, *People*'s editors informed its readers that their goal was "to peer into" people's "lives" and ask "Who is this person?"[24]

The Revolution Will Be Televised

Television deserves a special section — indeed a separate book — in the larger conversation about authenticity in post-1960s American politics. The television was not an invention of the 1970s, but it was essential to spawning an age of authenticity in that decade. By 1954, half of all American households owned a television set. Thus, the majority of young adults in the 1970s had been raised in a new age of televisual authority. This shaped the ways in which they understood themselves and one another, their cultural products, and their political representatives.

The paradox of television was that it created mediated realities divorced from the immediate exigencies of authenticity. Television simultaneously presented images that could be seen (and therefore authenticated) and images that were manufactured, produced, and skillfully edited to achieve intended responses from targeted audiences. Although televised sounds and images were reproduced, television also created live format viewership and fabricated an atmosphere of viewer choice. Thus viewers' relationships with television altered and complicated their conceptions of real and fake, mediated and immediate, authentic and inauthentic.

As a political tool, the television evolved dramatically since Harry Truman first employed the medium, since Dwight Eisenhower introduced the short-form spot advertisement, since Kennedy bested Nixon in the 1960 presidential debates, and even since Lyndon Johnson gained free exposure for his controversial "Daisy Girl" advertisement. By 1976, the campaign season in which this study begins, upwards of 97 percent of U.S. households owned at least one television set.[25] Importantly, 1976 was also the first cycle in which there was a decline in newspaper consumption aligned with positive percentage growth in television ownership.[26] Thus, although television played an important role in campaigns dating back to 1952, by 1976 it had become *the* accepted medium for American political participation.[27]

Television complicated citizens' relationships to their politicians. Television simultaneously distanced candidates from, and brought them closer to, their constituents. As a result of television, public figures regularly appeared in viewers' most private spaces — their living rooms, bedrooms, and dens. Voters did not need to see them in person, shake their hands, and make first-hand measure of them in order to believe they understood them. Campaign professionals, pundits, and political observers all noted this transformation as it happened. In his witness to the 1984 campaign, Jonathan Moore noted, "When a shift occurred from voting based more on party affiliation to voting based more on the personal qualities of individual candidates, it was aided and abetted by the culture of television."[28]

As television came of age, it produced increasingly personalized and individualized forums for public discourse. Even if the Walter Cronkites of TV news did not disappear as television matured, such austere and authoritative voices were required to compete in the marketplace with other kinds of questioners and other kinds of legitimate questions. In the late television age, talk show hosts, ordinary citizens, and soft news interviewers participated in analyzing and mediating candidate images for viewers at home. Their modes of inquiry transformed requisite standards of self-representation in public life. Take, for example, a typical framing question from the interviewer, Barbara Walters, in 1996: "Who are these two men? What people and events shaped their thinking and even now inspire the decisions that will ultimately affect you?"[29] This was not Cronkite.

Even as interviewers like Barbara Walters delved into probing personal questions, the medium, and voters' relationships to it, remained complicated. As much as viewers interrogated the images presented to them, they also probed the image-making function of television itself. Americans' relationships to television became even more complex as the medium came of age. Television required particular lighting and makeup and color schemes in order to convey images — in some ways viewers came to understand it as a purveyor of inauthenticity. In other ways, however, people came to trust their own ability to cut through the stagecraft of TV. As Jonathan Moore noted, despite the fact that television required "scripts, props, makeup, special effects, and acting ... over time" television "allows little hiding; the essence and the character of the person is liable to get through."[30] Transformations in television format also made this possible. As television came of age, it became more interactive, allowing viewers to at least *believe* that they were witnessing the *real thing*.[31] These transformations — from call-in programs to talk shows — democratized political television and broadened the range of legitimate participants.

Roderick Hart and others have argued that television transformed citizenship from an exercise in thinking to an occupation of feeling. In the television age, voters and thinkers became viewers and feelers. Voters came to expect that they would understand candidates intimately and psychologically. As a result, voters expected to have feelings (rather than mere thoughts) about candidates. As Hart argued, this meant that candidates had to express themselves in new and more intimate ways in order to pass the primary threshold for electability. Hart argued, "Important rewards now go to emotionally confident people like [Bill] Clinton, people who seem vulnerable even as they seem powerful. Like Ronald Reagan before him, Mr. Clinton proved that television's power lies not in the *number* of people it reaches but in the *depth* with which it reaches them. When Bill Clinton felt your pain, you felt him feel it."[32]

The trade-off, of course, was that the boundaries between public and private space became mutable and often indistinguishable. Joanne Meyrowitz has argued that television changed politics because it "decreas[ed] the distance between the politician and the voter."[33] As a result of television, the old style of campaigning, which required a candidate to be "an imposing physical presence ... or an accomplished orator" became increasingly unpalatable. As intimacy replaced austerity, it became "imperative to know how to" express oneself across "the more intimate medium of television."[34] In her study of television and speech patterns, Kathleen Hall Jamieson found that "the intimate medium of television requires that those who speak comfortably through it project a sense of private self, unself-consciously self-disclose, and engage the audience.... Once condemned as a liability, the ability to comfortably express feelings is an asset on television."[35]

The line between public and private was redrawn — if not blurred — as a result of television. As public space became increasingly personal, personal space became increasingly public. "For much of the twentieth century, most Americans only saw their presidents as presidents, performing executive functions and acting presidential. There was a zone of privacy surrounding presidents and their families, adding to the aura of executive control and imperiousness."[36]

By contrast, "as more and more private and personal information about presidents [became] public, citizens [we]re able to see these individuals as men with flaws and problems painfully similar to their own."[37] Voters "expect[ed] to see their candidates in increasingly intimate contexts." In order to adapt to these expectations, "the politician" had to "willingly accommodate an audience of voters accustomed to a televisual diet of intimacy and personal display."[38] As a result, our definitions of "presidentiality" necessarily changed, making the standard benchmark for presidential images more familiar and vernacular. Thus, rather than a "presidential" figure appearing formal, aloof, lofty, and majestic, presidentiality was re-constructed as more personal, open, and vulnerable.[39]

The transition to confessional, sentimental, and intimate forms of communication happened as television came of age. Until the mid-1970s, televised politics was still a matter of trial and error.[40] But "Beginning with ... Jimmy Carter, presidential politics ... turned confessional."[41] Politicians could no longer hide behind the artifice of official austerity. Instead, "because the mass media are fixated on differences between the private and public self of public figures, a comfort with expressing rather than camouflaging self, or at the minimum an ability to feign disclosure, is useful for a politician."[42] In sum, since 1976, voters have become increasingly preconditioned "to consider and use various personality traits in their evaluations of the candidates."[43]

I Am Not a Crook

In the 1970s, Americans became aware of what had once been the closed and secret world of elite politics. Voters could now witness the often unseemly and undemocratic processes through which their country was governed. This was evident in the televised experience of the 1968 Democratic National Convention in Chicago. As protesters battled police on the streets of Chicago, inside the convention hall, party leaders anointed one of their own, Hubert Humphrey. Humphrey had served as vice president under outgoing president Lyndon Johnson. He maintained the support of many party bosses. His challenger, Eugene McCarthy, had garnered a great deal of popular support at the grassroots, but had not won the favor of the state and national party leaders who oversaw the nomination process. To his supporters, it appeared as though his nomination had been hijacked by operatives in smoke-filled backrooms. Entering the general election, the Democratic Party was torn apart by the Vietnam War, the status of race relations, and a nominating process that was closed, elite, and undemocratic.

Following the election, the Commission on Party Structure and Delegate

Selection (the McGovern-Fraser Commission) was established to recommend reforms to the nomination process. The commission advised the party to reallocate delegate power within the party, requiring states to adopt democratic delegate selection processes, and recommending that the national party adopt new rules to make candidate selection more representative.[44]

The result was a transformation in the party's power structure, shifting influence from party bosses to party members. Prior to 1968, few states held primary elections. Among the states that did hold presidential preference primaries, the function was merely "advisory" to the state delegation. Following the McGovern-Fraser Commission Report, states began adopting alternative modes for designating presidential preference. Although the commission had not mandated that states hold primaries, binding party primaries seemed to be the most democratic means of awarding delegates. Between 1968 and 1980, the number of states selecting delegates through primaries increased from seventeen to twenty-eight. The number continued to increase after 1980, to a system that is now dominated by binding primaries.[45]

The new nominating system created the potential for outsider candidates to claim party leadership. As scholars of the transition found, "The shift to primaries gave party outsiders an unprecedented chance to run and win."[46] The culmination came when the Democratic Party nominated an unknown outsider who had based his nomination bid almost solely on winning support at the grassroots. Jimmy Carter's nomination in 1976 would have been impossible in a previous election year.[47]

Thus, Jimmy Carter emerged at a time of great transition. The structural, procedural, and cultural upheaval that made Carter's nomination possible, however, resulted from more than McGovern-Fraser Commission recommendations. The election of 1976 marked a great turning point because it was also the first post-Watergate presidential election. The publicity of the crime and its aftermath had lasting structural, cultural, psychological, and political impacts on American voters.[48]

Structurally, the post-Watergate election reforms changed the process and power balance of American elections. Campaign contributions and corruption became the new focus of reform, further changing the influence of moneyed fat-cat influence-peddlers and cigar-smoking party bosses. In 1974, the Federal Election Campaign Act of 1971 was amended to require limits on campaign contributions, limits on overall campaign expenditures, and to establish a new independent oversight agency, the Federal Election Commission, to enforce the regulations.[49]

As Kenneth Hacker noted, these reforms made individual candidates more important than political parties. Post-Watergate elections were increasingly candidate centered, with voters choosing between personalities and images, rather than parties and ideologies. "With the declining importance of political parties ... candidate images have become more important in presidential elections. Candidate-centered presidential campaigns entail less potent roles for political parties and greater needs for candidates to [personally] appeal to voters."[50]

Watergate also exposed the backstage of political campaigns. As the story of Watergate began to unfold, Americans learned about political machinations required of modern campaigning. Exposure to the extraordinarily dirty tricks unique to Nixon's campaign operations made Americans savvier and more cynical in general. Although they could not eliminate the smoke and mirrors and deceitful charade, they demanded access to and knowledge about the processes of campaigning.

This created a broad craving for "authenticity" as the stagecraft of politics became apparent. Thus began the postmodern campaign about the campaign — if voters could not always distinguish between real and fabricated, they could at least demand access to the process. In order to negotiate increasingly complex realities, voters demanded to know everything about the campaigns themselves — campaign managers became celebrities, the horserace became news, and campaign tactics became a legitimate topic for debate and discussion. Once hidden and secret, campaign managers, pollsters, and speechwriters became public figures. By 1976, these once anonymous operatives were expected to make themselves available to the press and the public. As Gil Troy noted in *See How They Ran*, "Franklin Roosevelt smuggled experts, including ghost-writers, into the White House." By the time Ronald Reagan was president, such advisors were "openly embraced.... Ghost-writers like Peggy Noonan ... achieved celebrity as 'speech writers.'"[51]

As a result of these changes, the lines between audience and producer, creator and receiver, were inverted. Voters not only interrogated the candidates, but also reconstituted their relationships to campaign messages. Prior to the 1976 election, voters were more likely to accept or reject campaign slogans and images, "largely view[ing] campaigns from the outside in."[52] By contrast, in the post-Watergate, postmodern, hyperreal election, "images show us the inside out version of the campaign experience ... as viewers are taken into the intimate, backstage regions of politics, they are ... invited to believe that what they see is the reality of the political experience. These viewers find themselves watching political actors in previously private sites ... they are asked to suppose that the ... events they witness are authentic."[53] In order to evaluate candidates in a world where "real" and "mediated" were often indistinguishable, voters demanded not only increased access to candidates, but also access to the candidate-making process itself.

Americans' wariness of politicians and widespread cynicism about politics engendered other transformations in their expectations of campaigns and candidates. Voters demanded, and the press delivered, increased access to politicians' whole lives. Perhaps to protect against electing another crook, personal information about politicians became a matter of public access. Because voters were now more interested in a candidate's character than his qualifications, every aspect of a candidate's life became relevant to his fitness for office. Therefore, Americans' expectations about the kinds of access — what information and standards of communication were permissible, acceptable, and requisite — fundamentally changed. "Contemporary politicians, particularly presidential candidates, have their personae and performances scrutinized to an extraordinary degree."[54] As personal information proliferated, the forums for public discourse changed as well. Talk shows and personal interest stories put candidates on the couch, making psychological assessment an expected part of political campaigns. In political journalism, "campaign reporters have become amateur psychologists, probing the candidates ... trying to discover the 'real' person."[55]

The impact of these events — psychological, structural, cultural, and political — made the age of authenticity not only possible but also necessary. People no longer cared merely about what candidates believed, but also *why* they believed it and *where* those beliefs came from.

Don't Trust Anyone Over Forty

In the 1970s, the culture of authenticity became evident in new patterns of public engagement as Americans renegotiated the terms of political participation. In general, they became less likely to affiliate with political parties, more likely to evaluate candidates on the basis of personal qualities, and unwilling to separate themselves personally, emotionally, and culturally from their political choices.[56] Americans redefined political knowledge and political awareness, creating a unique interchange between civic participation, personal representation, and popular culture.

In order to navigate the complicated terrain of authentic and inauthentic, real and imitative, natural and manufactured, Americans began to rely on emotional judgments more often than at any time in the past. New patterns of emotive decision making in the late twentieth century have forced political scientists, neuroscientists, pollsters, and cognitive linguists to reconsider models of political behavior. To voters in the late twentieth century, trust came from feelings — operatively "gut feeling[s]."[57] As Charles Lindholm argued, "The dominant trope for personal authenticity in modern America is emotivism — the notion that feeling is the most potent and real aspect of the self."[58] In public life, this transformed voting patterns and preferences. The turn to emotive or expressive choice allowed some voters to ameliorate, mitigate, and negotiate the harsh realities of political life in post-Vietnam, post-Watergate America.

Expressive Choice

In his 1994 study of voting behavior, *The Reasoning Voter,* Samuel Popkin examined a broad range of cognitive behaviors involved in candidate selection. Evaluating recent trends in voting behavior, Popkin discovered that, for the most part, most Americans assimilated political information using a process of low-information rationality, which favored emotional stimuli over factual information.[59] Despite the fact that information was increasingly available and accessible, the majority of voters did not make judgments and decisions about candidates based on issue-specific information. Instead, voters relied on cultural cues and symbols when selecting candidates.[60]

Economizing consumption in the political marketplace, voters tended to value different sets of information differently. Popkin found that the most valuable, lasting, influential, and potent information disseminated in campaigns was personal information about candidates. In examining political psychology, Popkin found that individuals gave heavier weight to personal information because it was the most available, most stimulating, and easiest to understand. "Small amounts of ... personal information can dominate large amounts of ... impersonal information, permitting hitherto unknown candidates to surge ahead of better known candidates."[61] This bifurcation of priorities in voters' decision-making process was therefore essential to understanding why voters preferred particular candidates.

The preference for personal information, however, was not merely a product of American laziness. Instead, personal information contained within it multiple clues to assessing a candidate's authenticity. "Ultimately ... individuals reference their own experience, much of which is gained interpersonally, to understand political candidates ... individuals look at a candidate and wonder what sort of person he or she is."[62] In this way, American voters' premium on personal details about candidates should not be reduced to mere fluff and icing. Voters gauge a candidate's authenticity and sincerity as a tool for predicting the unknowable — his future performance in office. Thus a voter's attempt to measure a candidate's authenticity is a means of placing an informed wager on the country's political future. As Popkin argued, "We care more about sincerity and character when we are uncertain about what someone will do."[63] As voters can not predict the future behavior of any political candidate, they rely on easily absorbed social cues to make reasoned choices.

Thus, voters care about candidates' personal lives because they want to understand whether office-seekers share their values, and because it is the best way to "estimate public morality and character from private morality and character, assuming in the absence of better information that candidates treat their constituents like they treat their own spouses and children."[64] Therefore, a candidate's ability to relate to an audience "is not ... the best test of a candidate's policy stands.... But neither is it merely symbolism, devoid of content and without meaning for the political process.... A president who understands and is familiar with" the foodways, habits, and patois of particular groups of voters "is more likely to understand" their "sensibilities and the ways that presidential behavior affects them than one who doesn't even know how to cope with their foods."[65] In this way, when voters vet candidates on the basis of authenticity, they make choices that are simultaneously emotional and rational. "When a candidate is in some sense a neighbor, the voter at least has a better chance of knowing whether he or she is a blatant crook or an obvious fool."[66]

To a large extent, using emotional and personal information to evaluate candidates, voters in late-twentieth century elections redefined political knowledge. Moving forward from Popkin, part of the difficulty has been in measuring voters' emotional evaluations of candidates and their absorption of personal details about candidates. This new political information is more likely to appear in *People* and on *Oprah* than in *Newsweek* and on *Meet the Press*. Using a variety of interdisciplinary methods and approaches, scholars of voting behavior have just begun to fully understand the nature of new political knowledge.

Campaigning in the Early Television Age, 1952–1972

The chronological framework of this study should not suggest that campaigning was devoid of authentic images prior to 1976. Indeed, as multiple studies have shown, one of the oldest and most dominant political campaign themes was the Log Cabin myth; later came the Algeristic rags-to-riches American story, which became central to portrayals of a uniquely American brand of "authenticity." Nonetheless, the historian observes a sharp distinction in the ways in which authenticity is currently employed and the ways in which it was deployed in earlier eras. Prior to 1976, such myths were most frequently used to prove a candidate's extraordinariness of character, rather than his ordinariness of circumstances, as is the case today.

That is, there was a certain American heroism attached to the men who could rise from hardship. Prior to 1976, few candidates offered their "just plain folk" sensibility as a major credential for election. I cannot delve into every campaign from 1796 through 1972, however, a brief history of campaigning in the early television age might provide a useful prelude to the chapters that follow. This brief history is not comprehensive; it is offered as a comparative framework through which the following chapters may be better understood. As a result, it emphasizes only those television media through which a baseline may be established for understanding authenticity in the chapters that follow.

In the early television age, from 1952 to 1972, candidates used the medium to demonstrate their political, but not always personal, credentials. For the most part, campaigning on television prior to 1976 required candidates to demonstrate expertise and experience. Even as candidates showcased personality and charisma, these were offered in service to more dominant messages about leadership and policy. In the television age, campaigning became increasingly visual, and candidates often offered familiar images to audiences and voters. Prior to 1976, however, such familiar images were relatively sparse as political professionals adapted to new texts and formats and learned to use the medium to its best advantage. At times television made politicians more austere and more reserved, as broadcast images provided a means of communicating authority. There were, nonetheless, multiple examples of televisual "averageness" injected into campaign communication. A few examples from television campaigns preceding 1976 offer glimpses into the ways in which presidentiality was visually constructed and reconstructed in democratic campaign appeals.

Eisenhower Answers America

The 1952 Eisenhower campaign's invention of the short political spot transformed ideas about what was expected and acceptable in political campaigning. In the hands of the Eisenhower campaign, long, textually focused speeches became short visually centered appeals. These spots were largely not political, and more closely resembled soap commercials than the Stevenson spots. Compared to advertisements that emerged in 1976, however, the visual focus of these spots was rarely the candidate himself.[67]

Eisenhower's Madison Avenue advertising team did create a series of spots in which the candidate was injected into the advertising, albeit in ways meant to promote his accomplishments rather than illustrate his personal narrative. The "Eisenhower Answers America" spots featured average citizens posing questions to be answered by Eisenhower. He did so expertly, with a touch of folksy wisdom and common sense.[68]

Although Americans saw no shots of Ike at home or with his wife, Mamie, the verbal template of "Eisenhower Answers America" approached the everyday vernacular. In one spot, Ike referenced his own life in average everyday terms, informing voters that "my Mamie gets after me about the high cost of living."[69] In these spots, Ike was ordinary — he was a husband whose wife worried about prices at the grocery store. Compared to the Stevenson advertisements, Eisenhower was more person than politician.

However, despite the injection of the candidate's own experience, for the most part Eisenhower came across as a teacher or a preacher — a man to whom people turned for advice and support.[70] The Eisenhower campaign's central message in 1952 was based on the candidate's heroic qualities, not his averageness. As illustrated in "The Man from Abilene" spot, Ike's personal life was not important to his candidacy. While the advertisement briefly referenced Ike's Midwestern roots, the fleeting image of a humble home in Kansas was contextualized by an overriding Superman theme. Using a superhero tone and announcements paralleling those of superman ("faster than a speeding bullet") the narrator told the story of America's own real life superman. Shadowed text shot upward on the screen, leaving a flight path behind, as the camera panned skyward from Abilene — a direct reference to Superman. The spot then launched into a series of heroic images of Eisenhower's performance in World War II. This series of images culminated with reference to contemporary problems — the country, embroiled in Korea, looking to the only man who could save it. The narrator announced: "The nation ... looks to Eisenhower..."

The "Superman" portrayal of presidentiality was Eisenhower's big ticket. Eisenhower was an experienced general who would skillfully expedite victory in the Korean War. Americans had turned against the war, and Eisenhower offered his World War II leadership experience as proof that he could end the war quickly. The campaign's personal appeals in 1952 were extras, aimed at the repetition of a brand name during popular television programs such as *I Love Lucy.*[71]

Eisenhower's most authentic personal appeal in 1952 did not come from the candidate himself but from his floundering running mate, Richard Nixon. The "Checkers" speech was the first televisual example of the potent appeal of ordinariness. In 1952, in jeopardy of being dropped from the ticket over a fundraising scandal, Nixon appeared on television and radio to absolve himself. Explaining that he was not a wealthy man, that his wife wore a "plain Republican cloth coat," Nixon informed voters that he *had* taken an illegal campaign contribution — a dog named Checkers, sent to his daughters from a man in Texas. Nixon's 1952 "Checkers" speech was effective not because it inspired sympathy but because Nixon appealed to his audience as a father and as a humble man whom the forces in Washington were trying to name, blame, and defame. People — dog lovers, parents, and owners of cloth coats everywhere — could see something of themselves in Nixon. His battle against establishment interests in Washington became their battle against the forces of power.

The "Checkers" speech was an early example of a politician using television as a mirror; that is, politicians found that they could send themselves directly into people's living rooms using images that closely resembled the kind of folks already there. The reverse construction of authority was effective because people trusted and understood people like themselves. In the "Checkers" speech, for a brief moment, Nixon was them. While it was effective, the "Checkers" speech was also an aberration — in political circles it was widely viewed as a last act of desperation.[72] Nixon's wife, Pat, was reportedly mortified at the image she was expected to portray during the televised speech. To Pat Nixon, poverty was not a prize, but an embarrassment.[73]

Nixon would not repeat that humbling appeal in his own campaign in 1960. All of Nixon's 1960 spots featured a well-dressed vice president speaking about his leadership and knowledge from a professional-looking office. His opponent, John F. Kennedy, produced spots set in more humble settings, although they were other people's average homes and not his own. While Kennedy's commercials featured a candidate listening to, empathizing with, and offering solutions for average folk, he did not relate to them. He would be their savior, but not their neighbor.

Like Nixon's "Checkers" speech, the Kennedy example was complicated by competing forces of ordinary and extraordinary, reserve and exposure. Even as the Kennedys deployed footage of family recreation, they also represented an unattainable ideal. There was no better depiction of the conflict between average and austere than in *Camelot*, the Kennedys' favorite musical. As the song goes, "They stare at the castle and ponder. Whenever the wind blows this way, you can almost hear ev'ryone say: 'I wonder what the king is doing tonight?'"

At last, the democratic impulse in *Camelot* was constantly at odds with nobility and grandeur, made clear in the duet "What Do Simple Folk Do?" Facing multiple challenges, Queen Guinevere wondered how regular people confronted personal struggles. Arthur replied, "I've been informed by those who know them well..." reflecting a substantial distance between the crown and ordinary folks. To most people, the Kennedys' *Camelot* came to represent an unattainable ideal, which mixed personal nobility (beauty, style, and grace) with political democracy (the Round Table). Thus, even as Jacqueline Kennedy opened the White House to camera crews, most Americans did not see themselves reflected in the Kennedy image, but admired it for its unattainably extraordinary grace.

Lyndon Johnson has become best known for his humble Texas roots and crass vernacular revealed in the White House tapes. At the time, however, the dominant image to emerge from Johnson's campaign in 1964 was that of the president in the Oval Office. Aware of the circumstances that brought him there, following Kennedy's assassination, the 1964 Johnson campaign opted to show, as often as possible, the president at work in Washington. Absent personal narrative outside his professional work in the White House, Lyndon Johnson might have actually been crude and "authentic" by 2010 standards, but this was decidedly not the image his campaign opted to display in 1964. By 1976, there would be a reverse impulse in campaign communication. While Jimmy Carter kept his training as a Naval engineer relatively hidden from public view, and instead highlighted his down-home-humble southern heritage.

By the time Nixon ran for president in 1968 and 1972, both the technology and national mood had changed substantially. Wary of political promises and political stagecraft, voters demanded participation in the process. As a result, candidates began presenting a kind of staged "backstage." For example, Nixon's 1968 campaign featured an element of televised authenticity — a live phone-a-thon complete with visible television cables and a set littered with coffee cups. Nixon's remove from this "real" display, however, lent authenticity to the phone-a-thon, but not to the candidate himself. More to the point, in both 1968 and 1972 Nixon's major campaign message was his foreign policy expertise, not his personal connection to real life outside Washington. While "authenticity" began to reveal itself in television production values, neither of these elections bore any resemblance to personal branding of authenticity that would come to dominate campaigning only a few years later.[74]

In 1972, Nixon's managers continued to believe that expertise, rather than personally revealing images, was the ticket to the White House. While in later years convention documentaries would feature candidates' lives outside of Washington, a short film produced for the Nixon campaign in 1972 showed the president *only* in the White House. Moreover, character witnesses employed to speak on Nixon's behalf stuck to the official image and professional script. Nixon "thrives on work" and was "heroic ... about how he conducts his business." This support came not from wives or children or childhood friends but rather from such ordinary Americans as Henry Kissinger. Nixon did continue with the live phone-a-thon format, which had proved exceptionally popular. Nonetheless, the goal was always to prove his responsiveness to voters and expertise in answering their questions.[75]

As will be illustrated throughout the chapters that follow, there was a marked change in campaign style in 1976. While previous campaigns had involved citizen questions and live call-in programs, prior to 1976 there was an obvious dimension of authority: the voters had the questions; the candidate had the answers. The answers were always framed as expert solutions for problems facing the country. In 1976, Jimmy Carter's live call-in show featured the candidate answering questioners, as Nixon before him. There was a remarkable difference, however, in the format, tone, and structure of the program. In the 1976 call-in program, Carter always responded to callers by first name and always answered with anecdotes from his own life: "My mother Lillian is seventy-eight years old." Carter's expertise did not come from his years in the Navy or his service as governor, but rather from his experience as an average American. Where Nixon would have tried to prove his extraordinary knowledge, Carter's goal was to prove his ordinariness.

That is what this book is about: the major transformation in the ways in which presidentiality has been projected, depicted, and defined through general election campaigns since 1976. Presidentiality is no longer a balance between expertise and removed responsiveness. Instead, the projection of presidentiality now requires authenticity — personal, American, and human authenticity projected and displayed in authentic ways — on talk shows and with behind-the-scenes exposure. What follows is an illustration of how this played out and evolved over nine election cycles from 1976 to 2008.

1

People Just Like Us: 1976

In June 1976, Jimmy Carter returned home to Plains, Georgia, for his first public appearance as the Democratic Party's unofficial presidential nominee. "I've met a lot of folks around the country — people just like us, people who know what it means to have to work for a living, who live close to one another ... who have deep religious faith...."[1] The candidate's repetitious invocation of the first person plural — the "we" of Carter's America — was essential to his representation of human and American authenticity. Carter's "people just like us" included ordinary, small-town folk who knew a hard day's work in the dirt. Like Carter, they did not live or work in Washington, were not lawyers or big city power brokers. Throughout the summer and fall of 1976, Carter would consistently appeal to the "we" — honest, hardworking Americans — as he campaigned to be *their* president. He fancied himself one of them and never failed to remind his audiences of that fact.

Past and Present in 1976

Gerald Ford came to the Oval Office in 1974 following the resignation of Richard Nixon. Forced out of office as a result of scandals, lies, cover-ups, and ethical lapses that became public as a result of the Watergate break-in, the Nixon presidency was mired in disgrace. The president, who had declared that he was not "a crook," was, in fact, a crook. Nixon's first vice president, Spiro Agnew, had himself resigned in disgrace as a result of tax fraud and bribery allegations.[2]

It was under these circumstances that Ford became president. Although the American people, on the whole, initially welcomed Ford's presidency despite its inauspicious beginnings, they began to sour on his leadership after he pardoned Richard Nixon in September 1974. Beginning with Lyndon Johnson's Vietnam War furtiveness, and continuing with Nixon's paranoid approach to leadership, the country had suffered a decade in which the White

House was seen as a bunker of secrets, lies, and backroom negotiations. Thus, the American people were on high alert for conspiracy. To some, it appeared as though Ford had traded his pardon for the presidency. While he tempered fears and worked to regain trust in the office and in his leadership, Ford entered the 1976 election under unprecedented circumstances. New measures of fitness and new models of desirable leadership had begun to form as a result of a decade of turbulent leadership.

The presidential race of 1976 was a character election.[3] The national tragedy of Watergate had not merely tested the people's faith in the presidency, but had served to expose the bowels of campaign machinery. Through Watergate, Americans became privy to the internal workings of political campaigns, from fundraising to ghostwriting.[4] This inured not only a sense of powerlessness among the people, but also an awareness that presidents were politicians — with speeches written, campaigns financed, and television makeup applied.[5] In short, the presidency came to represent a kind of evil unreality in the minds of many voters.[6] The end of electoral innocence drove their desire to locate a more "authentic" candidate and a more honest kind of campaign.[7] By selecting the man who was most "like" ordinary voters, both the public and the Carter campaign hoped that decent, honest folk could somehow take back the government and reclaim the presidency.[8]

In the first post–Watergate presidential election, both camps recognized the force of image. It was to be a competition of personalities rather than policies. Evaluating the tenor of the campaign at mid-season, the President Ford Committee advised, "Personal perception is several times more important to voting than the perceived position on issues.... Voters are far more influenced by the perceived personal traits of the candidate than their substantive position on even that issue which a given voter considers most important."[9] Prioritizing the campaign's fall advertising expenditures, another memorandum instructed, "It is particularly important to note that the people are far more influenced by their own feelings about the candidates' personal traits — than by the candidates' positions on issues."[10] Both campaigns recognized that character and honesty would drive voter preferences in November 1976. Neither candidate could afford to be perceived as a prevaricating, double-dealing, power-hungry Washington politician.

While dodging explicit exploitation of Nixon, each candidate used the symbolic power of Watergate against his opponent. When the Ford committee articulated its opposition strategy, central to the counter-branding campaign was an attempt to portray Carter in a Nixon–esque way: as a demagogue and as a partisan political animal; the plan was to "show that he [was] ... driven by personal ambition in ruthless pursuit of power."[11] For his part,

Carter frequently referred to the president's tenure as the "Nixon-Ford Administration."

Thus, while both campaigns hoped to burden the other with the albatross of dirty-dealing and win-at-all-costs campaigning, each also tread carefully to avoid making its own candidate appear overly political, ambitious, and mean-spirited. Each campaign's strategy reflected the eggshell quality of opposition branding in the first post–Watergate election. The President Ford Committee feared that its candidate would appear mean, partisan, and power hungry. The Carter team worried that it would inspire sympathy for the president and promote favor for the Cincinnatus who had come forward during a time of great national tragedy.

The pursuit of the presidency in 1976 was unlike any previous election cycle. While earlier campaigns had focused on candidate image, it was never as central as it was in 1976.[12] If Watergate represented the excesses of politics, greed, and the pursuit of power, voters would look to elect an anti–Nixon.[13] To the extent that Watergate had exposed Americans to the vast behind-the-scenes machinery of electioneering and campaigning, voters would privilege the more open and deconstructed style of campaign. Mostly, they wanted an authentic human being to whom they could relate.[14]

Jimmy Who?

Jimmy Carter was well suited to campaign as an anti-politician. Carter's own campaign advisors noted that his election would likely have been impossible had it not been for Watergate. The mood of the country had shifted; voters, disaffected and cynical, cast their lots with an unknown "one of us."[15] Emerging out of relative obscurity to capture the Democratic nomination, Carter had achieved his success in a seemingly old-fashioned way: by shaking hands, making speeches, and introducing himself to voters at the grassroots.[16] During the general election, Carter often reminded voters that he had bested his own party's establishment by taking his campaign straight to the people. His status as a Washington outsider, however, was not enough to capture and sustain national support. The campaign team had to construct an "authentic" narrative for its candidate and create "authentic" advertising to sell the relatively unknown Georgian.[17]

Veritas

One of Carter advisor Gerald Rafshoon's most notable contributions to American campaigning was his innovative use of cinéma vérité style advertising during the 1976 election. If the core of the Carter campaign was an anti–Washington message of openness in government, a "de-pomping" of the White House, and greater citizen access to a citizen president, the deconstructed cinéma vérité style commercials offered a less polished, less slick, and less "manufactured" appeal to viewers.[18] The spots allowed the campaign to emphasize its perceived strengths: the candidate's personal narrative, his kind and casual (and decidedly un–Washington) demeanor, and his one-of-you-feel-your-pain everyman message. Most of all, the cinéma vérité spots felt more *honest* and authentic. Many of Rafshoon's 1976 television spots included home video-style shots of the candidate, his family members, and ordinary citizens.[19] Rather than speaking directly to the camera, they would converse around the camera, seemingly caught on film. Much of Rafshoon's work included recycled clips of the candidate on the campaign trail meeting with ordinary citizens and talking to average voters. Watergate made voters suspicious of the overly produced candidate and campaign and Rafshoon's television spots offered a return to a more humble type of politics.

The style had several effects: first, it distanced Carter from the harder edge of political commerce. To this end, the campaign repeatedly reminded voters that Carter was running for office out of a sense of service, not for personal gain: "Jimmy is honest and unselfish and truly concerned about the country."[20] Second, it introduced a level of reality and an element of authenticity that was appealing to voters in the post–Watergate era. Because the candidate did not appear scripted or made-up, the "human element" came through on the television screen.

One of the more effective uses of the technique appeared in the campaign's "Bio" spot. The advertisement included a clip of Lillian, Jimmy Carter's mother, describing her son's early life to someone out of camera range. To whom she was speaking was not clear until she began discussing the family's use of corporal punishment. In the background, her son faintly disputed his mother's recollections. The two shared a nostalgic laugh as Lillian eventually agreed that she had probably spanked him on occasion.[21]

The clip did not seem scripted, but appeared to embody a genuinely embarrassing Carter family moment, as the ever-authentic Miz Lillian wistfully recalled her son's boyhood. The scene seemed human and *real*. That mother-son conversation in the "Bio" commercial worked because it was personal and apolitical and could have been any man's mother disputing the details of any family story. That the Carter campaign wrote, shot, and included the clip in its longest commercial is instructional about the campaign's method, message, and mood on a more important level.

The cinéma vérité style commercials frequently featured non-political legitimizers and advocates, like Carter's wife and mother. Others used man-on-the-street interviews, typically with "average" voters, speaking on the candidate's behalf.[22] Many included footage of Carter speaking to supporters on the street. The media approved. *Time* told its readers that Carter's advertisements illustrated "the nominee's vision of America. They show him mingling with voters, caressing corn stalks near his farm, and extemporizing upon his stands on specific issues."[23] Rafshoon later recalled his emphasis on recycling video footage from the candidate's hand-shaking, whistle-stopping trip across the country. "If you remember those spots in '76, they were mostly Carter talking on the road."[24] This was meant to produce two results. First, it established Carter's legitimacy, as the footage often showed crowds of people cheering for the candidate. Second, the footage seemed honest; they had the feel of documentary rather than produced and polished commercial material.

The medium matched the message perfectly. The campaign wanted to establish Carter as an anti-politician, an average guy, an outside the Beltway farmer, and a peanut-pickin' Ragged Dick, and the cinéma vérité spots accomplished this in format, rather than merely content.

The campaign needed to establish Carter's essential authenticity as an American and as a human being. In previous years, voters had been privy to the basic outlines of candidates' biographies; beginning in 1976, the intimate and personal details became something of an obsession.[25] Rather than brushing aside questions about its candidate's religion, family, and preferred breakfast cereal, the Carter campaign encouraged this kind of press attention and worked personal details into the bulk of its commercials.

In order to establish the candidate as an everyman, the campaign emphasized Carter's human dimension and life story from humble beginnings in rural Georgia to family man and peanut farmer. It has become a truism in campaign analysis that candidates must become personally familiar to the voting public. This began with Carter — rather than listing his political and professional accomplishments as a means of introducing himself through political résumé, the campaign wove images of Plains, Georgia, evidence of Carter's modest childhood, and descriptions of his small-town lifestyle through much of its promotional materials. The public wanted to know about Carter as a person, as a Baptist, as a father, as a husband, and as a son — a desire thoroughly satiated by a willing candidate and campaign staff.[26]

People

People debuted in 1974 to feed Americans' growing desire to collapse the boundaries between personal and public. *People* was not the first celebrity rag, nor the first to cover political candidates as celebrities. However, *People* fed a different kind of fame fetishism — it presented newsmakers as people rather than figures. While there had been public obsession with the Kennedy family and the Kennedy lifestyle, it was a public fixation on something out of reach, something grander and glamorously out of touch. Fetishizing the ordinary details of extraordinary people was something different altogether — this was the difference between a photo spread in *Life,* and a tell-all in *Playboy.* Part of the Carter campaign's brilliance was that it understood this sea change. It not only managed its candidate's image, but promoted interest in all things Carter. The best evidence of this comes from a July 19, 1976, cover story granted to *People.* The story sold the candidate as a farmer and as family man, featuring a cover photograph of "Jimmy" with his daughter, Amy. The head-line offered an adorable role reversal: "Amy Carter and Daddy," which per-formed exactly the cultural work the campaign intended — this candidate is not too proud to play second fiddle to his eight-year-old daughter. The article began with a folksy portrait of Plains, Georgia, a clichéd story line that was, by then, familiar to most voters. The article quoted Carter on his neighborly attachment to the town's 683 residents and included testimony from Carter's sons about their father's struggles to make a living in the peanut business. "'Dad did everything himself,' says Chip."[27]

Despite the Carter family's business success and long-standing status as one of the town's leading families, every effort was made to make the family seem ordinary and humble, from the family's adventures in sidewalk peanut peddling to a Carter cousin's hokey description of the family's worm farming business: "a lowdown, crawlin' callin.'"[28] As in the campaign's biographical television advertisement, Lillian Carter offered a typical account of her son's upbringing. "'We didn't have much money ... but we had everything we needed. Jimmy's book [*Why Not the Best?*] makes us sound so poor you want to get out a hat and take up a collection.... We made a Christian home, read the Bible and had prayers, but Jimmy was no different from other children.'" It was a story to which most veterans of the Depression–era South could relate. Careful to avoid anointing her son, Lillian added, "'But he did slip away the last day of high school and go to Americus with a bunch of boys. That kept him from being valedictorian.'"[29] He was not perfect. He was like you. He was just a hardworking small-town kid who made big on the national stage.

The most significant part of the article included assurances from Plains residents that Carter had remained true to himself despite his political success, a requisite stroke in establishing any celebrity's authenticity. "I've been know-ing Jimmy Carter since I was a child.... He's just like you see him — smiling. I've never seen him mad. The Carters are a fine set of people. You see them today and you see them tomorrow and they're the same. Jimmy don't change."[30] The "Jimmy don't change" story line was retold by multiple media outlets, cosigned by Lillian Carter's frequent public appearances, and repeated by the candidate's advocates and surrogates on the campaign trail. Carter's running mate, Walter Mondale told audiences that Jimmy Carter had come from the people and "stayed with the people."[31]

The sense that Carter was a regular guy, unchanged (uncorrupted) by politics was bolstered by the campaign's emphasis on (and the media's occasional obsession with) the Carter family. Reporters repeated the candidate's claim that he "hated being away from his family" on the campaign trail.[32] Covering the Carters as much as the campaign, nationally printed stories assured the public that, like them, he was "happiest when ... home with his wife and family."[33]

Members of the press frequently peppered their stories with quips from the family matriarch, who could be relied upon to offer heavily accented downhome aphorisms with a touch of Southern pride. A self-described "country hick," Miz Lillian could also cut the candidate down to size and serve up authentically embarrassing stories about her son.[34] In New York for the Democratic National Convention, "Jimmy's mother, 'Miss Lillian' gave a continuous round of interviews.... A little too much perhaps for her son's taste. She offered a novel account of how he first declared his intention of seeking the presidency. Clad only in his shorts ... he put a foot on her bed and started to speak. 'Take your foot off the bed,' Miss Lillian commanded. When Jimmy said that he would run for president and win, she thought he must be joking."[35]

As the press poured into Plains, town residents shared their own stories about the Democratic nominee, a man they knew to be a regular guy. A longtime resident of Plains recalled to the national press, "Jimmy was just an ordinary boy. He had to milk cows before he came to school, just like everybody else."[36] More than just reprinted accents and rural/regional dialect, these kinds of articles made readers genuinely believe that Jimmy Carter was a man to whom they could relate — a candidate who was one of them.

The Carter campaign attempted to take this a step farther in its controversial *Playboy* interviews. Perhaps the *Playboy* affair was an over-reaching attempt to establish Carter's authenticity. Carter was a well-known born-again Christian, an asset, to be sure, in a country where evangelicalism was on the rise. Nonetheless, Carter advisors feared that his frequently vocalized profession of faith made him seem straight-laced and self-righteous to the uninitiated. On the whole, the *Playboy* interviews included very few dirty details, but in an attempt to relate to his perceived audience, Carter created controversy where none existed.

It was an off-hand comment at the conclusion of the final interview that caught the most attention: Jimmy Carter had "lust" in his "heart."[37] He admitted to having "looked on a lot of women with lust. I've committed adultery in my heart many times.... But that doesn't mean that I condemn someone who not only looks on a woman with lust but who leaves his wife and shacks up with somebody out of wedlock."[38] Despite the perhaps scandalous content of his words, Carter's point was on target with the goals of his campaign message and the expected outcome of the interview: Carter was a good man and a good Christian, but he was "not ... condescending or proud."[39] It was the candidate's attempt to prove that he was a regular guy to an anticipated readership of over five million.[40]

While Carter may have had lust in his heart, cows in the barn, and peanuts in the field, his Depression–era upbringing was not nearly as shoeless and replete with hardship as the story was told.[41] To be sure, Carter was a peanut farmer, but the campaign also constructed the narrative it wanted voters to hear. Carter was from one of the two leading families in Plains, Georgia, and lived in relative comfort throughout the 1930s. Similarly, while Carter did return home to rescue the family's business after his father's death, he was much more a businessman than an active soil-tilling peanut picker.

Whatever success he had achieved, Carter sold through bootstrapping metaphors: he had *earned* it through honest toil. As his wife Rosalynn put it in the short spot, "Rose," "When people say, 'How did Jimmy Carter come from nowhere to where he is today?' I tell 'em it's *hard work*.... I think he'd be a great president."[42] Rosalynn's emphasis on hard work achieved two points. The first was a point of comparison: Carter was not a member of the East Coast elite who had risen to power on the force of his name and the reach of his connections; he was a political outsider whose life story bore more similarities to the farmer down the road than to the lawyers in Washington. The second was a point of connection: Carter, like average Joe voter, made his way uphill on his own two feet. During a campaign stop in Minnesota in September, Walter Mondale described Carter as "this marvelous man who's from the soil himself, the first full-time farmer to be a President of the United States since Thomas Jefferson."[43] This appeal worked equally among midwestern and southern farmers, as it did with blue-collar workers who felt they had something in common with Candidate Grunt.

In the four-and-a-half minute "Bio" commercial, Carter narrated a life that was strongly rooted in both soil and hard work: "My folks have been farmers in Georgia for more than 200 years. And we've been livin' around here for ... oh ... 150 years." Carter's mother, Lillian, picked up the story in Log Cabin fashion: "He had to work every afternoon ... we didn't have a car for him and he had to come home every afternoon and work, work real hard out in the field." The commercial then cut to Carter, in a casual blue shirt sitting by an old shack in a wooded area explaining how work and common hardship had kept his family close. Another clip showed Carter in a plaid work shirt in the fields on his farm, as he explained his good fortune in having had the opportunity to get a good education. "Nobody in my family before my generation ever had a chance to finish high school. We've always worked for a living; we know what it means to work." Americans could relate to his story — he was not from a politically privileged family; he harbored no sense of entitlement and had worked (with his own hands in the dirt) for his success like every other ordinary American growing up outside the seats of status and palaces of power.[44]

Many media outlets picked up on these campaign themes and repeated them. An October 1976 *Time* article quoted Carter's campaign biography, *Why Not the Best*: "My life on the farm during the Great Depression ... more nearly resembled farm life of fully 2,000 years ago than farm life today." The article went on to describe that "like most rural Southerners in those days, they had no running water or electricity."[45] The sense that the candidate was a "self-made man" was trumpeted by *Newsweek*, where one account glowed, "More than any contemporary presidential politician he [Carter] is a self-made man — a creation raised up out of nowhere by his own will."[46] *The New York Times* even offered evidence of the campaign's authenticity by highlighting the candidate's unscripted "spontaneity," and the ways in which his honest "human frailty" came through on the campaign trail. The *New York Times* gave voters an account of a candidate who preferred to "'wing it' without notes or text."[47] Noting voters' attraction to his "sincerity," other publications underscored Carter's self-identification as an "anti-politician campaigning against the Washington establishment."[48]

This theme was repeated in the short commercial, "Lawyer," which pictured Carter, in casual farm attire, looking off to the side of the camera. The camera panned away from Carter and showed clips of the candidate working on his peanut farm. He walked through the fields, picked at the soil, and manned a peanut shelling machine. In Southern drawl, Carter asserted, "I think it's time to have a non-lawyer in the White House for a change; somebody that's had to work with his hands."[49] The campaign's repeated references to "lawyers" also included coded digs at the ethical lapses of the Nixon administration. If any candidate understood the plight of average Americans, surely it was the peanut farmer more than the lawyer and twenty-seven-year veteran of Washington politics.

In the campaign's own tracking, Carter had "very strong appeal on the attitudinal sorts of questions — the 'he cares about people like me,' 'he's close to me on the issues' sorts of things.... Out of that came that combination of attitudes that had to do with the traditional American virtues, if you will, of honesty, sincerity, frugality."[50] Even as Carter's overall poll numbers began to slip in the fall of 1976, voters continued to identify Carter as the candidate who "shared" their values. In a survey conducted after the first debate, 53 percent of respondents said that Carter was more sincere and that they were more personally comfortable with him.[51] Responding to a poll taken after the second debate, voters selected Carter by a margin of just over two to one on the question "I think he really cares about people like me."[52] Even during his fall surge, Ford never scored higher than Carter on these essential measures; Carter consistently outperformed the incumbent on these types of questions.

The Ford campaign watched these "attitudinal" advantages for Carter closely. "In the recent national poll, people place Carter near themselves on the issues wherever they are. Because of his ... personal appeal, they *want* him to be close to them."[53] Thus, even when voters began to question Carter's specific positions on policy issues, they continued to identify with him on a personal level. A late–October *Time* magazine-sponsored panel found that voters from both political parties felt that "Carter's closeness to the common man" was "one of his chief virtues."[54] By comparison, the same group of voters identified "experience" as Ford's greatest asset.[55]

Carter's attempts to appeal to voters as "one of them" was particularly effective in the South where the candidate *was* actually one of them. As Carter stumped in the South, he assured voters: "When I'm in the White House, you'll have a friend there."[56] To be sure, he appealed to midwesterners as a farmer and to small business owners as a man who had rescued his family's business from near collapse. But it was in the South that Carter made the broadest appeal to a sense of regional pride and religious faith.

Beyond his status as a born-again Baptist, he effectively targeted a deep sense of Dixie pride. "Only a Southerner can understand what it means to be a political whipping-boy. But then only a Southerner can understand what Jimmy Carter as President can mean."[57] The Ford campaign could not defeat a native son of the Deep South who was campaigning hard as an authentic southerner.

Puttin' on the Dog

Carter did not change his accent, nor, very often, his casual style of dress. He preferred casual settings for campaign events, offering an alternative to what the Carter people called the "pomp" of presidentiality. The campaign preferred to present Carter as "himself.... This is what was appealing to the American people. And it was ... what the country was looking for."[58] During the Democratic National Convention in New York, the major newspapers made light of the culture clash that ensued as Plains speak met Park Avenue. Rosalynn Carter was mocked for wearing the same dress twice, a critique that backfired with ordinary Americans for whom such wardrobe choices were necessary.

Carter frequently carried his own bags and preferred to be photographed working on his farm.[59] During a campaign stop at the University of Illinois, running mate Walter Mondale proved his own chops by eating at the school dining hall and spending the night in a student dormitory room, thus establishing his own down-home bona fides.[60] The Carter campaign so frequently cultivated this image that the *New York Times'* Russell Baker satirized: "My name is Jimmy Carter and I'm Mister Regular Guy."[61]

The public and the press took notice. The *New York Times* devoted a multi-page article to Carter's preference for casual clothes in general, and blue jeans in particular. Quoting authorities on the pressing campaign issue of denim, The *New York Times* interviewed a North Carolina man who advised: "The important thing.... If you try to dress up, people will say you're puttin' on the dog."[62] Put on the dog, Carter did not. "Jeans are an authentic part of Carter's character ... and the well-worn fit of them proves that he feels at home in the Plains, Georgia, uniform of the day."[63] His persistent casual dress worked, not only among blue-collar voters, themselves no strangers to denim, but among the youth as well. Young voters not only yearned for authenticity, but were able to identify with a candidate in dungarees.[64] "Not lost on his political advisers is the fact that jeans register contradictory impressions with the young people around Harvard Square and the farmers in Iowa."[65]

A casual language matched the campaign's working-class attire. No fan of the final G, Carter made no attempts to mask his accent or incorporate technocratic jargon or four syllable words. As one voter said, "I had seen all the candidates on local television and had made a judgment that I liked this guy Carter. He didn't speak that well but what he said made a lot of sense and he seemed thoughtful."[66] The taped footage of Carter often included audio of the candidate employing southern accent and colloquial language. His best advocate, his mother, Lillian, did not speak with the affectations of wealth or education, but in plain-spoken, heavily accented southern vernacular.[67]

This also served to fill what was perhaps the most important thread in the 1976 Carter campaign: clearly branding the candidate as a Washington outsider. In the four-and-a-half minute "Bio" commercial, both Rosalynn and Lillian Carter were employed to establish not only Carter's strong sense of family, but also his anti–Washington bona fides. In a laugh line that she would repeat on the campaign trail, Rosalynn Carter equated the election season media circus to small-town busybody gossip mongering. She joked, "People ask me every day, 'How can you stand for your husband to be in politics and everybody know everything you do?' And I just tell 'em that we were born and raised and still live in Plains, Georgia. It has a population of six hundred and eighty-three, and everybody has *always* known everything I did." The laugh line was a good one. As Rosalynn equated national celebrity with a small-town rumor mill, national politics was humbled, and the campaign was brought firmly down to earth.

Rosalynn made these assertions explicitly on the campaign trail, comparing her husband to his out-of-touch opponent. At a campaign stop in Pennsylvania, she argued that "no way a politician could stay in Washington since 1948 as Mr. Ford has done without losing perspective." By comparison, "Jimmy" was "a farmer ... he knows what it is to work for a living."[68] According to the campaign, a vote for Carter was a vote to reclaim the government for the average citizen. One commercial asserted, "A year ago, people scoffed at the idea of Jimmy Carter running for president. A farmer and small businessman, Jimmy Carter certainly wasn't one of the Washington politicians usually picked for the job. As a working man, he's never served in Congress."[69] Experience, typically an asset to a campaign, had become a liability.

The sense that people would "scoff" at Jimmy Carter played particularly well in the South, where the anti–Washington message of the Carter campaign carried particular regional significance. In one radio ad, which played in the South, an announcer made this appeal: "It's like this.... Are you going to let the Washington politicians keep one of our own out of the White House? The South has always been the conscience of America — maybe they'll start listening to us now."[70]

It was not, however, mere southern pride that sold the anti-elite message of the Carter campaign. It was also a timely instruction to voters and a reminder of the scandal of Watergate and years of political secrecy. "We've seen walls built around Washington. And we feel like we can't quite get through to guarantee the people of this country a government that's sensitive to our needs. That we can understand and control."[71]

Carter frequently wove this theme into his stump speeches and television advertisements, explaining that his was a "vision" of a "de-pomped" presidency, accessible to ordinary citizens: "I have a vision of America ... I see an American president who ... is not isolated from our people, but a president who feels your pain and shares your dreams."[72] He promised to rid the office of much of the pageantry associated with the presidency. During the inauguration,

Carter continued this theme by "cutting ... the limos, walking down the street ... was all part of the 'I'll never lie to you' part of the campaign."[73]

The connections between grandeur, show, excess, and dishonesty had been made tangible by Watergate. The pared-down and casual aura of the campaign implied not merely an absence of excess, but also a commitment to openness and a direct connection between the people and the candidate. Ford's own opposition research found that Jimmy Carter's strengths among voters included the perception that he was "a new kind of politician who is against the corrupt Washington system and will not lie." More importantly, voters did not seem to think that Carter was a "politician" at all, as they responded that he was a leader who would not "let the politicians run over him."[74] The pervasive message was that regular people needed to be not merely represented in government, but reflected in the people running the government. On the campaign trail, Mondale summarized this mood, making the pitch for his running mate as a "people's President."[75] More comically (and potently), Tom Wolfe theorized that "Carter ... had stumbled upon a fabulous terrain for which there are no words in current political language. A ... politician had finally wandered into the Me Decade" gaining currency by reflecting the cultural priorities of the day: "Me."[76]

The Evolution of Jerry Ford

Although it was not an overwhelming mandate, Jimmy Carter's victory as the "people's President" in November 1976 was hardly a surprise. While it might be argued that Carter's nomination was a political upset against the Democratic Party establishment, any Democrat ought to have won the general election against Ford. That he did so by such a small margin is worth further investigation. In July 1976, Carter held a thirty-three-point advantage over Ford in the polls.[77] By election day, he bested Ford by a margin of only 51 percent to 48 percent.[78] Scholars have accurately assessed Carter's narrow win in multiple ways. Votes for Carter were soft, reflecting votes against Ford. Carter may have overstepped in the *Playboy* interview and lost crucial conservative votes. Carter also might have fallen into the trap set by the Ford campaign, revealing serious weaknesses as he was forced to articulate specific positions on issues. Some have argued that support for the risky candidate (insofar as Carter represented an unknown quantity) was always ephemeral; it inevitably weakened as Election Day neared.

All of these might be true to some extent. One point that has not been fully analyzed, however, was the dramatic re-packaging effort undergone by the Ford campaign, of which the main thrust was to humanize the president. Indeed, the 1976 Ford Campaign was one of the most effective re-branding efforts in the history of political television. An analysis of the 1976 election through the lens of authenticity adds another layer to our assessment of the first post–Watergate election and sheds greater light on the Ford campaign's dramatic surge in public opinion polls during the fall of 1976.

The Rose Garden Strategy

Both the President Ford Committee (PFC) and the Carter campaign team reversed strategies in the late summer of 1976. The PFC strategy came to resemble Carter's early campaign, while the Carter team encouraged its candidate to be more deliberate and more "presidential." As Carter began articulating specific policy details, the Ford campaign turned to more general, personal, and attitudinal messages.

Early in the campaign, the PFC had followed a "Rose Garden strategy," which lasted through the early summer of 1976. The Rose Garden strategy employed the advantages of office in order to picture the president being "presidential." Ford would achieve free media coverage by doing the things that presidents do — signing bills, meeting with foreign diplomats, and traveling on Air Force One.

When the President Ford Committee initially devised this strategy, it encouraged the president to avoid campaigning. Campaigning, it was believed, would make the president appear overly political and perhaps un-presidential. The PFC believed that the office was its one advantage over its opponents. The Rose Garden strategy was not only based on old assumptions, but also on its analysis of Ford's unique position as the only non-elected president in United States history. The Ford campaign initially believed that it needed to establish Ford as a strong leader and a good president, given the unusual circumstance of trying to reelect a president who had not been elected in the first place.

The team's initial analysis was that the president often appeared incompetent, that he shouldn't appear political, and that "the best way to control" the problem of exposing the president "is by keeping him in the White House."[79] During the 160 days of the primary season, Ford spent 115 of those in the White House.[80] One campaign memo from July 1976 advised that when the president did go out on the campaign trail, he must always appear "presidential" and be seen in "presidential settings." If Jimmy Carter wore cowboy hats in Texas, plaid shirts in Iowa, and ripped jeans in Harvard Square, Ford would step out of black limousines in blue suits and striped ties. Deriding

Ford's attempts to relate to voters as one of them, a campaign memo advised: "The President looks non–Presidential when he wears hats and jackets presented to him."[81]

The PFC learned, however, that the Oval Office, tainted by Watergate, was not a winning image in 1976. By the Ford campaign's own admission, the benefit of the doubt traditionally granted to incumbents was "substantially diminished as a result of Vietnam and Watergate."[82] The problem with the Rose Garden strategy was clear: in 1976 symbols of the presidency were contested emblems of power. President Ford's presidency was already inextricably linked to Watergate because both supporters and detractors understood Ford's presidency, to some extent, as a product of Watergate.

By late summer 1976, the campaign team began to formulate a new strategy agenda that addressed Ford's experience (both in the White House and as a long-serving congressman) as the weakness it was rather than the asset it was not. In an age when voters favored the "real" guy, Ford was disadvantaged by the White House. The Rose Garden strategy had cloistered the president and made him seem unapproachable and unavailable. One campaign memo concluded: "Based on studies ... we find that people do not relate to President Ford."[83] Focus group and polling results found that the president seemed shut off and political. The campaign's own list of negative characteristics most often associated with the president included: "Spends too much time on politics ... too much of an old politician ... seen as part of the old-time, do-nothing Washington establishment.... Appointed by Nixon, whom he pardoned."[84]

In August 1976, the Ford team feared that the president was seen simply as a Washington insider and party hack, "as part of the old Washington establishment."[85] According to one internal campaign analysis, one of Ford's major problems was that he was "coming to be seen as just another politician" who was "overexpose[d] on political matters."[86] The campaign acknowledged that it needed to abandon the trappings of the office in order to "bring President Ford closer to the people ... and move Jimmy Carter further away from them."[87] Advisors recommended significant re-branding in order to "break the President out of the Washington establishment mold."[88]

In order to do this, key aspects of the previous imaging campaign became anathema: "We should avoid symbolic acts such as bill signings, submitting legislation ... and the like, which simply reinforce the perception of the President as part of the Washington establishment."[89] To that end, the first goal of the August 1976 advertising strategy was to "strengthen the human dimension of President Ford."[90] Of the seven characteristics deemed essential to changing perceptions about Ford, four were notable for their identification with authenticity: "honest, strong character, compassion, perceptive/vision."[91] This would be necessary in order to get a second look from swing voters who, they hoped, would "reevaluate their assumptions about the President's personal characteristics."[92]

Running Around Like Jimmy Carter

The public did perceive that Ford had good qualities, which the campaign could emphasize in its re-branding effort. Poll results consistently showed that people thought Ford was honest, even if voters pitied him and found him to be a bit of a klutz, an image made famous by *Saturday Night Live*.

It is interesting to note how much of the Carter strategy was eventually adopted by the PFC just as the Carter team began backing off its earlier campaign themes. According to Gerald Rafshoon, his candidate's slide in the general election began when Carter abandoned the authenticity of his earlier campaign: "He became too much of a regular Democrat."[93] The Carter team at large agreed with this analysis: "The conclusion they reached ... was that ... Jimmy Carter was not being Jimmy Carter."[94]

By contrast Ford began campaigning more like Carter, Ford's poll numbers began to pick up when his team abandoned its emphasis on "Presidential leadership" and instead incorporated the populist flavor of Carter's early campaign. "Gerald Ford was running around the country acting like Jimmy Carter. Ford had become a regular guy, getting out and milking cows and going around the country and saying, 'I know what's good for America.' He was becoming the Jimmy Carter."[95] The Ford campaign had, indeed, created a strategy plan that included branding Ford as more of a regular guy.

Essential to this effort was a renewed emphasis on character, humility, and openness in government. Voters needed to believe "that the President has character."[96] Moreover, they needed to be reassured that the Oval Office was not a place of unrestrained "pomp" as Carter had charged, but that its occupant "knows that government needs ... to be restrained by humility."[97] Rather than locking Ford in the White House, he would be deployed to key swing states in order to communicate with voters on a human level. He would need to repackage his tenure as "An Open Presidency. A Shared Presidency."[98] This would mitigate the albatross of Watergate by portraying Ford as a president of the people.

In order to be a president of the people, however, people needed to get to know Ford as a human being. To this end, his best advocates were the members of his family. They could speak to his human qualities and vouch for his character. Most importantly, the image of Ford with his family was immediately ordinary and authentic. In the fall of 1976, the PFC "implement[ed] a major First Family media blitz aimed particularly at the swing voter."[99] The private life and personal acquaintances of Ford would be used to maximum extent. Front and center would be his family. "We will show the various members of the family not just as campaigners, but as warm, interesting individuals. We will show how they relate to each other and how they relate to their father. We would like to place heavy emphasis on Mrs. Ford — filming her in relaxed, personal conversation about traditional American values, about the feelings she has about her children and husband."[100] The First Family would soften Ford's image and add a human dimension to the accidental president. The First Family would not be pictured as prim or stuffy or perfect, but as casual and caring and human. The Ford family granted the president personal legitimacy and made him a man more than an office.

This was demonstrated in the "Family" television spot purchased by the PFC. The advertisement began with cinéma vérité–style home video footage of a young woman's birthday party. The clip was grainy and unpolished, replete with guests walking in front of the camera, blocking the view. A few seconds into the film, President Ford came into view to hug the young woman, his daughter, Susan. A narrator instructed, "Sometimes a man's family can say a lot about the man. That's why we want you to meet the Fords." Both the narrator's invocation and the home video footage gave a glimpse of the Fords as a regular American family. A series of father-son clips followed. The final such clip included an important message from one of the Ford boys. According to his son, President Ford often instructed his family that "this political year is not nearly as important ... as the thought of every one of us ... representing ourselves truthfully and honestly." Nothing, including his job, was more important to Ford than his family.[101]

In another scene from the same commercial, the camera panned over a still image of Ford and his daughter as she offered insight into the man who most viewers knew only as the president: "He's a typical, fun-loving, caring father." The spot ended with a shot of Betty and Jerry Ford walking their dog on the White House lawn as the narrator summarized, "The Fords: a close, loving American family."[102] The Ford family offered a human dimension to the campaign and allowed viewers to get what seemed to be an "inside look" at the man.

In addition to the First Family, the PFC hoped to construct a symbolic and easily identifiable, retellable, and relatable personal narrative for the president. In an effort to make him more "authentic," the campaign staff advised, "It is important to introduce the real Jerry Ford to America. We want America to meet his friends.... What are his roots? What are his likes and dislikes? How does he react to and with people in private? What kind of sense of humor does he have? Finally — we think the American people should hear how the President himself feels about the things that are important to him — his religion, his home town, his youth...."[103] It became an anti–Oval Office media blitz, as the Ford team constructed a campaign that would de-emphasize issues and the office in order to focus on personality and character.

As part of this effort, the campaign released a biographical advertisement that offered as credentials the president's experience as "an Eagle Scout, an honors student, he was the most valuable player at Michigan ... he served courageously in World War II...."[104] While the spot mentioned that the candidate had to work his way through law school, unlike the Carter "Bio" commercial, the Ford spot was brief, and included as well the candidate's long service in Washington, contextualized and softened by his life story. Unlike previous election years, however, Ford's service was highlighted not for its own sake, but for the sake of emphasizing his sacrifice.

Always Shuck Your Tamales[105]

Like Carter's efforts in the South, the PFC intended to use Ford's Michigan roots to bolster his appeal in the center of the country.[106] Just as Plains provided a useful backdrop for Carter's campaign, Ford replaced the Rose Garden with the Midwest. This would allow Ford to identify with people on a personal level, as he attempted to assure them that he was, in fact, one of them.[107] On a trip to Michigan late in the campaign, Ford was advised to "point out that you are a product of the state, its institutions and its people ... you know this state and its citizens."[108] It was further recommended that Ford repackage his long service as a member of Congress: "Your twenty-four years as a Representative gave you in-depth knowledge of the entire state."[109] In this way, Ford's service in Washington helped him to better understand his neighbors; he had not become an out-of-touch politician, but a better citizen. He also began to speak about his service in humble ways. To this end, Ford was advised to use nostalgia by sharing "stories from" his "first campaign."[110]

He was further instructed to establish his hometown bona fides by "refer[ring] to Michigan geography ... to identify with the state and the listener.... In Grand Rapids, personalize with people and boyhood, mention schools and teachers."[111] This would play to the local audience and also to newspaper readers across the country, who would come to identify Ford with Michigan, rather than Washington. There was a way in which the Ford campaign adopted a kind of "we're in this together" message on these nostalgia tours: as president "it is your hope that they shall be as proud of you as you are of them.... The honors you hold you want to share with them and that is what makes it all worthwhile."[112] It was both humble and humanizing. This strategy was later employed not merely in Michigan, but in other states as well where Ford could reasonably deliver "I'm one of you" messages. The president could play in the Midwest and the farm belt by employing geographic authenticity.

The campaign believed that voters would look for an easily packaged brand with which to identify its candidate. In short, symbols were more powerful than policies. "We were able to do better in some nominally Republican rural areas because of the President's rural background.... You had to get out to those people ... that array of things ... traditional values ... efficiency ... which came to be symbolized in the campaign when you could get away with symbols to do things."[113] As Carter had done, the Ford team attempted to bring it home by identifying the candidate as "of" rather than merely "for" various constituencies. In one memo Jack Marsh reminded Ford that "in Kansas City" the message should be: "'It is from your ranks that I come and on your side I stand.'"[114] Closer to Washington, DC, Ford would claim other places as "home." "When you were in Richmond, your remarks about Virginia being your second home went over quite well."[115]

The PFC poached not only parts of Carter's image and message, but also its advertising style. According to Gerald Rafshoon, the master of the technique, one of Ford's more effective media tools was his adoption of cinéma vérité, "probably the best spots were certainly his man on the street ones."[116] The Ford campaign agreed. Advisors found that they could use cinéma vérité to make Ford appear more authentic and also as a proxy for the candidate's negative attacks on Carter. "The latest television commercials for the President 'make heavy use of the man-in-the-street interviews — in the streets of Atlanta, especially — in order to underscore the doubts that voters most often voice about Jimmy Carter.'"[117] It allowed Ford to undercut his opponent without directly attacking him, which could have appeared mean in a year when cutthroat negativity seemed dirty and dishonest, and most of all, political.

Conclusions

The more authentic candidate's narrow victory in 1976 proves little in and of itself. The campaign included some thoroughly inauthentic moments, most notably both candidates' unwillingness to break professional pose during the September 23 debate's famous twenty-seven-minute technical delay. Of that half-hour staring contest, Ford would later recall, "I suspect both of us would have liked to sit down and relax while the technicians were fixing the system, but I think both of us were hesitant to make any gesture that might look like we weren't physically or mentally able to handle a problem like this."[118] Instead, they stood there, in fear of the medium, recalling Nixon's problematic appearance during his televised 1960 debate against Kennedy. More important than the twenty-seven-minute silence was the terms on which it was judged at the time — using the vocabulary of authenticity. Unmediated and unscrutinized political stagecraft was a thing of the past.

Nonetheless, while some of that emphasis on presidential stoicism remained during the 1976 campaign, the trajectory of the campaign styles, and each campaign's ultimate emphasis on authenticity, is telling. On Election Day, voters selected the risky, but more authentic candidate. The CBS/*New York Times* post-election survey found that voters preferred Carter to Ford on personal qualities, but not on most issues and policy questions.[119] For example, when asked which candidate respondents were "more comfortable with ... as a person ... more at ease," 56 percent selected Carter. Asked which candidate "is more likely to do a better job handling our country's foreign relations," 53 percent of respondents identified Ford,[120] despite his famous gaffe about Soviet domination of Eastern Europe during the debates.[121]

Ultimately both campaigns' internal analyses focused on voters' preference for authenticity. The Carter campaign blamed its fall slump on the candidate's attempts to display leadership and expertise, abandoning the earlier emphasis on personality. Campaign insiders believed that Carter had lost the authentic character of his campaign following the Democratic National Convention. The reason for the change was clear. Mainstream establishment Democrats had urged Carter to come into the fold. President Ford had begun to question Carter's ability to articulate specific policy solutions to the country's foreign and domestic problems. In response, the Carter campaign moved away from its generalized personal appeal to voters. As this happened, however, public opinion polls reflected increasing dissatisfaction with the Democratic nominee.[122] As the polls showed softening support for the candidate, even the anti–Carter forces in the Democratic Party, who had initially encouraged Carter to invoke ideological purity and party orthodoxy, eventually advised a reversal, of course, begging Carter to "return to his 'personal' style."[123]

It is also instructive to note that Carter's major gaffes in 1976 came when he overreached in his attempts to be authentic — including, most notably, the *Playboy* interview. It was here that the born-again Sunday school teacher tried, perhaps too hard, to relate to his perceived audience. There was also a growing perception in the fall of 1976 that Carter was attempting to be all things to all people all over the country. It was one thing to relate on a personal level, another to "put on the dog" in someone else's doghouse. His successful identification with farmers and southerners did not carry over when he attempted to fit in with urban ethnics, the East Coast liberal establishment, and the readers of *Playboy* magazine. The polls reflected this concern among voters who began to identify Carter as "wishy washy."[124]

For his part, Gerald Ford could overcome neither the taint of Watergate nor the trappings of the Oval Office. Delivering a barely audible election night address from Air Force One, Ford appeared to be a man trying to appear to be presidential. While a good-humored nature, honest smile, and occasional lack of coordination might have humanized the president, there was also a way in which he appeared to be a hapless man who had stumbled into somebody else's Oval Office. Ford, either through his own campaign's effort, or as a result of the Carter campaign's failures, made up a great deal of ground between the Republican National Convention and election night.

More important than the election outcome was the terms on which the campaign discourse was mediated. For the first time, a candidate's qualities of authenticity seemed to trump other factors on which previous candidates had been judged — experience, ideology, policy, and issues. If voters did weigh these factors heavily in their final decisions in 1976, this was not clear from the overwhelming emphasis on the candidates' qualities of authenticity in the months leading up to Election Day. It was clear that the campaigns prioritized this value. As Jimmy Carter gained traction with his everyman image, Gerald Ford adopted similar language and campaign styles to construct his own candidate image. Although journalists initially responded with surprise at Jimmy Carter's use of the vernacular, they ultimately came to evaluate both candidates using those terms. In the final analysis, the 1976 campaign season was dominated by enduring images of candidate authenticity.

2

There You Go Again...: 1980

In the early years, Jimmy Carter's presidency resembled his campaign and its organization in important ways. Carter came to Washington to change politics, not to fit in with the lawyer class against whom he had run his campaign. His advisors were almost all Georgians, and included very few "Washington insiders." They arrived in the capital in blue jeans and tee-shirts, intending to bring openness and informality to the White House. It was to be "the people's house" once again — free from years of remote secrecy, austere privilege, and immoral graft. The Carter administration symbolized that transition in its inauguration; the new president walked to and from his inauguration, opting to forgo the pageantry of limousines and inaugural balls. He even sent his daughter, Amy, to public school. It was a new day in Washington.

Although the initial optimism of the Carter administration lasted for more than that one day, trust in his leadership in particular, and in America in general, eroded over the course of his tenure. The country underwent more upheaval than renewal in the late 1970s. High interest rates and recalcitrant stagflation characterized the struggling economy. In late 1978, the Iranian revolution led to the second oil crisis and eventually the hostage crisis, which began in late 1979 and lasted through the final days of the Carter administration. These twin crises, and Carter's apparent inability to manage them, led many Americans to fear for the country's future.

Politically, Carter's leadership was disappointing at best. From the beginning, Carter suffered challenges in dealing with Congressional leaders. Believing it was a failure of message, rather than a failure of policy, Carter brought two campaign advisors (his pollster, Pat Caddell, and his advertising producer, Gerald Rafshoon) into the White House. After this overtly political act, of bringing the campaign inside the White House, Carter came to be seen as another politician, in the vein of Richard Nixon.

Existing interpretations of the 1980 election analyze Jimmy Carter's defeat in multiple ways. Scholars of the election point to Carter's failure to manage the economy, the hostage crisis, or both. Others argue that Reagan's victory was a triumph of working-class conservatism, a result of babyboomers' maturity, and a decisive moment in the Republican Party's twenty-year coalition-building project.[1]

While all of these are very good explanations for the outcome of the 1980 election, it is also true that Reagan was a more congenial, telegenic, authentically appealing, likable guy. Where Reagan spoke to the American people, Carter seemed to speak above them; where Reagan harkened morality, Carter moralized; where Carter hid in a Rose Garden, Reagan wore rose-colored glasses. Reagan offered voters something that they wanted — hope. They had reached for it with Carter in 1976, but caught a bad case of malaise instead.

By 1980, the charming peanut-picking long-shot candidate of 1976 had become the persona onto which the nation projected its woes; he had become the single symbol of "national malaise." Less visible in scholarship on the 1980 campaign is that Carter faced a crisis of authenticity in 1980. Carter's first hurdle was one that all sitting presidents must overcome in modern campaigns — he had to stand accountable for promises made and broken; he was forced to answer for moments of failure, dishonesty, and political compromise. He also had to run as the ultimate Washington insider — the president of the United States.

As illustrated in the previous chapter, Jimmy Carter's "personal characteristics contributed significantly to his victory in 1976."[2] If Carter had found success in 1976 with the everyman image, the current occupant of 1600 Pennsylvania Avenue could not believably recycle those winning images from the first campaign. Carter's media advisor, Gerald Rafshoon, bemoaned the position: "We were the incumbent establishment candidate."[3]

Not only would Carter have to run as president and not as a peanut farmer, but he would also have to do so under trying circumstances. The hostage crisis created a catch–22 campaign situation for the incumbent. On the one hand, he could not abandon the ship of state for the campaign. On the other hand, holed up in the Rose Garden, Carter looked like he was avoiding the public. It was a public, after all, that had been set in opposition to its president. Carter's much maligned 1979 "malaise" speech seemed to blame ordinary folks for the problems of the country. Not only was Carter *not* one of us, he was against all of us, and hiding out in the White House.

The outcome of the 1980 election, however, did not reflect merely Carter's failures as president, but also the political genius of the Republican opposition. While Reagan's campaign and leadership style was often described as regal and detached, on the campaign trail in 1980, he was not nearly so aloof and monarchical as he is sometimes remembered. Reagan's speech patterns were more informal than formal, incorporating conversational transitions such as "Well now," "but," "so," and "I guess." These colloquialisms made Reagan seem more ordinary, and although his image was thoroughly manufactured, he came across as less constructed. As Reagan himself told reporters on November 3, 1980, "Would you laugh if I told you that I think, maybe, they see themselves and that I'm one of them? I've never been able to detach myself or think that I, somehow, am apart from them."[4] Far from aloof, Reagan was able to parlay his past into an appealingly authentic American image for the 1980 campaign by using personality and charisma, plain language and common sense solutions, and by drawing from national myth and memory to create an appealing image of America with himself at its center.[5] As Reagan's friend Michael Novak noted, "Perhaps this is why Reagan always sounded ... so genuine and authentic.... 'What you see is what you get,' those who knew him well often said ... [and] most of the American public" trusted him.[6]

The Reagan campaign, and its candidate in particular, understood the importance of image and style in political retail. His aides and advisors understood the magic of their man — his charisma — and used it to their advantage. As Reagan's political advisor Lyn Nofziger noted, "People instinctively like and trust Ronald Reagan, and they'll vote for him."[7] Rather than forcing Reagan to get down in the weeds over policy and particulars, they allowed Reagan to run on personality and trust almost exclusively.

These Last Few Hours in My Life...

Unlike Ronald Reagan, Jimmy Carter could (and would) not construct his campaign around personality in 1980. This marked a striking departure from his smiling, congenial outsider-bid in 1976. To illustrate the differences, it is useful to contrast Carter's 1976 convention film, *Jimmy Who?* with the 1980 production, *This Man, This Office*. Although both films were produced by Gerald Rafshoon, the images were strikingly different. *Jimmy Who?* depicted a humble populist, whose roots in the Georgia soil connected him to average Americans. By contrast, *This Man, This Office* connected Carter not to ordinary Americans, but to iconic leaders of America's past. Where in the earlier film Carter was endorsed by his mother, his wife, and the plain-spoken folks of Plains, Georgia, Rafshoon now opted for more illustrious endorsements. In 1980, Carter's endorsements came from the very Washington insiders and powerful elite against whom Carter had run in 1976.[8] This shift was evident in the polls. Whereas in 1976 Carter polled strongest on questions of sincerity and empathy, in 1980, he outscored Reagan only in experience and expertise.[9]

Given these circumstances and the realities of incumbency, in preparation for the 1980 campaign, Carter's advisors laid out the president's perceived strengths and weaknesses: "Strengths: (1) peace, (2) trust, (3) safety, (4) moderation, (5) incumbency, (6) courage."[10] Notably absent were empathy and personality. As they ought to have learned from their own 1976 victory over Gerald Ford, incumbency and moderation alone could not win a campaign for president. In choosing a head of government, Americans required expertise, experience, and moderation. But a head of state needed to be a symbolic and inspiring figure. Jimmy Carter represented neither of these things on the campaign trail in 1980. If Carter had tried to build his campaign around image and personality in 1980, he might have found it an insurmountable challenge. By 1980, most Americans did not see the president as a plainspoken peanut farmer, but as a Washington insider and a power-hungry political animal.[11] No longer a humble Cincinnatus, but now a powerful professional politician, Jimmy Carter's actions were interpreted differently in 1980 than they had been in 1976. A campaign trip down the Mississippi River, for example "was highly criticized as a huge shameless media event."[12] Another time, "somebody did a piece about how the President had kissed a baby ... which just showed what a conniving SOB this guy was."[13] There was a catch–22 to both the media's interpretation of and voters' responses to Carter's campaign. As focus groups research found, on the one hand, a Carter advertisement showing the president at a kitchen table helping his daughter with her homework was perceived as phony and contrived.[14] On the other hand, efforts to show the candidate in the Oval Office were viewed as attempts to take advantage of "the incumbency by showing Carter handling the affairs of state."[15]

Although the public had come to expect access to the political backstage, Carter did not help his case when he granted public access to internal campaign decision making, which served to expose his own political calculations. Carter's "admission" that he was torn between campaigning and maintaining an image of leadership in the White House during the hostage crisis "deepened public cynicism."[16] This perception was not unwarranted. Because Carter framed his choice in political terms — campaigning for votes versus "appearing" presidential, the president exposed his own political machinations. In short, as journalist Martin Schram commented, Carter "no longer seemed decent and honorable, but manipulative."[17]

Rose Garden Redux

Part of this was the problem of the presidency as a platform for campaigning. There was an underlying assumption of inauthenticity attached to the address, 1600 Pennsylvania Avenue. For example, when Carter attempted to conjure the spirit of '76 by saying in one advertisement that "nothing is more important to me than spending time with you," focus groups reacted with alternating laughter and skepticism. "Some respondents commented that the words of the President" were "corny and unrealistic."[18]

The campaign's "Light" advertisement met equal disdain. The commercial featured a dimly lit, early-morning West Wing. Carter emerged from the ground floor, scurried up a flight of stairs, and entered a door. Moments later, the viewer could see a light turn on in a second floor window.[19] Carter never faced the camera, but a voice-over narrator explained that Carter worked day and night on behalf of America. In one Baltimore focus group, respondents disliked the advertisement, noting that it was "phoney"[sic] because "Carter could not have turned the light on in the Oval Office himself." Another respondent found it contrived, noting that the "light in the Oval Office is corny."[20] Others disliked the spot because they believed that an honest man would have faced the camera. Instead, Carter ran off, never offering to confront the camera, which made him seem "dishonest." [21]

The responses to these two commercials offered insight into the problematics of the Rose Garden as both image and office. On the one hand, citizens knew that presidents did very little for themselves (turning on a light, cooking food, spending time with ordinary people, etc.). Efforts to portray Carter in flagrante appeared fake, contrived, and inauthentic. At the same time, the image of the White House, as in the second response, immediately framed Carter in a political way — he was, after all, a politician. The fact that he appeared to be sneaking in the back door reinforced their already dismal views of politicians.

But the president *was* a politician — no longer a Georgia peanut farmer crisscrossing the country on a long-shot bid to become a citizen-president. In retrospect, Carter's own advisors admitted that they had missed the point in 1980. "There is an art of running for an office when you're the insider. You can't run against the outsiders, which presented a new dimension for him."[22] And thus, in an attempt to use the office, the Carter campaign employed a traditional Rose Garden strategy through the primaries and into the early general election campaign. Aides wagered that the hostage crisis called for a moment of sober leadership. While the gamble paid off in the primaries, by the summer of 1980 Carter appeared to be hiding in the White House, out of touch with the American public.

Most of all, as a man who had been, for four years, pictured in limousines surrounded by Secret Service and an entourage of advisors, Carter was no longer a human being but a *figure*.[23] The Reagan campaign's opposition strategy framed Carter in exactly that way: "Presidents get out of touch. They become isolated. They learn of the world's reality through the people who work for them, which is to say that all too often they don't learn of it at all.... By the time" anything "is presented to the President, it is not the view that the rest of the world is seeing. He ... lost contact."[24] This was markedly different from the hand-shaking, whistle-stopping, homegrown, Georgia peanut farmer who ran for president in 1976. Jimmy Carter's White House had seemingly forgotten many of its own campaign assertions of 1976. Wrapped up in the internal politics of the Beltway, Washington insiders "have a hard time realizing that people in St. Louis don't give a damn about what's in the headlines of the *Washington Post*."[25]

Themselves students of the 1976 campaign, Reagan's managers knew that Carter was running a losing strategy and they used the Rose Garden against the president. In a 1980 debate-briefing memo, for example, Reagan advisor Ed Gray instructed his candidate to hammer home the following point: "Perhaps Mr. Carter has spent too much time in the Rose Garden. He seems unaware or unconcerned about the extent of the suffering of the American people."[26] This line of attack must have been familiar to the Carter campaign team, as they had employed it in 1976 against Gerald Ford. As Carter advisor Gerald Rafshoon admitted, "In some respects we probably forgot the lessons that we taught the country in 1976."[27]

Carter's other advisors, too, admitted that the president had become cloistered in the Rose Garden: "The people like him when they see him, but they don't like him now."[28] Advisor Bert Lance later surmised, "The Rose Garden strategy was a mistake.... He's been the fellow who's been saying, 'Look, the insiders have done you bad. That elite establishment up there in Washington are crazy...' Then he gets to be the establishment and they make it be unnatural in his campaign situation by saying, 'It's really better that you stay in the Rose Garden.'"[29]

Billy Beer

It was not merely the image of the Rose Garden or a cloistered president that caused a backlash against the White House in 1980. Jimmy Carter had promised change, hope, and honesty. Running against corruption in 1976, Carter's fresh-faced former self had made promises for which he would later be held accountable. When the new administration first arrived in Washington in 1977, decked out in blue jeans and promising to "de-pomp" Washington, the Carter team was the anti-establishment. Soon, however, the "Georgia Mafia" became a cabal of nepotism, ineptitude, and corruption.

With respect to corruption, a series of high-profile scandals dogged the administration for much of its tenure. Carter's Office of Management and Budget director, Bertram Lance, was fired amid corruption allegations in 1977. Billy Carter, the president's brother, was initially a nuisance, but later became a serious threat to the president's reputation. Using his brother's fame for profit, in 1977 Billy Carter began promoting Billy Beer. The failure of Billy Beer must have been a relief for the administration. More seriously, during the so-called Billygate scandal, the president's brother registered as a foreign agent of the Libyan government, expressed anti–Semitic vitriol, and accepted a loan from the Libyan government. While the administration had done nothing wrong, in an effort to mitigate the fallout, the Carter team was less than forthright about Billy Carter.[30] Combined, all of this contributed to a sense that Carter had not held himself accountable to the standards by which average folks were required to live.

Beyond the headliner scandals, Carter's appointments and associations became problematic on another level. While Carter had campaigned on an anti-political platform, he brought two important Georgians into the White House with him. Gerald Rafshoon, an advertising producer out of Georgia, had made the commercials for the 1976 campaign and was brought to Washington first as an advisor, and later as communications director. Carter became the first president to employ a full-time ad man. Pat Caddell, Carter's pollster, also joined the team. As Rafshoon later acknowledged, "Bringing your pollster into the White House full time was bad publicity. We had enough criticism. People were saying the president reacted to Caddell's advice too much. It was almost like you were bringing a pollster in to tell you how to conduct public policy."[31] These two appointments became symbolic of the White House's political style, and reminiscent of Nixon's constant campaign.

What was initially seen as an anti–Beltway spirit came to be portrayed as nepotism at best, willful ineptitude at worst. As the Georgia team became the establishment, it lost its appeal. A memo circulated within the Reagan campaign noted, "As you are aware, President Carter campaigned against the Washington bureaucracy. But 80 percent of his appointments ... have been people ... who ... do not have the practical experience necessary to turn this country around."[32] This became obvious in the administration's inability to work with Democrats in Congress. Notable challenges from within his own party, including the Kennedy candidacy, embarrassed the president and made it seem as though he was too busy taking care of his own to properly manage the country's problems. More importantly, it gave the Reagan campaign and the media a tangible point of attack against a man who had become overtly establishment.

Meanness

The humble, kindly, peanut farmer to whom Americans were introduced in 1976 was not a candidate in the 1980 cycle. Three years in Washington and a post–Watergate adversarial press had removed much of Carter's smiling sheen. But a tough primary battle within his own party had brought out a more ruthless side of Jimmy Carter. In the fall of 1980, Jimmy Carter was more likely to be portrayed in the media as small, mean, and cutthroat than the wide-smiling hick caricature of 1976.[33]

In October 1980, Jimmy Carter's nice guy image of 1976 was undercut by the "meanness" debate. The charge began after Carter accused Reagan of racism and divisiveness. As the *Christian Science Monitor* reported, "In Atlanta ... Mr. Carter was taken to have linked remarks by opponent Ronald Reagan to 'hatred' and 'racism.' The result at the news conference was the spectacle of a President of the United States repeatedly having to deny that he was running a mean campaign or attributing hatred and racism to Mr. Reagan."[34] Reagan's aides, Gerald Ford, and the press began to report Carter's personal attacks against his opponent as "mean." As *ABC World News Tonight* reported, "Carter campaign officials are deeply worried tonight that the President's re-election is slipping away because, as some of them see it, the press and public are focusing more on something called the President's meanness in discussing Governor Reagan's positions than on Governor Reagan's positions themselves ... [they] seem to be saying the press reports what it hears, and the loudest sound these days seems to be that of a strident Carter rather than a dangerous Reagan."[35]

Malaise

If he could not be nice, at least Carter could still claim knowledge, experience, and expertise — qualities on which Reagan never bested Carter in national polling. However, Carter's emphasis on facts and lists and statistics and information made him, for lack of a better term, boring. Although the campaign reversed its Rose Garden strategy mid-way through the fall campaign, Carter's stump speeches seemed out-of-touch and technocratic. He bore little resemblance to the empathetic preacher of 1976. Even his commercials were different. Whereas in 1976 people responded personally and emotionally to spots featuring Carter and his mother in a Georgia field, in 1980 he offered up commercials featuring graphs rather than farms. As one Reagan advisor summarized, Carter's advertising "lack[ed] the personal identification factor."[36]

Part of this was the problem of the position — Carter was the president of the United States during a time of overlapping national crises — the economy, the hostage crisis — he needed to be serious and controlled. Although Carter played the hand he was dealt, the dull campaign style hindered Carter's ability to reach audiences through emotion. As Gerald Rafshoon later commented, "Carter's a preacher. One of the things I used to say to Carter was, 'More preacher, less engineer. Follow your own instincts. When you're a preacher, you're great. When you're an engineer you put me to sleep. You put yourself to sleep.' And that was our fault in the White House by giving in to the thought that you had to start policy in those speeches. Reagan does it with thematic speeches. You don't have to give a list of regulations you're going to cut when you say, 'I'm going to get the government off your back; there are too many regulations. I'm going to cut red tape.'"[37]

Trying to remain serious, steady, and sedate during the hostage crisis and primary challenge, Jimmy Carter lost the personal human qualities that had made him so attractive in 1976. According to his advisors, Carter's biggest problem in the 1980 campaign was his failure to inspire (and feel inspired). Bogged down in policy specifics and overzealous speechwriters, Carter's speeches read like "laundry lists" and were delivered as such. "When he'd go off the cuff he was so good. When he ran for Governor and when he ran for President so many of those speeches were without a text. Impromptu speeches were usually good because he internalized the subject... [the 1980] speeches were different. There was something about a teleprompter and about a list of details that made him so boring."[38]

Even when the moment called for humor and personality, Jimmy Carter fell short in 1980 where he had not in 1976. At the Al Smith dinner in 1980, Lyn Nofziger recalled, "Reagan did his usual funny job, and Jimmy Carter [was] serious."[39] Thus, while Reagan spoke to voters' emotions through humor, metaphor, and symbolism, Carter attempted to prove his expertise and intelligence. As Rafshoon acknowledged, "I think when he became President he felt, *I've got to*" prove "*how much I know. I'm not going to use metaphors. I'm not going to be folksy.*"[40] Just when the country needed something to believe in, Carter offered graphs and complex foreign policy credentials.

Carter seemed to suffer a malaise of his own. He had become humorless and unappealing — no longer the hopeful farmer, but now the serious president. This was a problem of his presidency more generally. The American people had come to know their president over the previous four years as a grim spokesman for bad medicine. Throughout his term, Carter was the man in his administration who delivered bad news, while others were able to take credit for good news. "Carter had a policy about not making somebody else say the bad things."[41] As a result, nearly all of Carter's speeches were "gloomy. Energy crisis, cutbacks, rising inflation, no easy answer. Lowered expectations."[42]

The now-famous July 1979 "Malaise" speech continued to dog Carter during the 1980 campaign. While he never used the phrase "national malaise," to many, this speech shifted blame from a failure of leadership to a failure of national will. Carter appeared to blame the country, rather than himself, for the economic crisis: "In a nation that was proud of hard work, strong families, close-knit communities and our faith in God, too many of us now tend to worship self-indulgence and consumption."[43] Just when Carter could have used metaphor and symbolism and folksy charm to lift the people, he gave voice to their malaise instead. As vice presidential candidate George H.W. Bush told an audience, "The President was in Ohio yesterday ... and this is what he" said: "'You know ... people tend to dwell on the temporary inconveniences that our nation faces.' Those were the President's exact words.... Talk about insensitivity — talk about lack of understanding.... Your President says your misery is just a 'temporary inconvenience.'"[44] The Reagan campaign had clearly captured Jimmy Carter's distant remove from the American people.

Debates Debate

Carter postponed the one-to-one charisma comparison between himself and Ronald Reagan by ducking the first debate, citing the commission's decision to include independent candidate John Anderson. While Carter might have avoided one debate, he created another. Carter's refusal to debate both Anderson and Reagan made the incumbent look political and calculating.[45] By the time Carter agreed to debate Reagan on October 28, his poll numbers were down and falling. Although Carter could prove himself a master of facts and figures, he was no longer the master of an appealing image. As Carter later noted, "I thought that I was much more a master of the subject matter.... I knew that he was a master of the medium, that he was perfectly at ease before the television cameras."[46] Nonetheless, Carter believed that lengthy debates would shift the balance and make "substance rather than style ... more prevalent."[47]

The president did attempt to conjure the 1976-style Carter at moments during the 1980 debate, but these moments appeared contrived at best and dangerous at worst.[48] For example, when Carter revealed that he had consulted his daughter on the issue of nuclear arms control, he came across as more absurd than authentic. "I had a discussion with my daughter, Amy, the other day, before I came here, to ask her what the most important issue was. She said she thought nuclear weaponry — and the control of nuclear arms."[49] It is not clear whether the public would have forgiven Carter the comment had he been a mere challenger. It is clear, however, that the comment came across as patronizing, disingenuous, and unprofessional. Surely, as president of the United States, Carter had access to more expert advice. Incumbents did not enjoy the luxury of playing down to the audience. His attempt to come across as a folksy family man seemed at best thoroughly inauthentic, and at worst, grossly incompetent.[50]

Finally, in light of Carter's absence from the Anderson debate, when he began his closing statements by thanking "the people of Cleveland and Ohio for being such hospitable hosts during these last few hours in my life" the president appeared more pained than grateful.[51] Like a forced guest at an awkward dinner party, Carter's grudging acknowledgment revealed a great deal to television viewers. Carter's poll numbers dropped ten percentage points in the final week of the campaign.[52]

Jimmy Who?

The president lacked the personal identification with the people that had made him so popular in 1976. The long advertisements from the 1976 campaign focused on homey, personal stories about "Carter the Man." In 1980, the long advertisements featured Carter avoiding direct communication with anyone, including the camera. Using other politicians as his surrogates, viewers felt disconnected from the president. Focus group analysis found that "Carter's long ad met with general disapproval.... One of the major complaints was that Carter never addressed the audience. Someone else did the talking for him.... The respondents pointed out that receiving endorsements from fellow politicians did not increase President Carter's rating in their eyes."[53] While Carter could not have convincingly attempted a series of "Carter the Man" commercials in 1980, Americans largely forgot who he was as a human being — they no longer related to him, and did not feel that he understood them. When voters went to the polls on November 4, 1980, they chose the man who offered hope and comfort, whom they had come to know and love on a personal level over the course of the campaign.[54]

The Creative Management of Ronald Reagan

Ironically, the 1980 Reagan campaign took many of its cues from the 1976 Carter campaign. Although he had been involved in politics since the

1960s, Ronald Reagan was very much a Washington outsider in 1980. His campaign managers knew and understood that this was an advantage rather than an obstacle to successful campaigning.[55]

When the Reagan team devised its strategy for the "Creative Management of Ronald Reagan," they came up with a key phrase that would become the organizing principle for much of the campaign: "We were so new we didn't know what 'couldn't be done'—so we did it."[56] This not only highlighted Reagan's outsider status, but it also inoculated him against charges of inexperience. It was, however, more than just an excuse — it elevated inexperience to the level of political desirability.

As a Beltway outsider, Reagan could frame the campaign as "us the people" in ways that Jimmy Carter could not. There was very much a "you and me" and an "us together" zeitgeist in the Reagan camp that, measured against Carter's oppositional tone in the "Malaise" speech, seemed not only authentic but also refreshing. An early draft of Reagan's "Vision" speech included the following highlighted text: "Beyond ... reforms ... there is something more, much more, that needs to be said tonight. That's why I want to talk with you — not about campaign issues — but about America, about us, you and me.... Together, tonight, let us say what so many long to hear: that America is still united, still strong, still compassionate, still clinging fast to the dream of peace and freedom."[57] Running as a citizen-candidate, Reagan managed to create a sense of togetherness with his audiences. As the anti-establishment campaign, the Reagan team often used its outsider status to strike a chord with American voters. Not merely a campaign ploy, the Reagan team was more in touch with average Americans than the Carter campaign, which was (more or less) cloistered in the Rose Garden.[58]

Reagan's advisors emphasized the importance of portraying Reagan as a regular guy. Frequently this meant prepping the candidate to be one of "them" when he was "there." Although these preparations were meant to make the candidate seem more comfortable and authentic, often the memos read like stage directions. In the campaign's advance materials for a visit to Detroit, Michigan, for example, the prep sheet advised: "Dress, Monday: Western Attire, Tuesday: Business Attire* Should remove jacket, loosen tie and roll up sleeves."[59] A skilled actor, Reagan was able to seem spontaneous and genuine even when following such scripted instructions.

Because Reagan was a former actor, he had to do more than just show up where people lived, dress as they dressed, and use vocabulary they understood. More than that, the campaign believed that it needed to bolster Reagan's image with a personal human story for the candidate — not an actor playing a role on a national soundstage — but a human being with a life history and a compelling personal narrative. In planning for the convention, for example, the campaign's advisory committee "Recommend[ed] at least ½ day of R.R.'s time be allocated for 'Reagan the Man' interviews in Los Angeles before convention."[60] These interviews were to focus on humble personal and childhood stories, rather than grand conquests and acting pursuits.

To be sure, Ronald Reagan was already well known to many Americans. As illustrated in the convention memo, however, his advisors did not believe that the people knew and understood Reagan *the man*. The Reagan campaign knew that voters required personal narratives in order to establish a basis for trust. This was evident in focus group responses. For example, the focus group results for one personal narrative spot produced by the Reagan campaign revealed that Reagan "was well-received" when he told his personal story of growing up as an ordinary midwestern kid. "The old film clips at the beginning were good" because they displayed a personal and human dimension to which voters could relate.[61]

We Sure Married Up

Unlike Jimmy Carter, Reagan claimed a life and a family outside of Washington. To highlight Reagan's human and personal side, the Reagan children were profiled in a July 1980 issue of *People*, which anointed the Reagan clan "an authentic American family." To the delicious joy of both readers and campaign advisors, *People* observed that the Reagans "invite judgment in a refreshing new way: not as the campaign PR experts would have them be — neatly pressed, hair slicked back, all smiles — but as they actually are."[62] Such an endorsement of authenticity was like gold to the Reagan campaign.

Certainly more experienced with public relations, and decidedly more cooperative than her children, it was Nancy Reagan who became the sum of her husband's personal narrative and, at many times, the central figure in his 1980 campaign. The Reagan campaign used Nancy in multiple capacities. She offered voters an "inside" look at the candidate as a human being, and stood as his enforcer and advocate. She was so good at this that campaign advisor Richard Wirthlin asked the speechwriters to "develop a speech with Nancy Reagan that will highlight her husband as a caring, compassionate and strong individual."[63] Across the country, Nancy was used to highlight Reagan's "personal side" and to assure voters of his "kindness, compassion, sense of humor. The governor is the candidate who, in his private and public moments, is genuinely committed to these values and planning for ... shoring up the family, the neighborhood.... The entire speech should be smothered in personal examples"[64]

A campaigner in her own right, Nancy Reagan's stump speech was used to "cite problems which indicate she listens to the people."[65] To that end, Nancy Reagan's speechwriters were encouraged to address issues by using personal examples "(e.g., 'I met a grandmother who is concerned about inflation and her fixed income; I met a student who is worrying about draft registration interfering with his education," etc.— her examples)."[66] Nancy Reagan devoted most of her speeches to incorporating as "many personal anecdotes and vignettes as she can pack in.... Nancy has got to use examples, examples, examples.... Nancy's sincerity 'always shines through' and, if that's the case, that in itself will help reinforce the Governor's image in the needed ways. Plus, it will reveal aspects of their relationship."[67]

The relationship between Ronald and Nancy Reagan was particularly important to consultants who rightfully understood that it would feed the public's interest in Reagan's private life and further soften his image. "There are a lot of heart-warming sorts of personal glimpses ... that could be used: 'He is a very sentimental man. How can you resist someone who sends flowers to your *mother* on *your* birthday, thanking her for making him the happiest man in the world?'"[68]

Although the Republican ticket was not likely to win a majority of female voters, the campaign used Nancy Reagan to appeal to women as the kind of woman to whom they could relate. Nancy's speeches proved that her husband would "deal with all of those concerns that the wives, mothers, working women, daughters and the other women of the nation have. We can think of no better vehicle to deal with women's concerns in all the aspects than the informal, unstructured dialogue among those women that we have proposed as hosted by Nancy Reagan."[69]

But perhaps the most powerful thing that Nancy Reagan contributed to the campaign was her now-famous admonition of President Carter. One of the more savvy commercials produced during the 1980 campaign season featured Nancy Reagan alone, looking straight into the camera, reprimanding Jimmy Carter for being mean to her husband.[70] Although it was a straight-on shot, it felt relatively unscripted as Nancy quietly fumed and stumbled over words with a calm inner rage. She scolded the president for being mean. That was family values, and she was their ticket. In this way, Nancy Reagan could serve as an attack dog because she negotiated her attack on authentically feminine grounds — niceness.

In later campaigns, when candidate wives became public figures, they were forced to authenticate their images as both women and public figures. For reasons that will be discussed in depth in later chapters, for Nancy Reagan and Laura Bush, this was a much simpler task than it would be for Hillary Clinton and Teresa Heinz Kerry.

Citizen Reagan

Running as the outsider, Reagan acted the citizen-candidate. Much in the way that Carter had in 1976, Reagan commented, "I went into politics in part to put up my hand and say, 'Stop.' I was a citizen politician, and it seemed the right thing for a citizen to do."[71] In this frame, Reagan was not running in order to obtain power for himself, but rather to restore America to his vision of what it should be.

The campaign's "Suggested Introduction of Ronald Reagan" to be used by advocates at various campaign stops, introduced Reagan as a regular guy concerned about the country: "A little over 10 years ago, a new kind of leader came on the scene. He wasn't a professional politician. He was a citizen who had been speaking out about the need to ... return more decision-making to the people." [72] In this narrative, Reagan did not pursue power; he did not want power. Surrogates were reminded to inform audiences that Reagan had gladly left office and returned to private life after serving his duty as governor. He had only returned to public life because he was asked to do so. "He said no Governor should serve more than two terms. He kept his word and in 1975 returned to private life.... At the urging of thousands of his fellow citizens, he became a candidate for the Republican nomination for President.... It is a pleasure to introduce him to you now."[73]

As polls showed, Reagan needed more than a citizen-campaign to best Carter in the fall of 1980. After a June 1980 survey revealed that "notably absent from the volunteered positive responses to the Reagan image are mentions of 'concern for people,'" the team set to work to construct a more empathetic image for the candidate by adding elder care to the candidate's stump speech.[74] The master campaign plan included additional speeches and images that would show "an outward concern" for people, which was deemed "necessary to project the image of concern for the common man which will allow him to cut into the Carter voting base."[75]

The Reagan campaign also began to soften the candidate's empathy deficit. In order to authenticate Reagan's values, advisors recommended that Reagan articulate his positions through personal narrative and human experience. "When addressing the 'war and peace' issue he should say he has sons and a grandson; he too worries about their safety." Reagan was encouraged to use such personal examples — from his own life and from the lives of ordinary Americans he met on the campaign trail. As one campaign memo advised, "Governor Reagan should focus on his powerful personal reasons" for seeking the solutions he offered to the American people.[76]

In Reagan's televised "Peace" speech, for example, the candidate was not a politician but a neighbor, a father, and a grandfather: "I'd like to speak to you for a few moments now, not as a candidate for the presidency, but as a citizen, a parent — in fact a grandparent — who shares with you the deep and abiding hope for peace.... I have known four wars in my lifetime — I don't want to see a fifth.... Recently, I was on the campaign trail in the state where I was born and raised, Illinois. Nancy and I traveled by bus and car in a motorcade down through the central and southern part of the state stopping at lovely towns; we visited a coal mine ... toured a productive family farm.... It was a beautiful, crisp autumn day and thousands of families had come out to see us at every stop. It was a moving experience, but I was most moved ... by the youngsters.... They are what this campaign is all about."[77]

Video Killed the Radio Star

The Reagan campaign was not just a good show. Entering the debates, Reagan's advisors recognized that the issue-specific policy polling numbers were stacked against their candidate. As a result, the debates could become problematic for Reagan. Nonetheless, Reagan's advisors knew that if voters liked the candidate, if they identified with him as a person, if they could relate to him, even the most committed New Deal Democrats might be persuaded to vote for a Republican in 1980. Although such voters would never be convinced to agree with Reagan's positions on many issues, polling and survey results found that when voters responded to the candidate emotionally, connecting with him on a personal level, they did not always appreciate ideological differences.

Reagan's advisors called this "the 'He's just like me!' syndrome" and hoped it was contagious.[78] As Dick Wirthlin predicted, Reagan could win many voters simply by being personally appealing. If a voter liked Reagan personally, he would be inclined to favor him, regardless of his positions on issues. In this way, voters would align Reagan's positions with their own, even when faced with evidence to the contrary. There was "a recognizable bias that moves the candidate closer to the respondent than is usually warranted."[79]

To that end, the Reagan campaign knew that symbolic gestures and broad statements would be more effective than policy specifics and boring lists. As Stuart Spencer advised, "It's the presence ... more than the substance."[80] Reagan did offer his generalized views on major issues, but with the understanding that, as Ed Meese advised, "issues are essentially vehicles for conveying image traits. Thus, the Governor needs to project both verbally and non verbally" in order to establish human connections with voters.[81]

In its debate analysis, CBS reported that Reagan was confident that his ability to connect with voters would play better on television than "Anderson's rhetoric or Carter's fine detail."[82] Perhaps proving the point, the most memorable moment of the 1980 debates was not Carter's expertise, but a short four-word phrase that became embedded in national memory: "There you go again." As a way of brushing off Carter's attacks, Reagan came across as more casual, collegial, personable, and reasonable. Reagan, Carter had charged, was an untrustworthy extremist whose ideology and character were outside the bounds of the American mainstream. These allegations lost their bite when Reagan repeatedly came across to audiences as a nice, friendly guy. In the 1980 debate against Carter, Reagan did not lose his head or viciously attack the president, but instead used casual dismissiveness to deflate his opponent. "There you go again" was more genuine to ordinary conversation than either the formal tone of a rehearsed debater or the aggressive tone of a right-wing nut job.[83] Reagan's advisors knew immediately that their candidate had won. "When Reagan said, 'There you go again,' in effect calling him a liar ... just wiped him out ... I think that we would have won anyway, but we won it a lot more handily because Reagan showed that he could stand up to the President of the United States."[84] Jimmy Carter's analysis was that "it showed that he was relaxed and had a sense of humor."[85]

And much of the debate did come down to style over substance. Jimmy Carter later admitted, "The debate was not a victory for me, but I still think that if you analyze the debate or listen to it on the radio, or see a transcript, there's no doubt that I won. But if you look at the television play of it, I think it's accurate for me to say or admit that Reagan won."[86] Recalling the 1960 debate between Nixon and Kennedy, the Carter team had little left but to accuse Reagan of lacking substance.

What the Carter team did not realize, however, was that the American people had learned to put little faith in the specific promises made during campaigns. Instead, voters preferred the candidate who made them most comfortable on a personal level. One internal Reagan campaign debate-prep memo advised: "In the '60 debate ... Kennedy did not respond to each of Nixon's points as Nixon was trying to do — rather he used the moment to speak directly to the American people ... our candidate should obviously not ignore the points made by his opponent ... but [he] must view this not as an opportunity to outpoint someone but an opportunity to speak directly to the American people."[87]

Reagan did speak to ordinary Americans, and he did so on their terrain. A memo circulated within the Reagan campaign argued: "The undecided voter is looking for ... the candidate they are comfortable with and for ... something positive, something practical and something they can believe in —

something, that when they hear it they say: 'That's right, that makes sense and I'm gonna vote *for* Governor Reagan."[88] Beyond budgets and numbers and lists and programs, Reagan wanted to reach voters where they lived. "To the extent possible, statements should not be in terms of billions of dollars and millions of jobs; but in supermarket food basket terms."[89]

The People Business

The Reagan team set out to capture human emotion. A memo to speech-writer Ed Meese from Andy Carter advised, "Politics is very much a people business. Human emotions, human responses, human morale, can be and usually are, far more important than technical considerations.... The campaign direction should be more broadly based, more people sensitive, more politically aware."[90] To that end, "While it is important that the candidate be able to recite some facts, ... facts ... are not important in political persuasion.... The voter wants to know whether a given candidate shares the individual voter's concerns, experiences, and hopes."[91] In this way, Reagan's candidacy would be presented in shared terms and on mutual terrain: "Governor Reagan [should] personalize his responses, show shared experiences, project common concerns."[92]

In contrast to Jimmy Carter, Ronald Reagan was advised to "let voters know that he himself has experienced the hardships of a bad economy. During the depression his father was fired and without a job.... Those are powerful images.... Here is a man who ... is not just some wealthy country club Republican with white shoes."[93] In this way, Reagan could use personal images to create a stark contrast between himself and Jimmy Carter. More importantly, Reagan needed to distinguish himself from established images of the Republican Party. Without that personal connection between himself and the experience of hardship, Reagan's advisors doubted that their candidate could win key blue-collar support from its traditional base in the Democratic Party.[94]

Impressions, empathy, and authenticity ultimately prevailed over laundry lists and policy positions. "It doesn't take a rocket scientist if you've got the touchy feely understanding of politics."[95] The Reagan campaign knew that it had a winner in the figure of Ronald Reagan. "The one thing Ronald Reagan has going for him in this election is Ronald Reagan ... speaking to all those Americans who ... want to get to know [him].... Facts, figures and coaching are fine as long as they don't screw up what we have going for us: Ronald Reagan. Let's not over coach."[96] A master of the preferred communication medium of the day, Reagan could best any opponent on the small screen. A Carter advisor concluded that television "contributed a great deal to both the oversimplification of matters and issues and questions, and so forth.... And what they get from television, I think, quite often is more impression than anything else."[97] But it was the impressions that voters remembered at the polling booth.

Reagan's advisors also believed that the "touchy feely understanding of politics" would reach more people, namely nonvoters, and inspire them to vote.[98] Nonvoters were rarely persuaded to vote on the basis of a campaign platform. Instead, they needed to be moved to the ballot box. An internal Reagan report on a Tarrance survey of nonvoters found that among target voters, most "are ... [not] dead-set against voting — it's just that they feel, apparently, that nobody pays any attention to them.... If one candidate or another is ever able to tap this hidden political resource, the shape of American politics would be changed forever."[99] By inspiring people, connecting with them intimately, Reagan intended to change "the shape of American politics."

A Folksy Common Man

The Reagan campaign's emphasis on values was not merely a reflection of the candidate's ideology and homegrown nostalgia, but a focus-grouped leitmotif that captured the spirit of the country.[100] Believing that problems "can be solved by sending those to Washington who share the values that you and your family hold dear," Reagan appealed to people on the level of moral compass and shared vision.[101] Through a broad-based appeal to an older values structure, Reagan related to people, a majority of voters, who wanted to see a different kind of America emerge in the 1980s.[102] One Reagan campaign memo advised, "The most serious failure of the Carter Administration is not in the specifics of rempid [sic] inflation, high interest rates, rising unemployment, uncertain and ineffective foreign policies, but in the failure of the American president to" reflect and anticipate prevailing value structures of ordinary Americans.[103]

While Jerry Falwell's Moral Majority would become a basis for the Christian right in the Republican Party, some of the previous scholarship on realignment in 1980 has overstated the importance of Christian fundamentalism in the values debate of the 1980s. Reagan's appeal to values was as much about an older, more patriotic, pre–1960s, pre–civil-rights-era America as it was about an America rooted in Christianity. Stuart Spencer later surmised, "The sum total of [Reagan] is simply this: here's a man who had a basic belief, who thought America was a wonderful, great country."[104] Reagan became the center of that America, offering his candidacy as a solution and himself as a kind of all–American folk figure.[105]

What Americans were looking for in the figure of Jimmy Carter in 1976, they eventually found in the figure of Ronald Reagan in 1980. As Richard Wirthlin predicted, "In the aftermath of Watergate and Vietnam, an exhausted public elected an honest, compassionate, even folksy common man to restore the country's confidence in itself. But in 1980, the national mood continues to be disenchanted and pessimistic; and therefore, not significantly different than it was before President Carter took office four years ago. The single most devastating domestic political failure of the Carter Administration has been the President's inability to provide the necessary political and moral leadership to restore the country to its proper bearings."[106]

These "proper bearings" included an idea about America that was familiar to Ronald Reagan — part imagined Midwestern childhood, part idealized small town — it nevertheless appealed to people who wanted more from their country and more from their leaders. "What we are seeing is a growing determination on the part of voters to be seen ... as human beings with values that they hold dear ... in the suburbs where the values of the old neighborhood have been preserved and in the neighborhoods themselves — this is the new coalition and it is coming our way." Giving voice to this message with a touch of anti–Washington sentiment, Reagan intoned, "For too long, your values ... have been mocked and ignored and exploited. The Washington bureaucrat and the Congressional majority have bussed your children, picked your pocket through inflation, ridiculed your desire for a strong national defense.... I say to you today: your time has come. Your values will be at the heart of the decision-making in Washington.... This is what you want and this is what you deserve."[107] It was neither right wing hyperbole nor antistatist paranoia. Instead, Reagan gave voice to a citizen candidacy, allowing voters to believe that he was with them — that they were in it together.

Conclusions

Although that kind of "in it together" rhetoric has come to be identified as uniquely Reagan, it was not so far from what Carter preached in 1976. Indeed, both men were successful for similar reasons. In the end, voters were not looking for something vastly different in 1980 than they had been in 1976. On the whole, as in 1976, voters remained skeptical of anything that was overtly political. The focus group responses to Carter and Reagan advertisements, press conferences, and debate appearances mirrored those of 1976. For example, one focus group leader reported that "people are very skeptical of" and "have a general distrust of politicians and of advertisements. A political advertisement doubles their skepticism."[108] On the whole, viewers preferred

Reagan's advertisements not because they were flashy, but because they came across as more genuine and more believable. A DMI national survey found that "Reagan spots" were "more... believable ... than Carter spots."[109] The quest for genuineness, honesty, and authenticity was the same in 1980 as it had been in 1976.

Although his advertisements were better, and his debate appearances softer, Reagan could not have won the election without pursuing that cornerstone of authenticity: trust. It was what voters were looking for in Carter in 1976; it was what they found in Reagan in 1980. Reagan built that trust by offering his personal narrative, appearing genuine, and providing a vision of America to which voters could relate. Voters were also skeptical of political sales tactics. Early in the campaign, Reagan's managers had created a grassroots organization, Commitment '80. Rather than using high-profile surrogates to endorse Ronald Reagan, the campaign would rely most heavily on citizen advocates. In the final weeks of the campaign, these citizen advocates were asked to share with their friends and neighbors "personal observation[s] of Ronald Reagan.... I am here tonight to tell you that I, my wife, my family and our friends trust Ronald Reagan."[110] It was political without being overtly political. Reagan's image was bolstered by genuine support from people who could speak to Reagan's authenticity, honesty, and trustworthiness.[111] As their friends and neighbors vouched for Reagan, many Democrats voted Republican for the first time in their lives.

Americans, on the whole, bought the image they were sold by the Reagan campaign. While voters might have remained ideologically and politically uncertain about Reagan, they liked him personally and trusted him implicitly. Deaver and Hannaford's internal post-election campaign analysis found that "Jimmy Carter, who had promised much and delivered little, was personally rejected by the voters."[112]

He may have been "personally rejected" at the polls, but more instructive is the ways in which his candidacy was interpreted and internalized throughout the course of the campaign. Voters may have been primed to reject Jimmy Carter on many grounds and for a range of reasons in 1980. Still, a good deal of the national discourse revolved around comparisons between the two candidates' authenticity and personal availability. Reagan would be remembered as one of the greatest candidates in the history of modern campaigning for this very reason. He could speak to voters on their turf and in their terms, endowing his candidacy with an unforgettable American, personal, and human authenticity.

3

Morning in America: 1984

It was a star-spangled summer. From the medal podium in Los Angeles to the briefing room podium in Washington, the national mood was patriotic, its spirit reified in the authentically American figure of President Ronald Reagan.[1] As Reagan toured the country during the summer and fall of 1984, he was greeted with the familiar chant, made popular and possible by the Los Angeles Olympics: "U.S.A! U.S.A!" The parallels between the two — Reagan's reelection rallies and the '84 Olympics — has been widely noted by political scientists and historians. Working synergistically throughout the summer and early fall of 1984, the heightened patriotism of each bolstered the emotionalism of both. There were multiple common threads between the Olympic spirit and the reelection spirit; ABC's Olympics promotional slogan mirrored Reagan's reelection slogan. The broadcast network's "rebirth of a nation" was easy to equate with Reagan's "New Beginning." In many ways, the Olympics and Reagan's campaign sustained and fortified one another, inspiring patriotism and peddling optimism.

To be sure, Reagan would have won reelection without the Los Angeles Olympics. Nonetheless, his version of America was broadcast in living rooms across the country throughout the Olympics. Reagan's intonation, "America is back and standing tall" was clearly displayed on the medal podiums in Los Angeles, reifying the president's campaign message and authenticating his narrative.

Americans cheered their president as he embarked on an old-fashioned whistle-stop, indulging his new era of good feelings. In their best flag-waving, bunting-hanging, balloon-dropping, U.S.A.-chanting zeal, crowds energetically adopted the Reagan zeitgeist. To mark the end of the summer and the beginning of his fall campaign, the president celebrated Labor Day at "a park in California ... in a sun-washed patriotic extravaganza that showcased his casual, upbeat brand of oratory."[2] Amid a crowd of "50,000 true believers"

Reagan asked the audience to support his bid for reelection, promising, "'You ain't seen nothing yet!'" His audience returned the enthusiasm, responding, "'Four more years!'" Ever charming, and with oodles of "aw, shucks," Reagan replied, "'You talked me into it!'"[3] The crowd laughed and cheered and fell in love with Reagan again and again. Captured this way in the national media, few Americans could avoid Reagan's spirited return to the campaign trail.

Although Walter Mondale had witnessed a balloon drop or two in his day, the summer of 1984 was decidedly less sweet for the Democratic challenger. His nomination still insecure heading into the Democratic National Convention, the only sunshine in his summer had been a brief, brilliant, wag-the-dog moment when he announced his running mate, the first major party female vice presidential candidate, Geraldine Ferraro.[4] On the whole, however, things were less than star-spangled for Mondale as he entered the fall campaign.

Mondale's Labor Day offered an illustrative diptych. As Reagan was rousing crowds in California, back on the East Coast, there was no upbeat oratory, no festive picnic, and no cheering crowds for Walter Mondale. The Mondale campaign assumed it had carefully set the stage for a successful rally on Labor Day 1984. Mondale and Ferraro were to be the center of New York City's Labor Day Parade — a city that ought to have been the center of their support, a union crowd that was supposed to form their base. But the crowd never materialized. As *Time* reported, the Democratic pair was met by a city that was "eerily empty." Despite the absence of an audience, however, they kept to script: "Smiles fixed, they wave[d] energetically at no one in particular."[5] The *New York Times* groaned, "*ABC* even showed Walter Mondale and Geraldine Ferraro waving from a reviewing stand to a parade that wasn't there."[6] ABC was not the only network to air the humiliating scene; within the news cycle, reports of Mondale's Labor Day catastrophe had reached far and wide. The image of Mondale was devastatingly unpresidential. Mondale not only appeared to be a leader without followers and a fool without friends, but also an over-scripted politico unable to adjust to his circumstances and environment.

Are They Choosing a Leader, or Going to the Movies?

The Labor Day incident underscored the importance of televisual imagery in modern campaigning. Because television was the primary medium through which they experienced the campaign, it was only natural that voters responded to the images presented to them. The *New York Times* captured this experience of the campaign: "The evidence in the polls so far is that they are not thinking much about the issues, but mainly about the personalities. Are they choosing a leader or going to the movies?"[8] As television privileged symbolic gestures and iconographic images, Mondale's advisors whined that Reagan enjoyed an unfair advantage in the contest. Throughout the 1984 campaign, Democratic leaders grumbled about their unfortunately untelegenic nominee: "'Next time' they would have to field a candidate who was a much better television performer than Fritz Mondale."[9]

In fairness, television did favor the candidate who could better project a visual persona. At the conclusion of the campaign, Mondale joked, "I think you know I've never really warmed up to television, and in fairness to television, it's never really warmed up to me."[10] It was a display of honest self-deprecating personality that had not been present during the campaign. Humor aside, Mondale's joke revealed a reality of circumstances. As television served to amplify candidates' social ease, grace, and style, Mondale's inability to warm to the medium did put him at a disadvantage.[11] After all, he was challenging a man who was arguably the most telegenic candidate in the history of American politics. As Howell Raines observed in The *New York Times* at the height of the campaign, "Mr. Reagan had the luck to come on the political stage at a time in history when Presidential contests increasingly seem to hinge on personality.... Measured against the incumbent, then, Mr. Mondale is a Presidential candidate with a double problem. He is the quintessential issues politician, and he is uncomfortable with television."[12]

The television did not make Reagan nor did it break Mondale. Their abilities to appear natural and project presidentiality across the medium, however, did very much inform voters' decisions at the ballot box.[13] Midway through the fall campaign, The *Christian Science Monitor* determined that "voters watching the" campaign on television "will make their judgments based first on the candidates' personalities and images.... Apparently the way a candidate expresses a view has been more important to voters than the view itself."[14] The statement was not unfounded. In polls, Reagan's personal popularity always surpassed his job performance ratings.[15] As Reagan's advertising manager Phil Dusenberry acknowledged, "We had a great product, President Reagan, telegenic, a national grandfather. Whether you liked his policies or disagreed with him, you liked him.... So it didn't matter whether you disagreed with his policies so much as everyone just really gravitated toward the guy, and because he was telegenic.... When [voters] go in there to pull that lever, they ... are often swayed purely by their emotional judgment. If you bring an emotional component to political advertising and do it very skillfully, you can really make a difference for your candidate."[16]

The Reagan Revolution?

None of this is meant to suggest that voters were duped by a slick adman. Nor should it suggest that they were shallow and mindless in their candidate-selection process. It ought to suggest that there was no real "Reagan Revolution" in any permanent and political sense. In the days following the 1984 election, pundits wondered whether Reagan's overwhelming electoral landslide represented permanent party realignment and the ultimate triumph of the conservative movement. While there were more self-identified Republicans in 1984 than there were in 1964, there is no evidence to suggest that the country underwent any permanent party realignment in 1984.[17]

Further, there is little to suggest that 1984 marked the triumph of the forces of conservatism. Although Reagan has been remembered as a right-winger, the architects of Reagan's reelection campaign carefully opted to make the campaign about optimism and personality, rather than about partisanship and ideology. Realizing that any hard-line position on social and economic issues would likely alienate otherwise persuadable voters, Jim Baker determined to make the election about Ronald Reagan, but not about divisive issues.[18] As historian Gil Troy noted, Reagan "knew he was more popular than his program."[19]

This was acknowledged even among Reagan's top advisors. According to Bob Teeter, the 1984 election "was not a realignment.... This election very simply represented a choice.... This was a vote up or down on Ronald Reagan. That includes his leadership, which in turn includes both his personality and personal characteristics."[20] While many argued that the 1980 and 1984 elections represented a conservative shift and a political realignment, Teeter believed that "the uniqueness to this election ... is Ronald Reagan.... He has the ability to communicate." Reagan was able to communicate with "voters in a way that no politician in my experience ever has. It is a very rare politician who can sit down before a television camera, look at the voters, and talk to them directly, and be perfectly understandable to them and have them absolutely believe and trust in what he says."[21]

In the months following the 1984 election, the Brookings Institution also doubted the realignment theory of the Reagan landslide. Arguing that the 1984 election was more reflective of Eisenhower's victory in 1956 than Roosevelt's in 1936, James Sundquist interpreted Reagan's mandate as the "personal victory of [a] popular" president "with no significant lasting impact on the party system." Indeed "the landslide Republican triumph ... did not extend to a *party* sweep in the contests for other offices."[22] While House Democrats lost only a few seats, maintaining majority control, in the Senate the opposition party managed a net gain of two seats.[23] These figures, combined with the data from the 1982 midterm election (in which Democrats enjoyed a net gain of seven governorships and twenty-six House seats) suggested that American voters were not wholeheartedly on board with the Republican agenda. In short, Reagan was able to project sincerity, communicate with voters, and embody their image of presidentiality. Over four years, he was not only able to portray himself as a believable president, but he was able to redefine many voters' ideal representation of presidentiality — so much so that voters offered Ronald Reagan more electoral votes than any candidate in American history.

In the final analysis, it is not clear that the 1984 election represented the endgame of conservative realignment, but it is clear that voters selected the man they liked better — who connected with them personally and who touched them emotionally. At the time, political scientist Gerald Pomper surmised that the most obvious "explanation of Reagan's victory is Reagan himself. The President's success is not due to his record or his philosophy, but to his 'image.' In this interpretation, tens of millions of Americans voted for a likable individual."[24] As John Anderson noted, "The parties don't stand for anything.... Increasingly, everything revolves around personalities."[25] Ultimately, the 1984 election firmly established Ronald Reagan as America's president.

You May Have Heard of Me...

Although Walter Mondale was a former vice president, a former senator, and a former Minnesota state attorney general, he did not exude presidentiality in the way that Ronald Reagan did.[26] Walter Mondale's résumé ought to have made him a believable candidate. But in an era when voters needed to discover personal stories and human capacity in order to establish a candidate's presidentiality, Mondale's well-known penchant for privacy put him at a distinct disadvantage. Walter Mondale did not emotionally represent Americans as they saw themselves, nor the national mood as they wanted it to be. Instead, he appeared to reflect Garrison Keillor's caricature of Minnesotans: "We come from people who brought us up to believe that life is a struggle ... if you should ever feel really happy, be patient. This will pass." His résumé included a lifetime of public service, but it was rarely enough to attract large crowds or favorable attention from the press.[27] Most importantly, Mondale was unable to structure his candidate image to suit the new terrain of campaign discourse.

Wobegon

The 1984 Democratic National Convention was Walter Mondale's opportunity to showcase his personal narrative and private life in order to establish a human connection with viewers at home. Compared to his contemporary opponent (Ronald Reagan), and former running mate (Jimmy Carter), Fritz Mondale's convention did little to convince voters of his inherent personality. His campaign film, which was not aired by the major networks, did little to explore, explain, or describe the candidate as a person.[28] Instead, after brief footage of Fritz fishing alone and playing tennis with a staff member, the nine-minute spot offered its case for Mondale's candidacy: "A lifetime of leadership."[29] Still photographs from Mondale's career in politics were followed by a series of clips from Mondale's campaign. Beginning with a lengthy speech in an auditorium, and continuing with a series of lectures on taxes, fairness, and defense, the film told voters very little about Mondale the man. To be sure, most Americans did not see the film, as it was not aired on the networks. The few who did have the opportunity to view Mondale's cinematographic résumé were left with no strong impression of the man's authentic character, personality, or presidentiality.

In the convention hall, the campaign video was followed by Mondale's acceptance speech, which was aired by the networks. Like the film, however, Mondale's speech offered policy instruction, but not personal illustration. Mondale did not even approach the topic of himself until the second part of the speech. When he did broach the topic, he discussed his life story passionately, but only briefly: "You may have heard of me — but you may not really know me. I grew up in the farm towns of southern Minnesota. My dad was a preacher, and my mom was a music teacher. We never had a dime. But we were rich in the values that were important.... They taught me to work hard; to stand on my own; to play by the rules; to tell the truth; to obey the law; to care for others; to love our country; to cherish our faith."[30] Except for those brief personal remarks, Mondale's speech was substantive — focusing on the Reagan record and the Democrats' prescriptions for a better future.

This was to be the extent of what most television viewers learned about Walter Mondale during the Democratic National Convention. The preceding days' speeches (by Mario Cuomo, Jesse Jackson, and Geraldine Ferraro) not only upstaged Mondale's presentation, but also failed to mention the candidate in any meaningful way. Mario Cuomo's famous speech focused on Ronald Reagan's record; Jesse Jackson used his address to introduce the Rainbow Coalition; Geraldine Ferraro used her speech to claim her place as the representative of the underrepresented.

Gray Suits

Unfortunately for him, Mondale's convention was representative of his campaign as a whole. Mondale's speeches were substantive, proving his workhorse reputation and commitment to public service. While essential to good governance, neither of these qualities were enough to hold an audience. His speeches delivered substance and specifics, but little by way of personal connection and human experience. Compared to Reagan's rousing and uplifting rallies, Mondale offered voters a standard stump speech that was, the press reported, "long, focused on complicated issues" and typically delivered "to a group about one-fortieth the size" of crowds at Reagan rallies.[31] This was not necessarily the experience of Mondale's campaign events, but it was the impression projected by the media. As Mondale's press secretary, Maxine Isaacs, moaned, nightly news broadcasts featured Ronald Reagan delivering patriotic messages, based purely on symbol and image. Then the broadcast would cut to "Mondale explaining something terribly complicated about the deficit or about arms control."[32]

As polls revealed that Mondale was consistently trailing by ten to twenty points, Mark DiCamillio of the Field Institute analyzed the race this way: "Right now the public is looking at the race in the personality sense, and if it makes its decision on that level, Ronald Reagan has the edge.... I don't know if the public makes up its mind on just issues."[33] Mondale's campaign advisors were not unaware of this disadvantage. They feared that they had lost the election when Reagan decided to launch a campaign based on his personal connection to voters "rather than programmatic, issue-oriented things."[34]

Another of Mondale's failures was his inability to illustrate his commitment in any emotional or personal way. As Richard Leone, senior advisor to the Mondale campaign recalled, "Our fundamental weakness was" that Mondale was perceived as "bland and uninspiring."[35] Voters had learned to tune out campaign promises, which rarely came true. Instead they had learned to trust the feeling behind a candidate's platform and his ability to project sincerity in both the diagnosis of and prescription for social, economic, and political problems. As analyst and pundit John Merriam noted, "'Mondale might have been able to make an issue of fairness, but he never dramatized it'.... Many political pros have long believed that Mondale's problem is not his message but his manner. 'For the race to turn into a personality contest is devastating for Mondale.... Mondale's only hope was to win on the issues.... But ... issues have just about dropped out of sight.'"[36]

Mondale's lack of enthusiasm, passion, and personal connectedness were apparent in his campaign events. The few who attended these events felt it. Many more at home read and heard about it. As one columnist informed his readers, Mondale "has been about as exciting as a shopping center on Sunday afternoon."[37] In contrast to Reagan, whose ratings in the polls improved every time he campaigned in a particular area, Walter Mondale's numbers plunged as he traveled the country. The Reagan campaign's internal tracking polls showed that Mondale lost support in key states after making campaign appearances.[38] Mondale did not attract valuable local press, nor could he stack up to Reagan's vibrancy and charisma in campaign stops.[39]

A nationally syndicated narrative about Mondale became the story of his campaign. On *ABC World News Tonight*, Brit Hume chided, "Sometimes Walter Mondale is so formal, even at home ... his closet may have more gray suits than some stores and those suits seem a metaphor for his campaign style ... dull.... With Mondale now pitted against the amiable and telegenic Ronald Reagan ... there is another related problem for Mondale: the television camera is unkind to him.... The image that comes through the TV screen ... is of a paler, older and wearier man."[40] It was clear that, at least in the media, human authenticity was the central organizing principle for the campaign story. Mondale suffered as a result.

If Mondale failed to present his positions on issues with passion and enthusiasm, he also failed to expose his personal narrative, which was integral to successful modern campaigning. The media coverage reflected Mondale's almost single-minded focus on substance. Not known for its heavy discussion of politics, even *People* was forced to get into the policy weeds when its reporters interviewed Mondale. Although *People* offered an article about Mondale in late July 1984, the piece did not resemble earlier, more lighthearted articles about the personal lives and personalities of Jimmy Carter and Ronald Reagan. The article did describe Mondale's poverty-stricken childhood in World War II–era Elmore, Minnesota, but only as a means of discussing his deep commitment to liberal values. The reporter contended that Mondale's congressional work was the result of years of struggle, beginning in childhood when Mondale first learned to defend the poor people of Elmore. The only reference to Mondale in the present was a less than flattering portrait, "It's hard to recognize the poor preacher's son of 40 years ago in the polished, starched politician Walter Mondale has become."[41] Compared to previous articles about Reagan and Carter, the story was a flat re-telling of Mondale's childhood hardships, without lively anecdotes about the candidate's children, hobbies, or private life. Although readers learned that Mondale was a playful child, the thesis of the article was much heavier: a poor preacher's son learned the work ethic and moral values that eventually allowed him to become a stilted, dry, liberal crusader in his adult life.

People was not the only media outlet — print or broadcast — to ignore Mondale's family and personal life. The Mondale campaign itself all but hid the candidate's children, hobbies, and supposed sense of humor.[42] The *New*

York Times complained, "When it comes to personality, Mr. Mondale has refused to open himself to the probings of the camera. Instead, he has left it to the cartoonists and the Republicans to limn him as the embodiment of what Mr. Reagan calls 'the unhappy past.'"[43] Reporter Meg Greenfield all but begged Mondale to expose his private life for public consumption. "If Mondale is such a terrific guy, it is up to him and no one else to prove it. America is not going to be bused into his living room.... If he is not, as the current criticism has it, a whiner and a yielder and a guy who can bore you to death, then let him show it."[44]

Garrison Keillor would say that Mondale was burdened by a touch of the Midwest-Norwegian-Wobegon antipathy to publicity. Wobegon or not, both the press and public refused to give Mondale a free pass. "On the stump, the public Mondale is almost always impeccably groomed, his silver-gray hair meticulously combed, his blue suit always pressed.... Privately, senior aides concede the problem of Mondale's public image, as conveyed by the television camera, the preachy, whiny, overly serious politician with deep lines rimming his eyes."[45] It was not enough for his campaign aides and friends to vouch for his personality.[46]

David Broder informed his readers, "There is ... a more subtle kind of forgiveness the Mondale campaign is seeking from voters — a willingness to accept a presidential candidate with a less vivid and attractive personality than the incumbent."[47] Even within the Mondale camp, advisors realized that "Mondale's chance of success was linked directly to getting the voters to feel 'comfortable' with him as he is.... Unless swing voters get 'comfortable' with Mondale," the Democratic candidate would not be able to defeat Reagan. "They have to ... get past feeling uncomfortable about Mondale."[48]

We Luv Yah, Gerry!

For a brief moment in the summer of 1984, the Democrats did best the Republicans in the personality contest. When Walter Mondale introduced his running mate, Geraldine Ferraro, Americans were rapt. While much of the press attention focused on the novelty of her gender, a good deal of the attention was lavished on Ferraro's undeniable authenticity. After the Ferraro choice, Mondale's campaign chairman James Johnson told *Time*, "Walter Mondale has never experienced a day like this before. People were actually crying. He has never had this kind of response, this same kind of excitement."[49]

Ferraro was all Queens, with a thick accent and a New York vernacular. She was a straight-shooter who appeared to say exactly what she meant. Lee Atwater, the deputy director of the Reagan campaign, admitted, "I was afraid that if she had the right message, she could have more credibility ... than Mondale would."[50] For a moment, the Democrats appeared to be fighting (and winning) on the Republicans' turf. "Mrs. Ferraro's personality contrasts starkly with Mr. Mondale's cautious, buttoned-down style, and audiences watch her and respond to it.... At a sweltering rally at the state capitol in Austin, Mrs. Ferraro was welcomed with a surge of applause by as many as 8,000 people. 'Oh, you're incredible!' she shouted. A moment later she told the cheering crowd: 'Texans are confident, tough, tender people. They don't make excuses. They get results. And that's the kind of Vice President I'm going to be.'"[51]

As Ferraro began her post-convention media blitz, she was a refreshingly authentic addition to the Mondale campaign. Walter Mondale offered little more than a policy-oriented stump speech at his events, but Gerry Ferraro could rouse an audience with a heavily accented call-and-response. "The crowds have begun to pick up on her familiar phrases and lob them back. Signs reading 'We Luv Ya, Gerry!' have begun popping up, and supporters yell back her familiar exclamation with assumed New York intonation, 'Yer teh-rif-fic!'"[52] *New York Times* columnist Maureen Dowd marveled, "The candidate was asked why Walter F. Mondale would be more successful than Ronald Reagan in a parley with the Soviets. 'Lemme just put it to ya this way,' Geraldine A. Ferraro began.... Syntax and thoughts were flying, vowels were flattening and syllables were dropping. But the audience ... was listening raptly and admiringly, caught up in the tough and sassy Queens speaking style that has become the surprise hit of the campaign season."[53]

America's love affair with Gerry was short-lived. Reports detailing Ferraro's inauthenticities caused voters to wonder about the woman they had so recently admired. When the press began digging into Ferraro's background, they uncovered the story of a politician who rose up through a political machine, who had used her power and the patronage system for personal gain. Among other things, the press began reporting that Ferraro had reverted to her maiden name because it carried more clout in Queens politics. According to widespread reports, she used that clout to become enmeshed in dirty politics. As Margaret Shapiro wrote in the *Washington Post,* "The Queens Democratic organization ... like its counterparts in other boroughs in this city or old cities like Chicago ... still doles out judgeships ... spots on the Democratic ticket and money-making assignments at the courthouse to the party faithful.... The political world of Queens is the base from which Ferraro rose to play a historic role as the first woman to run on a major national ticket. As politicians here tell it, she has excelled at maneuvering through the intricacies of an old-school political system," which still acts as "funnels for the patronage system. They place allies in jobs ranging from a $50-a-day poll watcher on election day, to parking inspector, assistant prosecutor or on the ballot for judge.... Geraldine Ferraro has had the right sort of connections for Queens," and Ferraro's Husband, John Zaccaro, was one such beneficiary of the patronage system, securing jobs and connections as a result of his wife's position."[54]

As the press began to dig into her background, Ferraro became defensive. Once accused, Ferraro "reverted to a combative, impersonal" style that ultimately "undercut her credibility."[55] Voters began to question her authenticity, suddenly turned off to her charms. Indeed, Ferraro came to be seen as thoroughly inauthentic as she appeared to squirm and prevaricate when questions were raised about her husband's finances and her own connections to the Queens political machine.[56] Suddenly viewed as the beneficiary of patronage and special privileges, Ferraro was further damaged by her responses to the charges. As Reagan campaign aide Lee Atwater noted, "Once she got on the defensive, she could never get her own message out."[57]

In the end, Ferraro ended up hurting the Mondale ticket. Reagan's pollsters found that "of those people who voted for Reagan because they did not like Mondale, 10 percent said they voted against Mondale because of his selection of Ferraro."[58] Unfortunately for the Mondale campaign, which was hoping to gain momentum following the Ferraro nomination, the damage had been done. "To the extent there was a Ferraro phenomenon, this ended it for the rest of the campaign ... because it politically took the varnish off her, and she was never able to get it back."[59]

There You Go Again... Again

Following weeks of negative press attention resulting from Ferraro's financial fallout, the Mondale campaign needed something to make it relevant again. Walter Mondale achieved this in Louisville, Kentucky, on October 7, 1984. Although debating had never been Reagan's forte, he had performed well against Carter in 1980—displaying sharp wit and commonsense responses to the then beleaguered president. Reagan was far from beleaguered entering the debate against Walter Mondale in 1984. However, when the two went head-to-head on national television, the entire balance of the campaign shifted—if only for a few hours. Where Mondale was sharp and witty, the president seemed slow and confused. Going into the debate, few expected that Reagan would be able to best Mondale on the basis of facts and figures, but most assumed that Reagan would be able to charm his way through the debates. When he did not, the "age issue" became the media's new favorite fascination.

After the first debate, Walter Mondale experienced a brief period of popularity and connectedness with American voters. Having faced attenuated crowds throughout the early fall, Mondale was suddenly attracting audiences with more supporters than hecklers. In an interview with *Time*, he gushed about his now crowded campaign rallies: "Enormous crowds, but not just that; the nature of the crowds too. Every time you shake hands, it's like a pile-up on the goal line. Several hundred people trying to get to you. I've never experienced anything like that."[60] Displaying a charming, self-deprecating sense of humor, Mondale remarked, "'If I were the person I'd read about in the paper [before the debate], I wouldn't vote for me. Suddenly they saw me; the contrast between what I'd been described as being."[61] Mondale knew that it was a campaign for authenticity and personality. Where he would take his newfound popularity was another question altogether.

Mondale's poll numbers suddenly rose, as if voters were just then discovering that there was a Democratic challenger. For the millions of Americans who opted to skip the Sunday night spectacle, the news media filled in the gaps. In a *New York Times/CBS News* survey taken immediately following the debate, 43 percent thought Mondale had won, while 34 percent preferred Reagan. By Tuesday, respondents "awarded Mondale the victory by an overpowering 66% to 17%."[62]

Despite his poor showing in the first debate, the president remained personally popular. In a *News Hour* panel following the October 7 debate in Louisville, Dick Lugar offered this analysis: "The negative Reagan numbers ... also indicate that by a full 20%, the people ... think [Reagan is] more likable; in short on all the things on which people vote in the elections, the President came out well ahead."[63]

Reagan did need to improve in the second debate, if only to dispense with the "age issue." He needed to return with the same easy, self-assured sense of humor that he had shown in the 1980 contest against Jimmy Carter. Despite anxieties within the Reagan campaign, there were some advantages to the president's position. First, going into the second debate, the threshold for Reagan's performance had depreciated; the president only needed to prove that he was not too old for the job. Second, entering the debate on October 21, 1984, all eyes were on Reagan. Where Mondale had been the unknown, the man who needed to introduce himself, most viewers tuned in to get a glimpse of Reagan — to see if he was still up to the job. Finally, owing to the spectacle of post-debate coverage following the first debate, more viewers

tuned in on October 21, 1984. Mondale might have offered his best performance in the earlier debate, but fewer Americans spared their attention to watch
it.[64] By contrast, the second debate was the fourth-highest rated presidential
debate since 1960.[65]

Mondale's advisor, Jim Johnson, agreed with this calculus: the threshold
for Reagan's performance in the second debate decreased as a result of the
first debate. While Mondale needed to represent himself as a plausible and
desirable president, Reagan needed only to assure voters that he was not
senile.[66] Although the Mondale campaign attempted to raise this threshold
by attacking the president's competence, the Reagan campaign did much to
create favorable conditions for its candidate in the intervening period. In the
period between the two debates, voters were reminded about "Ronald Reagan's
personality and [his] connection to the American voter."[67] Thus, while Reagan
was forced to pass only the most minimal test in the second debate, Mondale
was still forced to prove himself— on issues, leadership, strength, and personality.[68]

While Mondale remained a strong debater, Reagan did pass the minimum
test in the second debate. When the "age issue" arose during the course of the
second debate, Reagan handled it with grace and wit, joking, "I am not going
to exploit for political purposes my opponent's youth and inexperience." Eras-
ing the age issue with humor and ease, Reagan was back. The media
announced that Reagan was not, after all, too old to be president.[69] Using the
vocabulary of authenticity to vouch for Reagan's personality, journalists hailed
the president's second debate performance. As *Time* reported, "Flashing a bit
of folksy humor, sounding hurt more than angry at some of the Mondale
sallies and committing no harmful gaffe, a reassuring Reagan" regained command of his audience.[70]

In the end, the debates benefited Reagan. According to Reagan campaign
manager Ed Rollins, the debates "probably helped us a little bit." According
to the campaign's internal polling, Reagan's lead had stagnated in the early
fall; his position vis-à-vis Mondale was neither improving nor deteriorating.
Immediately after the first debate, the president's daily tracking numbers fell.[71]
Despite (or perhaps because of) this, the president emerged from the second
debate with a lead greater than what he had enjoyed prior to the first debate.
Internal polling found that, despite an adequate performance, Mondale's
numbers dropped eleven points the day after the second debate.[72]

Thus, despite his obvious qualifications and clear commitment to public
service, Walter Mondale's 1984 challenge largely fell flat. But not because voters disagreed with him on the issues. George Gallup's analysis of the
mid–September polls found that "if it were not for the personality factor, we

would have an exceedingly close race indeed."[73] But alas, there was the personality — more accurately Reagan — factor to consider.

Going to the Movies

It was not a close race, but neither was it preordained. In November 1983 it was not clear that Reagan's presidency would even survive the first term. Reagan's first team was characterized by poor economic growth. His party had suffered losses in Congress in the 1982 midterm election when Democrats charged that Reagan's economic program was "unfair." The Democrats had struck a nerve — many Americans felt that "unfairness" in their everyday lives, as the country shed jobs and suffered continued inflation on everyday goods. The first Gallup Poll of 1983 found Reagan's job approval rating at an abysmal 35 percent.[74]

While the Democrats might have won on the fairness platform in the 1982 midterm, such policy-based, issues-centric campaign tactics were no match in a head-to-head contest against Ronald Reagan. Even when less than 40 percent of Americans approved of his job performance, his personal approval ratings soared at 60 percent and above.[75] First of all, as the economy began to pick up, the issue of "fairness" lost its salience for many voters. Second, with a majority of Americans voting on the basis of presidentiality, it was difficult to contest the man who would come to define the term.[76] Finally, Democrats enjoyed a great deal of issue salience on fairness when their charges were levied against an institution (the Republican Party, the Republican Congress, the institution of the presidency). When these charges were levied against a popular individual, however, Democrats lost the debate. In short, the personally popular individual (Ronald Reagan) was difficult to best in a national campaign, even when the issues privileged his opponent. Many voters, even those who disagreed with his programs — who were disadvantaged by his economic policies — felt personal affection for the president.[77]

Ronald Reagan's reelection campaign, indeed his whole first term, was managed far differently from those of his defeated predecessors. Like Jimmy Carter in 1976, it was relatively easy for Reagan to run as an authentic outsider in 1980. As an incumbent, however, Jimmy Carter attempted to project an image of strength, control, and expertise — a Washington image. By contrast, Reagan was able to maintain his outsider image throughout his presidency. As president, he signed his first bill into law on his California ranch, wearing blue jeans and a cowboy hat. As campaign advisor Stuart Spencer said of Reagan, "Ron was a westerner. He was happier on a horse than he was in the

Oval Office."[78] He was able to project this throughout his first term in office and amplify that image during the campaign. Distancing himself from Washington and its odious institutions, Reagan constantly reminded voters that he did not like the beltway any more than they did. At home in California in September 1984, Reagan told the hometown crowd, "I can't help but thank you for giving me an opportunity to get away from those puzzle palaces on the Potomac to return home to kick off our campaign."[79]

A New Beginning

When he was pitted against Walter Mondale in 1984, Reagan appeared to be the man of America, and Mondale the senator of the Beltway. Although Reagan did not seem a likely candidate for "everyman" mythology, there was a way in which Reagan did reflect voters' self-images.[80] Beyond the charisma and charm and red-white-and-blue bunting, voters identified images of Reagan with images of everyday life on Main Street America. Throughout his first term, but particularly during the crucial twelve months leading up to the election, Reagan remained highly visible, revealing himself to voters in comfortable settings — namely, their living rooms. As Martin Schram reminded his readers, "Reagan appeared before the nation of television watchers ... doing what he does best — making people feel he is at one with them."[81] Despite the fact that he was the president, despite the fact that he had come from Hollywood, Reagan's image was rarely interpreted that way by voters, who overwhelmingly saw him as a loveable, likable authentic American. Reagan coveted and nurtured that image. Fans at the Daytona Beach 400 must have been surprised and delighted when, on July 4, 1984, they heard the president's voice over the intercom announcing, "Gentleman, start your engines!" Viewers at home caught a glimpse of Ronald Reagan celebrating the nation's birthday from the announcer's booth at a stockcar race.[82]

Thus, Reagan remained connected to Americans, and they to him, throughout his first term. In devising the 1984 media strategy, Reagan's media director, Doug Watts, decided to make the campaign "a series of conversations with the president ... conversations between the president and the people directly."[83] As a result, people felt personally comfortable with Reagan; they trusted him, they believed in him, and they felt they knew his heart. Take, for example, one voter's impression of Ronald Reagan: "I think he's just doggone honest. It's remarkable. He's been on television — what have I heard? 26 times?— talking to us? About what he's doing? Now he's not doing that for any other reason than to make it real clear. And if anybody has any question about where he's headed, it's their fault. Maybe they don't have a television."[84]

That voter was not alone in trusting Reagan and feeling personally connected to him. Cognitive psychologists studying voting behavior in the 1984 election found that Reagan "personified a popular image of 'the neighbor next door.' Perhaps voters identified so much with him in part because he was viewed as someone who saw life as they did and who experienced and talked about the world in a way that they could comprehend readily. He was not the best or the brightest among us, rather he was the best of the most typical among us."[85]

In sum, Reagan did not appear to be "another politician" in the odious vein of Jimmy Carter or Richard Nixon. As Reagan's long-time campaign strategist Stuart Spencer noted in an interview, what set Reagan apart was that he was always "an outsider in Washington.... He never los[t] his ear for what's outside."[86] Indeed, Reagan was a Hollywood actor, but he was never of Hollywood. He was president, but he was never entrenched in Washington. After spending his adult life in the most public and powerful positions, he still came across as a small-town boy from the heartland. As the *New York Times* proclaimed, "No one has been that saturated — marinated — in middle America, not even William Jennings Bryan."[87] It was, perhaps, Reagan's best asset in the 1984 election.[88]

They Sense That I Like Them

In a letter to the editors, one reader of *Time* magazine wrote, "We are seeing a love affair blossom between a President and his people.... After what we have been through in the past two decades, the change is welcome."[89] More importantly, if the people came to love Ronald Reagan, he professed to return the affection — with interest. In a *Newsweek* interview at the beginning of 1984, Reagan was reminded of the road-weariness of campaigning. He replied, "There's one part that you can't dread at all. And that is the opportunity to meet again the people of this country that I think are so wonderful. I love 'em ... if there is anything, maybe they sense that I like people. I like them."[90] Although many continued to perceive Reagan as an aloof marionette, a right-wing nut job, or a dangerous monarch, to many Americans, and to the national press at large, Reagan was a lovable personality. Throughout the 1984 campaign, the media grasped for description, attempting to articulate the president's indescribable qualities, often brimming over with praise. Reagan was "a public presence so pleasantly familiar that it dismisses normal scrutiny; people like to have him around."[91] Whether it was deemed charisma or telegenia, Reagan's ability to appear natural and lovable on television and at campaign rallies was difficult to quantify. As Reagan's gun-toting friend and colleague, Charlton Heston noted, "He has that ability to kindle enthusiasm in people. His skills as a communicator are widely dismissed as an actor's trickery, but ... the performance factor is a large part of a successful political leader's job."[92]

Democrats might have dismissed Reagan's affability as "actor's trickery" but to many, Reagan was humanly authentic and genuinely presidential. "I can hear the protests about how much of Reagan's ability to connect with voters "is simulated, feigned, conceivably even memorized and how some of it comes from old movie scripts. But whatever goes into it, it is Reagan's authentic style and it comes out looking plausible to people as" an expression of his genuine self.[93] Allaying voters' fears that the president was just a good actor, his press secretary, James Brady, argued that authenticity was the source of Reagan's telegenia. Reagan liked the medium of television because it permitted "one-on-one communication" with voters. "You really hear what he is saying.... He will just look into the boob tube and tell people what's on his mind."[94]

Ordinary voters viewed him as something more than an actor — many understood him to be a national symbol, a strong figurehead, an empathetic friend, and a kindly grandfather. As one interviewee told *People*, "He reminds me of my grandpa when he tells stories about when he was young."[95]

One journalist described how Reagan could connect with voters at campaign rallies, even in the largest settings, amid thousands of strangers.[96] His audiences laughed hard at his jokes, rode high on his soaring rhetoric, and wept as he described his love of country. One reporter recalled the emotional scene as Reagan concluded a stump speech in 1984 — members of the audience were so moved that "tears formed, to be rubbed quickly away, lest a neighbor see. It had been another bravura performance, calculated to make everyone feel good, very good — and to keep Ronald Reagan in the White House four more years."[97]

Unlike Walter Mondale, Reagan was able to make the country "feel good" by avoiding contentious and potentially divisive issues ... like politics.[98] True, elections were political contests, but Reagan managed to almost completely avoid serious discussion of policy specifics. Part of the magic in his antipolitical political campaign was that it was less likely to inspire antagonism. Another part was that he was able to run above — rather than with — a partisan platform and a political contentiousness that made voters loathe politics. His feel-good, good-guy image depended on it. As one observer told *People*, "Reagan never played the bad guy in the movies. It's ingrown in us that he's always going to be the good guy."[99] Indeed, when Reagan was his most political, most adversarial, and most negative in 1984, his poll ratings plummeted. People preferred the Reagan who was above the fray.[100]

His approach was not universally appreciated. In a *Washington Post* editorial, Martin Schram condemned the emotionalism of the Reagan effort. "His nightly news appearances are supplemented by campaign ads that are compelling in dramatics, soft on sell and high on good feeling. And that is apparently the way we like it, because voters are telling poll takers in overwhelming numbers that they are for Reagan."[101] On the whole, however, Reagan was more warmly received when he stuck to his anti-political campaign. For one thing, voters appreciated the tone of Reagan's campaign. For another, anti-politics came more naturally to the candidate. Reagan's national campaign director, Ed Rollins, argued that the president's success was due to the fact that he "is not a political man, but has superb people instincts."[102]

Reagan had the advantage of avoiding politics, to some extent, because the country was not confronting the same kind of immediate and exigent challenges as it had during the 1980 campaign. In the absence of pressing issues, the president could largely avoid the issues-based campaign. Nevertheless, it was surprising to many that Reagan enjoyed support among those who did not enjoy his economic and social programs.[103] It is clear that Reagan did not owe his 1984 victory to economic forces alone. The so-called "Reagan Recovery" was not a reality for many voters, whose personal economies did not improve during Reagan's first term. In her study of audience responses to presidential speeches, Lyn Ragsdale found that "the low-income group ... liked Reagan as a person and, perhaps" supported the president on a "personal level, despite their criticisms of his performance in handling ... unemployment. Although they disapproved of, and were disadvantaged by, Reagan policy decisions, they nevertheless increased their support of Reagan, perhaps gaining symbolic reassurance from his communications, including economic speeches dealing with the very policies that distressed them."[104]

Indeed, the Reagan recovery was uneven, and the Reagan economic record was mixed, at best, in rust belt states like Michigan.[105] But as the *Grand Rapids Press* predicted, "Through force of personality, determination, skilled handlers and inept opposition, the president, even in a state which overall owes little to the administration, could win big here in November."[106] Reagan's positive personal approval rating among unemployed and low-income underemployed voters was striking to some. Among groups of voters who ought to have formed Mondale's base of support (for example, rust belt union voters) Reagan was exceptionally popular.[107] Even the Michigan United Auto Workers (UAW) had difficulty rallying member support for Walter Mondale. Using the vocabulary of authenticity, one labor leader conceded, "Reagan comes across as being honest, fair, sincere and a flag-waving American. And that sits well with blue-collar workers. Mondale doesn't have that charisma and flair."[108]

In Ohio, where unemployment increased during Reagan's first term, stabilizing above 10 percent throughout 1982 and 1983,[109] "people thought Mondale would" provide the things that the state desperately needed: "more jobs, a better economic future." Consequently, the Reagan campaign feared that it might lose the state, "unemployment being what it was."[110] After a targeted personality campaign in that state, Reagan won Ohio by over 850,000 votes — nearly nineteen percentage points.

Reagan's support went far beyond economically depressed rust belt states. In the *Washington Post*, David Broder marveled at Reagan's popularity among small farmers struggling to survive in an era of corporate farms: "Rich Landon, 62, a wheat farmer from Hastings, said the agriculture situation is 'terribly bad,' with the price of wheat barely above 'the $3 a bushel my dad got in 1932 ... when bread was 9 cents a loaf.'" Nonetheless, the voter told Broder that he intended to vote for Reagan because of his human authenticity: "'When he talks to you, he laughs and jokes and seems so reasonable; Mondale, he said, 'screams and yells like a loud preacher' on television."[111]

The Tuesday Team

Reagan had the advantage of working with an advertising team that understood the power of the "soft sell." Rather than selling campaign promises (about which voters were skeptical anyway) the Tuesday Team sold the man, Ronald Reagan. As Tuesday Team member Phil Dusenberry noted of his 1984 media campaign, "Over time people are numbed by facts and figures and promises, most of which don't come true, and I think people are more powerfully moved through a sense of feeling good about a particular candidate."[112]

This was reflected in Reagan's campaign commercials, most of which were decidedly anti-political.[113] Understood better as movie trailers than as political advertisements, the spots sold an experience rather than a product or a set of promises. Featuring icons of Americana — quaint towns, smiling shop owners, and flag-waving children — these spots peddled a hopeful patriotism based on nostalgia for the present.[114] In 1984 Reagan connected viewers to a mythical present. The Tuesday Team wanted viewers to emotionally connect with Reagan's portrait of small-town America.[115] Most Americans did not live in small towns where barbers greeted everyone by name, where neighbors were always helpful, and where flags decorated every lawn, but they felt at home there in Reagan's advertisements.[116]

Take, for example, the Tuesday Team's campaign commercial, "Train." The spot opened with video footage of small-town folks smiling and taking off early from work. Syrupy music played in the background as a kindly sounding narrator began to tell the story of townsfolk coming together to greet Ronald Reagan as his train passed through. The images of the town were old-timey, preparing the viewer for an equally old-fashioned-looking train. Long gone were the days of the old-fashioned whistle-stop, abandoned for the convenience of airplanes. But at the conclusion of this spot, viewers saw Reagan, smiling and waving out the caboose of a train, as onlookers smiled and waved. The personal exchange between the president and the people was invested with emotion, as the narrator advised: "While some folks might have come so they could tell their grandchildren they saw President Reagan, most of them just stopped by to say 'thanks.'"[117]

Utilizing the same syrupy background music, the more famous "Prouder, Stronger, Better" spot (commonly called "Morning in America") offered an equally homey and hopeful portrait of Ronald Reagan's America.[118] Like "Train," "Prouder, Stronger, Better" captured the spirit and temperament of a movie trailer. A video montage of American life — a paperboy on a bike, a farmer in his field, a man in a station wagon, a young bride at her wedding — filled the screen as the narrator described one day in the life of the country. "Nearly 2,000 families today will buy new homes.... This afternoon, 6,500 young men and women will be married." Reminding viewers of the hope, patriotism, and optimism of Reagan's campaign, the spot closed with the key question: "It's morning again in America.... Why would we ever want to return to where we were less than four short years ago?"[119] Even for viewers who had not enjoyed the economic bounty of Reagan's first term, the commercial offered an experience that they had enjoyed.

While these spots were beautifully made, the most emotionally charged episode in the Ronald Reagan Show came during the Republican National Convention. The same Tuesday Team worked to create a masterpiece of modern political film, titled *A New Beginning*.[120] Using the vocabulary of authenticity, Tom Brokaw of NBC attempted to discredit the Reagan marketing machine, informing his viewers that what they were about to see was "an evening of scripted, colorful pageantry, kind of like an old-fashioned MGM musical." By 1984 Americans were well versed in the political stagecraft of election campaigns.[121] After all, they had been living with an actor-president for four years. What they wanted from Reagan was a sense of connectedness (we're in this together) and perhaps a peek backstage (to ameliorate their fears that he was acting). They would get both from the 1984 convention film.[122]

In the film, Reagan directly addressed the audience at key moments, creating the illusion of unmediated intimacy. While he remained "presidential" throughout the film, he offered viewers a glimpse into his private thoughts and feelings. Narrated by Reagan himself, the film offered a brilliant diptych between well-known and official video footage, for example, the video footage from Reagan's inauguration in 1981, paired with Reagan's own private thoughts and feelings about the events. Of his inauguration, for example, Reagan said, "Yes, it was quite a day. A new beginning."

The diptych allowed voters an intimate perspective on a public life — a glimpse into the private thoughts of a public man. For example, Reagan offered these thoughts about the Oval Office and the presidency: "Sitting in the Oval Office, you look around and sometimes you can't help but choke up a little bit." To most Americans, the Oval Office was one of the most grand and official symbols of the presidency. In just a few moments, Reagan opened the office to the American people, personalizing both the president and the presidency. Like most ordinary people, Reagan, too, was in awe of the office.[123]

A New Beginning was a stunning film — its content and production stirred emotions, inspired patriotism, and unified a nation, if only for a brief moment.[124] Its message was decidedly anti-political; its producers opted to portray Reagan as a unifying figure, rather than a divisive politician.[125] Even Walter Mondale's campaign aides and advisors were moved to tears as they watched the convention film. As Martin Schram reported in the *Washington Post*, "There are tears in the eyes of the Mondale workers ... so moved were they by the emotional" impact of *A New Beginning*. "It wasn't just the young and impressionable... a well-known liberal Democratic political adviser found herself in tears as Reagan said.... 'Everywhere we go, Nancy makes the world a little better.... I can't imagine life without her.' And in suburban Bethesda, a hardened middle-aged Mondale advisor found himself sitting alone in his den crying. 'It got us all.... We don't have anything to compete with that.'"[126]

On the whole, the production had an aura of intimacy and viewers left the experience with the impression that they *really knew* Ronald Reagan. In addition to Reagan's own performance in the film, viewers were also exposed to the thoughts and opinions of ordinary voters, who assured their peers that they liked and trusted Ronald Reagan. According to Trevor Parry-Giles and Shawn Parry-Giles, the verite interviews with average voters suggested "a similarity or unity between Reagan and the 'average' voter. Reagan also emerge[d] as the 'people's' president, and the interplay between what Reagan discusse[d] and what the 'average' voter conclude[d] manifest[ed] the symbiotic relationship between candidate and voter."[127]

Conclusions

Unlike Jimmy Carter, Ronald Reagan was able to remain connected with voters throughout his first term in office, reminding them of their mutual affection throughout the 1984 campaign. Other differences between the two incumbents — national mood and economic factors — also changed the stakes for Ronald Reagan in 1984. Despite overwhelming evidence that the economy had improved, however, it was not clear that Reagan fought for reelection on the basis of the strong economy. Reagan instigated, encouraged, and nurtured the patriotic spirit in 1984, placing himself and his personal story at the center of the American narrative. The president did not merely ride national spirit to the ballot box on November 6. Reagan was able to inspire patriotism and good feelings because the people liked him, they trusted him, and they were therefore willing to put faith back into the country and the economy.

More importantly, it was increasingly clear that the boundaries of public discourse and the vocabulary of campaigning were in part determined by a candidate's ability to project, if not embody, authenticity. When Mondale appeared more comfortable, he won praise from the press and approval from the people. When Reagan was able to connect with voters, share his intimate thoughts, and bring an air of casual informality to his representation of presidentiality, he won the overwhelming approbation of the country. Similarly, when Reagan stumbled in the first debate, appearing tense and ill-at-ease, the people and the press raised questions not only about his image, but about his fitness to lead. In the end, both of these men were frequently judged on the basis of their authenticity. While the result of the election may not have depended on this particular projection of candidate image, much of the national discourse about the election of 1984 was articulated in these terms.

4

Belgian Endives, Quiche Out of a Can: 1988

If the 1984 campaign themes embodied good feelings and patriotism, the 1988 campaign was a different kind of experience altogether. Most analysts judged the debates useless, advertisements negative, and candidates boring. A CBS/*New York Times* post-election survey found that "fifty-four percent of Americans rated this campaign as dull.... Americans also rated this year's campaign as abysmally negative: 63 percent thought this year's campaign was more negative than past campaigns.... Strikingly, two-thirds of Americans said they wished there had been choices other than Mr. Bush or Mr. Dukakis this year."[1] Indeed, the contest pitted two of the least charismatic figures in American politics against one another, resulting in the second lowest voter turnout rate in the post–Watergate era.[2]

Despite its lack of compelling characters and uplifting narratives, the 1988 campaign was an important and interesting case study in the history of American political authenticity. First, the media's heavy emphasis on campaign management gave voters a procedural view previously unappreciated by average citizens. Second, the media's heavy emphasis on the "horserace" offered a useful way to analyze voters' reactions to the contest over the contest. Finally, the heavy emphasis on negative campaigning suggested that in the absence of any overwhelming purchase on authenticity, each side resigned itself to bringing down the other.

At the 1988 party conventions, the Republicans nominated Vice President George Bush. The Democrats selected Massachusetts governor Michael Dukakis. Despite the scandals of the second Reagan term (Iran Contra, HUD scandal, and the savings and loan crisis)[3] the economy was stable and many Americans were satisfied with Ronald Reagan. As a result of this complacency, George Bush faced few serious challengers in the 1988 primaries, despite the fact that he was often portrayed as a bureaucratic hack for his more popular commander-in-chief. By the conclusion of Super Tuesday, George Bush was the presumptive nominee of the Republican Party.

On the Democratic side, early frontrunners were forced to withdraw their candidacies. Gary Hart was marred by marital infidelity. Dick Gephardt was crippled by attacks from his opponents. Two candidates, Michael Dukakis and Jesse Jackson, lasted until the nominating convention. The two men represented seemingly opposite styles, factions, and directions in the Democratic Party. Jackson was a charismatic but polarizing figure. Dukakis was the consensus candidate, who selected Texan Lloyd Bentsen to mitigate his Northeastern credentials. Despite Dukakis's overwhelming victory at the nominating convention, Jackson remained a force, and a point of comparison, for many voters. Where Jackson inspired passion, Dukakis was a much steadier hand. Where Jackson offered fire-and-brimstone, Dukakis presented lists of policy proposals. Neither party offered the American people its most charismatic candidate. Both Bush and Dukakis were safe, consensus choices. George Bush had been a force, if not a face, in American politics for decades. Although he had served in Congress and later in the vice presidency, he had spent much of his career in relative bureaucratic anonymity. Michael Dukakis was the governor of Massachusetts. In and outside of his home state, Dukakis was seen as a technocrat, best known for overseeing less-than-flashy improvements in mass transit and technology.

The Vision Thing

The campaigns of 1988 were interesting, if not unique, because of the extent to which managers, pundits, and ordinary voters in focus groups openly discussed the value of likeability and authenticity. As in previous campaign seasons, but more frequently and more publicly in 1988, these figures observed that the candidate most likely to win was the one to whom voters could most easily relate. As one California Republican operative noted, "The average guy wants someone in the Oval Office he can relate to."[4] Unlike previous seasons, however, neither man had any natural claim to authenticity. Voters looked for signs and clues from both men, forcing the campaigns to project "authentic" messages and images. As a result, each campaign offered emotional appeals to voters highlighting the candidates' personal narratives and personalities.

In response, pundits began to locate authenticity as a key predictor of success in presidential elections. As one noted, "In the past few years, some useful working theories have emerged" to pinpoint candidates' relative likeability. These "working theories" mostly involved "comfort level ... it's not surprising to discover that this homey feeling may be the engine driving history."[5] Voters became used to seeing candidates on television and hearing intimate details about their personal lives. "Thanks to television and a press corps that is infinitely more diligent in reporting about the personal lives of candidates than it used to be, American voters know infinitely more about the people who want to be president. A candidate's personal life can blow him out of the water. So can his personality, which is another word people use when they describe the comfort-level factor.... The man who will win is the one whom a majority of Americans think they will feel comfortable with in the White House as we head into the 1990s."[6]

Focus groups and polling results confirmed the correlation between likeability, relatability, and emotional connection to candidates. "Research on the 1988 campaign" showed "strong relationships between specific emotions elicited by Bush and Dukakis ads and audience evaluations of candidate images."[7] Part of this, however, may have been a result of the media's emphasis on thematic messages and emotional appeals. In order to earn free media, campaigns had to capture the attention of newsroom editors, who favored the stories that were most appealing to viewers. As a result, campaigns often willingly dumped issue spots and policy speeches, which had become expensive burdens. Advisors to both candidates ultimately determined that issue spots and issue-oriented stump speeches were in fact potentially harmful detractors in the contest to win the news cycle.[8] Thus, as *Time* magazine readers learned, Americans were "forced to depend on factors of character and personality to predict presidential performance."[9]

In the 1988 contest, remarkably, George Bush was able to best his opponent in the likeability war, if only because it was Michael Dukakis headlining the Democratic ticket. As Roger Ailes later noted, "In the final analysis, the people vote ... for somebody they like better than the other person. There's a 'like factor, in there." George Bush was able to convey a "kinder, gentler side" to the voters and "that kind of vision did catch on to some degree. We saw it in our tracking."[10] To that end, George Bush's consultants and advisors understood that they needed to remodel their own candidate, and ultimately recast Dukakis, in order to win the likeability war. "You can present all the issues you want on the air, and if at the end the audience doesn't like the guy, they're not going to vote for him."[11]

Handlers

Much of the network, print, and cable news coverage of the 1988 election focused on the influence of campaign managers and the force of political advertisements. More than ever, journalists sought to expose campaign tactics for their readers. They turned major campaign managers into minor celebrities and offered a running narrative of the campaign about the campaign. *Time* called on the political communication scholar, Kathleen Hall Jamieson, to introduce its readers to campaign tactics of the political backstage. Jamieson concluded that a campaign's ability to convey its candidate's likeability was a central factor in strategic planning. Likeability, "the ability to disclose a sense of the private self in public," would need to be central to campaign planning and media messaging because "in the television age, candidates have to be comfortable with public intimacy and self-disclosure."[12] To the latter point, the election hinged on each candidate's ability to portray himself as authentic. Ultimately, the whole country was made aware of the fact that "presidential candidates ... get elected because voters liked them more than they liked the other fellow who was running."[13] Such articles provided evidence of the increasing importance of authenticity in candidate image construction. They also provided evidence of a pervasive hyper-self-awareness that was indicative of national discourse during the 1988 campaign season.

In the non-stop campaign about the campaign, the candidates' commercials became events. Perhaps because the spots were so negative, or perhaps due to increased interest in the political backstage, "the high visibility of television spots in the 1988 campaign was unprecedented. The spots themselves became a major aspect of media reporting about the campaign. In 1988, there were more stories on network news covering political spots than in all the presidential campaigns from 1972 through 1984 combined, suggesting that the extensive coverage may have legitimized television ads as voter decision-making tools."[14] As forceful and controversial advertisements gained free media airtime, campaigns reallocated funds to support those spots that would garner the most attention.

News outlets did not merely critique advertisements, they also obsessively covered the people responsible for crafting them. Campaign professionals, in particular Lee Atwater, became minor celebrities. Despite their own role in immortalizing the "handlers," editors and reporters criticized both campaigns for offering voters little more than carefully scripted events. Both candidates were depicted as slaves to their advisors, consultants, and "handlers." Journalists determined that Bush and Dukakis suffered from "passive and uncritical acceptance of the premises of modern political manipulation ... as the backstage puppeteers pull the strings, and Bush and Dukakis dangle before TV cameras obediently reciting their memorized themes for the day."[15] Thus authenticity, or, more so, inauthenticity, became an issue of national concern as voters attempted to parse the messages and dig underneath the stagecraft for something real.

Even as they made celebrities out of "handlers," journalists also tried to offer a caveat in both print and television coverage. "Something has truly gone awry in 1988, as the election becomes transformed into a handlers' handicap. More than any other race in history, this has become a narrow-gauge contest between two disciplined teams of political professionals."[16] Walter Shapiro of *Time* worried that "at the very moment the voters are asked to place their future in the hands of one of these men, the campaign staffs of Bush and Dukakis are trying to prevent their candidates from uttering a spontaneous thought in public."[17] Other journalists also blamed handlers for the overall lack of spontaneity and authenticity in 1988: "The candidates perform simulations of encounters with the real world, but the exercise is principally a series of television visuals, of staged events created for TV cameras."[18]

Skeptical voters learned about campaign managers' "skillful use of television to project a narrow and often negative message, rigid control over every other aspect of each day's communications, avoidance of the press and off-the-cuff remarks."[19] In such an environment, voters' lack of enthusiasm came as no surprise. Their lack of enthusiasm, however, was very much targeted at the two candidates' perceived inauthenticities. Whether the candidates wholly lacked authenticity, whether their events had become more scripted, whether the media was hyper-focused on campaign tactics, or whether authenticity was simply more important to voters and journalists, the construction of authentic candidate image became the underlying plotline of the 1988 campaign.

Despite campaign managers' efforts, both candidates in the 1988 election were deemed cold and unrelatable by the press, the pundits, and the people. In July 1988, a *Christian Science Monitor* article examined the ways in which the candidates could become more personally appealing to voters. "Dukakis and Bush (and the consultants they've hired) understand that the voters wish them to be 'human.'" To that end, "a Democrat consultant ... suggested that Dukakis" ought to free "up his body language ... making chummy little gestures and eliminating those hostile orator's karate chops." Bush, too, attempted to become "unfrozen."[20] Even as George Bush managed to put on some personality in the fall of 1988, observers and voters remained wary and skeptical of the vice president's scripted authenticity.

Atwater's America

The presidential race of 1988 was condemned as the most negative election in recent American history. Both teams, but particularly the Bush campaign, and especially Lee Atwater, came under attack for the conduct of the contest. To be sure, there was not much to commend about the conduct of the 1988 election. Analyzed through the lens of authenticity, however, the negativity of the campaign is essential to understanding voters' desires for something "real." Many scholars have looked to the candidates' advisors (particularly on the Bush side) or to the campaign organization (or lack thereof on the Dukakis side) to examine the pervasive negativity of 1988. Some scholars have argued that the tight race, voter apathy, alienation from process, relative peace and prosperity, power of campaign managers, and the lack of major policy issues contributed to the gross negativity of the 1988 campaign.

While all of these might be true to a certain extent, examined through the lens of authenticity, we can understand the negativity in 1988 in a different way: neither Bush nor Dukakis was particularly charismatic. Neither had any natural claim to authenticity. Bush, a Beltway insider born of privilege, had no obvious connection to the general population. Further, he lacked both the telegenia of his predecessor and the charm of his son. Dukakis, son of immigrants, but nonetheless a product of Harvard, lacked not only charisma, but also a willingness to fake it. It was to be a battle between the wimp and the robot.

Because we understand 1988 as the most negative campaign of recent times, it is important to closely study the attacks themselves. Most of these attacks, particularly from the Bush side, focused on branding the opposition as inauthentic. Indeed, the 1988 election was a Pyrrhic victory for its victor, who would forever be linked to the Willie Horton advertisements, for which his campaign was not directly responsible.

De-Veeping

Bush did build up his "like factor" during the course of the campaign. In order to relate to voters, Bush, who had spent much of his adult life in Washington, and the previous eight years in the White House, needed to "de-veep" himself.[21] The campaign found that its polling results improved as the candidate "shed his vice-presidential skin."[22] He was "a scion of wealth ... who complained that media people were not reporting his love for country music and pork rinds."[23]

Pork Rinds

It was not easy, even for the likes of Lee Atwater, to turn George Bush into a regular guy. Consultants and handlers made every effort to portray their candidate as a man to whom voters could relate. The campaign offered video footage of the Bush family, BBQ stops in Texas, and homespun stories told through outside-the-Beltway, anti-elitist populism. In them, Bush downplayed his privileged background. As *Time* reported, Bush "jettisoned his g's, touted his taste for pork rinds and successfully put himself across as a regular guy. Bush persuaded voters to forget his background by pushing to the foreground the themes of cultural ... populism.... At the same time, the Bush campaign depicted Dukakis as a 'Harvard elitist.'"[24]

Atwater pushed this image so forcefully that, as one associate later recalled, the Yale graduate and Connecticut–born "[Bush] even had a syntax problem when he was speaking."[25] Reporters following Bush noted that his stump speeches were increasingly "filled with masculine sports metaphors and ... qualifiers like 'all that sort of stuff.'"[26] The Bush team reinforced its regular guy image with downhome campaign appearances and Tex-i-fied paid media. The Bush team knew that it had to both establish Dukakis as an out-of-touch liberal, and to remake Bush into a regular kind of guy. On these two points, the team was both consistent and persistent. As Republican campaign consultant Doug Bailey noted, "Every day, there's a photo opportunity and sound bite to reinforce the first message and a photo op and sound bite to reinforce the second."[27]

George Bush chose the unlikely Dan Quayle as his running mate. Quayle was a plainspoken man whom many hailed as a "VP for Average folks."[28] Even as he was ridiculed by the press, many voters personally identified with the Indiana senator. As John Harris wrote in the *Washington Post*, "I don't think Dan is any kind of raging intellect, but he's an average guy.... He's got the capacity that all the rest of us average folks have got, and I don't worry about him at all."[29]

More to the point, the Bush campaign's internal post-election poll analysis found that, rather than hurting the Republican ticket, Quayle contributed to Bush's election. In the end, 1988 was a numbers game of voter turnout, and Quayle's position on the ticket brought out "Middle American" and evangelical voters who otherwise might have stayed home.[30] Given that so many voters were "unenthused" about the candidates, the smallest bump in voter turnout had a powerful effect on the overall margin in 1988. Further, the Bush campaign found that attacks against Quayle rallied otherwise apathetic midwesterners, conservatives, and evangelicals who felt that the elitists in the media were assaulting one of their own.[31]

Although many still saw him as wimpy and patrician, Bush's forceful defense of Dan Quayle disempowered caricatures of the candidate's "wimp factor."[32] To this macho end, the campaign also employed the state of Texas (symbolically at least) as Bush's second running mate. Bush was not originally from Texas but the state's immediately identifiable symbolic value offered Bush two things. First, its identification with ruggedness helped to mitigate the vice president's "wimp" factor, a trait that had been exposed by *Newsweek*.[33] Second, it granted the Yankee–born vice president a kind of down-home legitimacy, which Connecticut could not supply. Maximizing his connection to the Lone Star state, George Bush displayed his familiarity with Texas's famous folkways as frequently as possible. Even prior to its post–Labor Day media blitz, the Bush campaign team set itself up for the fall, hoping to establish the candidate's authenticity by "mov[ing] Bush away from his image as a white-shoe elitist."[34] George Bush made public show of getting his hands dirty, eating pork rinds, and wearing cowboy boots in order to relate to average (white male) voters and legitimize his connection to Texas. Not lost on the media, the vice president's new love affair with pig byproducts became breaking news.

To achieve the goal of out-regular-guying Dukakis, "the message from Bush headquarters was that their fella was a regular guy, too, someone who eats pork rinds and listens to country music." In the *New York Times*, Lee Atwater asserted, "'It's not a defense.... He eats pork skins.'" The *Times* story offered equal parts ironic humor and political journalism.[35] As exemplified in this article, journalists approached the new Bush in multiple ways, often with tongue-in-cheek disbelief, even as they reprinted the stories and replayed the video footage.

One reporter dealt with it by qualifying a quote from the candidate with a sarcastic dig at his attempts to play Average Joe. "Thursday, in a speech in Texas, George Herbert Walker Bush, regular guy, tried to set himself apart from Michael Dukakis, Northeastern liberal and elitist. 'When I wanted to learn the ways of the world, I didn't go to the Kennedy School [at Harvard], I came to Texas.'"[36] To add legitimacy to this claim, the campaign offered the media witnesses to Bush's Texas authenticity. "A close Bush associate swears that the candidate would rather reach for a pork rind than a canapé, but admits that Bush's patrician background makes voters reluctant to accept the idea that 'he really is a regular guy.'"[37]

The campaign played its candidate's newly acquired down-home roots outside of Texas as well. Questioning Bush's authenticity, *Time* reported on an October excursion to the Midwest, revealing Bush's attempts to be every man's everyman. "Sometimes Bush's speech has a chameleon quality ... at a stop in the town of Wenona [Illinois], Bush told the crowd that" he "'thought'" he had "'died and gone to heaven.... George Bush, out of Kennebunkport and Houston, out of Andover and Yale, had a little mountain twang in his voice when he said it, standing in twill trousers and a cowboy shirt." His own country act was followed by "Loretta Lynn, the coal miner's daughter" from Kentucky, who endorsed the candidate and "told the crowd she love[d] George Bush 'cuz he's country!'"[38]

The extent to which journalists framed Bush's campaign appearances using the terms of authenticity revealed a great deal about the terrain on which the campaign was fought in 1988. Such reports exposed the irony of Bush's appeals to the trailer set and this kind of hyperreal reporting played to voters' sensibilities. The journalists with the best sense of irony and taste for political punchlines mediated Bush's image in the national discourse. In his post-debate analysis, for example, Walter Shapiro chortled, "Bush, whose privileged background is alien to the life experiences of most Americans, kept harping on the word values as he proclaimed that he was in tune with 'the heartbeat of the country.'"[39]

A Thousand Points of Light

Even as the staged politics of Bush's pork-eating adventures were unveiled by journalists, the more Bush campaigned, the more his Texas narrative became embedded. Thus, Bush might not have been "country," but, with the assistance of Lee Atwater, he managed to maintain his pickup truck message, despite his Andover education.

One of the ways in which the campaign authenticated his image to voters and the press was through genuine expressions of human authenticity. Even as it tied up the Texas image, the campaign sought to prove that George Bush was a real man of human emotion, not some technocratic Washington insider. Beginning in August, the Bush campaign alternated images of tough–Texas Bush and grandfather Bush, who was a kinder, gentler man.[40] To some extent this was necessary, given the dramatic gender gap found in early polling. Both the Bush campaign's internal numbers and the polling results of independent surveys found that women were put off by the hard macho image.[41]

The "kinder, gentler" George Bush image was also used to temper his negative attacks against Dukakis that the campaign launched beginning in the summer of 1988. If voters could identify Bush as a good person first, the campaign could survive the bad press its attack ads would surely elicit. Thus, in addition to peddling video footage of the candidate indulging in fine Texas BBQ, the campaign also made efforts to show George Bush as a family man and as a person with a heart. To that end, the campaign unleashed the candidate's large family to present his human authenticity beyond the Beltway.

As reported in the media, Bush's advertising guru Roger Ailes prepared "a series of ads depicting Bush as a gentle grandfather" in preparation for the fall campaign.[42] Bush's managers "arranged for him to be photographed amid his photogenic grandchildren," who were not only cute, but who also contextualized the candidate as a man rather than a politician.[43] The campaign produced documentary-style footage of the family for dual use in paid television spots and the Bush convention film. Because they would be documentary-style images featuring family, their authentication was not required. From this footage, the campaign produced several long-running emotional, biographical spots, including its original sixty-second "bio" spot, a short thirty-second ad, and a sixty-second spot that Roger Ailes called an "ad with the kids."[44]

In the Bush team's biographical advertisement (called the "workhorse" of the campaign by Roger Ailes), images of George Bush playing with his grandchildren were set to emotional music.[45] Interspersed with this footage was video of Barbara Bush, who informed viewers, "I wish people can see him as I see him and as thousands of people see him."[46] The candidate's wife went on to frame the national election in ways better suited to small-town local election humor. When asked about her husband's constituency, Barbara was confident that her husband could win on the friends and family vote alone. "I've got a great big family and thousands of friends and that's what I have."[47] The commercial concluded with an emotional shot of George Bush, smiling and laughing as he lifted one of those many granddaughters in the air. The spot humanized Bush and legitimized his personal authenticity. Managers believed that although George Bush had been in the public eye in an official capacity for decades, the American people needed to get to know the candidate as a human being, as a husband, and as a grandfather.[48]

The emphasis on family was not merely an effort to show a kinder man but also an effort to present his human authenticity — glimpses into his private life, which only family could provide. In this way, the Bush family offset troubling media images of Bush's inauthenticities. Few journalists questioned the family portrait. As the *New York Times* reported, Barbara Bush vouched for "her husband's true personality — 'loving, caring, smart and funny,'" all qualities that "came through just as the public began focusing on the candidate. 'They saw a side they haven't seen before.'"[49]

At the Republican convention, Bush highlighted both his family and his human authenticity. Having effectively shed the "wimp" label, Bush now had the opportunity to highlight his personal side. In a joint interview with CBS's Dan Rather, George and Barbara Bush were "invited ... to tell the audience what a nice, warmhearted, affectionate, generous, humorous person the real

George Bush is."[50] Other reporters picked up on this thematic shift: "In recent weeks, as he has stressed his vision of a 'kinder, gentler nation,' the Vice President has tried to portray Mr. Dukakis as cold and calculating, guided more by abstract theory than common sense.... 'I wish it would be a campaign based on personality,' he said. 'I would win.'"[51]

The issue of personality advantaged the candidate Bush had become. Ultimately both Bush and his campaign managers played to public perceptions about George Bush the human being. "George Bush was seen as awkward, wimpish, maladroit. So Bush's handlers engineered a makeover. They had him utter self-deprecating cracks about his lack of charisma."[52] Even as the media poked and prodded, the softer image of the vice president began to stick. None of this ought to suggest that George Bush rode Lee Atwater on a Lone Star to victory in 1988. He did improve as a candidate over the course of the campaign — what political analyst David Gergen called the "personal transformation of George Bush."[53] Although his opponent was weak, and Bush looked better by comparison, George Bush did make good work of both the process and the media.

This was particularly notable during the October 13, 1988, debate, when George Bush very clearly "upstage[d] Mr. Dukakis personally."[54] Although much was made of a serious gaffe by Dukakis, discussed later, Bush did perform in the second debate.[55] *Time* reported it to its readers this way: "George Bush strode onto the stage in Los Angeles determined to prove with an avuncular assortment of smiles, chuckles, winds and asides that he was the affable heir to Ronald Reagan.... Bush won the debate largely because he triumphed in the congeniality competition."[56] Corroborating the Bush image, Walter Shapiro informed his readers that Bush could, indeed, establish a human connection. He did not merely offer a favorable contrast against the robotic Democrat; Bush really did appear to be himself on television that night. "Bush ... was as relaxed and confident in Los Angeles as he has ever been on a national stage. His efforts at humor seemed mostly spontaneous rather than the spoon-fed one-liners of backstage handlers.... The Vice President interrupted moderator Shaw, who was trying to pose a hypothetical question about Dan Quayle's becoming President following Bush's death. 'Bernie!' Bush interjected at just the right moment, conveying with that single word the natural human reluctance to dwell on one's own mortality."[57] Even Dukakis's hometown paper gave Bush high marks on the October 13 debate. The *Boston Globe* reported that "George Bush 'niced' it up. Mike Dukakis let him get away with it. The Vice President, so goofy in his first televised confrontation with the more articulate Massachusetts governor, went for the grandfatherly image last night, and pulled it off."[58]

All Hat and No Cattle [59]

Although he did improve his personal image, George Bush's dubious claim to Texas authenticity did not escape the media; Bush was not without his own lingering inauthenticities. Some found him fake and packaged, others believed that he was simply uncomfortable acting as both candidate Bush and regular guy Bush. Poll analysis found that voters interpreted the Bush campaign image through the framework of authenticity. Respondents found that Bush often came across "as insincere."[60] More broadly, many voters were put off by candidate Brahmin: "What comes across ... is a mannered preppie ... his attempts at humor often fall flat ... when he tries to be humorous under pressure, his face gives way to a false smile, a lopsided grimace that does not involve his eyes."[61]

Many of George Herbert Walker Bush's "regular guy" moments were mocked by the media. Reporters occasionally commented with tongue-in-cheek disbelief at the vice president's new populism. Bush suffered an authenticity gap in rural and anti-intellectual Republican crowds, with whom the candidate had nothing in common, beyond, of course, a love of pork rinds and pickup trucks. "George Bush ... sometimes seems to ... be ... trying out different accents, different styles of thought, as if seeking his own authenticity.... He ... panders unapologetically to the Know-Nothing instincts in the crowd, but one listens to him always with a smudge of doubt: Does he really believe that?"[62] Coming from the centrist, pragmatic wing of the Republican Party, George Bush courted cultural conservatives and Republican populists on their own turf, and his efforts to relate often fell flat. By far his biggest problem was that, while accusing Michael Dukakis of being "Kennedy School," Bush himself had enjoyed all of the privileges of the Yankee elite. And thus, as skilled as Lee Atwater was, the Bush campaign team was not always able to control its candidate's image, although advisors tried. Roger Ailes recalled that when *Newsweek* requested photographs for its "wimp" cover article "they said they would like a shot of George playing tennis. I think somebody smelled a rat on that and eventually sent one with him in a speed boat."[63]

Dukakis did not sling mud on Bush's white golf shoes until late in the campaign. Perhaps there was a missed opportunity for the Democrat to attack Bush's authenticity early and effectively. Adopting his own populist tone in the fall of 1988, the Dukakis camp began to connect Bush's policies to his privilege: "Dukakis ... suggested that Bush's" economic policies "would help the privileged few 'hire a second butler.' He derided it by "pointing to the beneficiaries of proposed capital-gains tax breaks, one of whom was George Herbert Walker Bush."[64]

In addition to whatever inauthenticities a home in Kennebunk might symbolize, Bush also suffered from an over-exposed campaign machinery. In a year when the process was more interesting than the candidates, the media paid close attention to the internal machinations of both campaigns. The issue of Bush's "handlers" often headlined election analysis.

Much was made of these "handlers" during the 1988 campaign. Lee Atwater became a celebrity, as both the press and the public began to question how much of Candidate Bush was pre-fab political architecture. After focus group results showed that voters were primed to receive such a message, the Dukakis team wrote and released negative advertisements to highlight this aspect of the Bush campaign. As Dukakis advisor Susan Estrich explained, "we were seeing in focus groups a reaction to the manipulation of the campaign, to the role of handlers."[65] Although some of these Dukakis spots suffered their own lack of authenticity (examined in greater detail in the next section), the general idea of the spots was solid, and they articulated concerns that voters already had about George Bush and his campaign, namely, that Bush was a puppet in the hands of expert consultants.

The Dukakis campaign's "Packaging of George Bush" spot informed voters that "the George Bush and Dan Quayle you see on the stump are packages created by Roger Ailes. Quayle made that point extremely clear in the debate, offering only programmed answers."[66] Another spot, titled "Crazy" focused more heavily on Dan Quayle, as the Dukakis team continued to make issue of the vice-presidential pick. The original script read: "Packager #1: We've got a disaster on our hands. Packager #2: After all that rehearsal I thought we had Quayle totally programmed. Anncr: They'd like to sell you a package. Wouldn't you rather choose a president?"[67] These commercials addressed some of the focus group participants' concerns, and were meant to highlight and legitimize voters' previously held misgivings about both Bush and his campaign.

Belgian Endives

Ultimately, Bush could not generate enough evidence of his own authenticity. As a result, much of his campaign focused on bringing down Dukakis. Bush enjoyed some advantage in this respect, not merely because of Dukakis's inability to respond, but also because he was able to use attack ads as few candidates could. In this regard, "The Wimp Factor" liberated George Bush. When Bush began to hit hard against Dukakis, some even championed Bush's newfound strength and boldness. Second, as many believed he was "handled" by Lee Atwater, few believed that George Bush approved of the worst aspects of his campaign. Thus, negative ads allowed the Bush campaign to walk a careful and contradictory line, and, despite the gross negativity of the Bush campaign, many still believed that he was a good-hearted man. As one analyst surmised, "This election voters may have to choose between a candidate [Bush] with too soft a heart and another [Dukakis] with one that is ... too cool."[68]

The extent of the negativity in the 1988 campaign highlighted both candidates' real weaknesses. As Republican campaign consultant Roger Stone noted, "If you let the campaign be about Bush, he probably would have lost. The campaign had to be about the values you project onto Dukakis. It was an early example of the culture war."[69] While much has been said and written about negativity in 1988, little focus has been paid to the overarching nature of that negativity. In short, the Bush team spent more time and money showcasing their opponent's human, personal, and American inauthenticity — branding Dukakis as an inauthentic, robotic, out-of-touch Massachusetts liberal — because they were unable to fully sell their own candidate's personality. "Lee Atwater knew that that sort of east coast, elite, liberal ideology and persona was going to be problematic for Dukakis."[70]

The irony was not lost on many voters and has not eluded the attention of historians. Kennebunk-Andover-Beltway Bush counter-branded Dukakis as out of touch and Ivy League. The matchup was about as NASCAR as the Harvard-Yale Regatta. Failing to completely convince voters that its own candidate was a de–Kennebunked Texas good ole boy, the Bush team needed to brand Dukakis as an elitist; code: Massachusetts liberal. Bush frequently used these charges on the stump and in his campaign commercials. "Governor Dukakis, his foreign policy views born in Harvard Yard's boutique, would cut the muscle of our defense and I will never do that."[71] This particular accusation was potent because it linked many of the negative symbols already associated with "Massachusetts liberal": weak, elite, out of touch. Thus, even if Bush could not construct an entirely authentic image for himself, his portrayal of Michael Dukakis did ring true for many voters.

As Lee Atwater informed the national press, the Dukakis campaign was "reflective of the kind of out-of-touch crowd they are. They probably sat up in Brookline eating Belgian endives and quiche out of a can."[72] Although many Americans had difficulty with George Herbert Walker Bush's claim to Texas, most were also willing to believe that a governor from Massachusetts was bound to be some kind of Ivy–covered commie. "See, it works because there's a ring of truth to it. They probably think, you know, Dukakis — they were a bunch of elitists."[73] In Texas, George Bush repeated this message on the stump, at county fairs, and at rallies. Mike Dukakis was "A nice WASP kid, born in Milton." By contrast, Bush was "from" Texas and "Texans want a Texan as president, not someone from Massachusetts." Then, displaying cowboy boots, Bush added, "Don't let them tell you I'm no Texan. Take a look at that."[74]

Of these attacks, Dukakis would later recall: "Well, obviously [Atwater] and the folks around Bush were trying to make me a kind of Northeast liberal who was out of touch, and that kind of a thing. I mean, the irony of this is that, you know, I'm the guy who is the son of Greek immigrants who came over here and lived the American dream. Nothing against Yankee Brahmins, who were here since 1630."[75] But Dukakis could not convince the country that he was more "in touch" than Bush, despite many voters' doubts about the Republican's authenticity.

Michael Dukakis, Regular Guy

None of Dukakis's campaign advisors matched the fame or exposure of George Bush's handlers. Indeed, it did not always seem that his managers knew how to engage the new politics of campaign politics. Not only was his campaign organization unstable, but Dukakis often refused to resort to the politics of symbols, which Lee Atwater had used so masterfully for Bush. Internal campaign records make clear that the candidate came to the competition determined to avoid changing his personality and feigning likeability. As a result, many voters perceived him as an ice-cold Eastern liberal, a brand that would remain throughout the campaign.

The Dukakis team did realize that it would need to transform the candidate into someone to whom voters could relate. The original June strategy, which was loosely followed throughout the campaign, included a three-pronged message intended to create an attractive Dukakis brand. "The three elements of" the Dukakis message were "[he] cares about people like you; [he is] making the case for change; and [he has] leadership character."[76] The campaign believed that voters would identify Dukakis as "their" candidate. Going into the Democratic convention, advisors hoped that the week of free and paid media coverage would focus on the image of "Michael Dukakis, the man of American roots and a product of the American dream. And ... it was the emotional closing argument that Michael Dukakis is on your side."[77]

While the campaign nominally emphasized issues, particularly those important to Reagan Democrats and the Democrats' blue-collar base, Dukakis advisors knew that, first and last, they had to make a case for Dukakis as a human being. The Atwater attack machine sidetracked those efforts, but Dukakis's managers did understand that a winning strategy had to include personal appeal. "Dukakis felt it was very important to establish a substantive base ... so that in the last three or four weeks of the campaign, when he said, 'I'm on your side, I am the person who really cares about people like you,' he would have the credibility."[78]

Dukakis and his staff attempted to craft a more appealing image going into the general election. Although he would not go so far as to eat a pork rind, the team realized it needed to soften the image that had been constructed during the primaries. During the primaries, Dukakis was seen as "aloof, cerebral and technocratic." He changed his themes and tone during the general election. Although his transformation was not nearly as dramatic as George Bush's, Dukakis was nevertheless mocked in the press: "Mike Dukakis, Regular Guy. 'He's taking off his coat AND rolling up his sleeves,' one Dukakis aide said with deep satisfaction last week."[79]

Explaining the candidate's makeover to the *New York Times*, Dukakis media consultant Dan Payne explained that while his candidate was "still not a 'shot-and-beer kinda guy,'" the general election campaign would project an image of Dukakis "as a neighbor, a man who lives in a modest home in the suburbs, cuts his own grass, lives a life like millions of Americans.... 'This guy understands your life; he lives your life.'"[80]

Although usurped by media coverage of Jesse Jackson, the Democratic National Convention offered the best opportunity for Dukakis to present his new image to a large audience. The media reported that Dukakis's convention video was "folksy" and "carefully produced to have the look of a home movie."[81] The convention film featured images of Dukakis's modest upbringing as the son of immigrants. The film offered footage of "the humble Dukakis homestead" and the candidate's "25-year-old snow blower."[82] As Dukakis later joked, "Little did I know my 25-year-old snow blower would become overnight a symbol of efficient frugality in this country."[83] The snow blower was proof that Dukakis still lived as ordinary Americans lived. Unlike the vice president, Dukakis still removed snow from his own driveway, still scrimped and saved like average folk.

Although the campaign made attempts to identify the candidate as a regular guy, Dukakis often fell flat. As much as they had mocked George Bush's makeover, journalists seemed to at least appreciate the Republican's efforts. If both campaigns were handling the candidates and constructing makeovers, at least George Bush was succeeding. As *Time* reported of the Democrat's efforts, "The Dukakis camp came late to the likeability war ... he sometimes seemed to be running for Accountant in Chief."[84] This stiff image of the Democrat stuck; by late October many believed he had become a caricature of his icy self.

Despite campaign manager Susan Estrich's claim that they emphasized emotional appeals, it was clear that the campaign's message of substance, expertise, and sober competence was repeated more often and more broadly. Unable to compete on the grounds of likeability, ultimately the campaign promoted reliability at the expense of relatability. This was borne out in the polls. Following the first debate, a *Time* poll revealed that most voters believed Dukakis had won, but that Bush was more likable (by a margin of 44 percent to 38 percent).[85] Even his close associates deemed him "the Mr. Spock of politics, a totally rational alien bemused by the passions around him."[86] While Bush had friends and associates vouching for his authentic love of backyard cuisine, Dukakis suffered dearly the modern politics of authenticity.

Even the Democratic National Convention, typically a candidate's opportunity to own the media, was a mixed bag for Dukakis. His efforts to portray a relatable image often seemed scripted, particularly when compared to the ever-authentic Jesse Jackson. The Dukakis campaign's own post-mortem memoranda on the convention argued that the one highlight of Dukakis's performance was "when he thought he was off camera and mouthed 'I love you,' to his wife, Kitty.... We need to see more of that. Instead I suspect Dukakis is afraid of smiling all the time because every time he starts to break into a smile he stops it midway and comes out looking more like a sneer. I would work on his smile.'"[87]

Compared to Bush's consultants, the Dukakis team made only meager attempts to out–Joe the opposition. When it did, the campaign had a real case to make. Dukakis could emphasize his immigrant roots and his twenty-five-year old snow blower. Moreover, it missed the opportunity to reframe his Harvard education as a bootstrapped American dream. While his advisors believed that Dukakis had greater purchase on blue-collar authenticity than his opponent, this was often lost on voters who did not receive the message. Of George Bush, Dukakis advisor Dan Payne said, "'He couldn't take us to Kennebunkport. He couldn't take us to the Houstonian Hotel. He hasn't had the experiences of ordinary citizens. Dukakis has a real advantage because he's lived the life of the average, suburban American."[88] This message, however, would never be a dominant theme for the Dukakis campaign.

Because Dukakis was so uncomfortable playing to the politics of personality, he was unable to make full use of the soft media. He was uneasy on talk shows and cold in magazine interviews; both the public and the interviewers were left with an icy impression of the candidate. For example, a *People* cover article released in July 1988 ought to have been Dukakis's opportunity to dish authentic. The content of the article did not follow through with the message conveyed on the cover, which headlined, "Kitty and the Duke." The cover photograph featured the couple smiling and embracing. "He mows, he cooks, he shops — he even *does the dishes!*"[89] To be sure, Dukakis could not have hoped for a better headline than household chores. Despite the fortunate headline, the campaign did little to follow up on this charming aspect of the couple's life, and did not push the issue, even in the *People* interview. Indeed, Dukakis was unable to take full advantage of the cushy anecdotes requisite for *People.* The article concluded, "To look upon Dukakis is to learn little, for his face is remarkably inexpressive. His visible range of emotions is unimpressive, a wan smile representing delight and a slightly raised voice indicating anger."[90]

Liberals and Lobsters

For the most part, Dukakis was strangled by too few "Kitty and the Duke" moments, and too many ice man caricatures. The Bush campaign's negative assaults on Dukakis centered on one major theme: Dukakis was a Massachusetts Liberal, out of touch with American values. As conservative commentator George Will noted, "The premise of the Bush campaign is that many people west of the Berkshires think that only two things come from Massachusetts, liberals and lobsters, and pretty soon they're going to wake up and say that's not a lobster."[91] This played not only to Middle America's ideas about itself, but to a broader sense of American authenticity.

Spokespersons for the Bush campaign and Republican Party began describing Dukakis as a Massachusetts liberal during the Republican National Convention. George Bush ran with that message in an August 26, 1988, speech in Texas, where he accused Dukakis of opposing both gun ownership and the Pledge of Allegiance.[92] This was followed by comments and attack ads condemning the infamous Massachusetts prison furlough program. The Republican campaign and conservative support groups continued this theme in their paid advertisements, painting Dukakis as a fringe candidate — a man to whom most voters could not relate.[93] At a November 1 speech in Indiana, George Bush told a live and television audience that Dukakis was "disconnected from common sense ... guided more by abstract theories and grids and graphs and computer printouts and the history of Swedish social planning."[94] The Bush campaign discovered that the more inflammatory comments were more likely to be repeated on the nightly news.

Gaining traction with the "fringe" characterization of his opponent, Bush attacked Dukakis directly on this point at the University of Notre Dame: "One of us holds mainstream views and stands for mainstream values and one of us does not ... mainstream isn't just the middle: it's the big, full-hearted center, it's the traditions and the faith and the beliefs that have guided this country for 200 years.'"[95] In short, Dukakis was out of touch. Bush's comments got airtime, but Dukakis failed to respond. His inability to address this fact led even some leading Democrats to wonder whether their candidate fully understood the "values that Americans hold dear.... He shows his lack of understanding of the utility of political symbolism." [96]

The infamous "Willie Horton" advertisement, not produced by the Bush campaign, received the most attention of any paid spot produced during the 1988 campaign.[97] It received such national recognition that the Bush campaign produced two follow-up spots, making similar charges. The campaign's "Revolving Door" spot set menacing images of prisoners against the threatening voice of an announcer who informed viewers that "as governor, Michael Dukakis vetoed mandatory sentences for drug dealers. He vetoed the death penalty. His revolving door prison policy gave weekend furloughs to first degree murderers not eligible for parole.... While out, many committed other crimes like kidnapping and rape, and ... many are still at large. Now Michael Dukakis says he wants to do for America what he's done for Massachusetts. America can't afford that risk."[98] Another spot, produced along the same story line, offered Dukakis in his own words. Taken from debate footage, the "Credibility" spot showed Dukakis seemingly laughing at himself as he claimed to be "tough on violent crime."[99] Both spots questioned Dukakis's personal, human, and American authenticity by making him appear to be cold and out of touch with both his own record and with mainstream American values. The spots also suggested that Dukakis was either lying or wholly unaware of himself and his work. The fact that these were replayed in subsequent news reports made the charges difficult to overcome.

Throughout much of the campaign, Dukakis appeared defensive and defenseless against such attacks. Using coded and not-so-coded language, Bush managed to frame Dukakis as "a 'Harvard elitist.'"[100] The Bush campaign characterized Dukakis as the embodiment of "a liberalism that is ... exotic as a Harvard boutique yet stealthy enough to win an election by misrepresenting itself to the American people."[101] Because these images became so deeply entrenched, when Dukakis did attempt to defend against such attacks, he appeared inauthentic, as though he were trying to deceive voters about his background and Harvard education. Roger Ailes promoted a theme that "Dukakis was being deceptive about his past, trying to deny his liberalism, to mask the menace to the nation presented by his softness on crime and defense ... Dukakis made these absurd accusations credible by his refusal to take them seriously."[102] Seemingly unable to effectively defend himself, Dukakis instead "played right into that perception."[103] His hometown paper's assessment of the October 13 debate judged the liberal label more damaging than charges of incompetence: "Duke got to remind everybody that Bush picked Dan Quayle, but Bush got to remind everyone Duke is a liberal."[104] Lee Atwater had effectively conjoined the words "liberal," "elite," and "out of touch."

Next to the Willie Horton spot, the famous "Tank Ride" opposition advertisement received the greatest amount of attention in the national press. The Dukakis campaign itself was responsible for the event that produced the embarrassing video footage. Attempting to shore up his muscular chops, Dukakis allowed himself to be filmed while campaigning at a General Dynamics plant in Michigan. Dukakis wore an oversized helmet, making him look like a small child playing at war, as he drove the tank in circles around a dirt lot. Dukakis looked silly. The Bush campaign pounced on it, creating a paid advertisement to keep the free media loop moving. The footage ran as an announcer asserted, "Michael Dukakis has opposed virtually every defense system we developed ... and now he wants to be our Commander in Chief. America can't afford that risk."[105] Dukakis's tank ride seemed inherently inauthentic. He was a man not merely playing at guns, but pretending to be someone he was not — a hawk. The video footage of Michael Dukakis's "tank ride" was already famous by the time it was used in the Bush advertisement. Its replay capacity was both effective and potent in portraying Dukakis as an out of touch liberal who had not likely ever touched a gun, let alone a tank, in his life.

Today I Shall Torment an Intellectual[106]

Dukakis's inability to display any sense of humor about the charges levied against him made him an easy target. His lack of personality itself became an object of ridicule for both the Bush campaign and the media. When Bush referred to his opponent as "ice man" during the September debate in Winston-Salem, North Carolina, the charge may have been mean, but not necessarily unfair. As one reporter joked, "All too often the candidate" took "wooden prose and tired arguments and, miraculously" made "them even blander."[107] Republican campaign consultant Edward Rollins believed that part of Dukakis's problem was not that he did not allow his personality to show in public, but that he had no personality to begin with: "What this campaign really came down to is ... I don't think there's anybody ... who doesn't say Mike Dukakis is a very cold, calculating man ... he's very cold, he's not warm."[108] In the absence of personal appeal, the press and many voters had little reason to pay attention to Dukakis.[109] Instead, the press found it easier to mock the seemingly defenseless Democrat. *Time* ridiculed, Dukakis "tout[ed] such eye-glazing proposals as the Pan-American summit on drug trafficking."[110] As a result, both campaigns came to understand the danger of focusing on issues in a year when free media attention was lavished on gaffes, negative advertisements, and emotional appeals. By attempting to elevate the national discourse, Dukakis often appeared to be above the national conversation. Bush advisor Vince Breglio observed of Dukakis, "Competent people are sometimes seen as arrogant.... He's made competence his emblem. But competence is only a part of image. A President has to be open and caring, as well as tough and hard. He must project a comfortable image. It's tough for Dukakis to retrace his steps now and make himself nice."[111]

Even among members of his own party, there were few who could vouch for Dukakis's personality. In a survey taken among delegates at the Democratic National Convention, "288 said he was dull or described his personality as cold, aloof, humorless or arrogant. 'How can I say this politely? The one weakness is he is boring,... He lulls his audiences to sleep.... You start out listening to him, but by the middle of his speech, you've forgotten what he's said.'"[112]

To be fair, at the Democratic National Convention, Dukakis was forced to measure up not only to his Republican opponent, but to a more charismatic figure within his own party. Jesse Jackson had built a grassroots movement based in equal parts on his politics and on his force of personality. While political scientists are still analyzing the impact of protest nonvoting among Jackson supporters, it was clear that the attention given to the challenger, particularly in the period leading up to the convention, detracted from the feel-good free media Dukakis might have enjoyed in the week preceding the Democratic National Convention. Dukakis advisor John Corrigan noted that the campaign's internal analysis found that Jackson received twice as much free media coverage leading up to the DNC as the nominee himself.[113]

The typically unadulterated media attention around the convention generally offered candidates complete control over both image and message. Excepting dramatic vice-presidential selections or platform committee infighting, in the absence of the smoke-filled back rooms of yore, campaigns used modern conventions to send messages of hope, unity, and strength. The conventions were designed to hype the candidate's biography and exploit the free media coverage. The conventions were almost entirely scripted by the nominee.

Jackson's continued popularity diminished the Dukakis campaign's ability to take full advantage of the convention. Equally important, Jackson's continued media attention not only detracted from the amount of time spent discussing Dukakis, but offered a startling diptych of images: the charismatic, relatable, grassroots mover, Jackson versus the dull, cold, Dukakis. At a time when the Dukakis campaign ought to have been peddling soft music, delightful home videos, and adorable childhood anecdotes, the candidate was forced to measure up to the naturally charismatic Jesse Jackson.[114] Deputy Dukakis campaign manager, John Corrigan noted, "There are only so many minutes ... you are trying to teach people as much as you can about Mike Dukakis ... and what his values are. Our 15 minutes ... was being consumed by" Jesse Jackson. "We were in a position where we couldn't control the media coverage because Jackson is much better at it."[115]

Jackson was also simply a more likable and interesting man than Dukakis. As one political cartoonist commented, "Dukakis is so controlled and he plays his cards so close to his chest that he's hard to get a fix on for voters, not to mention cartoonists,... He's so dull that cartoonists tend to caricature that dullness. I just did one on sheep counting Dukakises."[116] At the Los Angeles Times, Paul Conrad added, "I've only done Dukakis three or four times. There's really no need, as far as I'm concerned. There's nothing there, other than the fact that he's never said anything."[117]

Late in the campaign, Dukakis granted an interview to Nightline's Ted Koppel. It was meant to be Dukakis's opportunity to "'give the people the sense of who the real Mike Dukakis is.' But when encouraged to talk about himself, he talked about Bush.... He seemed to be looking only for openings to repeat well-worn lines from his stump speech and to use gray words like 'concern' and 'tough.'"[118] Ted Koppel recalled: "I was saying to him, 'Governor, you know, here's a chance to get a network audience for one hour in which you are being asked questions,' and he kept saying the same things he had been saying in the campaign throughout. I didn't mean it to be rude, but it came out that way. And he missed that opportunity, too."[119]

Dukakis's problem was not merely his lack of personality but also that he was inept at faking it. Ironically, this made him appear even more inauthentic than George Bush at a rib-eating contest. One reporter summed up Dukakis's struggles with personal authenticity in this way: "Michael Dukakis trying furiously to grin, with meager results."[120] Another reporter joked that Dukakis's "eerie grin had the spontaneity of a Dale Carnegie student practicing before the mirror."[121]

According to Republican campaign consultant Edward Rollins, George Bush won the election in large part because Dukakis was "arguing intellectually on certain points" whereas Bush was "arguing on emotional issues."[122] The most obvious example of Dukakis's inability to convey human emotion came during the October 13, 1988, debate. CNN's Bernard Shaw opened the debate with a question that has been widely criticized, asking Dukakis whether he would support the death penalty were his wife, Kitty, raped and murdered.

A reference to the Massachusetts prison furlough program, Dukakis might have used the question (fair or unfair) as an opportunity to display the requisite human emotion associated with personal tragedy. He did not, saying only that he had "opposed the death penalty" his "whole life." Many believed that he came across as a robot or, more famously, as an "ice man."

Conservative linguist William Safire concluded that Dukakis's response was a "mechanical reaction like that of the mentalist in *The 39 Steps*."[123] Safire was not alone in his evaluation of Dukakis's performance. Another pundit analyzed the debate gaffe in this way: "Dukakis fed his own worst stereotype as a technocrat with ice in his veins when he gave that passionless answer to the question of whether he would support the death penalty for a man who had raped and murdered his wife. And he resisted advice that he dramatize his commitment to fighting crime by citing two crime victims in his own family: his brother, who was killed by a hit-and-run driver, and his father, who was bound and robbed in his office."[124] To Dukakis, law and policy were academic. To voters seeking assurance or reform or security, Dukakis's remote responses were simply not enough.

But the now infamous Kitty–rape gaffe, however, was only one example of Dukakis's poor performance that evening. As the *New York Times* reminded its readers, "Mr. Dukakis was asked at least two questions that might have evoked emotion: a question on rape and one about his heroes. He responded with passionless laundry lists."[125] Throughout the debate he "performed ... routinely and stiffly ... seemed ... programmed, even strangled."[126] It is unclear whether Dukakis could have salvaged the debate after his response on the death penalty, "muster[ing] all the emotion of a time-and-temperature recording."[127] He was unable to relate policy in a human, empathetic, and self-disclosive narrative, as required in modern campaigning.

A CBS/*New York Times* survey confirmed negative personal perceptions of Dukakis resulting from the debate. Neither Republicans nor Democrats surveyed could muster much enthusiasm for their respective candidates. But while 55 percent of Republican respondents acknowledged that they would prefer a different set of candidates, the number was much higher among Democrats. Seventy-two percent of Democrats said "they wish there were choices other than Bush and Dukakis."[128] The post-debate October poll also "found that Mr. Dukakis's personal ratings had dropped to their worst point all year.... Mr. Bush's ratings, in the meantime, have risen to their highest level since 1984. For Mr. Dukakis, 32 percent of the electorate said they had a favorable view of him and 43 percent said their view was unfavorable. For Mr. Bush, it was 47 percent favorable and 30 percent unfavorable."[129] The same poll showed a strong preference for other candidates, particularly among

Democrats, who preferred the more charismatic and authentic Jesse Jackson. Late in the campaign, as Dukakis's failure appeared certain, more Democrats indicated that they preferred Jackson to Dukakis.[130]

The morning after the debate, at a breakfast with Jesse Jackson, Dukakis reportedly turned to his fellow Democrat and said, "Jesse, there's a new word in the political lexicon — 'likeability.'"[131] Facing such long odds on the likeability question, the Dukakis team knew that it would have to go negative against George Bush. Opposition branding was most effective when it addressed ideas that voters were previously primed to receive. In the case of George Bush, voters were open to charges that he was a patrician in cowboy's clothes, and that he was being "packaged" and sold by Atwater and Ailes. The Dukakis camp attempted to capitalize on this knowledge. However, Dukakis himself was unable to repackage his opponent. The charge was instead made by a surrogate at the Democratic National Convention. Ann Richards, governor of Texas, delivered one of the more memorable laugh lines in a mostly humorless campaign: "Poor George, he was born with a silver foot in his mouth." This attack, however, received only sparse follow-up by the Dukakis campaign and did not become a major narrative at any time.

Another mismanaged attack addressed the inauthenticity of the Republican candidate and his campaign. The "handler" ads, discussed previously, might have targeted a ripe market, but suffered major flaws. Most obviously, the advertisement titled "Handler" used bad actors to deliver an over-scripted message. Rather than making its point, the commercial seemed hokey. The purpose of the advertisement was to frame Bush as a mere packaged front man for the Lee Atwater organization. Instead, it counterproductively offered viewers packaged actors to deliver the message. If the content of the commercial was meant to re-focus viewers on Bush's deceitful inauthenticity, the cinematography, actors, and script management undermined that message.

Conclusions

The 1988 campaign may have been the most negative in recent memory simply because neither candidate had any real claim to authenticity. Even as Bush underwent a personality makeover, the team, admittedly, could not have won on its guy alone. Instead, it required the public to refocus its attention on the greater inauthenticity of the other guy. Bush was fortunate to be advised by an organized and diligent campaign team staffed with brilliant opposition branders. They were assisted by a campaign-obsessed national media, which turned its attention to the mechanics of the campaign. In so doing, the media often legitimated attacks against the Democratic challenger.

It is not clear whether Dukakis might have won with a more organized staff and a more focused message. While scholars have examined the Dukakis camp's inability to muster effective campaign organization, in the final analysis, this was merely a procedural problem in a campaign that suffered much greater difficulties. Dukakis may have been a brilliant manager and a competent leader, but this story became secondary in the face of continuous loop video footage of the governor in a military tank. Instead, as the press focused on the campaigns as much as the candidates, journalists had a difficult time summoning enthusiasm for Dukakis's more reserved managers and their sober campaign tactics. It is not surprising that the most negative campaign was the one in which neither side had any real basis for positive, thematic, and emotional advertising.

Additionally, with the national press determined to report on campaign tactics in order to uncover the political backstage, journalists grasped for the easiest brand and most consistent narrative to frame the election. Getting little from the Dukakis side, the story line was provided by the Bush campaign's negative advertisements, which offered a believable counter-image of Dukakis as inauthentic on multiple counts. His Massachusetts liberalism was portrayed as out of touch with American authenticity. His inability to portray emotion branded Dukakis as lacking human authenticity. His ill-fated attempt to drive a tank was portrayed as insincere. These were the most enduring images of the campaign.

5

The Man from Hope: 1992

If Democrats were disgruntled with their lackluster candidates in 1984 and 1988, they found a solution in 1992. The heart-warming, sax-playing, pizza-eating, feel-your-pain candidacy of Bill Clinton was a welcome departure for beleaguered Democrats. In many ways, Clinton was a man of that moment. Just as Americans began tuning in to talk shows for a dose of introspection, self-help, and scopophilic insight into the personal lives of public figures, Bill Clinton arrived on the scene, pre-made for the talk show set.

There were multiple reasons for Clinton's victory, not the least of which was the economic recession that dogged the final years of the Bush administration. Those who have evaluated Clinton's 1992 victory within the economic framework had good evidence to support their claim.[1] The president's initial campaign strategy focused on his foreign policy credentials, emphasizing his leadership during the brief and popular 1991 Gulf War. However popular the war was, a year after its conclusion, most Americans were not focused on foreign policy in a time of peace, and this emphasis was out of touch with Americans' pocketbook concerns. Nonetheless, it would be misleading to focus solely on the state of the domestic economy or on Bush's seemingly misguided emphasis on foreign triumphs to explain the national discourse surrounding the 1992 campaign.[2] More central was Bush's inability to understand ordinary voters and connect with them. What was more notable about the 1992 election was what the candidates revealed about themselves. Like never before, candidates were asked to answer increasingly personal questions in increasingly intimate venues.

The Election of Larry King

The standard format of political communication was upended during the 1992 campaign as talk shows and electronic town halls became the preferred venues for political media. Voters craved authenticity and intimacy;

the talk show style allowed viewers to probe the deepest depths of candidates' psychologies, personalities, and biographies through the media of eager hosts and live studio audiences.[3] The format proved so popular and so powerful that it was adapted to official campaign events; the second debate was modified to create a Donahue–esque atmosphere. Each of the three candidates eventually adopted the style (with more or less success) in their own campaign events and commercials. The talk show, however, was not an equal playing field. The conversational, pseudo-psychological, intimate virtuality favored the Democratic challenger, who came across as comfortable and familiar. "The 1992 campaign demonstrated that responsiveness" and "intimacy ... were the keys" to successful campaigning.[4] No one did this better than Bill Clinton.

Initiating the talk show campaign, Clinton appeared on MTV, *Donahue*, *Arsenio Hall*, and *Larry King Live*.[5] When Clinton first incorporated these free media into his campaign, such programs were not traditional settings for politicians. Clinton played the saxophone, engaged hosts and audiences, and came across as a regular guy in casual, conversational settings. Voters not only appreciated Clinton's willingness to appear on their favorite shows, but came away feeling that they had earned a relationship with him. This ultimately worked to his advantage even as he was often, as a result, forced to account for personal shortcomings.

Despite Clinton's occasionally difficult public confessional, political scientist Lance Bennett demonstrated that Clinton's nontraditional television appearances strongly correlated with tangible support in national polling. Using a double overlay graph of Clinton's nontraditional television appearances and statistical data compiled from major national polls, Bennett showed that Clinton's appearances correlated with positive favorability numbers.[6] While these data suggested a correlative, rather than a causal, relationship between the two, Bennett made clear that voters responded positively to Clinton's campaign style and availability.

Although the television talk show best suited the stay-at-home, pop-psychology, celebrity-culture mien, it was not surprising that it eventually invaded the world of politics. In the often uneasy marriage between the two, however, politics did not enter the world of talk shows as much as talk show topics and question formats entered the world of political campaigning. As campaigning became confessional, talk show hosts and eager members of studio audiences posed personal questions, probing for intimate details about candidates' lives. As political communication experts Shawn and Trevor Parry-Giles noted at the time, "Confessional politics has been central to this year's presidential contest, as political oratory has become indistinguishable from interviews with Oprah."[7]

Despite the fact that television talk shows were thoroughly manufactured environments, the format added at least an aura of authenticity to viewers' interactions with candidates. According to communication psychologist Richard Jackson Harris, talk show appearances "opened new avenues for the candidates to present themselves as 'real people' who were very approachable."[8] The talk show style changed the campaign and challenged traditional campaign interactions. Even as the candidates met the demands of the format, voters came to expect increasingly revelatory and intimate disclosure. By August of 1992 it was clear that the format had changed politics. "While politicians once kept their emotions and the intimate details of their lives under wraps, voters and the news media increasingly have demanded that public officials show and tell all."[9] Janet Hook of *Congressional Quarterly Weekly* observed that voters had come to prefer "candidates that people can 'relate' to."[10]

It seemed that the voters craved something more authentic than standard campaigning could offer. While the virtual world of television talk shows and electronic town halls crafted a manufactured intimacy, voters felt that they could get closer to their candidates *as people* through the structure of a give-and-take televised conversation. In his post-election analysis, political reporter Joe Klein summed up the mood of the season: "Anything that seemed ... authentic ... had far more resonance than any pro might have predicted."[11]

Although the "pros" might not have predicted it, they quickly switched strategies to capture it. In a late-summer analysis of the campaign, the *Boston Globe* reported that "authentic" images were the keys to the campaign. "Today's political operatives are on a quest to find what it is to be real. Both President Bush and Clinton have attempted to strike the delicate balance recently — using the sophisticated tools of modern political warfare to project determinedly "authentic" images."[12]

He's Just Like Us. Only Richer

One man attempted to present voters with an "authentic" campaign from the very beginning. Ross Perot changed the stakes of campaigning in 1992. After his dramatic fall from grace in the early summer of 1992, Perot could not recapture many voters. However, his early and somewhat sustained popularity reified what was essential about Ross Perot: voters found him attractive because he seemed to be an authentic alternative.

Early in the campaign, Perot presented himself as a boot-strapping Ragged Dick — a grassroots Texas everyman who had struck it rich and wanted to take back the country on behalf of regular folks. "Perot ... fostered the image of himself as the very embodiment of the Horatio Alger myth, a man of very humble origins who rose to become a billionaire by dint of hard work."[13] His supporters were attracted to the anti-politician who was at once a billionaire and a guy next door.

Nonetheless, there was more "truthiness" than truth in Perot's mediated self image. Perot's "humble" origins were mythic versions of the truth — stories from Americana that Perot had worked into his own autobiography. "Perot emphasized his father's frugality, despite the family's comfortable economic circumstances, citing the fact that his father drove the same Dodge for twenty years. In shaping the Perot legend, he has referred to his own hard-working industriousness, placing it in the context of the Texas cowboy." On the campaign trail, he often repeated the mythified false "story that he delivered papers from horseback." [14]

While Perot managed to garner a great deal of support, besting both Clinton and Bush in polls through the late spring of 1992, Perot's dramatic fall came as reporters began to dig into the truth about the political phenom. Early in the election season, Perot's high poll numbers began to drop. In the late spring and early summer, media outlets began to pay close attention to the dark horse Texas billionaire. In June, the *Washington Post* ran one of the most damaging stories, revealing that Perot was more of a Washington insider than he had led voters to believe. In addition to Washington lobbying efforts on behalf of his company, Perot had held some amount of influence in the nation's capital as far back as the Nixon administration. Included in the *Post* story was a quote from former Nixon advisor Peter Flanigan, who revealed that Perot was "the ultimate insider.... He knows his way around the corridors of power almost better than anybody I know."[15]

As other journalists began to probe into Perot's background, the increased media attention did more harm to the candidate. His notorious paranoia, prudishness, self-aggrandizement, and dictatorial leadership style were but a few of the unflattering psychological details disclosed about Perot. His humble childhood and authentic anti–Washington rhetoric were soon revealed to be thoroughly inauthentic as investigative journalists began writing about Perot's embellished childhood stories and extensive connections in Washington. In addition to media revelations about the Texan, Ross Perot turned out to be neither a charismatic public speaker nor an authentic everyman. The more he spoke, the worse he polled. Although he appeared multiple times on *Larry King Live*, fielding softballs and speaking in platitudes, he could not seem to rally, rouse, and excite his once passionate supporters.

Perot's inauthenticity was borne out in his advertisements. Although his famously long advertisements were relatively successful in introducing a mythologized version of the candidate, they suffered some serious problems. Because Perot did not launch his advertisements until mid to late October, most viewers were already wary of his alleged unsavory personal qualities. Further, Perot's big-budget advertisements belied the candidate's emphasis on the "grassroots" nature of his campaign. The media coverage of Perot's advertising did not focus on Perot's ideas or biography, but rather on his personal wealth and self-financed campaign.

Of the few short advertisements purchased by the Perot campaign, only two even featured the candidate. One, "Best Person Independent," featured a clip of Perot's closing remarks from the October 19, 1992, debate. While in the context of the debate, Perot's remarks were relatively standard; when clipped for a TV commercial, Perot seemed more like a personal injury lawyer on a low-rent local TV commercial than a grassroots man of the people. In a straight-on headshot of the candidate speaking and pointing his finger, Perot asked, "Who's the best-qualified person up here on the stage to create jobs ... I suggest you might consider somebody who's created jobs. Who's the best person to manage money? I suggest you pick a person who's successfully managed money. Who's the best person to get results and not talk? Look at the record and make your decision. And, finally, who would you give your pension fund and your savings account to manage? And, last one, who would you ask to be the trustee of your estate and take care of your children if something happened to you?"[16]

Despite his failures, the Ross Perot phenomenon gave insight into the cultural story of the 1992 election. First, Perot's candidacy found a home in the talk show media environment. Perot used *Larry King Live* as his platform to announce his candidacy in February 1992. Second, the rise and fall of Perot was negotiated using the vocabulary of authenticity. At the height of his popularity, the press attention focused on his down-home, grassroots citizen campaign. His downfall was equally mediated using the standards of authenticity. Finally, when Perot supporters began to sour on their candidate's grassroots everyman image, they looked for a truly authentic Ragged Dick. They found him in Bill Clinton.

Although Perot was nominally a conservative, he shared more crossover support with Bill Clinton than with George Bush. In August 1992, the Pew Research Center found a "virtual wholesale shift of Ross Perot's constituency to the Clinton side."[17] This finding was confirmed across polling organizations and was sustained throughout the fall. A September 1992 Times Mirror survey found that "former Perot supporters who say they would be very likely to vote for the Texas businessman, now support Clinton over Bush by almost a two to one margin."[18] While both made the budget deficit a theme in their campaigns, few voters thought that Bill Clinton was likely to decrease federal government spending. Instead, much of the crossover was due to the fact that voters were looking for a candidate to whom they could relate.

Read My Lips

That candidate was not George Bush. By 1992, George Bush had been in Washington for most of his life; he had been serving in the upper echelons of the executive branch for twelve years. While the early Bush strategy attempted to capitalize on the president's foreign policy successes and executive credentials, his advisors quickly found that they were losing to not one, but two ostensibly authentic outsiders. The media portrayed the president as dull, wonkish, and out of touch. He had successfully overseen the conclusion of the Cold War and the first post–Cold War military operations, but the patrician president was no match for the Double Bubba ticket emerging on the Democratic side. The Texas good ole boy image that Lee Atwater had effectively constructed for George Bush in 1988 might have worked against Michael Dukakis, but it had no force against Bill Clinton.

Although it was a pithy line, "Read My Lips" was also easy to mock when George Bush signed the Omnibus Budget Reconciliation Act of 1990. The "Read My Lips" caricature was the most famous symbol for voters' discomfort with Bush whose authenticity gap went far beyond his inability to deliver on his promise to prevent tax increases. To be sure, Americans were dismayed with the Bush tax increase. However, the tax increase itself was less important than the fact that voters lost faith in Bush as a result of his unkept promise. But Bush's authenticity gap also came from more pervasive and endemic qualities: Bush was a relatively dull, easily mocked, uncharismatic patrician who was bad at playing ordinary.

Buying Socks at Penney's

When Bush attempted to appeal to middle Americans as one of them, he appeared to be play-acting. In an ill-fated attempt to encourage shoppers to buy their way out of economic recession, Bush purchased four pairs of socks at JC Penney, a store carefully selected for its budget appeal. The scene was simultaneously callous and ridiculous. What the cameras captured was a patrician man ill-at-ease in an unfamiliar department store. For its readers, *Newsweek* characterized the president as inauthentic and embarrassingly out of touch. "Bush is accident-prone at it because, I think, his own natural idiom is so alien to the idiom of those he is aping and/or with whom he is seeking to establish photographable rapport. Often when he tries to adopt what he imagines to be the local vernacular it comes out wrong. But even when the transaction is straightforward, as in buying those now famous socks, what the encounter, by its very nature, must say to the bemused onlooker is not 'Hey, look at the president out there buying his own socks at Penney's ... what a guy!' but. "Look, there is George Bush pretending to be a regular guy buying some socks at Penney's."[19] This was to be the case in many of his 1992 campaign ventures into ordinary America.

Although the Bush team made efforts to change his image, Bush's authenticity gap remained. As one political consultant noted, "The smartest thing the White House could do right now is to declare Tuesday night bowling night and make everyone go to a bowling alley in suburban Virginia every week to spend some time with regular guys."[20] As was evident in the JC Penney incident, despite his aides' efforts to show Bush as a beer-drinking bowler, the media did not passively absorb the Bush campaign's cowboyed-up images. On the contrary, Bush's efforts to be a Bubba were inauthentic in the extreme. That the press used the terms of authenticity to determine the acceptable boundaries of his candidate image limited Bush's ability to appeal to the bowling classes. "The candidate with the biggest authenticity handicap is obviously George Bush. A preppy droppin' his g's to be one of the guys? Shoppin' at Penney's? Munchin' pork rinds.... He's a bad faker."[21] Voters, however, did not need journalists to tell them that Bush was a bad faker — in television speeches and campaign stops, he could not seem to connect to average Americans.

Trying to appear more Texas and less Beltway, in September the president began longer campaign trips to the border South. Unlike 1988, however, journalists did not buy the act. A *Washington Times* journalist mocked the president's efforts to make a "determined appeal to the nation's good ol' boys and gals" by employing country musicians and southern vernacular. "President Bush, in his best redneck-lovin,' hi-y'all twang, swept through" Tennessee "in an effort to win America's beer drinkers, bass fishermen, veterans and country music fans."[22] The jokes were pervasive — they were featured on *Saturday Night Live* and reprinted in countless newspaper and newsmagazine articles. Democrats, of course, caught on to Bush's authenticity gap early. As Democrat Patricia Schroeder informed the *New York Times,* "Instead of wrapping himself in pig rinds, now George Bush is always on the golf course.... In their world, I guess, the golf course is the place where a lot of business gets done. But if they want to know about real folks, they should watch the Roseanne Barr show more. She's not out on the golf course.'"[23]

Wrapped Up in Pork Rinds

Bush's attempts at ordinary became a major national joke. A CNN analyst ruthlessly ridiculed Bush's faux Bubba forays into the real world. "Right now ... we got one too many Bubbas in the race. And when you start talking about Bubbas, I mean, there is George Bush and Dan Quayle, and what are they — off fishing and eating pork rinds or something this week.... George Bush is not a Texan. It's just that simple. The man lives in a hotel there.... He just ... doesn't come through as a Texan."[24] Making matters worse, the Connecticut–born patrician Bush attempted to wield a typical Republican weapon against an atypical Democratic challenger. "Bush has been talking a good deal lately about [Bill Clinton's time at] Oxford University in England.... Oxford to Bush is a den of left-leaning, Big Government types, schooled in tricky debating tactics and busily hatching schemes to run America through an 'elite of the so-called best and brightest.'" On the whole, the media did not share Bush's disdain for the Rhodes Scholarship, nor did they accept Bush's right to criticize Clinton as a parvenu. They cheered when Clinton exposed the president's hypocrisy: "He went to a country day school and prep school in Connecticut, and Yale.... Where does he get off looking up to me as an Oxford man?"[25]

Perhaps owing to the president's unpopularity, or perhaps as a result of his opponent's authentic claim to blue-collar roots, newspaper reports about Bush's upbringing were more pervasive in 1992 than they had been in 1988. In September, the *Washington Post* stated bluntly what most already knew: "Raised in the wealthy community of Greenwich, Conn., Bush was chauffeured to day school during the Depression, then prepped at the elite Philips Academy in Andover, Mass., and matriculated at Yale University. With his summer house on the Maine coast and his passion for golf and tennis, he might make a good illustration for 'The Preppie Handbook.'"[26] Stories like these kept public attention on Bush's privileged, cloistered upbringing.

Unlike in 1988, any attempt by Bush to be "Texas" became fodder for political humor, and Bush had a difficult time shedding his patrician demeanor. As longtime Reagan and Bush aide Stuart Spencer noted, "George Sr. in late life was in Texas, but was really a New Englander. He was an Ivy Leaguer."[27] According to Spencer, Bush had a great deal of difficulty acting the part. To prove the point, different news outlets offered humorous articles and segments about the president's attempts to be Texan. *CBS This Morning* dished up a segment featuring a real live Texan who informed viewers that "real Texans do not use the word 'summer' as a verb.... Real Texans never wear those navy slacks with the little green whales all over them. And no real Texan has ever described trouble as 'deep doo-doo.'"[28]

When conservative commentator William Safire noted Bush's authenticity gap, readers of the *New York Times* agreed. In a letter to the editor, a resident of Silver Spring, Maryland, responded, "Safire comments correctly that the patrician Bush 'clanks falsely when he puts on Joe Sixpack nonairs...'" The reader went on to puzzle at Bush's attempts to appeal to a media environment in which "ungrammatical, macho-posturing" was a prize.[29] Bush was clearly not alone in feeling pressured to appear ordinary, but he was the worst at faking it. In her analysis, political scientist Betty Glad argued that Bush was "a patrician who liked to be liked." As a result, the candidate Bush "tried too hard to look hip or ordinary or tough or to be a good ol' boy. Oftentimes the result was a series of non sequiturs," complete with misused blue-collar patois and cringe-inducing references to passé popular culture.[30] While his pork rind posturing was tolerated in 1988, in 1992 it had the opposite of its intended effect: Bush looked phony.

Bush Encounters the Supermarket, Amazed

Bush's problems went beyond ill-fated attempts to eat pork rinds. As President of the United States, Bush was cloistered from the ordinary world encountered by average people every day. The Oval Office could be both a blessing and a curse for a candidate. For Bush, it was a curse. George Bush was a career politician; as president, he was the ultimate Washington insider.

Bush's privilege alone did not crash his candidacy. Stories about his privilege often highlighted a bigger issue with his candidacy and presidency: he was completely out of touch with the experiences of average voters. As the "out of touch" critique became more pervasive, Bush's campaign managers encouraged him to lay off the yacht during the campaign. Those inside the Republican Party, desperate to hold together the Reagan majority, encouraged Bush to push a low-rent image of himself. Republican Al D'Amato criticized Bush for spending so much time at his Kennebunkport, Maine, summer home. "People think he's spending all his time on the golf course or his boat," D'Amato said. "That's not the way the average guy spends his time.... He's portrayed as having a good time and being out of touch with the problems of the country."[31]

And he was. The best illustration of Bush's inability to understand and connect with the experiences of average Americans came during an early campaign stop at a National Grocers Association convention in Florida. In an event that would become caricatured throughout the election, Bush wondered at the experience of the grocery store checkout. He had never seen an electronic scanner — and announced that he was "amazed by some of the technology."[32]

The electronic scanner had been introduced some twenty years earlier and, in 1992, most Americans were familiar with the scanner system at the grocery store checkout. Voters understood that presidents were cloistered — they did not drive, they did not go to the grocery store, they did not even commute to work. Regardless, for a president to be so out of touch with an everyday experience — the grocery store checkout line — was remarkable and illuminating.

As a result, Bush was never quite at home with the everyman style of campaigning. Perhaps more than any other recent incumbent, George Bush was disadvantaged by the trappings of the office. As a result of Bush's failed encounters with the real world, his managers opted to revert to an Oval Office strategy.[33] Despite the obvious failures of the approach, the Bush team locked the president in the White House until late in the campaign. It was only after the president's abysmal showing in the second debate that the campaign decided to abandon the Oval Office as its organizing strategy.[34] While Bush might not have fared well in his encounters with ordinary America, closed up in the White House, Bush appeared even more aloof and out of touch. Even after the campaign abandoned its Oval Office strategy, Bush had difficulty reforming his image. The figure of the ultimate Washington man, Bush became the symbol of what people most detested about politicians — that the rules by which ordinary Americans live do not apply.

The Clinton campaign struck a chord with voters in its "Maine" attack spot for this reason. Illustrating what many voters already disliked about Bush, the "Maine" spot captured George Bush's privileged lifestyle at his family's sprawling vacation home in Maine. The spot opened with an establishing long shot of the Bush estate at Walker's Point. As the voice-over narrated Bush's leisure activities, viewers were presented with video clips of the candidate golfing, boating, and looking like a clueless dandy. Adding injury to insult, the narrator revealed that, while Bush enjoyed his life in Maine, he did not pay taxes on his vacation home. "You can find George Bush doing just about everything at his home in Maine except paying Maine taxes.... For tax purposes he calls Texas his home. In fact this Houston Hotel has already saved George Bush over $165,000 in Maine taxes.... And when George Bush saves $165,000 in taxes, guess who makes up the difference? You do."[35] Given the recession in general and the relative poverty of rural Maine in particular, George Bush's world seemed blatantly unavailable to ordinary voters. Further, the attack ad recognized and justified most voters' deepest fears about the Washington elite — they were hypocrites who thought that they were above the system. By comparison, then, the Washington outsider with a southern accent and an authentically humble childhood was not only refreshing, but also necessary.

While the Clinton spot was damaging, George Bush's own "What I Am Fighting For" spot might have been far worse. This advertisement powerfully illustrated the campaign's inability to recognize the importance of authentic imagery to average voters. The spot featured the president giving a speech about job creation and national defense.[36] As the president spoke, the video of his speech was cut with clips of airplanes and factories and a pervasive scrolling green computer-generated Courier–type text. The image of the scrolling words was meant to demonstrate Bush's technology-driven forward thinking. In fact it served to highlight voters' concerns about politicians in general (and George Bush in particular). The words on the computer scroll followed the text of the president's speech as he was giving it. Even though voters were well aware of the TelePrompTer, it was as though the candidate were speaking words provided for him by a robotic computer-generated speech-making machine.[37] This worst possible connotation amplified what voters already believed about George Bush: that he was out of touch and utterly devoid of imagination. Even worse, as a party hack, a career bureaucrat, and a Washington insider, Bush was just a computer-generated political talking machine.

A Teenybopper Network

Had Bush been able to come across on television and in person as a more likable and relatable guy, the negative charges against him would not have resonated so strongly with voters. George Bush never adapted to the talk show style of the 1992 campaign — he did not like the idea of talk shows. In contrast to Clinton, whose campaign made full use of popular television, Bush famously dismissed MTV as "a teenybopper network."[38] When he did finally succumb to the pressure to appear on that "teenybopper network," he was clearly uncomfortable and visibly awkward.

The most important talk show of the campaign was not a talk show at all, but the second debate, which followed the popular format. It was clearly not George Bush's best venue. Moderated by Carol Simpson of *ABC News*, the live audience was composed of undecided voters who were to pose questions to the candidates. One of the most replayed clips from the debate featured Bush stumbling to respond to a question from the audience. When Bush was asked how the national debt had personally affected him, he haltingly replied, "Well, I think the national debt affects everybody. Obviously it has a lot to do with interest rates. It has." Bush had not answered the question. Worse, it was not clear that he had the capacity to answer the question.

Carol Simpson interrupted the president to emphasize the question and pigeonhole the answer, "She's saying, '*you personally*.'" The audience member re-emphasized the point, "You, on a personal basis — how has it affected you?" Again the president attempted a response, "Well, I'm sure it has.... Are you suggesting that if somebody has means that the national debt doesn't affect them?" After failing to produce a satisfying response, the audience member was asked to clarify the question. "I know people who cannot afford to pay the mortgage on their homes, their car payment. I have personal problems with the national debt. But how has it affected you and if you have no experience in it, how can you help us, if you don't know what we're feeling?" The moderator clarified further, "I think she means more the recession..." For a final time, the president attempted a response, citing his experience with people who had suffered the recession; he had visited a black church in Washington, DC, and had received letters from the unemployed. After offering these fleeting examples of other people's difficulties, he returned to a discussion of the national debt, finishing with a nod to exports, investments, and "better education systems."[39]

The president's response stood in contrast to the preceding answer by Perot, who had spoken of his grandchildren's future and about his own Horatio Alger American Dream. More importantly, the president's response stood in stark contrast to the answer that followed, given by the Democratic challenger. Answering the question empathetically and personally, Clinton entered into a conversation with the voter, asking her about her own experiences and those of her friends, followed by a classically Clinton Feel-Your-Pain style Preach–n–Teach. Reflected in the exchange was the Democrat's talent for exposing what a citizen-president relationship could be in a Clinton administration. Finally, and most tellingly, Bush checked his watch. As Perot's advisor, Orson Swindle recalled, "The impression I got ... the most glaring thing that I saw was a President who had no passion. To me, he reeked passivity throughout all three debates.... It was as if he didn't want to continue and that bothered me greatly; it seemed like he had no fire, no enthusiasm for what was ahead."[40]

Bush did attempt to incorporate the talk show style into his own campaign, albeit late in the season. However, even in his most conversational and arguably authentically formatted advertisement, "Presidency: Plain Talk," Bush couldn't seem to come across as a comfortable, casual speaker. While the spot attempted to capture the talk show mien of the 1992 campaign, the candidate appeared uneasy with the format. In a small room, speaking to a group of gathered voters, Bush explained the importance of democracy and the responsibility of voting for president. Unlike Clinton's demeanor in such forums, however, Bush appeared more instructional than conversational. At first, propped on a stool while seated voters craned their necks to look at him, Bush informed the group that a voting choice was a "serious choice."[41]

The height difference, seating choice, tone of speech, and topic already made Bush appear to be a kindergarten teacher. Then, standing up to increase the vertical distance between himself and his audience, Bush continued his lecture.[42] The overlording figure of the president reinforced voters' fears that the Washington elite thought they were above ordinary people. More importantly, because of the president's condescending tone and the *mise-en-scène* of the spot, the ad failed to capture what people loved about the talk show format — an intimate venue wherein the audience was more important than the subject, who was put in a position of relative vulnerability. Instead, the staged awkwardness of the spot manufactured inauthenticity. In such a small venue, the viewer expected Bush to interact with his audience, but he barely looked at them as he talked over their heads. Overall, while it appeared that the Bush campaign was trying to adapt to the new talk show style of campaigning, their attempt made the candidate appear more inauthentic than if he had not tried at all.

A Little Bit of a Bubba Ticket

The Clinton campaign made good use of the talk show format and the (constructed) intimacy it required. Sharing personal stories, family anecdotes, and homespun childhood tragedies, Bill Clinton was a made-for-talk-show candidate. Analyzing the course of the campaign in August 1992, *Congressional Quarterly* observed that "the 1992 Democratic nominees — Gov. Bill Clinton of Arkansas and Sen. Al Gore of Tennessee — have made intimate details of their personal lives a key part of their campaign. Before Election Day arrives, the whole country will probably know that Gore's son almost died after being hit by a car, that Clinton's father died before he was born, his stepfather was an alcoholic and his brother was a drug addict."[43]

Slick Willy

While these personal stories inspired empathy and brought voters and viewers into an intimate relationship with Bill Clinton, the Democratic nominee was not without his flaws. To a large extent, Bill Clinton used the talk show forum and confessional style to ameliorate shortcomings that were revealed throughout the primary season. Many of the attacks against Clinton focused on categories of authenticity: honesty, character, family, and gender.

To the last point, Hillary Clinton was often portrayed as an ambitious, power-hungry ice queen. In his Republican National Convention address, Pat Buchanan spoke to Hillary Clinton's perceived inauthenticity: "Elect me, and you get two for the price of one, Mr. Clinton says of his lawyer-spouse. And what does Hillary believe? Well, Hillary believes that 12-year-olds should have a right to sue their parents, and she has compared marriage as an institution to slavery-and life on an Indian reservation."[44] Thus, Hillary Clinton was seen as political baggage for the campaign. As *Newsweek* found fit to report, the Clinton campaign hired image advisors and a costume consultant from the popular television show *Designing Women* to put her into a "less austere wardrobe."[45] In addition to altering her physical appearance, Hillary Clinton was advised to campaign in feminine venues and alter her speech to make herself more identifiable to middle-class mothers.[46] Clinton called on friends and family to corroborate, illustrate, and authenticate her image as a wife and mother. "Friends of the Clintons say that the public labeling of Hillary as an ambitious careerist misses her warmth and her playfulness....' She is a compassionate and loyal friend and a great mother.' 'A lot of the problems I face are the same ones all working women face,' she says. 'I ... am engaged in the same kind of juggling act that most women I know are.... People may not see it, but I play the same roles other women must play every eight seconds or whatever it is.'"[47]

Questions about Bill Clinton's authenticity went far beyond his wife's austere pant suits. Clinton's famous evasiveness — over alleged adultery, draft dodging, and marijuana use — earned him the nickname "Slick Willy." To the latter, Clinton's response that he "didn't inhale" came across as snarky or dismissive. In response to allegations about his Vietnam–era draft status, Clinton more successfully served up a classic American icon: "'I was raised on John Wayne movies.... I had always wanted to see myself fighting for my country.... It was very painful to have all that stuff brought back up.'"[48] Nonetheless, he was more dismissive than forthright, and the Republican ticket kept the charges coming. As Bush operative Mary Matalin recalled, "We kept trying to draw attention to the credibility issue.... We tried always to come back to, 'This guy has ... got a story for everybody.'"[49]

When the Bush campaign increased its attacks against Clinton in the fall of 1992, it focused primarily on issues of authenticity, character, and credibility. In order to maximize their effort, they drew from well-worn criticisms and familiar stories about the Democrat. However, the allegations often hurt Bush more than they damaged Clinton. One particularly unsuccessful line of attack revolved around allegations about Clinton's Vietnam–era antiwar activity. The Bush team wove together questions about Clinton's travel abroad, his antiwar work at Oxford, and his subsequent evasiveness about both. As Charlie Black, senior political advisor to the Bush Campaign contended, "Moscow was just part of the pattern of Clinton trying to hide what he had done during those [Vietnam War] years."[50] Clinton camp internal polling, however, found that the issue did more damage to Bush than it did to Clinton. "Both in the focus groups and polling, when the draft issue got extended to the Moscow trip" Bush was damaged by the line of attacks that "made the President look desperate and tended to discredit the whole line of attack."[51]

Although these questions about Clinton's honesty and authenticity did not evaporate — indeed they remained with Clinton long after his presidential term ended — it turned out that many voters could relate to the candidate's preference for dodging absurd questions with absurd answers. As we found during the 1998 impeachment hearings, most Americans believed that such charges, even if true, were trifling. Babyboomer voters evaluated sexual indiscretion, draft evasion, and pot smoking through a different lens. Less abhorred by Clinton's behavior than annoyed with the media, many voters became sympathetic to Clinton. Clinton could not have earned that sympathy, however, without appealing directly to voters.

Clinton on the Couch

By taking himself directly to the people, Clinton was able to bypass much of the negative press and also establish long-term emotional connections with voters, which ameliorated many of the charges against him. Further, by offering his own confessional, self-disclosive, personally revealing stories, Clinton came across as more open and less evasive. Voters who felt they knew Clinton could forgive or even dismiss much of the negative press. As mentioned in the introduction to this chapter, Clinton's appearances on talk shows and soft news programs were followed by positive poll numbers.[52] Between January and November of 1992, Clinton appeared on these programs more than the other two candidates in the race. In addition to his own televised town halls, Clinton appeared four times on *CBS This Morning*, three times on *Donahue*, twelve times on *Larry King Live*, twelve times on the *Today Show*, and sixteen times on *Good Morning America*.[53] Mandy Grunwald, the architect of the effort, knew that if Clinton took his appeal directly to the people, engaging them in discussion-style dialogue, embracing the self-disclosive and confessional style advantaged by talk shows, he could win the emotional support of many voters. As Clinton pollster Stanley Greenberg noted, "We set out first to go directly to people through whatever medium we could find."[54] Despite his obvious personal flaws, the Clinton campaign willingly exposed its candidate to human-interest hungry reporters and voters, seeking to create for Clinton "a human persona that was vulnerable, humble, and accessible to ordinary people."[55]

Clinton's appearance on the *Arsenio Hall Show* on June 3, 1992, allowed the candidate to showcase his human side in front of a massive popular audience. The fact that it was a nontraditional forum for a politician merely heightened the novelty of the program. But for Clinton's campaign it exceeded mere novelty — it allowed voters to see him as a different kind of candidate. Laughing and joking and blowing on the sax, "the act got Clinton badly needed front-page coverage around the country and allowed him to show the friendly, relaxed and engaging side of his personality."[56] When Arsenio joked that it was nice to "see a Democrat blowing something other than the election," Clinton broke into laughter and appeared to appreciate the joke. He proved that he did not take himself too seriously — he was a candidate to whom voters could relate.

Clinton also took his campaign to multiple popular programs including *Donahue* and MTV's *Choose or Lose*, perhaps the most path-breaking and nontraditional of all the programs. These appearances allowed voters to feel an intimate connection with the candidate, and many viewers found these appearances to be a refreshing departure from the aloof political tone of the Bush years. Bill Clinton's "aspiration to intimacy [wa]s, in part, a response to people's frustration with political facades" that characterized old-style political campaigning.[57] It worked. Voters began to feel that, for once, they had really come to know the candidate intimately. Underwriting Clinton's authenticity, *Time* informed its readers, "Clinton the candidate is closer to Clinton the private man than almost any other campaigner of recent memory."[58] Many voters felt the same way. Presenting his human side, "Bill Clinton ... display[ed] his private life to voters" in order to allow them "to get beyond the façade to uncover and authenticate the candidate, the president, and the man who identified as Bill Clinton."[59]

But Clinton coveted intimate venues beyond the popular talk show circuit. In a series of nationally and regionally televised town halls, Clinton took his preach-and-teach, feel-your-pain style directly to the voters. These town halls allowed Clinton to share his personal narrative, talk about his family, and get quizzed by voters on such everyday issues as consumer prices. In stark contrast to Bush's grocery store gaffe, Bill Clinton was not only aware of the electronic scanner, but actually knew the prices of basic commodities. In a nationally televised *CBS This Morning* Town Hall, Clinton aced the "milk quiz" by accurately reciting the prices of everyday items: "'Gasoline is about $1.20 depending on what kind of gasoline it is. Hamburger meat's a little over $1. A gallon of milk's $2. A loaf of bread's about $1 now.... And blue jeans run anywhere from $18 to $50 depending on what kind.'" The woman who asked the question "said she asked the question because 'I don't believe that politicians know what it's like to be in the shoes of the average American family.'"[60] The town halls felt real; they felt conversational. Although Bill Clinton was selling his candidacy, he managed to connect with voters, many of whom found him refreshingly authentic. At the conclusion of one nationally televised town hall in June, Clinton remarked, "This is what elections ought to be about. It was real.... It was unrehearsed. It was direct."[61]

It was to Clinton's advantage, then, that the second debate adopted the talk show style format. Stanley Greenberg recalled that "Bill Clinton, in that second debate, was with the people in that audience, he was relating to those questions. The President wasn't."[62] Clinton strategist James Carville agreed. Even as the talk show style disadvantaged the often aloof incumbent, it offered Clinton an opportunity to shine on his own. "Clinton ... is the best one-on-one politician that I've ever seen. This was his forum. This is the place he wanted to be."[63]

Clinton also took his case on the road, engaging voters where they lived. His campaign stops often felt like spontaneous, albeit large, live talk shows. While he repeated bits from a standard stump speech, the campaign was sure to remind reporters and voters that the candidate often made unrehearsed, off-the-cuff speeches.[64] He kicked off his general election campaign with a bus tour of the South, his home turf. As campaign manager David Wilhelm noted, "Bill Clinton's great strength was the energy that he ... gives back to average folks. What better way of doing that than the bus trip.... As it turned out, we won every single state along the bus trip. So it seems to have succeeded."[65] The bus tour also highlighted Clinton's departure from the president in both style and content. As a *Time* article reported, "The bus tours ... drew an unsubtle contrast between the patrician Bush's alleged loss of contact with heartland America and the Clinton-Gore close-to-the-people pitch."[66] They served a valuable purpose for that reason. As Stanley Greenberg noted, the campaign took its case directly "'to the people in a way that looks like you really want to get to them — not just use them for a photo opportunity.'"[67]

A Little Town Called Hope

Both the tone and preferred forums for the Clinton campaign made voters feel that "at a ... basic level ... [they] were introduced to their 'neighbor,' Bill Clinton."[68] Because it required a more conversational than oratorical presentation, the talk show format did a great deal to foster the image of Clinton as a regular guy. Dukakis's former press secretary, Patricia O'Brien, noticed the striking differences between the 1988 Democratic campaign and the images and messages put forward by the Clinton camp: "'What I think we have is an attempt now to give intimate images that are supposed to link' the candidates 'to the common man ... . We certainly have lost the image of the politician, the candidate as a person larger than ourselves.'"[69]

In large part, the campaign managed to accomplish this by re-telling the candidate's biography at every opportunity. The long-format convention film, *The Man from Hope*, offered the Clinton campaign a chance to highlight intimate details and personal narratives on a grand stage.[70] Indeed, Clinton's convention focused almost exclusively on biography. Stanley Greenberg recalled that the managers "had decided that biography was critical.... On the popular-culture talk shows you go directly to people, but more importantly, it was a format in which you could talk about biography, you could talk about your life, which you didn't get the opportunity to do on 'Face the Nation.'"[71] Political scientists Shawn and Trevor Parry-Giles called these moments "scripted intimacies." Such personal, self-disclosive, and confessional appearances allowed Clinton to reveal "himself to the larger public, crafting an image that was highly palatable and electable."[72]

Less palatable, it seemed, was political divisiveness. It is telling that Clinton's campaign film, *The Man from Hope*, featured no discussion of politics or ideology — it was pure biography featuring family members and personal friends of Clinton, all discussing the candidate's character, human qualities, and personal narrative. At the center of *The Man from Hope* was the story of a young man growing up in poverty in Arkansas. The media and voters alike loved the story and the marked contrast between the candidates. The *Washington Post* offered this contrast to its readers: While George Bush was being "chauffeured to day school," Bill Clinton "on the other hand, lived briefly as a boy in a house with no indoor plumbing — which his campaign points out fairly often. That's as close as anyone comes this year to the log-cabin credential."[73]

The film production in *The Man from Hope* created a visual intimacy with voters. As the camera moved in for close-ups of the candidate, the film offered viewers the feeling of a personal and sincere conversation. The words became almost secondary to the visual feeling of intimacy, as though a voter could look into Clinton's face and decide whether or not to trust him. As media scholars and political psychologists have recognized, the "camera's focus on the face promotes ... intimacy and encourages ... 'face watching,' as faces are turned 'into arguments.'"[74] If, then, the faces (of the Clintons) were the issues, voters would decide their votes on the basis of personal trust.

According to *Time*'s analysis of the convention, "The bio might have seemed corny to some observers, but it and the thunderous reception Clinton and his family received when they paid a dramatic visit to the convention floor on Wednesday night put the capstone on a remarkable transformation. The candidate who a few weeks earlier had been drawing only about a quarter of the total vote in polls now had a lead of more than 10 points, which quickly swelled to 24 points."[75]

Many felt an emotional connection to Bill Clinton. In a way that was reminiscent of the diptychs in Reagan's campaign film, *The Man from Hope* offered private reflections on public events. Memorably, Clinton asked his daughter how she had felt about her parents' *60 Minutes* interview in which they discussed their marital problems. Chelsea answered her father, "I'm glad you're my parents." Then, taking the audience back from the campaign, Clinton reminded viewers that he was a father first, a candidate second. Tearing up, Clinton commented that everything "would be alright" as long as the publicity hadn't ruined what was most important: his family.[76] The emphasis on personal narrative at the 1992 convention produced its intended effect. After the DNC, "People were beginning to say that Clinton was an average guy, somebody who might be good for them and for the economy."[77]

The theme, structure, and content of *The Man from Hope* was cut and adapted for the short spot, "Journey." According to Stanley Greenberg, "The most important thing we had as our goal was to introduce Bill Clinton in a personal way with biography."[78] Narrated by Clinton himself, the advertisement began with a well-known narrative line. "I was born in a little town called Hope, Arkansas.... I remember that old two-story house where I lived with my grandparents. They had very limited incomes.... I remember just, uh, thinking what an incredible country this was, that somebody like me, you know, who had no money or anything, would be given the opportunity to meet the president. ... I worked my way through law school with part time jobs, anything I could find."[79] In touching and revealing moments, the candidate was at once humble and unashamed of his boyhood roots in border-South poverty.

Voters in the American South particularly related to Bill Clinton's personal narrative. Hope, Arkansas, was a more familiar place than Kennebunk, Maine. This politics of place worked to Clinton's advantage. In 1988, George Bush had successfully branded Michael Dukakis as an out-of-touch liberal from Massachusetts. This line of attack would clearly not work against Bill Clinton, who, after selecting Al Gore as his running mate, joked about the Bubba ticket on CNN. "It is a little bit of a Bubba ticket in the sense that we both come from small towns where people have old-fashioned values.... There's a little bit of Bubba in both of us, and I don't think that's all bad."[80] As "Double Bubba" became media shorthand for the Clinton/Gore ticket, the candidates embraced the moniker.

Clinton's personal campaign focused on more than just his life history and claims to southern regional authenticity. The campaign equally emphasized Clinton's present-day family life for obvious reasons — rumors about Clinton's infidelity would be ameliorated by images of the candidate's real relationships with his wife and daughter. The ways in which the campaign highlighted these relationships, however, were illustrative of the country's mood. The Clinton family displays were foregrounded not only to offset stories about a philandering fop, but also to establish human connections with voters and create a thoroughly authentic image for Clinton. Of all the mushy mush, the most heartwarming and human moment was projected in *The Man from Hope*. Recalling the birth of his daughter, Clinton offered the following sentiment: "I remember how scrunched up she was when she came out. I still, uh, remember how profoundly grateful I was that, you know, Hillary was okay and that I had lived to see it. I mean, I was very aware at that moment that that's something my father hadn't done."[81]

A July 1992 *People* article about the Clintons carried the same theme about family. The article informed readers that Hillary Clinton missed her daily routine while out on the campaign trail. Readers learned that Bill Clinton longed for time with his daughter. The quotes from Hillary established an image that ameliorated negative images of a cold, hard, career woman. "'This has been the hardest part of the campaign,' says Hillary, 44. 'We have never spent this kind of time away from [Chelsea].' Early in the campaign Hillary tried to return to Little Rock every three or four days to be with Chelsea, playing tag-team parenting with Bill, home less often and still adjusting to the challenge of being a good father to a preteen amid a presidential campaign. 'We're sort of making it up as we go along,' he says.... I have driven her to school every day since kindergarten, unless I was away. The morning is our time.'"[82] Hillary was not an ice queen; she was a regular mother. Bill was not a self-obsessed womanizer; he was a loving father.

According to *People*, Hillary was also a wife, and Bill was also an adoring husband. They did not, however, attempt to construct an image of a perfect family. Instead, in their *People* feature, the Clintons presented readers with typical problems of parenthood — stories to which ordinary Americans could surely relate. "Adolescence is already being foreshadowed by early skirmishing over pierced ears. 'We really held out against it,' Hillary says, laughing. 'We've hung tough,' Bill agrees. Sort of. 'Well, we've walked back and forth on this.... So now we've agreed not to talk about it until her 13th birthday.' Bill: 'Until

February we have.'"[83] It was a charming story — not exactly newsworthy, but common and everyday and easily appertained by parents of preteen children. It was these kinds of stories about the Clintons that made so many people feel so close to them, despite the fact that they were a political power couple.

Feel Your Pain

People also felt close to Clinton because of his personal, emotional, and empathetic campaign style. As Joe Klein reported, Clinton made *real* personal and compassionate connections with voters across the country. Rather than discussing health care reform in terms of budgets and regulations, he encouraged voters to discuss their personal stories. "He asked the woman, what concerns you about drugs? The price of them, she said. What sort of medication do you need and how much does it cost? he asked. How much does Medicare cover? he asked. And, how much do you get from Social Security? The woman — her name was Mary Davis — seemed calmer, talking about it. But then, as she was saying 'We don't have enough [to pay] for drugs *and* food,' she burst into tears. Immediately, Clinton was down, hunched over her, his arms around her, repeating 'I'm so sorry, I'm so sorry ...' for what seemed an eternity. Then he stood, wiped his eyes and continued on."[84] This kind of oozing empathy was characteristic of the Clinton campaign. "Clinton was ... more likely than the other two candidates to discuss *compassion* as a quality he felt he could bring to the office of president."[85] He began incorporating the stories he heard on the campaign trail into his political speeches, describing the heartbreaking and heartwarming circumstances of ordinary voters.

In addition to endlessly sharing anecdotes on the campaign trail, Clinton offered emotional and personal appeals in his campaign commercials. Not surprisingly, an analysis of voter reaction to political television spots conducted in 1992 found that "the spots that received the most consistently high ratings from the audience ... were also spots that made great use of emotional appeal ... they were ... highly emotional and highly 'image oriented.'"[86] Clinton mastered the emotional appeal; even the campaign's more serious issue advertisements presented a familiar and friendly candidate. While offering positions on hard issues, these spots presented Bill Clinton as a casual, relatable guy — a new kind of politician who was *with* you, not just *for* you.

Take, for example, the short spot, "Leaders 2." In this advertisement, Bill Clinton and Al Gore were shown campaigning together. While the advertisement offered visual images of the candidates making campaign speeches, these shots were interspersed among video clips of Clinton and Gore talking and laughing with voters, high-fiving supporters, casually rolling up their sleeves, and sharing private moments with each other. Although the commercial was ostensibly an issues advertisement, the visual images were at once personal, hopeful, and authentic. While the camera rarely offered physical proximity in this spot, the visual narrative presented an emotional propinquity and intimacy. In the images presented, the viewer got the sense that Clinton and Gore's relationship with each other and with their supporters was real and that it was more personal than professional. Rather than closing the spot with a standard campaign logo (Clinton/Gore '92) the commercial concluded with a video shot of a handmade sign attached to a tractor on a rural roadside. These average citizens had taken the time and care to construct their own huge Clinton for President sign — not a mass-produced bumper sticker, but a homemade icon on display for passers by. As the video made clear, the supporters responsible for the sign felt personally committed to his candidacy.[87]

Clinton's issue spot on the economy was equally personal and personable. Bill Clinton's "Rebuild America" advertisement used a different visual context than "Leaders 2." "Rebuild America" created a physical intimacy using zoom shots and close-ups, presenting a casual, conversational candidate. Although it was an issues ad, Clinton presented his position in a way that referenced a political discussion between friends. With his shirtsleeves rolled up, Clinton punctuated his points with hand gestures, but not the kind of lectern-pounding, fist pumping gesticulations that would indicate political affectation. Instead, he waved his hand as regular people do when they are speaking to their friends about things that really matter. In a colloquial but passionately conversational vernacular, Clinton expressed what he felt many Americans felt about Republican economic credo: "Just keep taxes low on the wealthy and see what happens. Well, I'll tell you what's happened. Most Americans are workin' harder for less money."

Conclusions

George Bush was never able to overcome the authenticity gap between himself and Bill Clinton; people simply felt drawn to Clinton. Even voters who disliked Bill Clinton felt something for him on a personal level. Whether voters agreed or disagreed with George Bush's policies, few felt something for him. Bill Clinton was able to capture public affection and connectedness because he made himself personally available to voters. When voters felt that they knew Bill Clinton, that Bill Clinton was somehow a part of their lives, he became a more authentic character. George Bush, on the other hand, could only feign ordinariness. When he did attempt to put on "nonairs," he came across as a man attempting to eat BBQ chicken wings on Wedgewood China.

These things did matter to voters. Although it would be easy to take a *War Room* approach to analyzing the 1992 election, focusing almost exclusively on the economy, voters did not see the election in that way. As an August survey by the Pew Research Center found, "Most often (14%) people say that Bush stands for the '*rich, upper classes and monied interests.*' One in ten mention the President's credentials in the foreign policy area and 10% mention the Persian Gulf crisis specifically. Eight percent mention '*negative effect on the economy.*'"[88] Bush's inability to connect with voters' real life circumstances clearly had an effect on public opinion about him.

We also saw this in the ways in which voters understood their candidates. By late fall of 1992, Clinton was seen as the most likable candidate. His full court press on the talk show media made viewers feel a personal connection to him and gave him the opportunity to sell his personal narrative as he wanted voters to hear it. On these programs, Bill Clinton did not come across as an Oxford man playing hillbilly—he appeared to be the real thing.

The more he campaigned, the more voters liked him. After trailing both Ross Perot and George Bush in the likeability rankings early in the campaign, Clinton's poll numbers began to steadily improve. As a September 1992 Pew Research report found, "Since the Spring the electorate has reversed itself as to which presidential candidate is more personally likable. A late March poll found a 43% to 33% plurality thinking that Bush was personally more likable than Clinton."[89]

The September 1992 Times Mirror survey corroborated these findings when "decidedly more voters" reported that they personally liked Clinton (49 percent) more than Bush (32 percent).[90] In three key categories of likeability, honesty, and empathy, Clinton's poll numbers increasingly improved throughout the campaign. By September 1992, more voters were beginning to view Clinton as the "*more 'honest and truthful candidate*," and 49 percent of those surveyed (compared to 26 percent for Bush) found that Clinton was the "*candidate who cares.*"[91]

While these numbers might not offer absolute proof that Bill Clinton won the 1992 election because he came across as more authentic than George Bush, there was ample evidence in the Ross Perot phenomenon to at least suggest that Clinton's authenticity made him more attractive. When Ross Perot dropped out of the race in the summer of 1992, his former supporters who had opted to support Bill Clinton reported that they were more "satisfied (46%)" with their choice "than those who say they now intend to vote for the President (26%)."[92] In its internal polling, the Bush team found that there was a greater connection between his two challengers on the basis of personality. According to Dave Carney of the Bush campaign, "Perot's constituency" clearly "preferred Clinton on personality and cultural affinity."[93] The September 1992 Times Mirror survey found that "Former Perot supporters who say they would be very likely to vote for the Texas businessman, now support Clinton over Bush by almost a two to one margin."[94]

Clinton and Perot shared some important personal and cultural similarities that voters clearly preferred in 1992 — they both took their campaigns directly to people via the medium of talk shows and town halls. Neither was born into wealth, although revelations about Perot sent many of his supporters fleeing to the Clinton camp. In the final analysis, both were simply more authentic than George Bush who had never seemed to connect intimately with voters.

6

In the Kitchen with Bill: 1996

Bob Dole was a World War II veteran, a veteran of the Republican National Committee, the House of Representatives, and the United States Senate. He resigned from the Senate at the top of his career — he was the Senate majority leader and, after three attempts, had finally been selected as his party's presidential nominee. He had spent his life in service to his country. Nonetheless, when the eulogistic praise to his service on Capitol Hill subsided, the press and the American people wanted to know one thing: Who *was* Bob Dole? Bombarded by the media on his way out of his Senate office for the last time, he was not asked about his many legislative accomplishments, he was asked about his hobbies. Dole did not lack a political résumé, but he did lack pastimes. Bill Clinton's hobbies (both licit and otherwise) were well known; he liked to jog, eat junk food, spend time with his daughter, and watch sports on television. Bob Dole, who had bested his opponents in war and in Congress, was stymied.

He should not have been unprepared for the question. Announcing that he would resign his Senate seat on July 11, 1996, Dole informed the public that he would be a man "without office or authority, a private citizen ... just a man."[1] For a man who had not known private life for thirty years, it is not clear that Bob Dole knew what it meant to be "just a man." Stumped for an answer, his campaign managers quickly set to work trying to figure it out. When they finally mustered a response, the American people learned that Citizen Bob Dole, like any seventy-three-year-old American man, would retire to Florida where he would spend time with his wife, enjoy the sun, and stay physically fit. Family, fitness, and Florida. It was the perfect response.

It was perfect, that is, until Dole's managers opted to take advantage of their boss's new Citizen Dole makeover by inviting the press to see it for themselves — to observe Bob Dole in his natural habitat — at his home in Florida where he and his wife Liddy could be found, presumably, jogging, relaxing, and sunbathing. They were equal parts important — Dole needed to prove both his vitality and his ability to be ordinary. Unfortunately, neither these qualities, nor willingness to concede, came easily to Dole. In preparation for his fitness showcase, Dole's "aides had carefully chosen a running outfit for him to wear for the occasion." Unfortunately, between the time he was instructed to don the workout wear and the time the press arrived, "Dole ... had put on a button-down shirt over a pair of shorts, making himself look not only out of touch but also only half-dressed."[2] He could not, apparently, suffer the day without a dress shirt. To make matters worse, the candidate's preferred jogging regimen included an indoor treadmill and a television preset to C-SPAN. It appeared that Dole's retirement was to be spent watching his former life on TV. No doubt anxious for the sunbathing portion of the program, Dole's aides invited reporters to instead observe the candidate poolside, where he was to relax, pass the time, and soak up some rays. Wearing equally unfortunate and inappropriate businesswear, Dole spent the afternoon "hunched over" a notepad talking shop on the phone with aides and advisors and only intermittently sunbathing ... in a dress shirt.[3]

Bob Dole would wrestle with Citizen Dole throughout the 1996 campaign. His inability to bare his soul (and apparently also his arms) was instructive — Dole would always be more dress shirt than tee-shirt, more Beltway than Sunbelt, more party insider than partier. Compared to the president, who remained infinitely human despite the trappings of the White House, who lived *in* Washington but who was never *of* Washington, Bob Dole was a man who could not live without Washington. Moreover, he seemed a relic of politics past — a man who did not understand — or even want to understand — the hyperpersonal, self-disclosive, empathetic, modern campaign style.

The Status Quo

Historians have yet to fully examine the 1996 election. If early evaluations by journalists and political scientists are any indication, we may yet write it off as unworthy of our time and consideration. Dubbed one of the "most boring" elections in history even by its major participants, 1996 has largely been understood as a low-turnout, status quo, nonevent.[4] Even moments after polls closed on November 5, 1996, a consensus had already begun to form: two factors had kept voters uninterested and at home on Election Day. First, Republicans were unable to construct a cohesive opposition. Not only was the party divided in its message, but the Republican standard bearer, Bob Dole, was unable to craft a consistent and compelling argument for his own election. Second, relative economic prosperity afforded voters the luxury of silent consent to the status quo — Republican majorities returned to both houses of Congress and Bill Clinton returned to the White House.

Nonetheless, there is much evidence to suggest that Bill Clinton's reelection was not the result of economic factors alone. To be sure, most Americans were more prosperous in 1996 than they had been in 1992. The country was at relative peace, and all major economic complacency predicted future growth. Despite that rosy retrospect, however, many voters felt neither hopeful nor prosperous when they approached the ballot box in 1996. Indeed, a majority of Americans were discontented with their own economic circumstances and were circumspect about Clinton's ability to guide the economy in his second term. An October 1996 national survey by the Pew Research Center for People and the Press found that, nationwide, voters rated Clinton's performance as president only a C. Further, the Pew survey discovered that "a large percentage" of respondents "still say they do not earn enough to lead the kind of life to which they aspire (55%), and rate their economic situation negatively (44%)." In short, regardless of official economic indicators, voters continued to believe that the economy was "off track."[5] The 1996 election, therefore, might not have hinged on peace and prosperity alone. To fully evaluate voting behavior in 1996, then, we must delve deeper into what voters were saying about the candidates and their choices.

While voters did not wholeheartedly approve of Bill Clinton's politics, they continued to like him personally. Despite their wariness about the president's job performance, apprehension about the American economy, and fears about the future, they felt an emotional connection to him. A September 1996 national survey conducted by Pew found that voters personally preferred Clinton to Dole by a margin of 67–20 percent.[6] Even as voters gave Dole much higher marks than Clinton on character, honesty, and issues, they clearly felt personally and intimately connected to Clinton. Take, for example, Clinton's high marks on "Connects well with ordinary Americans" (Clinton 68 percent, Dole 21 percent) and "Cares about people like me" (Clinton 51 percent, Dole 29 percent).[7] As the Pew analysis discovered, voters were simply turned off by and tuned out to Bob Dole's personality.[8] Thus, even when they agreed with Dole's positions, they did not agree with Dole. As the Pew report noted, voters thought the economy was doing poorly "unless Bob Dole says so."[9] Their distaste for the Republican was personal, but not necessarily ideological or political.

In stark contrast, Clinton could capture an audience. The president certainly had shortcomings, both personal and political. Nevertheless, as Frank Fahrenkopf, then co-chair of the Commission on Presidential Debates, observed of the 1996 election, "There is something special people look for in their president. It has nothing to do with whether you're a Republican or you're a Democrat or you're an Independent.... It's the capability to speak for the American people."[10] Bill Clinton had it.

Anti-Politics Political Style

By 1996 American voters had developed an ironic self-awareness about their own voting behavior. On the one hand, using the language of political professionals, they critiqued the cult of personality that had come to dominate American elections. Bemoaning the fact that "other voters" favored youth and charisma, they nonetheless condemned Dole's utter lack of humor and openly acknowledged the importance of personality in their own voting choices. One letter to the editors of the *St. Petersburg Times* illustrated this. Simultaneously deriding and participating in the personality contest, the letter proposed an Elizabeth Dole candidacy: "We do want a Dole in the White House, but we want Elizabeth driving.... This is not to take away from the fine person that Bob Dole is; I just feel that he is not the man for the job. He will not be elected over a younger, charismatic Bill Clinton, regardless of how sleazy he, Clinton, is. It seems that the American people prefer youth, good looks and personality over character, honor and integrity."[11]

We don't know whether that particular Floridian's friends and neighbors voted on the basis of personality, but we do know that both Bob Dole's and Bill Clinton's campaign managers spent a lot of money assuming that they would. In 1996, personally affective texts and images dominated both paid and free campaign media. As one commentator noted, "The key to victory" in 1996 was "a kind of anti-politics political style."[12] Although in past years campaign messages "may not have been graduate-level seminars on policy issues" in 1996, more than in any previous cycle, the rhetoric was dominated "largely by emotional appeals — not intellectual discourse."[13] While Bill Clinton was vastly better at delivering self-disclosive personal narratives, in 1996 both campaigns understood that "the best politics is the least political."[14] Both campaigns, therefore, attempted to capitalize on their candidates' life stories and personal narratives. As a result, the campaign as a whole became more personal and less political. As will become clear, however, the inflated value of personal appeals advantaged Bill Clinton, who was unbuttoned, unplugged, and unreserved.

The overwhelmingly personal nature of the 1996 election was the result of multiple factors. Part of it was a product of historical learning. By 1996, it was clear that, more often than not, success had come to those candidates who were personable, likable, and accessible. Another part, however, was the constitution of the American electorate. Since 1976, voters had become increasingly independent — when they did identify with one or the other political party it was rarely with the kind of lifelong loyalty and allegiance that their parents and grandparents had felt.[15] Independent and swing voters were more likely to respond positively to personal, rather than political, information about their candidates for president. According to James Carville, an architect of Bill Clinton's 1992 victory, swing voters were more likely to be persuaded by soft media and human interest stories than by negative advertisements and issues-specific messages. More specifically, Carville identified empathy as the most important quality in capturing crucial swing voters.[16] As the electorate became increasingly independent, therefore, candidates had to become increasingly intimate in order to succeed. With the two political parties dividing the partisan electorate more or less equally throughout the late twentieth century, it was up to the swing voters to determine the election.[17]

This theory was borne out in the polls. Were experience, leadership, and ideology the most important qualities to voters, Bob Dole may well have won the election, as he consistently scored higher than Bill Clinton on the basis of these qualities. On the basis of personality and personal qualities, voters preferred Clinton. A summer 1996 *Wall Street Journal/NBC News* poll reported that respondents favored Clinton over Bob Dole as a man who was "'likable and friendly' by a margin of 56% to 14%."[18] There remained, however, a discrepancy between Bill Clinton's poll numbers on issues of character and leadership and his survey results on likeability and empathy.

"Respondents favor[ed] Bill Clinton over Bob Dole in caring about average people (51–23); having a vision for the country (40–29); being likable and friendly (56–14.)"[19] On the other hand, those same respondents preferred Bob Dole in three key categories, which, logically, ought to have served as a basis for support: "serving as commander in chief (45–32); being effective and getting things done (38–30); being a strong leader (40–32)."[20] As political scientist Robert Lovey summarized the 1996 polls, "Apparently a flawed but charismatic President Clinton looked like a better option to most voters than a stumbling and colorless Bob Dole."[21]

Reading these poll results and analyzing their own internally funded focus group evidence, both campaigns believed that they needed to showcase the candidates' authentic personal lives in order to win the election. The privilege of this saccharine campaign style was most apparent in the tenor and tone of political conventions. Since 1972, the major party conventions had been defined by their successively elaborate public displays of the private. Bill Clinton had set the new standard with 1992's *The Man from Hope*. Gone were the days of solving, resolving, and debating party business on live television. Off-air, out of prime time, and in pre-convention meetings, the public business of political parties had become private. Instead, private matters (the touching remembrances of hometown folks) became the prime time public business of the conventions. As the *Philadelphia Inquirer* noted of the 1996 conventions, "Not by accident did both parties build their quadrennial extravaganzas around images that seemed to be divorced from politics and policy.... Politicians have come to understand that people respond largely on an emotional level."[22]

Indeed, the public portions of the conventions, particularly those on display during prime time, had become more emotional, more personal, and more biographical than ever before. Bolstered by home videos and childhood photographs, spokespersons for each party competed on the basis of pathos, rather than policy. Both parties and both campaigns used the personal to connect to ordinary folks at home — to display their authenticity and remind voters that politicians were people too ... people just like them. As one media consultant noted, "'That is why Lamar Alexander wears a plaid shirt, or Clinton jumps on a bus.... They are all trying to seem like just plain folks.'"[23]

This was in evidence during both the Republican and Democratic national conventions in 1996. At the conclusion of the conventions, Ellen Goodman observed, "There is an emotional narrative in the air and on the air this year. The political has become thoroughly personal. The conventions were not the backdrops for ideas but for life stories that were touchier and feelier than ever."[24] Goodman continued to observe that party insiders and candidates alike offered stories to connect to ordinary voters: "The most authentic messengers" were "those whose own experiences validate their message.... One way to close the gap between citizen and politician — us and them — is with the personal touch."[25]

Beltway Bob

"The personal touch" did not come easily or naturally to Bob Dole. As evident in the campaign's ill-fated attempt to showcase Dole's post–Senate private life, the senator was inept at communicating the hyperpersonal textures required of modern campaigning.[26]

The absence of compelling narratives from the Dole camp, however, was not the fault of the candidate's personality alone. The campaign made several strategic errors, which contributed to Dole's unsavory public persona. Perhaps the most fatal was the candidate's lack of media presence following the Republican primaries.[27] Due to the frontloaded primary schedule and the candidate's early frontrunner status, Bob Dole became the presumptive nominee of the Republican Party on March 2, 1996.[28] As a result, the Dole campaign had an unprecedented opportunity to launch its general election campaign five months prior to the nominating convention.[29] For lack of funding, strategy, and message, however, Dole all but disappeared from the public consciousness until the announcement of his resignation from the Senate on June 11, 1996.

Called the "big lull" by his own campaign managers, and dubbed the "Black Hole" by Richard Berke of the *New York Times*, Bob Dole was absent from the public eye for five months.[30] As *Time* reporters moaned in mixed metaphors in early May 1996, "Bob Dole's campaign has yet to find its feet or its voice."[31] Moreover, except for its Floridian fitness exposé, the campaign largely squandered the opportunity to construct a compelling public persona and personal narrative around Dole's post–Senate "private" life. As former Reagan press secretary James Brady noted of the Dole effort, "This was a campaign without coherence, a message or a charismatic standard bearer. If Campbell sold soup this way, it'd be in Chapter 11."[32] James Brady may not have known it, but the Dole campaign actually *was* close to bankruptcy throughout the late spring and early summer of 1996.[33] With limited funding and fundraising opportunities, Dole's campaign was stymied in its ability to garner press attention.

Bob Dole's biggest chance to define his message and exploit free media came when he announced his resignation from the Senate in June. At this early point in the election, it was Dole's best opportunity to breathe life back into his already struggling campaign. The resignation afforded Dole an unusual opportunity in his adult life: the chance to define himself as a Washington outsider, a private citizen, and a man of the people. The symbolism of the gesture was not lost on a campaign that, despite its shortcomings, understood its weaknesses. The populist rhetoric of the announcement offered a perfect illustration: "It is my obligation ... to leave behind all the trappings of power, all comfort and all security. So today I announce that I will forgo the privileges not only of the office of the majority leader, but of the United States Senate itself, from which I resign effective on or before June 11. And I will then stand before you without office or authority, a private citizen, a Kansan, an American, just a man."[34]

On June 11, 1996, Bob Dole was a celebrated man. His Senate colleagues praised his service, and President Clinton took a moment to congratulate his opponent on a long and illustrious career. Leaving Washington, Dole was to make his way to his home to Florida by way of a few campaign stops in the South and Midwest. Basking in the immediate glow of his newfound populism, Dole made attempts at (and occasional references to) private life. To highlight the "New Bob Dole" the candidate underwent a retirement wardrobe change. Gone was his Senate uniform — dark suit, white shirt, and tie — traded in for casual collared shirts and slacks. As one reporter noted, "Since the day he quit the Senate and, briefly, traded his power tie for a sport shirt, Bob Dole has been trying to show that he's just a regular guy."[35] Nevertheless, Dole was ill-at-ease with the transition to casual clothes. Making it clear that he was merely wearing a costume, Dole instructed the traveling press corps to back off, saying, "We're trying to get good pictures. Don't worry very much about what I say."[36]

As illustrated in the Floridian fitness debacle, Dole took to retirement about as comfortably as he took to those reporters on his plane. On the morning after his resignation, Dole called his office. As he told the press, "I got a recording. Said nobody's here.... I knew I wasn't there."[37] The bad joke fell flat, but the fact that he had instinctually called the office on the morning after his retirement said more about Bob Dole than his inability to deliver a well-timed joke; no one doubted that Dole actually had called his office. As reporters traveling with him noted, the old Bob Dole had returned.[38]

And so, like his retirement, his casual wardrobe costume change was also short-lived. By the time he made it home to Florida he was back in his "usual ... business suit, plus matching shirt and tie."[39] Having squandered the resignation limelight, and with few campaign dollars to spare, Dole largely absented himself from public view, leaving it to Bill Clinton, the national press, and late night comedians to define his candidacy.

Even if the national press quickly tired of Dole, those comedians could not get enough of the former senator. Although the president had given them plenty of material with which to work, they could only serve up so many jokes about McDonalds, Whitewater, and Paula Jones. Even if he was undeniably stale and old, Dole offered comedians a refreshingly new punching bag. In September 1996, the Center for Media and Public Affairs found that throughout the spring and summer of 1996, the three major late night network comedians (Jay Leno, Conan O'Brien, and David Letterman) had offered almost two times as many jokes at Bob Dole's expense than at the president's.[40] In many ways, because he was neither present nor relevant throughout the summer months, these caricatures of Bob Dole became many voters' primary image of the candidate. As a result, his least flattering characteristics — his age, grumpiness, Washington temperament, and propensity to speak about himself in the third person, came to define him.

By the time the fall television season began, the comedians had defined his candidacy, even if his campaign had not. Offering innocuous caricatures of Bob Dole referring to himself in the third person, the comedians joked that he was dull, boring, and unlikable. According to Letterman, Bob Dole was as dull as the famously inconsequential 1996 All-Star game. "Presidential candidate Bob Dole, former Senator Bob Dole [was] at the All-Star Game last night. And the game was so dull ... fans turned to Bob Dole and started chanting, 'Speech! Speech!'"[41] Later in the season, *Saturday Night Live* made use of Dole's unpopularity to take a stab at Bill Clinton: "While jogging on the beach in San Diego this weekend, President Clinton was berated by tourist Valerie Parker who shouted at him, 'You're a draft-dodging, yellow-bellied liar and you're a disgrace to the office of the presidency, to your gender and to this nation!' adding, 'And I'm still voting for you.'"[42]

This portrait of Bob Dole in particular, and characterization of the electorate in general, may not have been exactly accurate, but it did affect voters' impressions of the Republican as a person and as a candidate. As one political reporter noted, "To the casual TV viewer, he's the guy in the dark suit who starts his sentences with verbs and looks grumpy a lot.... The consensus is that Dole must work on his warmth deficit."[43]

The Real Bob Dole

Struggle as it did with the "warmth deficit," for the most part Dole's campaign tried to make the election "about Bill Clinton."[44] While this might have worked to rally support among the base during the Republican primaries, it was an inadequate message when Bob Dole was actually running against Bill Clinton. Even if Bill Clinton had not been personally popular among voters, Dole gave them only something to vote against, not a reason to show up or a cause in which to believe. As lifelong Republican Mickey Edwards informed NPR listeners, "There's an old saying in politics that you can't beat somebody with nobody. Well, Bob Dole is clearly not a nobody. He has been one of America's most important public figures for years, but that's not enough. If the voters don't know who exactly he is, they're not going to vote for him."[45]

This was to be the task of the Republican Convention — introducing Bob Dole to American voters. In his pre-convention press release, Haley Barbour, Republican National Committee chairman, used the vocabulary of authenticity to prepare viewers for the evening's events. "Tonight America will get to know the real Bob Dole. A man who grew up in a small Kansas town, was raised in the Depression and wounded in war. A man whose character was forged by his perseverance and triumph against all odds. Through his own personal struggle, and his service to community and country, Bob Dole has come to understand the everyday problems of real Americans.... Like most Americans, Bob Dole knows the answers to ... problems lie ... in ... the ...

Main Street wisdom of the people. That's the lesson of true citizenship. That's the lesson of Russell, Kansas."[46]

The repetition of promises like Barbour's leading up to the convention offered insight into the media's obsession with biographical authenticity, and also indicated the Dole campaign's inability to deliver on personal narrative throughout the summer of 1996. In 1996, Bob Dole had been a national political figure for thirty years. He had run for president three times since 1980. Despite this, neither voters nor the campaign felt that the country really knew him. As one reporter wondered, "While the Dole people talk constantly about the need to 'introduce the candidate to the American people,' a question nags: Shouldn't Dole have connected by now? And isn't it a bit late to start?" Even among Dole's friends and advisors, there were doubts about whether it was too late, or whether the candidate was even up to the task. As Dole advisor David Keene admitted, "There's a reason why the public doesn't feel great empathy for him. He's a very private person, a backstage guy who can get a bit waspish at times. His problem is, he just isn't an attractive political figure who can swing [independent] voters to him."[47] It had, indeed, been a long, dry summer in the Dole campaign.[48]

Whether he was up to the task or not, by 1996 personality fetishism had become convention orthodoxy. To be sure, lines of policy and ideology would be drawn. But Bob Dole's political résumé was never a question of concern for voters; Dole clearly had the experience and expertise to perform the job. As a personality, however, he was not appealing, and the convention would need to attenuate the personality deficit.

To mitigate the candidate's lack of charisma, leading up to his convention speech and video, the campaign offered surrogate spokespersons, especially his wife, to highlight the Doles' life outside of Washington. As one newspaper reported at the time, "Perhaps the most memorable moment at the Republican convention occurred when Elizabeth Dole strolled triumphantly through the convention hall, extolling her husband in terms of small human anecdotes, rather than large political victories.... The trick is to appear to be outside the Beltway, looking suspiciously in, rather than inside looking out."[49] Elizabeth Dole lent credibility to the notion that Bob Dole had a life and a personhood outside the halls of Congress. As one newspaper reported at the time, "Elizabeth Dole ... gave a window into the person you're looking at to be president. Knowing that Dole took the time to say hello to the security guard every day tells you he is concerned about regular folks. He's not just someone dispensing policy."[50]

Devoting more time to the candidate's three years in a military hospital than his thirty years in Washington, Dole's convention film also served as a surrogate, illustrating Dole's personal and human qualities, all of which were centered on Russell, Kansas. The film was a video version of his campaign autobiography, *Unlimited Partners*, in which he had argued that he was not just *from* Russell, Kansas, he *was* Russell, Kansas. "Anyone who wants to understand me must first understand Russell, Kansas. It is my home.... It is a wellspring of small-town wisdom.... The Russell of my youth was not a place of wealth. Yet it was generous with the values that would shape my outlook." In the speech that followed, Dole repeated the most important theme of the film, "And there is no height to which I have risen that is high enough to allow me to ... forget where I came from and where I stand, and how I stand, with my feet on the ground, just a man, at the mercy of God."[51]

Dole's convention video and speech satisfied some. One post-convention survey respondent came away with the impression that Dole was "'a basic guy who's had a lot of hassles in his life and has had to overcome them.... He's seen the good in America because he's experienced the bad."[52] For the most part, however, Dole's convention speech received mixed reviews, even from conservative linguist, speechwriter, and commentator William Safire, who thought the candidate delivered a policy message, but nevertheless seemed nervous and ill-at-ease.[53]

Others were less kind. One reporter argued that Dole was the worst part of the convention: "Bob Dole's case for himself as the next president was an anticlimax to a week of knockout TV moments."[54] Another reporter was even more harsh: "Of all his campaign's failures to date," the worst failure was "how phony" Dole's convention film was. "Far from coming across as Mr. Authenticity, Mr. Dole often seems a forlorn Slick Willie wannabe — a politician ... pandering to voters ... and unlike his opponent, playing them ineptly."[55]

Uphill Both Ways

Inept or not, Dole suffered a failure of message. Aside from its anti–Clinton theme, it wasn't until the Republican National Convention that the Dole campaign would attempt to define its first (of many) organizing principles. Because both the press and the public privileged authenticity, candidates needed to offer consistency in both image and message. In his acceptance speech, Dole offered an overarching theme for his campaign, based on a Reagan–esque, values-loaded, past-meets-personal reminiscence of days gone by. According to Bob Dole, all the country needed was a bridge to the past. As he noted in his acceptance speech, "Age has its advantages. Let me be the bridge to an America that only the unknowing call myth. Let me be the bridge to a time of tranquility, faith, and confidence in action. And to those who say it was never so, that America has not been better, I say, you're wrong, and I know, because I was there. And I have seen it. And I remember."[56]

Dole attempted to duplicate Ronald Reagan's ability to tap into Americans' nostalgia for simpler, nicer, and humbler times. In early communications meetings, the Dole team hoped to "take advantage of Dole's age by saying that Dole could connect people to the values that they missed."[57] Unlike Ronald Reagan, Dole could not deliver on the emotional appeal of nostalgia. Where Ronald Reagan offered a vision for a future that referenced the past, Bob Dole appeared to grumble about days gone by. Where Reagan's past was sunny and inviting, Dole's past was impoverished, war-wounded, and bleak. Where Ronald Reagan wanted to take Americans there with him, Dole hearkened history, it seemed, only to condemn the present.[58] As an old curmudgeon would recall walking up hill both ways in three-foot snow drifts, Bob Dole asked voters to believe that their present could never compare to his dreary past.

Bob Dole repeated this thematic approach in his requisite interview with Barbara Walters. Walters, known for her probing personal interviews, had become sine qua non in the new campaign environment, offering viewers what they wanted most: intimate portraits of public figures. As a result, the Dole campaign knew that the Walters interview was an important venue for the candidate to showcase his human, personal, and private life. The prime-time *20/20* interview granted him a national stage and an opportunity to bring America home to Russell, Kansas.

Welcoming the veteran interviewer to his hometown, Dole appeared more comfortable than usual, walking through the streets of Russell, greeting his neighbors by name. As Dole had constantly repeated — on the campaign trail and in his autobiography — viewers could not understand him without understanding Russell, Kansas.[59] To his benefit, the second half of the Walters interview featured the candidate's wife, Elizabeth Dole, who was both captivating and charismatic.

The *20/20* interview, however, was more indicative of the media and the public's obsession with knowing the "real man" than it was of Bob Dole's capacity to appear vulnerable, disclose personal stories, and connect with average voters. Despite Walters's probing personal questions, Dole failed to offer an authentic, human portrait to which most Americans could relate. He discussed his past in terms of his superhuman expectations of himself, offering his willful, tough-minded recovery from war wounds as proof of character. Despite his admirable and inexorable fight to recover from those wounds, Dole's personal revelations remained almost aloof— for example, he informed

Walters that he always carried a pen in his right hand to prevent people from shaking his hand. More significant, however, was what he didn't tell Walters. In contrast to Clinton, who often allowed himself to appear vulnerable, Dole explained the failure of his first marriage by discussing his shortcomings glibly and in political, rather than personal terms: "Sometimes you get your priorities mixed up ... but in politics, you know, you do sometimes forget the important things. So it was a lesson."

Dole did try to use Walters as a mouthpiece for the soft campaign. Despite this, every attempt to go tête-à-tête with Bill Clinton's self-disclosive talk show style was met with cringe-inducing groans. Attempting to be homey and folksy, the Doles instead appeared old-fashioned and buttoned-up. Where Clinton revealed personal and marital struggles, Dole referenced his war wounds.

Better accustomed to the disingenuous postwar "this old thing?" style of feigning casual, the Doles could only reference personal stories where Clinton could really let it loose. When the Doles appeared on *Regis and Kathy Lee*, for example, one reporter commented that watching them was like watching a reenactment of a clichéd 1950s television couple. "It's a lot easier to watch Bill Clinton on MTV than Bob Dole with Regis and Kathie Lee.... Bill Clinton revels in" personal interviews in casual settings, whereas "If you dropped in on the Doles ... Elizabeth would have kicked off her high heels and Bob's tie would be loose, but they'd both look as though they were expecting a visitor."[60] In short, the Doles were too buttoned-up, too forced, too imitative, and too inauthentic. Although Dole made the rounds on *Regis*, highlighting the importance of the soft campaign, he had a difficult time adjusting to the expectations of the forum. As a result, voters did not feel that they knew him, beyond his projected political representation, and the candidate remained cold, aloof, and unknown to many voters. Toward the end of the campaign, one New Hampshire voter explained why she and her Granite State neighbors were likely to vote for Clinton in 1996, turning the historically red state blue in 1996. Using the terms of authenticity, she told the *Boston Globe*, "They need to show us who they are ... and with Dole I'm not sure you get that."[61]

Because he was unable to project a compelling persona, many voters perceived Dole as dull and inauthentic. To this and other voters Dole was a senator, a suit, a Republican Party man, and an old grump. A Pew survey measuring response frequency found that the most common adjective used to describe Dole was "old." Among the top ten were also "dull" and "boring."[62] The lack of enthusiasm was evident even at Dole rallies, where the crowds were notoriously small and surprisingly somber.

Even for Republicans resigned to voting for him, Dole was a lackluster choice. Using authenticity as its framework, the *Daily News* informed readers, "Those who admire him and say they intend to vote for him don't rave about his rhetoric and charisma."[63] In conservative rural Pennsylvania, one reporter found more enthusiasm for (or at least acceptance of) Bill Clinton, than support for Bob Dole. "This being the most Republican congressional district in the state ... one would expect Dole to be strong here. But ... interviews revealed a remarkable lack of enthusiasm for Dole.... On Dole's personality, some say he is too dour and his manner of speech too halting to match up effectively against Clinton, a gifted campaigner who manages to sound upbeat even when on the attack."[64] This quote offered an example of the ways in which authenticity played into the media discourse; such representations in turn gave readers a lens through which to interpret future interactions with the candidate.

Those future interactions would be many, as the Dole campaign attempted to narrow the gap by making use of soft media. Uncomfortable with the format, however, Dole often played into established expectations. At times, he appeared more bitter and paranoid than old and wise, as during a *Today Show* interview with Katie Couric. Because she was better known for human-interest interviews than hard-hitting journalism, viewers must have been surprised when Dole attacked Couric for her questions about his connections to the tobacco lobby. Confronted with an adversarial set of questions, Dole first accused journalists, including Couric, of participating in a left wing media conspiracy before turning his attention to the former surgeon general (and Dole supporter) Everett Koop whom Dole suggested was "brainwashed" by that same "liberal media." In sum, he came across as an old curmudgeon. As one Florida voter told a reporter, "To tell you the truth, I thought he was kind of a grouch.'"[65]

The *Boston Globe*'s David Nyhan agreed. In his review of the Couric interview, Nyhan found something troubling in the candidate's personality — resentment. Nyhan informed his readers that Bob Dole was not merely cranky, he was bitter. "Dole isn't as bad a candidate as we thought he'd be; he's worse. The Cranky Candidate went on morning TV with Katie Couric and snarled his way through an innocuous interview ... [Dole] gives off the vibes of a man who's always feeling sorry for himself, who sees enemies everywhere, who's always liable to fly off the handle because of his conviction that he's about to get dumped on.... Others think that Dole's acerbic personality stems from a lifetime of disappointments in national politics."[66]

It seemed that every time Dole made overtures to soft style and face-to-face campaigning, he fell flat. Worse, his failures were seized upon by an eager press corps. Using the vocabulary of human authenticity, reporters told their readers of Dole's latest adventure with America. "On the campaign trail, Mr. Dole can seem stiff and distant. His forays into the crowd often give off a forced-march quality that voters can hardly fail to notice. Many, including many Dole supporters, argue that his chances in the race depend critically on whether he can overcome his reserve enough to give Americans a hint of his private self."[67] As a result, nearing the end of the campaign, many Americans reported that they did not know the "real Bob Dole." Others feared that the "real Bob Dole" really was Beltway Bob. As *Time* noted, "So little has emerged of Mr. Dole's private persona that ... less than four weeks before the election, even his aides acknowledge that Mr. Dole has not provided voters with much of a picture of a life apart from politics."[68] To most, it seemed that "Mr. Dole is almost always pictured engaged in politics because that is almost always what he is doing.... Mr. Dole's private side has been all but invisible. As he has crisscrossed the country, Mr. Dole has rarely been shown taking part in any sort of activity that would conventionally be called recreation. Instead he has appeared ... making speeches and shaking hands — in other words, as a political candidate."[69]

Thus, despite the fact that Dole was the challenger, Bill Clinton seemed the more authentic outsider in the campaign. As the *New York Times* reported in the fall of 1996, "In polls and interviews beyond the Beltway, a startling number of them describe [Bob Dole] as mean or vindictive, shifty, too old, inept.... He is known, in short, as a partisan, in a day when partisanship is unpopular, and as a Washington fixture, in a day when Washington is unpopular."[70]

Just Plain Bill

Compared to Bob Dole, Bill Clinton was infinitely human. Few in the press, the Republican Party, and the administration ever let voters think otherwise. Warts and all, the president always remained a man whom Americans understood to be human. A gripping and humorous illustration of Bill Clinton's deep-fried down-home love of greasy, salty, fatty food, *In the Kitchen with Bill* offered a portrait of the appetite behind the presidential-sized Big Mac. The book offered its readers a few laughs, a few recipes, and a great deal of commentary on the president's food preferences. Although Clinton occupied the White House, Arkansas cuisine occupied his stomach — Clinton preferred cheese fries over caviar, Jell-o over crème brulée, and burgers over coq au vin. Readers learned that Clinton replaced the classically trained French-born executive chef of the Bush years with an American cook who understood the finer points of curly fries.[71]

Iconography of Ordinariness[72]

In the Kitchen with Bill highlighted the fact that the president liked the kinds of foods and hobbies that ordinary folks liked. Despite being in the White House, he did not "put on airs." People could relate to him, and he could relate to them. Stories about Clinton's propensity to sneak pizza past the eagle eyes of his wife and secret service detail made him accessible. As one reviewer astutely noted, "Far from the book harming the President, I strongly suspect he wrote it himself as an aid to re-election. In America, hearty eating is still a sign of being a regular guy."[73] His personal flaws reminded Americans of themselves, or of Homer Simpson, or of their charming but handsy neighbor. "Bill Clinton ... perhaps more than any other Presidential candidate and certainly more than any other President, exposed his casual side for public consumption. Over the last four years, Americans have watched him jog around Washington in shorts, indulge his appetite for doughnuts, even reveal his taste in underwear. Images of Mr. Clinton playing golf, or the saxophone, or his favorite card game, hearts, have become such standard fare that they have come to constitute what might be called an iconography of ordinariness."[74] In short, Bill Clinton did not suffer the trappings of the office during his first term in office. As a result, during his 1996 reelection campaign, the president was still personally appealing to many Americans. As one voter told the *Washington Post*, "'When I listen to Dole, I hear my grandfather talking.... [But]I could see Bill Clinton sitting around my kitchen in a sport shirt and a pair of slacks.'"[75]

Clinton's success, however, did not lie only in his ability to wear sweatpants or consume junk food, but in his ability to be both presidential and human, depending on the occasion. The humor, surprise, and allure of a president who would jog to McDonalds was that it was refreshingly and unexpectedly real. Throughout his first term in office, Bill Clinton was able to negotiate these often discordant requirements of the modern presidency. On the one hand, he benefited from the trappings of the office — the traditional Rose Garden backdrop lent an accepted and assumed seriousness and importance to his public images. On the other hand, Clinton was a master of popular media.

The rituals of the White House, combined with the austerity of the setting, framed Clinton within a serious, authoritative, and ceremonial context. In *The Invention of Tradition*, Eric Hobsbawm argued that "invented traditions," such as state dinners and Rose Garden ceremonies become potent because of their "symbolic nature, which seek to inculcate certain values and norms of behaviour by repetition, which automatically implies continuity with the past."[76] Thus, Clinton was able to use the Rose Garden in order to pass the threshold test for presidentiality; that is, people could envision and understand him as presidential. However, by projecting himself in antipodal environments, Clinton was also able to remain surprisingly and refreshingly "one of us" even as he was often pictured in austere and ceremonial settings.

To that end, his appearances on MTV, daytime talk shows, and *20/20* made Clinton more than a president — he was a public figure who was humble enough to meet Americans on their turf and in their terms. Where it seemed that Bob Dole only deigned to sit with Katie Couric, Bill Clinton reveled in it. Despite four years on Pennsylvania Avenue, Bill Clinton remained refreshingly public and accessible.

To many, what was authentic about Bill Clinton was that he was the same as he had always been — old friends and hometown folks could still recognize the president as "just plain Bill." Reporters helped Clinton to capitalize on that brand of authenticity. The *Philadelphia Inquirer* repeated the assertion that the president was still "just plain Bill." "To his childhood chums, Bill Clinton is the same now as he was then, hard-driving, modest... intimate and caring even if he doesn't have time, congenial, emotional, surprisingly shy and, most of all, their lifelong friend. To them, he is neither slick nor arrogant. They call him 'Mr. President' in public; otherwise, he's just plain Bill.... 'He's just an older version of the guy I knew in high school.'"[77]

Unlike Dole, he exposed "just plain Bill" in his requisite Barbara Walters interview in 1996. Admitting that he was still "in awe" of the White House, Clinton appeared star struck and humble as he spoke to Walters. Most of all, and unlike Bob Dole, Bill Clinton revealed himself as a husband and a father. In an "on the couch" kind of moment with Walters, Clinton joked about Chelsea's dates and admitted his pain and apprehension at the thought of her moving off to college.[78]

A Rose Garden by Any Other Name

Bill Clinton's White House might have been too casual and permissive for some people, inciting morals and ethics charges throughout his eight-year tenure, but that same lax style and sensibility allowed Clinton to sustain his connection with the American people, even from the confines of the Oval Office. As a result, even when Clinton was being "presidential" he maintained that human touch and that personal connection. Two major events of his first term illustrated his ability to redefine presidentiality in his own empathetic image. In the aftermath of the Oklahoma City bombing, and especially following the crash of TWA flight 800 in July 1996, Clinton exuded his very best "I feel your pain" empathy. If tears brought down Edmund Muskie in 1972, tears reaffirmed the nation's love for Bill Clinton in 1996. The news coverage of the event detailed Clinton's private meetings with families, quietly weeping as he embraced and comforted the victims' husbands, wives, children, and friends.

In moments like those, Clinton could be both man and president. Other moments called for a precarious negotiation between those two roles. Where others had failed to simultaneously project both personhood and presidentiality, a requirement of modern campaigning, Clinton could thread the needle like no other. He understood the symbolism of the White House and the importance of the presidency, but his ability to represent ordinariness in particular ways and on particular occasions allowed Americans to feel like they had one of their own at the head of government.

His relationship to ordinary life was on display in his 1996 convention film, *A Place Called America.* The film negotiated the themes of his first term with those on display in his 1992 video, *The Man from Hope.* His video highlighted important moments in his first term, woven through the narrative context of Clinton's extraordinary ordinariness. As political sociologists Shawn and Trevor Parry-Giles noted, "What [made] the film remarkable" was its ability to tap into viewers' emotions at "both the private and public levels."[79] For example, even as the film highlighted Clinton in his official capacity, there was a constant theme of a private man — an ordinary citizen — in awe of the office, enjoying his life, and trying to remain connected to both his roots and his countrymen.[80] At one point in the film, Clinton spoke about his nephews, who came to visit him in the White House. Clinton explained, "Even if I'm having a bad day, if I can see one of them, or even look at their pictures, it kind of connects me to what I'm really doing here."[81] Moments like those, whether on national television or the local news, allowed voters to understand Clinton both as a president and as a private man.

Despite his natural ability to connect personally — from the steps of the White House and across television sets into American living rooms — Bill Clinton had also learned from past failures. Since Richard Nixon, only one sitting president, Ronald Reagan, had won a bid for reelection. Rejecting the "Rose Garden" strategy, Clinton campaign manager Peter Knight recalled, "We took a look at the last four campaigns since '76 that had tried to run for the presidency from the White House, and only one of those had been successful."[82]

Clinton both exploited and rejected the Rose Garden. Although Clinton employed the office to punctuate his presidentiality and earn free media, the Clinton campaign did not follow a typical Rose Garden strategy. Dividing his time between official duties and shoe leather salesmanship, Clinton intended to harness his talent for face-to-face campaigning. "It won't be a Rose Garden campaign.... Campaign officials say Clinton is not planning a 'Rose Garden' strategy.... He is scheduled to be on the road 20 of the 30 days in September. If plans hold, these will not be fleeting rallies at local airports, but media events at sites where crowds can gather and where Clinton can "interact with voters."[83] Using the terms of authenticity, campaign strategist George Stephanopoulos revealed that the Clinton strategy was to ensure "that the real Bill Clinton could be seen ... by the American people."[84]

To that end, Clinton embarked on several long campaign trips across America, stopping in small-town living rooms and rural farms and heartland factories. In his 1996 whistle-stop trip from Washington to Chicago, Clinton wandered off tarmacs and train station platforms to shake hands and talk to voters. The campaign wanted images of Clinton's connection to local people to be the biggest story on the five o'clock local news. *CBS This Morning* followed the president on his whistle-stop tour and offered viewers a presidential special: "The whistle-stop tour was designed to take advantage of the ... trappings of small-town America.... Here, Bill Clinton is not the ultimate political insider, but the small-town boy who made good. Unidentified Woman #1: 'He makes you feel like he is one of us rather than all the big politicians that are in it, I think, for the money.'"[85] Whether they agreed with his policies or not, people across the country came out to see Bill Clinton. "The turnouts Clinton drew on his whistle-stop and bus tours so far exceeded expectations that it appears he has recaptured the 'chemistry' with voters he showed in the best moments of the 1992 campaign."[86] Even when the train did not stop, Clinton waved and shouted to people by the tracks as his train went by. As one reporter noted, "It was a down-home brand of retail politics, and nobody" enjoyed it more than the president, who relished his rapport with ordinary citizens.[87]

In these face-to-face encounters, voters became connected to and invested in Bill Clinton. Clinton's retail politics involved one-on-one conversations with members of the audience, whose stories he heard, and whose pain he felt. "The candidate who never saw a hand he didn't want to shake is once again reaching out to the crowds and letting them reach back for him — persuader, confessor, empathizer and king of the rope line."[88] Indeed, Clinton genuinely appeared to enjoy being out on the campaign trail. As Al Gore remarked in the 1996 convention film, "What energizes Bill Clinton is going out and being with the American people."[89] Voters felt that he liked them, and so they liked him. Moreover, they could identify with him. "Out on the campaign trail, President Clinton has been giving evidence of his talent for connecting with people's hopes and anxieties ... . His talent for identifying himself with voters has given him a considerable edge over Robert Dole."[90] As one Ohio Republican explained, voters preferred Clinton's personal style. This particular voter told a reporter that she intended to vote for Bill Clinton based on his personality and authenticity alone: "He seems to warm to the crowd, and the crowd warms to him.... He doesn't seem rehearsed."[91]

Thus, despite (or perhaps because of) his shortcomings, Bill Clinton remained a compelling figure and an eternally likable human being. Even Republican respondents narrowly favored Clinton on survey questions about which candidate was "personally likable" and which candidate "connects well with ordinary Americans."[92] These qualities, difficult to maintain from within the walls of the White House, allowed Clinton to remain connected.

Conclusions

Like Ronald Reagan, Bill Clinton was able to maintain his connection to the American people, despite the trappings of the White House. Also like Ronald Reagan, Bill Clinton was challenged by an uncharismatic Washington insider who often seemed more Beltway than the sitting president. Like Walter Mondale, Bob Dole had difficulty connecting with ordinary voters and exhibiting his personal and private life outside the halls of Congress. Also like Mondale, Bob Dole had an impressive political résumé— he was clearly qualified for the job professionally, but could not sell his candidacy personally. Absent other reasons (economic conditions, war) to oust the incumbent, Bob Dole could not convince voters that he was a more attractive choice than President Clinton.

Nevertheless, a great deal had changed between 1984 and 1996. Bill Clinton and Bob Dole negotiated their candidacies within a much different media environment. The talk show campaign had come to dominate political media, introducing new interviewers, new kinds of questions, and new premiums on candidate self-disclosure. As a result, voters interpreted the candidates through the story lines generated by the soft media. To most voters, Bill Clinton was the kind of guy with whom they would like to have a beer. Bob Dole, they imagined, was the kind of guy who would sit at the bar grumbling about the way things used to be. While voters appreciated his public service and military heroism, these were not things to which they could relate. Conversely, Bill Clinton not only offered hope for the future, but a president of the present moment who understood them experientially, if not politically.

Low voter turnout in 1996 suggested that voters were satisfied with the status quo. Some were reasonably satisfied with the president's performance, but not particularly passionate about him. They were even less inspired by Bob Dole, and thus had no reason to vote. Others had no compelling reason (war, economy) to prompt a trip to the ballot box. Still others were unmotivated by the preordained election outcome — it was obvious that Bill Clinton would win. Nonvoting was equally a vote for Bill Clinton as it was a vote against Bob Dole. Whatever the reason for widespread nonvoting in 1996, it seems clear that Bob Dole was an uninspired challenger. Even if nonvoters did not particularly care for Bill Clinton, they particularly disliked Bob Dole.[93]

There is some evidence of this in widespread ticket-splitting in 1996. Voters' decisions to reelect Republican majorities to both houses of Congress, while reelecting Bill Clinton, is evidence of Clinton's personal, if not political, appeal to voters. Split ticket voting indicated that voters did not approve of all of Clinton's political positions, even as they wanted to keep him as head of state, if not especially as head of government. The divided government that remained throughout the Clinton years, ironically, brought trouble to the Clinton presidency on the very terms on which he had appealed to voters in the first place — his personal life.

In sum, there is no doubt that the charismatic (if divisive) Bill Clinton was a man whom voters felt they understood and whose image they felt they owned. Clinton brought Arkansas, and therefore middle America, into the White House with him. He brought his experiences, which were, in many ways, ordinary Americans' experiences. Struggle as he might with the politics, there was no doubt that Clinton symbolically represented ordinary Americans.

7

Hanging Chad: 2000

After the most controversial election since Watergate, the 2000 contest ended in a stalemate. For weeks following Election Day, the country turned its eyes to the suddenly famous Florida secretary of state Katherine Harris, the suddenly important state of Florida, and its suddenly newsworthy hanging chads.[1] Republican candidate George W. Bush was ultimately determined the winner — but only after a month of national hand-wringing and head-hanging. A divided popular and electoral vote tally, a Supreme Court decision, and widespread condemnation of third party candidate Ralph Nader[2] ended in the inauguration of George W. Bush on January 20, 2001. It was an election result without historical comparison.[3]

Although the result was without comparison, the campaign season was fairly ordinary. To some extent the climate and conditions in 2000 resembled those of 1988; both were years of relative peace and prosperity. Both were also years in which charismatic two-term presidents delivered dramatically staged farewell addresses, handing the party reins over to their vice presidents. In his eight years, Ronald Reagan had seen dramatic improvement in consumer and market confidence, heightened patriotism, and a greater perception of national security. In his eight years, Bill Clinton had achieved budgetary surpluses; he prepared to leave his country in good fiscal health. Unemployment was low, prospects for peace were seemingly high, and crime rates had been reduced.[4] In such periods of optimism, the incumbent vice president ought to have enjoyed a distinct advantage. As George Bush's campaign strategist Karl Rove commented, any Republican candidate in 2000 would face serious disadvantages: "Absent a major downturn in the economy ... the party out of power was likely to have a very large uphill fight to win the general election."[5]

There were other similarities between George H.W. Bush and Al Gore from which we can draw accurate parallels between 1988 and 2000 — both were experienced politicians who had faithfully served president, country and

171

party, although neither could match the charisma and charm of his former running mate. Al Gore was disadvantaged by his president's very public personal struggles and by his own very public personality struggles. George H.W. Bush was disadvantaged by his connection to the most controversial policies of the Reagan administration and by his own public reserve.[6] Despite these obvious similarities, however, their opponents could not have been more different. Where George H. W. Bush ran against Michael Dukakis, Al Gore faced George W. Bush. George W. Bush was decidedly NOT Michael Dukakis.

George W. Bush bore physical resemblance to his father, former president George H.W. Bush, but shared none of his father's famous reserve. Unlike his father's 1988 opponent, Michael Dukakis, the laid-back governor's Texas accent and interesting syntax made him immediately endearing to many voters and obviously alluring to the hosts of countless talk shows.

The Beer Poll

Although the election results proved inconclusive, history may yet determine a winner in the 2000 election: Oprah Winfrey. By 2000, Bill Clinton's self-disclosive, therapeutic, pop-culture style of campaigning was sine qua non in the campaign world. The talk show couch was the perfect forum for a candidate to reach a mass audience, display his lighter side, and field hard-hitting questions about family and hobbies. As one reporter noted at the end of the 2000 election, "If you can't relax and ooze personality on *Oprah*, your hopes for the White House are dashed."[7] The element of surprise — at seeing a very serious person in a very casual forum — had not disappeared from the *Saturday Night Live* cameo but had nonetheless become a requirement for any serious candidate. This kind of campaign environment favored George W. Bush. The Texas governor may not have been able to name foreign leaders or pronounce multi-syllabic words, but he did "ooze personality" and appear comfortable in casual settings.

In mid–October 2000, the very scientific Sam Adams/Roper Starch poll found that more Americans would rather have a beer with George Bush than with Al Gore.[8] The Beer Poll offered no official tally of serious voter preferences, but it did provide insight into voters' perceptions about the candidates' lifestyles and personalities. It also provided insight into trends in American ideas about the boundaries between politics and culture — that is, the fact that a Beer Poll existed, and the fact that major news organizations considered its results newsworthy (if lighthearted), said a great deal about politics in American life. Essentially, through this single question, the Beer Poll asked Americans which candidate more closely resembled average American life outside of Washington. It cut to the heart of what many perceived to be American authenticity. It surveyed people's embedded candidate images. What was interesting was how accurate these polls were. This one question: "With which candidate would you rather have a beer?" combined a battery of character and personality questions typically asked by academic and professional polling organizations.[9] In 2000, the Beer Poll uncovered voters' remarkable ambivalence about presidential choice. Interestingly, more noteworthy polls uncovered similar results.

At the start of the fall campaign, Al Gore led Bush on nearly every major issue. A late August *Newsweek* poll, for example, found that more voters thought that Gore would do a better job handling the economy, Social Security, and education. They also believed that he would do a better job of upholding moral values, appointing Supreme Court justices, managing health care costs, and helping seniors with prescription drug costs. Despite this, polls repeatedly found that Americans preferred Bush when it came to personal characteristics: likeability, "understands voters like me," and "honesty." According to Gore's pollster Stan Greenberg, voters agreed with Al Gore on the issues that concerned them most. Indeed, Gore's internal polling found that on every issue category except taxes, voters preferred Gore by substantial margins (ten points or more). Most significantly, voters thought Al Gore would do a better job managing the economy, Social Security, and the federal budget. On only one issue, taxes, voters preferred Bush (by around four points, a record low margin for a Democrat). Despite this, George Bush bested Al Gore in almost every category pertaining to character — personality, honesty, and leadership.[10]

In mid–October 2000, the Associated Press condensed results from a variety of polling organizations and found that, while voters continued to prefer Gore on nearly every major issue, and while they thought that Gore was more intelligent, they preferred Bush's personality. "Gore retains the advantage on most of the top issues ... but Bush has gained ground on the public view of candidate traits." On leadership qualities, Bush bested Gore by a margin of 66–60 percent. On "straight talk" and "honesty" Bush edged Gore by a margin of 63–45 percent. On likeability, Bush continued to impress 75 percent of voters.[11] As Bush's character numbers improved, his overall voter preference numbers climbed at a corresponding rate. Explaining this phenomenon, Bush strategist Matthew Dowd noted, "The American public, to be honest, is making a decision based upon is this the kind of man that I want to lead this country, unrelated to a specific issue."[12]

Specific issues were rarely a hot topic on daytime and late-night television talk shows, forums privileged by both campaigns in the summer and fall of

2000. Both candidates appeared in-cameo on *The Late Show with David Letterman* to deliver the host's famous "Top Ten List." Proving how important such appearances had become, both Bush and Gore made the rounds on *Regis* and *Leno* and *Saturday Night Live*, where Bush pulled pranks and Gore unveiled a more easy-going side of himself. Both also appeared on *Oprah*, where Gore gushed about his wife and talked about his commitment to populist causes. Conversely, Bush gushed about tacos and shed a tear discussing the birth of his daughters.[13]

Gore's appearance on *Oprah* was illustrative of his campaign posture. On the one hand, both he and his campaign managers knew that he needed to appear in casual, intimate settings like *Oprah*. On the other hand, Gore seemed to have more difficulty straying from his campaign script than George Bush, a requirement on talk shows. A master of policy, Gore brought his expertise to the *Oprah* audience. Gore did dish with the host, but even when he engaged in personal banter, his performance was largely flat: His favorite book was an obscure nineteenth century French novel. His favorite movie was a relatively unknown film set in Scotland. Even his favorite cereal, Wheaties, was dull.[14] As one reporter noted of the candidates' talk show appearances, "The pursuit of likeability on TV worked for Ronald Reagan and Bill Clinton, but.... It's working against Al Gore ... and when push comes to shove" Oprah's viewers would surely "vote for personality."[15]

Despite Gore's shortcomings, both candidates did make their campaigns personal by making the talk show rounds. A reporter for Cox News Service acknowledged the campaign strategy: "The candidates' goal on the comedy and talk-show circuit, of course, is to show voters they're 'regular guys,' just like the rest of us."[16] Neither Oprah nor Leno was duped by the campaign managers, however. Not only were their viewers hungry for the dirty dish, but hosts, particularly comedians, were not passively usurped by the candidates.

The candidates were also the victims of late night television barbs. Jokes and caricatures and comedy sketches about the candidates were salient, perhaps more salient than stump speeches. Political jokes on popular television programs were both cutting and frequent. Although none of these programs could compare to average debate viewership (forty million), comedy shows featuring jokes about the presidential candidates were aired nightly and weekly, reaching a diverse and widespread viewership.[17] An average episode of *The Simpsons* alone reached around ten million viewers. Combined, Jay Leno and David Letterman averaged around thirteen million viewers per night in 2000. The late night program *Saturday Night Live* reached an average viewership of around eight million each week.[18]

More important than the ratings, however, was the reverb created by these jokes, which were often more memorable than the impressions left by the candidates themselves. In its October 7, 2000, broadcast, *Saturday Night Live* featured a presidential debate sketch in which Chris Parnell, playing Jim Lehrer, asked each candidate to summarize his candidacy in one word. Will Farrell, playing George W. Bush, responded with the made-up word, "strategery."[19] In that same broadcast, as in others, Al Gore was portrayed as a slow-talking, long-winded pedant. Clips of the skit were later replayed on *NBC News*, transcribed by the *New York Times*, and repeated by millions of Americans to whom the word "strategery" became synonymous with George W. Bush. As NBC's Brian Williams commented, "The parody ... entered ... the national consciousness. Certainly, the national conversation."[20] To the millions of Americans who followed *Saturday Night Live* or *The Late Show* or *The Tonight Show* or *The Simpsons* more closely than they followed the *New York Times*, George W. Bush was a lovable frat guy with only a passing familiarity with the English language; Al Gore was a long-winded know-it-all with a "real person" anecdote for every issue and a lock-box solution for every problem. The problem with (and benefit of) these caricatures was that they simplified the candidates to their most extreme characteristics — George Bush was funny and affable and simple. Al Gore's only connection to "real people" was through his never-ending, politically motivated examples. Like the mainstream media, these programs focused on authenticity as the framework through which candidate images could be interpreted. That they did so in an exaggerated form merely made the images more potent and more memorable. Moreover, for all their imperfections and exaggerations, these comedy programs did serve to introduce viewers to one set of realities about the candidates, which the candidates themselves reinforced in their own public appearances.

Really Authentic

In the final analysis, what was interesting about the 2000 election was its uncertain outcome. What was interesting about the campaign, however, was the extent to which national discourse was devoted to uncovering and analyzing the relative authenticity of the two candidates. Al Gore was deemed "stiff" and "wooden." He was praised when he cut loose on a talk show or at a town hall. He appealed to voters when he discussed his family. He caused a long-running cable news debate over whether his managers had scripted his convention kiss with his wife, Tipper. On the other side, George W. Bush was criticized for having been born with a silver spoon in his mouth. Some questioned whether he had learned ranching at Andover or at Yale. Reporters were taken with his personality, jovial nicknames, strange syntax, and paltry vocabulary.[21] He was praised for being "straightforward" and for reaching out to rural and blue-collar conservatives — speaking to them on their own level.

The media, voters, and the candidates themselves all seemed to come together around this one fact: personality, image, and authenticity were essential to constructive campaign discourse in 2000. Authenticity was also, perhaps, essential to the election outcome, uncertain as it was. At the end of the election, George Bush's campaign strategist, Karl Rove, postulated that the election had been Al Gore's to lose. Were it not for the overwhelming personal popularity of George Bush, the election would not have been close. After studying exit polls, Rove determined that "the undecided voters at the end were people who thought the country was going in the right direction.... They were disproportionately, by about two to one, thinking the country was going in the right direction, which was where the whole electorate was ... these were people at the end who were being kept from voting for Gore" by personality factors and gut feelings.[22]

Being Al Gore

Despite his relative lack of personality, perhaps the most compelling campaign media produced during the 2000 election came from the Al Gore campaign. The short film produced for the Democratic National Convention was unlike any campaign film ever produced. Like other campaign films, its goal was to "introduce" the candidate to average voters, but its style and content were exceptional. The campaign hired Spike Jonze, director of *Being John Malkovich*, to produce the film. Jonze had a keen grasp of viewers' delight in observing celebrities performing mundane and ordinary tasks. The convention film played into this scopophilic impulse, as Jonze shot (in pared-down, verite, home-video-style) a day in the life of the Gores. The film brought the Gores down to the level of ordinary — made them understandable and everyday. If Gore was unable to relate to audiences with comfortable, casual ease, the film performed that necessary duty on his behalf. The film seemed authentic — it gave viewers a seemingly real, secret, unfiltered, unplugged, behind-the-scenes glimpse of the Gores hanging out together.

The controversy over the film — it was said that Gore did not want it to air at all — remained unresolved. The film was ultimately played on Tuesday evening of the convention, rather than Thursday evening, as was standard. Whether the campaign hedged in order to authenticate the film, or whether Al Gore was honestly concerned about its airing, was never determined. Accidental or intentional, it was a brilliant strategy. While fewer viewers watched it live, many, many more saw it in full, or in clips, on news programs. The film was not the cinematographic genius of *A New Beginning* or *The Man from Hope;* it was another kind of political tool altogether — a masterpiece of documentary-style cinema. The film was so "real" that it opened with a shot of Gore's Secret Service agents asking the videographer to put down the camera; this was cinéma vérité in its most extreme. Viewers had little reason to doubt its unscripted authenticity.

In the opening scenes, Gore offered a guided tour through his mother's house, exposing his childhood bedroom — complete with still-unmade bed. In another scene, Tipper, embarrassed, entered a room, shocked to find her husband (and a camera man) looking through the family's personal possessions, "You're *really* showing him our house?!" Throughout the film, Gore's family members attested to his ordinariness, sense of humor, and personal characteristics. The Gore daughters were filmed poking fun at their dad, but also informing viewers that the "stiff" and "wooden" candidate was just the mask in front of a genuinely human and passionate man: "In a different context ... at the dinner table," Gore was eloquent and passionate.

Finally, after a day with the Gores, the film ended abruptly in true verite style. After a long day, finally, Gore announced, "I've got to go to bed ... do you want me to get up and cook breakfast for you?" The light turned off and the film ended. Some films (*The Man from Hope*) firmly rooted the subject in the American tradition to display American and personal authenticity. Others (*A New Beginning*) had brought viewers to the emotional edge to display American and human authenticity. Jonze's convention film, however, displayed American, human, and personal authenticity in perfect combination. It was a concoction expertly made to dispel the most salient myths about its subject. In this film, Gore joked about being wooden and displayed a life and family outside of Washington. Most of all, it cut through the opposition's most potent attacks — that he was a deceitful Washington insider who would say anything to get elected.

As the Associated Press reported, the film was but one "effort to humanize Al Gore's image" at the Democratic National Convention.[23] Throughout the convention week, the Gore campaign offered multiple character witnesses for the vice president, among them, an old army buddy who was employed "'to dispel the image of the vice president as wooden'" and a childhood friend who offered anecdotes from Gore's footloose past. The latter was offered up to reporters and anchors and viewers at home as a witness to Gore's inspired, but average, childhood in Tennessee. This particular man remembered frequently cutting loose with Gore, recalling "midnight skinny dips in the public pool, swiping Coke bottles from the porches of country stores to lob at street signs and ... getting into whatever we could.'"[24]

What was interesting was not that the Gore campaign acknowledged its candidate's personality deficit, nor that it made multiple attempts to ameliorate the problem. Instead, Gore's advisors realized that the kind of childhood deviance that might have been embarrassing or even dangerous in another generation (or to another candidate) was sine qua non for Gore. By contrast, in an effort to the opposite — to dispel images of its candidate's seedier past — the Bush campaign told its candidate's history in broad brush strokes. They absolved George Bush through a redemption narrative, which included the herculean efforts of God, Laura Bush, and the Reverend Billy Graham. For Al Gore, however, who was widely viewed as humorless and pedantic, the American people needed to see a more carefree human side.[25]

The characterization of Al Gore as wooden was so widespread, and the campaign's attempts to dispel that image so well known, that when the candidate and his wife enjoyed a long and passionate kiss at the convention, the ensuing media frenzy focused only on its authenticity — they cared less about the kiss than whether it was scripted. In the days following the convention, the candidate and his campaign operatives made the early show rounds, defending the Gores' spontaneity to the likes of Matt Lauer and Diane Sawyer. Rather than examining the acceptance speech, the poll numbers, or the post-convention campaign trip, the media scrutinized the convention footage and demanded to know whether Gore's advisors had mandated a timed practice run with the candidate's wife.[26] For Gore, who had learned to joke about himself, this provided an opportunity to discuss his family *and* his image with the likes of some of the country's most influential opinion-makers: talk show hosts.

According to Bush's campaign strategist, Karl Rove, the tactic worked. Going into the Democratic National Convention, most Americans saw Al Gore as a stiff, wooden, Clinton lackey. Coming out of the convention, "people saw him as a loose, warm personable individual, in a way that they hadn't seen him before."[27] CNN gave Gore a positive, if measured, review. "He was certainly personable, he was forceful. And one thing he didn't do was yell at the audience, which was something he has done in the past. He smiled a little more, he gestured, he looked a little less wooden than he usually does."[28] Al Gore did more than just avoid "yell[ing] at the audience." A spectacular post-convention bounce for Al Gore proved that the strategy of introducing Gore "as a warm, caring, family man with a terrific family" was effective.[29]

Al Gore's post-convention surge in opinion polls did not prove that any one of these tactics worked, but the numbers did provide evidence that the campaign's efforts to reintroduce the candidate as a regular guy resonated with some voters. Throughout the history of televised conventions, most candidates enjoyed a post-convention "bounce" in poll numbers. Thus, the fact that Al Gore's poll numbers improved was not surprising. More interesting was the extent to which each candidate in 2000 became more popular and more appealing in opinion polls following the convention. According to Gallup, Gore enjoyed a seventeen-point post-convention surge.[30]

The categories in which he improved were all personal categories.[31] Gore's overall favorability rating improved twelve points, with a corresponding decline in his unfavorability rating. According to Gallup, the "results suggest that the bounce in Gore's support is part of a more generally positive reassessment of the Vice President."[32] Specifically, Gore's net change in voters' assessments of personal characteristics was dramatic. The vice president improved twenty-six points in each of three categories: "Cares about people like you," "Is honest and trustworthy," and "Is someone you would be proud to have as president."[33] These gains were more than substantial — Gore had been trailing George Bush in *every* personal characteristic assessment category prior to the convention. Coming out of the convention, he outperformed George Bush in every category (except "is a strong and decisive leader") by a margin of between five and sixteen points. While it is not clear that any one aspect of the Democratic Convention moved these numbers, it is clear that the campaign's strong emphasis on "humanizing" Gore had an impact on many voters.

Strategically Real People

Following the Democratic National Convention, the campaign adopted a hyper-aware posture about Al Gore's reputation for being wooden. The campaign found that if they took a postmodern approach to this potentially big problem, they could neutralize its effects by authenticating the candidate's human credentials. The Spike Jonze film had featured several moments in which Gore and his family joked about his reputation as "dull" and "wooden." This was followed in the candidate's convention speech in which he acknowledged: "If you entrust me with the presidency, I know I won't always be the most exciting politician."

Following the convention, the candidate and his spokespersons continued this effort by joking about Gore's stiff and wooden image. An authorized story in *People*, which included internal campaign sources, illustrated the new effort. *People* reported that the vice president was prone to giving speeches in which he "droned on in all-too-familiar fashion about gas prices, trade unions, the possibility of water on Mars.... Though friends and family say that privately Gore ... is unfailingly warm, charming and witty, it is a side most Americans rarely see. What they have witnessed instead is an intelligent, if at times pedantic, public speaker whose aggravating verbosity has been fodder for the likes of Letterman and been known to push even his wife Tipper's buttons. 'When he's boring and goes on and on and on,' says a former aide, 'you can see her roll her eyes and go, "Enough already!"'[34] Gore's wife was in on the game — if she could joke about his long-winded speeches, he must have a sense of humor.

In another effort to humanize the typically "wooden" vice president, the Gore campaign surrounded the candidate with what they called "strategically real people."[35] Following the convention, Gore's campaign managers sent the candidate on a riverboat tour of northeastern Iowa and southwestern Wisconsin. Unlike the airplane, the riverboat allowed Gore to make frequent stops, garner local press coverage, and be pictured with and among "real people." They were the "realest" as it turned out — voters outside of the Midwest found them parochial and endearing.

Part of the "real people" effort employed an oratorical device made popular by Bill Clinton, as Gore tried to frame all of his issue positions through real-world, real-life, real-people, real-impact examples.[36] The campaign team attempted to saturate the press with images of "Al Gore sitting down with real people in their town."[37] Although "not enthused about real people, because we thought we were real people," Gore went along with the strategy.[38]

The strategy had worked brilliantly for Clinton, but Gore's lack of enthusiasm for "real people" examples was quickly clear — they soon degenerated into onerous, long-winded illustrations of Americans with whom Gore seemed horribly out of touch. Al Gore used "real people" examples so often that he mocked the strategy himself at New York's 2000 Al Smith dinner and was roasted for it on *Saturday Night Live* in October 2000. Thus, while the strategy worked in the short term, Al Gore continued to suffer a personality deficit. Although aided by the fact that people knew that Al Gore knew that he was boring, Al Gore was nonetheless ... boring.

Following the first debate, *Saturday Night Live* ran a mock debate skit in which Darrell Hammond, playing Al Gore, interrupted moderator Jim Lehrer (Chris Parnell) to offer the example of a tragic ninety-four-year old woman. "Jim, I'd like to interrupt here and answer that question as if it were my turn to speak. Jim, let me tell about a friend of mine.... She... She suffers from polio, spinal meningitis, lung, liver, and pancreatic cancer, an enlarged heart, diabetes, and a rare form of styptic acne. Now, several recent strokes, along with an unfortunate shark attack, have left her paralyzed and missing her right leg under the knee.... She tells me that some weeks she has to choose between eating and treating her Lyme Disease. Now, under my plan, Etta's prescription drugs would be covered. Under my opponent's plan, her house would be burned to the ground."[39]

A Wooden Soldier

Problematically, Gore's constant invocation of "real people" came across as scripted and inauthentic. When employed by Bill Clinton, this style of oratory seemed real and empathetic. In Gore's speeches, however, the candidate often seemed to be reading a laundry list of other people's tragedies. As the *New York Times* informed its readers, "Too often, Gore is just giving you boilerplate. He needs to speak with a certain genuineness of tone, which has been lacking."[40] Many voters and viewers began to interpret Al Gore's television appearances in that light. Through their own experiences watching him, and also through repeated press analysis of the candidate's lack of personality, voters began to view Gore as a stiff and scripted politician.

Journalists employed the "inauthentic" label when describing Al Gore. Quoting expert psychoanalysts, the *Washington Post* determined that Gore's lifelong quest to "fit in" in Washington had deprived him of authenticity: "Gore has spent 20 years trying to be the Establishment and seems inauthentic."[41] The *New York Times* framed Gore's lack of human connection with voters relative to Bill Clinton: voters "think they know Clinton but Gore comes off as inauthentic."[42] The *St. Petersburg Times* told its readers that "eight years in Clinton's shadow made him seem one-dimensional: faithful but dull, a wooden soldier."[43]

Absent context, the fact that Al Gore lacked charisma might not have damaged his chances in the election. By 2000, however, both voters and reporters had come to understand a candidate's "scripted" and "wooden" inability to relate to voters as somehow "political" and "staged" and "inauthentic." It was the "scripted" attempts at displaying human connection that truly damaged Gore: "There still are many times when he seems scripted. In ... interview[s] many answers were rote sound bites. Personal questions were batted away. He even seems scripted when he removes his coat at the start of campaign rallies. He peels off the jacket and says, 'I know it's a little chilly here, but I feel hot!'"[44] That such news analysis was scathing is obvious. That it was repeated so often is informative: this became the central organizing principle for press analysis of Al Gore.

An October Pew survey measured voters' reactions to Gore, finding that his personal image had tumbled since his post-convention high: "Gore's personal image has faltered.... Fully 45% of voters see him as a typical politician, compared to 37% who felt that way in September, when he held a slight lead in the presidential horse race. Just 29% now regard Bush as a typical politician. And while Bush's rating for honesty has edged up slightly since September (from 35% to 38%), Gore's has declined over the same period from 37% to 30%."[45] The Pew survey found that Gore's personal image had softened among the very groups he had been courting throughout the fall: "Gore's problems can be traced partly to the doubts some Democrats harbor about the vice president's personality and character." According to Pew a "sizable" portion of Democrats, 31 percent "regard Gore as a typical politician. On balance, independents view Gore this way (41%, compared to 29% who say Bush)."[46] Gore's increasingly negative image was the result of multiple factors, not the least of which was the portrayal of Gore by late night comedians and mainstream news organizations. But voters were not duped or manipulated by these media. These descriptions and caricatures resonated with voters because of their own experiences with the candidate.

An average of forty million viewers watched the presidential debates.[47] Although Gore was abundantly prepared to display his vast knowledge of American foreign and domestic policy, the debates were staged events in which viewers assimilated nonverbal messages and candidate interactions as much as they listened for political talking points. As Bush advisor Karl Rove noted, "heuristics, the visual short-cut to understanding what the person is about ... how [the candidates] appear to be, are almost as important" as policy prescriptions and ten-point plans.[48] Those who watched the debates on television saw a pedantic and impatient Al Gore. Over the course of the three televised debates, Gore sighed, moved awkwardly around the staged area, and at one point attempted to physically dominate George Bush by moving inappropriately close to his opponent.[49]

As a result, voters reported mixed evaluations of Gore at the debates. Following the final debate, Pew reported that "Gore continues to hold double-digit leads over Bush on health care, Social Security, prescription drug coverage for seniors and stewardship of the economy," which were the issues that voters reported were most important to them.[50] However, his "standing on character and personality traits has ... declined" as a result of his debate performances. Problematically, "more people have cited ... personality as a reason for not voting for him." In sum, while many agreed with the points that he made in the debates, many more reported that they did not like his posture and personality. As Pew reported: "Al Gore's personality may be costing him votes.

Although a plurality of voters believe he won the first presidential debate, he has lost his small September lead over George W. Bush. As the race has narrowed, an increasing number of voters ... say they dislike his personality."[51] As Gore campaign advisor Bob Shrum admitted, "I believe that Al Gore won the first debate ... on issues."[52] However, when people thought about the debates, they did not think about "the issues ... but things like Al Gore appearing overbearing in that first debate, sighing too much."[53]

The Bush campaign's internally funded debate focus group studies confirmed George Bush's advantage in the debates. While voters were more likely to prefer Gore's positions on substantive issues, they were more likely to personally identify with Bush. As Bush pollster Matt Dowd revealed, post-debate polls and focus groups augured well for a Bush victory. Women, who would be key to a Gore victory, were increasingly turned off by the Democratic candidate. "When women voters saw Al Gore sighing and acting the way he did, unrelated to issues, they were turned off by it. When you asked them at the end of the focus group, who do you think won the debate? They thought Al Gore won the debate. When you asked them, who would you rather have as President of the United States? They thought George Bush. It's a whole different question." Some in the media caught on to this discrepancy between image and issue preference. As the *Los Angeles Times* reported, "Most polls said that a majority of Americans thought that Al Gore won the first televised debate, but they liked George W. Bush better."[54] In all three of the debates, Gore was described as uncomfortable, smug, overbearing, moralizing, and annoying.

Those who did not watch the debates saw clips of only these most dramatic moments, heard jokes about them on comedy programs, or read newspaper analysis of the events, which tended to highlight Gore's lack of personality.[55] His much-mocked sighs became fodder for a sketch on *Saturday Night Live* and saturated post-debate discussion and analysis. It was a boon for the Bush campaign, which found that more voters heard about the sigh in the aftermath of the debate than actually watched it live on television. "Talk radio was on fire with the sighs ... we found on national morning shows and morning drive radio for about two or three days after that first debate, it was just all about" Al Gore's sighs.[56]

In its final debate analysis, Pew determined that "Gore's personality emerged as a real liability during the presidential debates, and those negative perceptions appear to have stuck. Fully 27% of Bush supporters now say what they like least about the vice president is his personality. This figure, virtually unchanged from early October, represents a substantial increase from September and Gore's post-convention surge."[57]

Inventing the Internet

Gore's image problem was not merely a matter of his stilted and wooden speech patterns. More seriously, voters came to believe that Gore was not honest. The Bush campaign used focus groups to target its attacks against Al Gore and found that three interrelated charges against the vice president resonated with voters: first, he exaggerated; second, he changed positions in order to be more popular; third, he was a Washington insider.

These charges worked well because they created a consistent portrait of the vice president and because they confirmed what voters were already prepared to believe about Al Gore. As Karl Rove noted, "When the conversation was about exaggeration, that had an impact" because it highlighted existing notions about the vice president.[58] The fact that Al Gore fed these charges did not help. Although Gore never meant to imply that he "invented" the internet, once the story caught on, all of Gore's self-promoting exaggerations were closely scrutinized — that he "started" the Love Canal case, that he was on the scene with FEMA during the floods in Texas, that he inspired the male lead in Erich Segal's *Love Story.*[59]

As a result, the Bush campaign did not need to spend much time on the attack. Once the press caught on to the story, voters and the media began to police Gore's record themselves. As the Gore campaign's Bob Shrum later admitted, "The Bush campaign did a brilliant job of ... changing the standard by which" the candidates were judged "by basically getting this exaggeration story up and going."[60] The story reverberated through nearly every media outlet. "From the *Washington Post* to the *Washington Times*, from the *New York Times* to the *New York Post*, from NBC's cable networks to the traveling press corps" America's journalists investigated and policed Gore's record, "freely denounc[ing] Gore as 'a liar,' 'delusional,' 'Pinocchio,' a 'Zelig' character who inserts himself into improbable historical events."[61]

Questions about Gore's credibility led directly to attacks on Gore's consistency. Because it was both believable and plausible, the Bush campaign made Al Gore's lack of issue homophily a central part of its opposition strategy. As Karl Rove noted at the end of the campaign, "For those [voters] who were up for grabs ... the idea that [Gore] would say something now that he rejected nine months before" was disconcerting, and it reinforced the Bush campaign's emphasis on Gore's tendency to flip flop and exaggerate.[62] These charges also counted against his alleged lack of personal consistency. These attacks were particularly salient because they made the Gore campaign's efforts to "humanize" its candidate seem sinister and politically motivated. Both the Bush campaign and critics in the press "said he changed personas as often as he changed his clothes. There was Business Suit Gore, Earth Tones Gore and now, Shirt–sleeves Gore." [63]

Together these attacks on Gore's character led to an overarching thematic attack against the vice president — that he was a Washington insider and a political animal. This was a line of attack that George Bush could make often, make directly, and make himself (without the assistance of surrogates and spokespersons). George Bush gained a great deal of traction when he accused Al Gore of being "of Washington, for Washington and by Washington."[64] Of his own qualifications to be president, Bush told Jay Leno that he was more qualified than Gore because "the more time you spend in Washington, the less qualified you are."[65] It was, perhaps, the most useful attack against Al Gore because it allowed George Bush to also create a positive contradistinction, with himself as the populist outsider.

Plain-Spoken Folks

The populist outsider was exactly the image George Bush had been projecting. Kicking off the fall campaign season with a stump-speech road trip, Bush began to condense his attacks against the vice president. At Bush rallies, Al Gore represented all that was wrong with Washington. On September 4 in Illinois, for example, Bush accused Gore of "Washington double speak," offering his own candidacy as an alternative to out-of-touch, lying, deceptive politicians-as-usual. He told his audience that his presidency would provide the opportunity to "get some plain-spoken folks in Washington, D.C."[66] To all Americans who were disgruntled with Washington, George Bush promised, "Help is on the way. It's time to elect some folks that've got good common sense ... we need plain-spoken Americans in the White House."[67] That kind of populist appeal was typical of the Bush campaign, which provided images of its candidate as a "regular guy" alternative to the entrenched powers in Washington. It was a perfect combination of human, personal, and American authenticity.

The 2000 campaign was not a joy ride for the Bush camp, however. According to internal polling sponsored by the Gore campaign, George Bush entered the general election season with a serious deficit in opinion polls.[68] Still trailing Gore in early September, it appeared that Bush's only assets were "that he won the nomination and people kind of liked the guy."[69] Working within that reality, Bush's strategists needed to construct a campaign that would emphasize the candidate's obvious strengths and attempt to ameliorate — or at least spin — his weaknesses.

Strategery

Matthew Dowd, director of polling and media for the Bush campaign, later said that "the fundamental strategy ... was really to try to convey why we loved this guy.... That really was the fundamental strategy for ... the campaign."[70] In retrospect, Matthew Dowd's recollection was a bit Pollyannaish. In a more hard-hitting summary, advisor Karl Rove believed that he could create an image of George Bush that would ameliorate most, if not all, of his candidate's perceived negative qualities — namely, that he was unintelligent and unprepared — and, hopefully, reframe them as positive characteristics. Even in his public comments, Karl Rove showed his hand. Prior to the debates, for example, Rove primed his candidate's performance by framing Bush's lack of experience as an authentic strength: "Well, he's a plain spoken person, he's not an accomplished orator, he's not a practiced debater, he's a person who, you know, says what he feels. And so look, there are people who are far more accomplished at debating, but he's a good strong leader, and that's what the American people are really looking for."[71]

In this way, the Bush campaign attempted to rewrite the playbook. George Bush's poor grammar and penchant for verbal blunder were reconstructed as qualities of spontaneity and authenticity — framed in opposition to the sleek and scripted oratorical smoke and mirrors employed by Washington politicians. At best, Bush's weaknesses would become advantages. At the very least, Karl Rove believed that none of these negative qualities would become a major factor in determining votes.[72]

A good part of the appeal was that, despite his family name, George W. Bush never seemed to be an Ivy League or Beltway kind of guy. Interviewing historians and psychologists, the *Washington Post's* Michael Powell reported that Bush was authentic, despite his upbringing. "Bush is more real because ... his insistent self-identification as a rough-and-tumble Texan has allowed him to frame his own myth.... He has become the Texas roughneck, a man who knows the roar of a sandstorm and the despair of a dry well. That he graduated nonetheless from Andover, Yale and Harvard, and that his chosen home of Midland, Tex., is an upper-middle-class place marked by money ache, that he is a millionaire baseball team owner, all this matters little."[73]

The rough and tumble was evident in George Bush's convention film, *The Sky's the Limit*. The goal of the film was three-fold: first, to introduce Americans to George Bush as a man from *Texas*; second, to capture the candidate's casual, thoughtful essence; finally, to dispel any notion that Bush was running for president because of his name or because he desired power —

instead, the film depicted Bush's authentic credentials and his personal commitment to his country.

The George W. Bush of *The Sky's the Limit* was at once humble and aspirational. The common thread throughout the film was home-video-esque footage of the candidate driving around his ranch in a pickup truck with his dog. Bush's media advisor Stuart Stevens said that he wanted to make a film that created intimacy and casual proximity between the viewer and the candidate. "Here you will be very intimate with him. It's like if Governor Bush said, 'Hey, let's ride around for half an hour around the ranch and let's just talk.'" The recurring pickup truck narrative firmly rooted this son of privilege in a more homespun personal history. As Stuart Stevens said, the film was meant to introduce Americans to a different image of George Bush: "A lot of people don't realize that he's from Midland, Texas. They think because he's the son of a President — they assume that he grew up in the White House."[74]

In the opening scene, Bush talked about collecting baseball cards as a small child — sending them off to players writing, "Hello, I'm George Bush from Midland, Texas. Would'ya sign the card and please send it back to me?"[75] It was the story of a regular kid growing up in a small town in Texas. Although Bush attended Phillips Academy in Andover, Yale University, and Harvard University, this part of his personal history was absent from the convention video. Instead, the candidate's mother, Barbara Bush, informed viewers that her son "went to public school and then on to high school."[76]

Giving the film the appeal of authenticity, with a sense of humor and the mien of casual conversation, the producers even included a clip of the candidate jumbling his words. Sitting on the ranch with his wife, Bush broke into an emotional narrative of his life as a father. His twin daughters "just graduated from high school and it just seems like yesterday that we were at the hospital having birth..." at which point George and Laura Bush broke into laughter. Bush couldn't get the words right but laughed at himself anyway, noting, "I like to laugh and I like to laugh with people, and you know sometimes I find myself, you know, I need to laugh at some of the things I say. I'm a person who likes to smile."[77]

From the humble images of Bush at home in his pickup truck in Midland, the film intertwined Bush's "ordinary" life with his dreams for a simpler America, filled with barbeque and baseball. These dreams of Americana moved swiftly into bigger American dreams — Reagan in Berlin, Kennedy's inauguration, and King's "I Have a Dream" speech. In the final minute, the film returned to the pickup truck in Midland, where George Bush was humbled by the opportunity to run for president of such a wonderful country. Expressing his sincere patriotism and sheer love of the "American experience," the final frame featured the candidate driving down a dirt road in the middle of nowhere, America.

Bushisms[78]

The Sky's the Limit was an anti–Beltway film depicting an anti–Beltway candidate. It was successful, in large part, for its depictions of Washington. If Washington was about double-speaking and double-dealing, Bush would be the opposite kind of candidate — plain spoken and straightforward. As Karl Rove revealed to the press, the Republican ticket would benefit from its refreshingly earthy candidate. "Bush comes across as someone who is straightforward and plainspoken, someone who is approachable and likable."[79] A late October *Pew* poll found that Rove had accomplished his task: "The GOP nominee has narrowed the qualifications gap, is seen as more likable, and as more of a straight shooter than his Democratic rival.[80]

In some ways, it was almost comical that Bush was so widely viewed as a straightforward straight-shooter when his language was so often a jumbled mess. "Bushisms" became an easy target and frequent fodder for the commentariat. The New York *Daily News* reprinted its own collection of favorite Bushisms, including the governor's insightful thoughts on poverty: "I know how hard it is for you to put food on your family," and education: "Rarely is the question asked: Is our children learning?"[81] *Slate* magazine offered its readers a special election feature titled "Bushisms of the Week." Each week, *Slate* editors selected a quote (some weeks more than one) directly lifted from George Bush's previous week's speaking engagements. The feature produced numerous gems, such as "I have a different vision of leadership. A leadership is someone who brings people together"[82] and "This is what I'm good at. I like meeting people, my fellow citizens, I like interfacing with them."[83] Multiple media outlets featured contests to rewrite famous quotes in Bush patois with jumbled syntax and mispronounced words.[84]

To his credit, George Bush proved that he could laugh at himself. When he went on the *Tonight Show*, he proved that he was not too proud to poke fun at himself, warning Leno not to light a candle around "highly flammabbabble" material.[85] On *Letterman* in October, Bush joked about his syntax and vocabulary, "A lot of folks don't think I can string a sentence together, so when I was able to do so, it uh — Expectations were so low, all I had to do was say, 'Hi, I'm George W. Bush.'"[86]

All of this made George Bush exceptionally likable to many — a clear natural asset. Even reporters who accused the Bush campaign of running purely on image had to admit that Bush's personality was a real asset. "'He's popular despite the fact that people don't know what he's done.... But people don't just vote on policy. If your position on Social Security is wrong, you can tinker with it. It's very hard for someone to say, 'I'm going to become likable.'"[87]

Thus, the Bush campaign vigorously guarded the contest over likability. Campaigning in San Antonio in July, Bush defended the personality contest: "You know, the presidency is more than just a popularity contest. It involves whether or not you're willing to fight for what's right, whether or not you're willing to spend popularity to do difficult, hard things."[88] He did so, it turns out, for good reason: "Bush knows that if the presidential campaign is contested on his personality against Gore's he wins hands down. Bush has an easy-going manner that seems to endear himself to a large segment of the population.... The problem is the Democratic Party clearly has the upper hand on policy issues that most Americans are concerned about. And after nearly eight years in the White House and unprecedented national prosperity during that time the Democrats, including Al Gore, can claim they know how to govern."[89]

In the absence of other factors, likability did translate into votes. Fred Meyer, the former chairman of the Texas Republican Party, told the *Dallas Morning News* that George W. Bush enjoyed a clear advantage, despite the fact that Gore consistently bested his opponent on every major issue: "It's the old Reagan story.... If you asked a lot of people, they would not have agreed with Ronald Reagan. But they voted for him."[90] In the end, people remembered little of long speeches, but they did remember their impressions of candidates. "'I don't remember policy at the Republican convention, but I do remember the candidate.... The question will be whether the personality of Bush will overcome the desire to vote for the successful policies of the Democrats.'"[91]

Regis and Oprah and ... NASCAR

In an era of talk show campaigning, Bush clearly had an advantage, as he had an outlet to display his personality. Although both campaigns courted the soft media stage, the Bush campaign clearly dominated the venue. As Howard Fineman joked, over the course of the campaign, "the Bushies were ... eager to talk" on "Regis and Oprah, where the man from Texas got all verklempt about his daughters.... The candidates, political princes who were prep-schooled and Ivy–trained, are obsessed with finding new ways to be convincing as regular guys with tender emotions, a good sense of humor, solid families and limitless empathy for average folks."[92]

Early in the campaign, Bush's advisors recommended a media strategy that would include "snapping up every chance to appear on 'non-news' TV shows; hosting their own, Oprah-style sessions in the round and preparing a debate strategy that stresses winsome personality as much as the mastery of briefing-book details.... The Bush campaign has assembled a long, blue-sky list of other possible TV targets: *Saturday Night Live, Baseball Tonight, Monday Night Football, The View*, Rosie and MTV."[93] Clearly reaching voters where they were and where they were most comfortable proved an important advantage for George Bush, whose image voters came to assimilate as common and everyday.

NASCAR was as common, everyday, and American as it got. When Dale Jarrett (of NASCAR fame) arrived at the Republican National Convention, George Bush was already familiar with his sport. As part of his effort to reach voters where they were, Bush made frequent use of the NASCAR circuit during the 2000 campaign. On July 1 in Daytona Beach, Bush embraced the Mecca of his blue-collar base, talking to fans and drivers — the kind of people who (according to Bush) "work for a living." Although he could not possibly have met every fan, they all heard his voice as he was awarded the honor of calling the race to a start: "*Gentlemen...*"[94]

Bush deployed important personal assets where they mattered most — in Florida. Bush's ability to connect to Florida voters (especially Spanish language speakers and the elderly) came largely through his mother and his brother who could authentically connect with old folks and Latinos, respectively. In October, elderly voters in Florida began hearing a recognizable voice on their home answering machines: "Hello, this is Barbara Bush. I'm calling to tell you about my son George W.'s plan to protect Social Security."[95]

Bush made use of another important asset in Florida — his Spanish language base. Although Cuban descendants in Florida had historically been a base for Republican support in Miami-Dade county, Bill Clinton had won about 40 percent of the Cuban vote in 1996, and their vote in 2000 was considered to be up for grabs.[96] More importantly, between 1996 and 2000, the Spanish–speaking population of Florida had increased, mainly due to Mexican immigration. Bush was a Spanish language speaker himself, a skill he employed in Florida and across the Southwest. In Florida he was able to showcase his brother's family (the Jeb Bushes) to highlight his close personal affinity to the Spanish language-speaking community. Bush's sister-in-law, Columba Garnica Gallo, was a Mexican immigrant. Their children had been raised bilingual, and the campaign made several short community-targeted Spanish language spots featuring Bush's nephew, who informed his community that George Bush was a man who was both with and for them.[97]

Conclusions

Alas, not everyone found Bush's Just Plain Folk image appealing. An NPR survey of voters revealed some amount of ambivalence about George Bush. Surprisingly, what most bothered some Independent and Republican-leaning blue-collar voters was not his syntax or cowboy hat, but his display of Bubba–faux. As one former Reagan voter said, George W. Bush was "the kid with the lollipop, golden lollipop in his mouth. He's got Daddy's hundreds of millions of dollars."[98] For those who did cut beneath Bush's patina of Texas dirt, there was something off-putting about an Ivy League son-of-a-president who ran a campaign based on mocking the Washington elite. To those voters, Bush was a man who had enjoyed a great deal of privilege for which he had never been forced to work. As one reporter noted, Bush was a "prep-school boy trying to be blue-collar."[99] While some rural and blue-collar voters found Bush's odd syntax refreshingly real, others wondered about Bush's free ride through Andover and Yale. Similarly, to some "values" voters, Bush's story of rebirth and redemption was inspiring; to others, he was a hypocritical former playboy. Despite these negative evaluations of Bush's inauthenticities, many continued to relate to George W. Bush as a regular guy who reflected their values, understood their lifestyles, and with whom they would enjoy ... drinking a beer. In this way, for many voters the Bush campaign was able to turn Horatio Alger on his head — George W. was just plain folk at heart, even if, by accident of birth, he had been born a Bush.

It was this story line that many in the press opted to repeat. To be sure, Bush was a complicated character, even if he seemed simple-minded. His charm was impossible to avoid, even if reporters sometimes wondered about his down-home authenticity. The dominance of this story line — Bush and Gore's relative and respective authenticity — both in print and on television — consumed readers and viewers in 2000. The 2000 election was so close and so inconclusive that it is difficult to draw conclusions about the result. Instead, perhaps it is more telling to draw conclusions about the campaign. In their 2004 book about the 2000 campaign, *The Press Effect*, Kathleen Hall Jamieson and Paul Waldman argued that reporters' affinity for George Bush (on and off the campaign trail) played a role in shaping the boundaries of national discourse in 2000. On his bus and plane, George Bush frequently mixed it up with reporters, joking, telling stories, and doling out nicknames. By contrast, reporters following Al Gore's campaign received limited access to a candidate who maintained professional reserve at all times. In effect, reporters were pre-conditioned to interpret Al Gore as heavy and wooden and George Bush as an intellectual lightweight. Thus, when selecting quips and clips for television and print stories about the candidates, reporters typically opted to frame the two men within these easily understood stereotypes.

The campaign was not waged in a vacuum. On issues of government spending, economic conditions, and social security, voters had no reason to reject the Clinton-Gore administration. By 2000, however, authenticity had become the single most dominant theme in campaign discourse. Gore's ability to relate to voters was an equally legitimate topic on which to evaluate his candidacy. If there was no definitive conclusion to the election *result* in 2000, perhaps authenticity offers at least a set of terms on which to evaluate the *process* through which voters and journalists evaluated the candidates.

8

Flip-Flopping: 2004

George W. Bush may not have garnered more popular votes than his rival in 2000, but he did manage to prove that a fun-loving, plain-speaking, grammatically challenged Texas "cowboy" could re-define the image of presidentiality. While many could not overlook his syntax, gaffes, and cavalier attitude toward foreign policy, in 2004 voters returned him to the White House ... by an indisputable electoral *and* popular vote margin.

The president's grammar did not improve, but much changed for both the country and George Bush between 2000 and 2004. Together, they weathered the transition to a new posture in the world. The man who loathed foreign policy and "nation-building" pursuits asked for his people's support as he oversaw two ground wars and a rhetorical "war on terrorism." They had not elected him for his diplomatic credentials, but stood behind him as he learned to negotiate the new realities of the twenty-first century. His tenure was to be defined by national security.

There is some evidence to suggest that voters balloted for George Bush on these grounds in 2004. However, the 2004 campaign was not fought on these terms. Instead, authenticity framed the terms of the election, at least on television and on the Internet, and arguably also in the private conversations that comprised the national public discourse.

Indeed, the transformation that took place between 2000 and 2004 was not limited to foreign policy. Although it played a role in the 2000 election, the Internet was still a relatively experimental political medium before 2004. From fundraising to advertising to Election Day GOTV efforts, the Internet created a new terrain for electoral politics in 2004. Campaigns continued to produce traditional spot ads, but in 2004 those ads were outnumbered by Internet appeals and viral videos made not only by the campaigns, but also by outside issue groups and ordinary citizens. Like the campaigns, the traditional media — television, print, and radio — were forced to keep up with citizen journalists, bloggers, and Internet pundits who demanded access to the conversation. They gained that access and, at times in big ways, drove the course of the campaign in 2004.

Another transformation, which had been building since 1988, became full blown in 2004. Americans increasingly situated themselves as participants in the backstage world of the political process. By 2004, they had fully adopted the vocabulary of the political analyst. Rather than reacting to messages personally and discussing their own feelings about the candidates, Americans analyzed their choices the way political professionals do: picking apart candidates' messages, gaffes, margins, and odds. By 2004, it was an entirely new environment. Voters had framed their choices using the grammars of the pundit in 2000. Four years later, lay punditry had consumed election-year discourse.

In the end, Americans returned George Bush to the White House. As polls show, they did not do so because they necessarily agreed with him, but rather because they liked and trusted him more than the other guy. As veteran pollster Stan Greenberg noted in his post-election analysis, "Very important things happened in this election to make Bush's victory possible, but support for the president's approach to domestic and world affairs is not one of them.... Bush asked people to vote their beliefs and feelings, rather than to judge his performance or ideas for the future."[1]

Reporting for Duty

The Democratic challenger was selected for his war hero credentials, which primary voters wagered would make him more "electable" against George Bush in the general election. Beleaguered Democratic primary voters cast off early frontrunner Howard Dean, whom they deemed likable and passionate but ultimately "unelectable," and went for the man who was widely considered to be the most believable hawk of the bunch. He was the safest, most stable, most moderate choice. Caucus-goers in Iowa set the stage, opting for Massachusetts senator Kerry over his more authentic rivals, betting that he was the best choice to beat George Bush. Following the caucus, *Time* yawned that Kerry was "easy to admire but hard to like. The consolation out of Iowa was that maybe it didn't matter if he wasn't all that likable if he's what voters think they need."[2]

A week later New Hampshire's Democrats validated the selection. On January 28, 2004, CNN determined that "Kerry, a decorated Vietnam veteran serving in his fourth term in the Senate ... benefited in New Hampshire by what some voters described as his electability.... Of the 33 percent in exit polls who said a candidate's electability was more important to them than the issues, more than half favored Kerry."³ *Time* chimed in: "Kerry, the statesman, won the people who cared most about beating Bush."⁴

Thus, Democrats selected the "safest" candidate — a former soldier who promoted moderate policies and who had voted for the Iraq War. But he was certainly not the most authentic option, nor the one about whom they felt most passionate. After New Hampshire, other states began to fall in line, and Kerry continued to win 50 percent and more of the "electability" vote. In *Slate*, William Saletan groaned, "Why has Kerry won these contests? Not because voters agree with him on the issues. The reason, according to exit polls, is that voters think he's the candidate most likely to beat President Bush." He continued, "Among voters who picked the candidate *they* wanted based on the issues, not the candidate they thought somebody *else* wanted, Kerry did not win the New Hampshire primary.... In the states that followed, voters applied the same theory to other candidates ... the people who gave Kerry his enormous vote tally in Missouri — and nearly two-thirds of the state's delegates — were the 'can defeat Bush' voters, who went for Kerry over Edwards by a ratio of more than 3 to 1.... In Arizona ... he crushed Clark among 'can defeat Bush' voters.... In Oklahoma, both Clark and Edwards beat Kerry by 13 points among 'agrees with you' voters, but Kerry got away with a competitive finish by thumping them among 'can defeat Bush' voters."⁵

What was intriguing about voting on "electability" was not that Democratic voters got it wrong by going "safe," but the extent to which political processes, once the domain of smoke-filled backroom pros, had entered into the voters' consciousness and decision making. By 2004, everyone was an analyst, pundit, and commentator. MTV's *Choose or Lose* broke it down for its audience this way: "Though endlessly examining candidates' strategizing, positioning and polling numbers was once the exclusive domain of political junkies, primary voters are now taking on the roll of election analyst. Issues are taking a back seat to the more high-maintenance task of determining "electability" — can a particular candidate win the general election in November?"⁶

Purple Hearts

Democratic primary voters were not the only ones who thought John Kerry could capitalize on a war hero biography and moderate platform. Early on, the Kerry campaign opted to contrast its bona fide veteran with the president. A Vietnam War veteran, John Kerry had received two Purple Hearts for his wartime service. Challenging a man whose Vietnam War service was shady at best, Kerry offered himself as a real war hero who could bring honor to American conflicts abroad.

Kerry did attempt to construct an "authentic" image in the war hero tradition. To Kerry's campaign, this image alone, particularly in a time of war, was an indisputable brand of American authenticity. As a result, the first spots produced by the campaign structured John Kerry's biography completely around his service — military and political — to showcase the senator as a believable commander in chief.

The tagline "a lifetime of service and strength" framed Kerry's personal biography. What Kerry told Americans, however, did not seem exceptionally personal (or relatable) to them. What they learned was that John Kerry "had a lot of privileges ... to go to a great university like Yale" and was driven by noblesse oblige to volunteer for service as an officer in the Naval Reserves. A professional narrator summed it up for viewers: "For more than thirty years, John Kerry has served America." The spot did include personal advocates — Kerry's daughter, Vanessa, and wife, Teresa, but neither offered much by way of a personal touch. His daughter added only items already on the professional résumé: "If you look at my father's time in service to this country, whether it's as a veteran, prosecutor, or senator, he has shown an ability to fight for things that matter."[7] The downfall was that Americans got to know very little about the Democratic challenger personally before the opposition began branding him.

Because the early campaign strategy staked its claim to presidentiality on Kerry's Vietnam War service almost exclusively, Kerry's opponents needed only to revisit his service record, and his subsequent anti-war activism, in order to undermine his authenticity. On May 4, 2004, an independent organization called Swift Boat Veterans for Truth organized to dispute Kerry's record. Using the Internet (and a well-timed book, *Unfit for Command: Swift Boat Veterans Speak Out Against John Kerry*, published in August 2004), the group sought to challenge, undercut, and ultimately turn Kerry's claims about his service in the war against him.

The Swift Boat Veterans charged that Kerry used his Vietnam War service only for the purpose of image and self-promotion and that he "misrepresented his service in Vietnam and lied about his claims of atrocities committed." According to the Swift Boat Vets, Kerry was "a liar and a fraud" who "invented 'atrocities' for his personal and political gain."[8] They took their case to the Internet, launching ads that, to some, seemed to tell a more authentic story, as they were produced by citizens, rather than self-promoting politicians. Their videos achieved instant mass penetration, completely upending the discourse around Kerry's image. The narrative forced the Kerry campaign to defend the candidate's war service and authenticity rather than reach out to voters and promote a positive image.

Although many did not buy the Swift Vets' story in full, the establishing narratives they told about Kerry created the dominant frame for his image: he was a political opportunist and self-promoting politician. In one story, the Swift Boat Vets charged that John Kerry appeared at their reunion only because it made a great photo op. When other veterans refused to participate in the publicity session, Kerry grabbed his few supporters in the group, snapped some pictures for promotional materials, and left before the group could get to the real business of the reunion: memorializing their fallen comrades.[9] And many were willing to accept this part of the story: Kerry dishonorably promoted his service in order to win votes. He turned his medals and fellow veterans into political commodities for the purpose of personal gain.

To those on the fence about Kerry, these charges were believable because he seemed more politician than human. As a candidate, he did not project sincerity, passion, conviction, or emotion. In one of the hokier moments in American political oratory, Kerry opened his 2004 convention speech with the line, "I'm John Kerry and I'm [dramatic pause] reporting for duty!" It was meant to reference the discrepancies between his own voluntary Vietnam War service and the president's intermittent National Guard duty. Even as the reference drew a cheer from Democrats gathered in the convention hall in Boston, on television he seemed staged and insincere. And this wooden insincerity was not limited to major events with large audiences. As Richard Corliss wrote, "Kerry talks with an interviewer as if he were addressing millions from the Washington Mall; Reagan chatted to the world as if it were his neighbor."[10]

Flip-Flops

The most enduring image of the 2004 campaign was the flip-flop. Many voters, including Democrats, feared that John Kerry lacked strong convictions. They could understand how a Vietnam War veteran returned home to become an anti-war activist, but his more recent positions seemed to lack staying power. Early in the Democratic primary campaign season, for example, Howard Dean gained traction for his solid anti-war position. The other candidates began shifting their posture on the war. As a senator, Kerry had voted for the war. He mitigated his position, engaging in a bit of rhetorical gymnastics, to please the primary voters. But without a knack for pith and the gift of charisma, it was difficult for Kerry to explain his nuanced positions and complicated vote history to a sound-bite-obsessed media. In his most famous "flip-flop," the senator tried to explain his decision to vote against an $87 billion Iraq War funding bill. When accused of endangering American soldiers by leaving them under-funded and poorly armored, Kerry responded: "I actually did vote for the $87 billion before I voted against it." It was technically true, and Kerry had important reasons for withholding support as a matter of funding. However, what most Americans heard was a linguistic Chinese finger trap: "I voted for it before I voted against it."

In his Republican National Convention speech, Dick Cheney summed it up for the blood-thirsty, chum-hungry crowd: "Senator Kerry has disagreed with many of his fellow Democrats. But his liveliest disagreement is with himself." In full-throated response, the crowd at the convention began chanting, "flip-flop! flip-flop!" Cheney continued, "Senator Kerry says he sees two Americas. It makes the whole thing mutual. America sees two John Kerrys." The crowd cheered wildly and the chants continued throughout the convention.[11]

At the same event, entrepreneurial vendors sold Kerry flip-flops, each shoe offering a different opinion. Throughout the summer and fall of 2004, heckling pairs of oversized, anthropomorphized sandals haunted John Kerry's campaign events. A man who supposedly wanted to have it both ways and more, taking positions for political expedience rather than his own strong convictions, Kerry could not catch a break from the taunting summer footwear. The Bush campaign had captured the perfect image for many voters. And it stuck.

Kerry did not seem to have a single position or a straight answer for anything: did he burn his Purple Heart medals during anti–Vietnam War protests, as he said at the time? If so, how could he rightfully use them for political gain? Was Kerry for or against the Iraq War? He had voted against authorizing mobilization for the first Gulf War — arguing that it gave the president unlimited and unchecked authority — but had voted in favor of giving President George W. Bush far more unlimited and unchecked power to invade Iraq. He had supported the No Child Left Behind Act when it was popular and expedient to do so, but when voters turned against it, he switched his position.

Kerry's flip-flopping became so embedded as a theme, it was taken as fact in the popular media. In its opening sketch of the 2004 season, *Saturday Night Live* presented a mock debate between Bush and Kerry. Will Forte portrayed Bush as a casual but flippant and dim-witted president. Seth Meyers depicted John Kerry as a robotic talking machine who did not have a handle on normal human expressions, making stiff and exaggerated gestures, waving his arms in an unnatural way. More cutting was *SNL*'s analysis of Kerry's consistency:

[Seth Meyers:] You know, this President likes to talk about how I called Iraq the wrong war at the wrong place at the wrong time. Then a few days later, how I say that anyone who doesn't think the world is a safer place without Saddam Hussein, is not fit to be Commander in Chief. But what he doesn't tell you is that when I denounced the war in Iraq, I was speaking to an anti-war group. And when I endorsed the war, I was addressing a pro-war delegation from the UGA. The fact of the matter is I have consistently supported the war in front of pro-war audiences, and condemned it when speaking to groups that oppose it. That is not flip-flopping, that is pandering! And America deserves a President who knows the difference. Thank you.[12]

Saturday Night Live was not the only popular show to point out Kerry's game of political limbo. The challenger's lack of strong convictions and inconsistency became *the* story about John Kerry. In a monologue on his show, David Letterman presented it this way:

You know, there's a lot of talk about John Kerry, who's running for president, and a lot of people say that he takes one side of an issue, and then a couple of weeks later, if it's politically beneficial, he'll take the other side of the issue. They're accusing him of flipping and flopping, and I think that that's just part of life, but in politics there is no greater sin to commit than flip-flopping on the issues.... Especially when they're important issues. As a matter of fact, did you see the C-Span? They were voting ... the Senate was voting today on an issue. Watch this. I think you'll find it fascinating.
   [COMEDY SKETCH] Mr. Kennedy? Mr. Kennedy votes no. Mr. Kerry? Mr. Kerry votes no. Wait, now, Mr. Kerry votes yes. Okay, now he says no. Back to yes. Now back to no.[13]

On the *Tonight Show*, Jay Leno quipped, "We make jokes about it, but the truth is this presidential election really offers us a choice of two well-informed opposing positions on every issue. OK, they both belong to John Kerry, but they're still there."[14] As *Saturday Night Live's* Amy Pohler joked, "Kerry scored many points with voters and pundits by finally putting to rest criticism that he's a flip-flopper. Kerry said, 'I have one position on Iraq: I'm for-gainst it.'"[15]

   It was clear that this framework had become central to the story about John Kerry. Late night comedy programs thrive on diverse audiences — including many viewers who do not follow political events closely. In order for these jokes to be presented with little context, comedians had to be sure that their audiences would get the joke. Thus, this image of Kerry had become so pervasive that even late night comedians took it for granted. These jokes were also powerful — they reinforced this frame for much wider audiences. Soon, "flip-flopping" became John Kerry's brand.

   As a result, when video cameras captured John Kerry windsurfing during a late summer vacation on the Cape, the image was not framed by Kerry's athleticism, but rather by his flip-flopping. The media pounced on the image. Jay Leno joked, "You see the pictures in the paper today of John Kerry wind-surfing? He's at his home in Nantucket this week, doing his favorite thing, windsurfing. Even his hobby depends on which way the wind blows."[16] The Bush campaign quickly followed with a paid television spot called "Wind-surfing." In the spot, Kerry was shown windsurfing back and forth in different directions. Each time Kerry changed directions, the narrator highlighted one of Kerry's alleged "flip-flops."

> NARRATOR: In which direction would John Kerry lead? Kerry voted for the Iraq war, opposed it, supported it and now opposes it again. [TEXT: Iraq War; Supported; Opposed]
>
> He bragged about voting for the eighty-seven billion to support our troops before he voted against it. [TEXT: $87 Billion for Our Troops; Supported; Opposed]
>
> He voted for education reform and now opposes it. [TEXT: Education Reform; Supported; Opposed]
>
> He claims he's against increasing Medicare premiums but voted five times to do so. [TEXT: Increasing Medicare Premiums; Supported; Opposed]
>
> John Kerry: whichever way the wind blows.[17]

The Authenticity Gap

The video footage not only offered the perfect analogy for flip-flop politics, but also illustrated an off-putting East Coast, Vineyard Vines, Cape Cod elitism. John F. Kennedy might have roused awe and inspiration with video footage of his sailing excursions, but in 2004, midwesterners did not assimilate images of a windsurfing candidate in any desirable way. At best, the image elicited a confused, "huh?" Many Americans received the footage as an illustration of all that was wrong with the East Coast elite. If the campaign meant to emasculate the floundering senator, it succeeded. More likely, if the campaign meant to show that John Kerry was a laid back and sporting kind of guy, it failed miserably. As George Bush cleared brush on his ranch in Texas, John Kerry was splashing around on Nantucket.

By early fall, Kerry could not do or say anything that did not seem staged and inauthentic. Even many Democrats felt more passionately about voting against the president than voting for the man they had chosen. As the media (new and traditional) began to pick Kerry apart, the Democrat became defined by an image that was increasingly staged, unnatural, and insincere. Early in the primaries, rumors began circulating that Kerry had received Botox treatments. While not a pressing "issue" debate, even the Grey Lady found it fit to report. *New York Times* columnist Maureen Dowd mused, "How could we elect a president who couldn't show his emotions?"[18]

The obsession with Kerry's personal image did not end there. When John Kerry arrived for the first debate with an orange-tinted tan, the media immediately scrutinized the authenticity of his questionably bronzed skin. The press picked him apart, interviewing "experts" on the subject and displaying before-and-after pictures for television viewers and newspaper readers. "Mr. Kerry surprised campaign-watchers this week by turning up with a sudden, orangey-bronze glow — one that beauty experts say is highly unlikely to be the real deal. 'John Kerry's tan is temporary — just like people say his opinions are,' said Cynthia House, CEO of Enhance Me, a brand of spray-on tanning products. 'I don't know what they tanned him with, but it's an artificial tan. They went a little overboard.'"[19] Reports about Kerry's manufactured face were so widespread that even the most die-hard Democrats had to wonder about the tin man's orange-tinged skin.

As in many elections, 2004 also prompted a direct comparison between the wives of the candidates. Their images, interpreted within frameworks of femininity, served to bolster previously established ideas about their husbands. Laura Bush was depicted as an innocuous woman with a sweet smile, a soft voice, and a big heart. She liked children's books and cookbooks and charity. By contrast, Teresa Heinz-Kerry was foreign. Literally. She was also strong, smart, and independent. She wore pants and spoke seven languages. Often depicted as cold and calculating, she did little to help her husband alter the terms of the contest for authenticity.

These images stuck with voters. When a focus group of swing voters was asked why they hesitated to vote for John Kerry, they responded, "He flip-flops." "Yeah, it's the trust, there's no consistency." "Lack of conviction, flip-flopping, going with what the public wants." "Consistency." "At least I know where Bush stands."[20] Other respondents said, "He's a politician." "Wishy-washy, votes only when circumstance is favorable." "He doesn't have his own stand on things. He says what you want to hear." "Just listening to him talk." "Don't like his wife, billionaire heiress." Even among Kerry supporters, respondents noted, "He flip-flops on every issue."[21] And it mattered. In its 2004 post-election survey, the non-profit polling group, Democracy Corps, found that the biggest single reason voters doubted John Kerry was "flip-flopping."[22]

At some point, voters had difficulty believing and trusting him because they felt they did not know him — he was cold and aloof, strange and unknown. "One reason the flip-flop charge has stuck is that Kerry, with his meandering, caveat-filled speaking style, often seems like a guy trying to avoid a straight answer.... As a result, while Kerry leads Bush on most domestic issues, voters turn sour when asked about Kerry the man. In last week's *Time* poll, Kerry's biggest deficit versus Bush was in 'sticking to his positions.' Only 37% of registered voters in the survey said Kerry does that, compared with 84% for Bush."[23]

Mission Accomplished

A September 2004 Zogby/Williams Identity Poll of undecided voters found that 57 percent would rather have a beer with President Bush than Senator John Kerry. The poll's questionable methodology aside, the result is less than shocking. As *USA Today* reported, "President Bush, despite his many problems, strikes most of the American people as a pretty nice guy — the kind of guy they would feel comfortable with if he showed up at their front door. The more standoffish Kerry projects little warmth.... While both were raised with silver spoons in their mouths and both went to Yale, Bush comes off as less pretentious and more down to earth. Kerry sounds like he is lecturing people rather than holding a conversation with them.... 'Snob' is a word often used by people when asked how Kerry strikes them. 'Nice guy' is the way many express their response to Bush."[24]

In any other year, George Bush would have faced long odds for reelection. He began his presidency under a cloud of illegitimacy. By 2004, the economy was sluggish. At the time of the election, only 34 percent of the population gave the economy a rating of "good" or "excellent." More importantly, by a significant margin, Americans did not believe that the economy was going to improve.

Half of those surveyed believed the economy was going to get worse, while only 39 percent believed that the economy was going to get better. The president's policies — particularly the Iraq War — were not incredibly popular in 2004. Approval of the war had dipped below 50 percent in 2004, and continued to drop. In the summer of 2004, for the first time, a majority of Americans began to say that the Iraq War had made the country "less safe from terrorism."[25]

Finally, in the year leading up to the election, the president's approval rating rarely hit the 50 percent mark; on Election Day, his approval stood just below 50 percent.[26] For comparison, at the same point in their presidencies, Bill Clinton's approval rating was 54 percent, Ronald Reagan's 58 percent.[27]

Just Plain Folk

The election was about more than policies, the war, and the economy, and this was highlighted in the media as in no previous election. Across mediums, just as John Kerry was fictionalized as an overly stilted, long-winded, inconsistent version of himself, George W. Bush was reduced to a caricature of a flippant and dim-witted, but ultimately plain-spoken, casual, likable, and ordinary guy. As Minnesota governor Tim Pawlenty said in his endorsement of the president, "President Bush is authentic. What you see is what you get."[28] As previous chapters have shown, it is difficult for a sitting president to remain "in touch" and "connected" to ordinary Americans. While his critics might have believed that his policies were "out of touch" with ordinary Americans' lives, as a person, many Americans continued to assimilate images of the president as "just plain folk." The campaign captured this and, at every opportunity, highlighted the personal differences between the president and his opponent.

To highlight his "just plain folk" credentials, the paid Bush campaign spots opened with the president's approval line, often delivered by the president on his ranch in Texas. These images showed the president and his wife, Laura Bush, leaning up against a rustic post, with the ranch in the background. While many of the 2004 Bush spots focused on the threat of terrorism and the challenger's inauthenticity, several ads produced by the campaign also aimed to remind voters that Bush was simultaneously a powerful president and human person.

To that end, George Bush made the rounds on talk shows, and was the first sitting president to appear on a daytime talk show, shooting an interview with his wife for *Dr. Phil* in September 2004. The show was not about policies or politics. It was about George Bush, father and husband. Dr. Phil and his wife, Robin, filmed the show at the president's ranch in Crawford. As the show's publicist noted, "We're not talking about Iraq."[29] The *Washington Post* ran this preview: "Today on the *Dr. Phil* show, voters can find out all sorts of unusual tidbits about their president, such as: Did Papa Bush spank Jenna and Barbara when they were little? How did Daddy feel when Jenna stuck out her tongue at reporters? And does Dr. Phil have any advice for the president on how to keep his 'Family First' while on the campaign trail?"[30] Viewers also learned about important matters of state — for example, that Jenna and Barbara Bush were sent to their rooms as punishment ("We were 'in-your-roomers,' as in 'get to your rooms.'") and that Jenna Bush was "working on her impulsiveness." As for his daughters' futures, George Bush said only that he hoped they would marry "someone I can go fishing with."[31]

In this way, to many voters, the president was able to remain grounded in a human life that was not completely framed by the White House. Some of his supporters even appreciated his verbal fumbling, believing he seemed more natural, less scripted, and more authentic. As a result, in a September 2004 Pew survey, George Bush beat John Kerry on every characteristic related to authenticity. More than half (56%) said that George Bush seemed like a "real person, not a politician."[32] Almost as many (54 percent) said that Bush didn't "over-complicate issues." Not surprisingly, Bush beat Kerry by a ten-point margin on which candidate seemed more "down to earth."[33]

If You Can't Vote for Me, Vote Against Him

However, the same Pew survey also revealed that voters largely did not agree with the president's policies.[34] As a result, aside from some conservative red meat for the flag-waving base, George Bush's reelection campaign was about John Kerry. Bush's policies were not overwhelmingly popular and, finding weakness in the opposition, the Bush team opted to run against Kerry rather than for Bush.

By 2004, support for the Iraq War had atrophied significantly. In July 2004, nearly half of all Americans said that "the Bush administration deliberately misled the American public about whether Iraq has weapons of mass destruction."[35] A majority (54 percent) said that "sending troops to Iraq" was "a mistake."[36] As *USA Today* reported, "Many Americans are uneasy about the war in Iraq and the mounting death toll. But polls show they trust Bush more than Kerry.... A lot of that has to do with personality. If they like you, Americans will give you the benefit of a doubt when things go bad. How else can we explain why Bush is hanging in there and even pulling ahead in the polls when the news over the past eight months has been so bad?"[37] As Jon Stewart joked, "With the economy still struggling, combat operations in Iraq dragging on, and the 9–11 hearings revealing damning information, even an opponent of limited political skill should be able to capitalize on those problems. The Democrats, however, chose to nominate John Kerry."[38]

Conclusions

Even as many images of authenticity remained stagnant and stable in 2004, the meanings of these images were contested on a new terrain. In 2004, the battle between competing images of presidentiality was fought, debated, and projected via the Internet. Between 2000 and 2004, the American media landscape changed dramatically. Voters increasingly accessed information from nontraditional sources, largely Internet–based media. In 2000, a Pew survey found that 9 percent of respondents regularly accessed information about the presidential campaign from the Internet.[39] By 2008, nearly a quarter of respondents reported learning about presidential candidates primarily from Internet–based sources.[40] Although the numbers were relatively small in proportion to traditional news sources, such as evening news programs and Sunday morning talk shows, the shifting source of origin for campaign news, from traditional media to the Internet, yielded a yet untold impact on American politics.[41] The advent of the Internet fundamentally altered voters' expectations of their political candidates. Candidates would need to become more available, more responsive, more open to new voices in the process.

Graying white men owned the image of political journalism through the 1980s. Still graying and now balding in the 1990s, these men were joined, with equal legitimacy, by daytime talk show hosts who preferred the grammars of pop psychology to those of political theory. In 2004, bloggers, citizen journalists, and kids with wireless connectivity demanded equal access to political topics, if not politicians themselves. While the networks were still dominated by aging men on Sunday mornings, new topics, new vocabularies, and new questions demanded their attention. Much of the debate in 2004 focused around "viral" information — Internet rumors, YouTube videos, and electronically disseminated documents. Debuting online, rumors about George Bush's National Guard service, the whereabouts of John Kerry's Purple Hearts, and the academic records of both candidates came to command the attention of traditional media.

It is important to note the extent to which the candidates, the press, and the people discussed candidate image in 2004 using the vocabulary of authenticity. To supporters, George Bush was consistent, honest, and earthy. He was straightforward and plain-spoken. To detractors, he had lied about his National Guard service, his personal history, and the Iraq War. He was an Eli playing at cowboy, manipulating rural Baptists and blue-collar hawks. To his supporters, John Kerry was a soothsayer trying to save the country from a dangerous president. He was a genuine war hero who cared more about his country than himself. To his detractors, John Kerry lied about (or at least embellished) his war record for self-serving political ends. He was the guy who attempted to trick voters with a chemical spray-tan substance, altering his physical image to seem more youthful and attractive. He was a Beltway establishment figure who left the nation's capital only to return to the liberal capital — Boston.

By 2004, the media had begun to pick up on the trend of authenticity and reported on it more regularly. George Bush was returned to the White

House for a second term, but the campaign in 2004 paved the way for an entirely new kind of election — one where the Internet was more influential than print, and one in which "authenticity" was the most dominant framework through which candidates were judged.

Conclusion

I began thinking about this book in early 2008. I was living on the New Hampshire seacoast where, just three miles from my house, Hillary Clinton mounted a comeback on the force of an emotional display at a café in Portsmouth. I had watched the media dissect images of the ordained establishment frontrunner with a critical eye. Chris Matthews, Tucker Carlson, and others employed gendered vocabularies of another time to mediate Clinton for their audiences. So, after her teary display in my own neighborhood, I was eager to hear what the punditocracy would make of the newly vulnerable Clinton. The great irony of Clinton's candidacy was that, despite the fact that she was the only female in the race, she was disadvantaged by a political culture that had become thoroughly feminized (in its hyperpersonalized content and talk show media formats).[1] As a woman, her campaign wagered that she needed to be more serious, more knowledgeable, more expert, less personal, and less emotional than her male opponents. At a time when rewards go to the most emotionally available and personally authentic contender, Clinton was running a losing strategy.

Clinton's fortunes did change when she opened up at that café in Portsmouth. Whether genuine or staged, the women in New Hampshire responded to the display, and their votes tipped the balance in the first primary of 2008. More troubling, however, was the debate that ensued in the aftermath of Clinton's emotional admission. The authenticity of the moment was challenged by most in the media. Take two examples from opposite ends of the political spectrum: On New Hampshire primary night, Bill Kristol explained, "It's the tears. She pretended to cry, the women felt sorry for her, and she won." And in her *New York Times* column, "Can Hillary Cry Her Way Back to the White House?," Maureen Dowd wrote:

> When I walked into the office Monday, people were clustering around a computer to watch what they thought they would never see: Hillary Clinton with the unmistakable look of tears in her eyes.

A woman gazing at the screen was grimacing, saying it was bad. Three guys watched it over and over, drawn to the "humanized" Hillary. One reporter who covers security issues cringed. "We are at war," he said. 'Is this how she'll talk to Kim Jong-il?"

Another reporter joked: "That crying really seemed genuine."[2]

Clinton's human authenticity was so thoroughly dissected by the media that it became the central frame for her candidacy. In time, Barack Obama faced his own battle for authenticity, as his claim to American authenticity was picked apart, beaten down, and torn up over questions about his birth certificate, religion, and alleged radical politics. Much of this debate entered into the mainstream media, but much of it also originated online.

By 2008, the electronic squawkers, talkers, and bloggers could not (would not) be ignored. These new interrogators, debaters, and video producers made themselves central to the debate. They produced their own campaign commercials ("I've Got a Crush on Obama"), asked their own YouTube debate questions (albeit mediated by the debate producers), and created their own candidate images ("Hope" by Shepard Fairey).

These new participants and opinion-makers often dabbled in the inane, but they also cared about the integrity of the process. As much as authenticity in 2008 came to reflect an aggressively blue-collar, assertively Palin-esque anti-elitism, it also meant access to the image-making process. The political backstage is often referred to as a sausage factory. Here *The Jungle* provides a crude, but serviceable example. In 2008, voters did not just want to eat the sausage — more than ever, they wanted to judge and police and gain access to the process through which it was made. They wanted to hear from David Axelrod as well as Barack Obama. They wanted to know about the poll numbers as much as the election results. They wanted to watch Barack Obama get ready for the big speech as much as they wanted to hear it delivered. As the Internet comes to dominate politics, it is likely that these new voices and new demands will gain increasing legitimacy.

It is impossible to determine what the advent of electronic media will mean in the future. If 2008 offers any predictions, it is likely that the Internet will make campaigns more authentic: more narcissistic, more scopophilic, and more democratic. Narcissism is an obvious part of the new media. It is clear that Twitter feeds, Facebook posts, blogs, and the self-indulgences of other fame-seeking, navel-gazing Internet pursuits have heightened and legitimized American self-probing. In that kind of world, there is potential for increased demands on "just like me" campaigning. Narcissism's reverse impulse, socopohilia, is an obvious product of the Internet. Users demand ever more access to the private and personal lives of public figures. From

Barack Obama to Rielle Hunter, the Internet offers an opportunity for access that cannot (will not) be denied.[3] Americans follow celebrity Twitter feeds and blogs, demanding more and more access to the personal thoughts of, and mundane details about, public figures.

The Internet, however, is also an incredible tool of democracy. More voices may mean that political topics are diluted, but it also means that there is less mediation between voters and office-seekers. Barack Obama was able to win the money campaign long before he won the actual election — Americans voted online in ones and fives by huge numbers. The YouTube debate offered voters (not only those lucky enough to access a prized seat in the audience) an opportunity to ask their own questions of the candidates. Free web-publishing offers citizen journalists an opportunity to make and analyze news. It is impossible to predict, but it is likely that we are at the dawn of a new age of authenticity.

Chapter Notes

Preface

1. Joseph Biden, Aug. 23, 2008, Springfield, Ill.

2. It would be much simpler to argue that the "boundaries of 'real America'" were drawn politically. In recent years, conservatism has become a popular topic for historians, sociologists, and political scientists. This book takes a decidedly anti-ideological approach. While popular discourse, election results, and the American National Election Studies survey data all indicate a rise in conservatism in the second half of the twentieth century, I contend that, regardless of the popularity of conservative ideas, conservatives have been more adept at adopting the *cultural* language of "real America." In this way, the boundaries of "real America" were not merely ideological, but rather drawn geographically, culturally, and socio-economically. I have contextualized and defined "real" America as an anti-elitist, anti-intellectual, anti–East, anti–Washington worldview. While this book focuses on the contemporary causes and effects of anti-intellectualism, this is not a new topic. In 1962, the historian Richard Hofstadter located its presence as part of the American tradition. Some 130 years earlier, the French visitor Alexis de Tocqueville also identified a particularly and peculiarly American brand of anti-intellectualism. Thus, while anti-intellectualism and anti-elitism are clearly constitutive to one strain of thinking about America and Americans, I focus on its incarnation in recent years, aided by the forces of mass culture, neopopulism, postmodernism, and the vocabulary of the culture wars.

3. In *See How They Ran*, Gil Troy articulated a constant binary between the forces of republicanism and the lure of democracy. He argued that, more often than not, voters preferred the popular (populist) democratic candidate over more stately republican choices. Gil Troy, *See How They Ran: The Changing Role of the Presidential Candidate* (Cambridge, MA: Harvard University Press, 1996).

4. It is tempting to condemn this style of political participation as ignorant, careless, and uninformed. In the course of conducting research for this book, I returned to Richard Hofstadter's *Anti-intellectualism in American Life*. Although Hofstadter's thesis appears more prescient and potent than ever, I nonetheless opted against including Hofstadter as a major source for this project. While this book is very much about the personalization and emotionalization of American political behavior, for the most part, I have deferred to my subjects, trying to understand their choices, rather than criticize the results. In examining anti-rationality, I also turned to Susan Jacoby's 2008 book, *The Age of American Unreason*. In her introduction, Jacoby wrote, "During the past four decades, America's endemic anti-intellectual tendencies have been grievously exacerbated by a new species of semiconscious anti-rationalism, feeding on and fed by an ignorant popular culture of video images and unremitting noise that leaves no room for contemplation or logic.... This condition is aggressively promoted by ... politicians ... whose livelihood depends on a public that derives its opinions from sound bites ... and it is passively accepted by a public in thrall to the serpent promising effortless enjoyment from the fruit of the tree of infotainment." See Susan Jacoby, *The Age of American Unreason* (New York: Pantheon Books, 2008), p. xx. Admittedly, this book is about all of these things. It thrives on infotainment, sound bites, and celebrity culture. Nonetheless, the historian must not condemn historical actors. I do not sit in judgment of the historical subjects and objects analyzed in this book. Instead, I have tried to understand why, how, and when American political priorities evolved.

5. Kathleen Hall Jamieson and Paul Waldman, *The Press Effect* (New York: Oxford University Press, 2004), p. 29.

6. Drew Westen, *The Political Brain* (New York: PublicAffairs, 2007), p. 208.

7. Arthur H. Miller, Martin P. Wattenberg, and Oksana Malanchuk, "Schematic Assessments of Presidential Candidates," *American Political Science Review* 80 (June 1986): 183.

8. Hacker, ed., *Presidential Candidate Images* (Lanham, MD: Rowman & Littlefield, 2004), p. 2.

9. By identifying this project as a study in can-

didate image, I do not to suggest that issues do not matter. As political scientists have moved away from the issues versus image binary, they have discovered the ways in which issue content and image projection interact in campaign discourse. "The sustained bifurcation of issue and persona perceptions has led researchers to neglect the ways in which messages about multiple types of candidate image content and how various forms of content affect each other and are interrelated" (Hacker, Zakahi, Giles, and McQuitty, "Components of Candidate Images: Statistical Analysis of the Issue-Persona Dichotomy in the Presidential Campaign of 1966," *Communication Monographs* 67: 236). Indeed, a candidate's positions on particular issues — his ability to articulate those positions and his passion for them — is a factor in the construction of candidate image. "When voters are presented with issue content, they habitually infer image-based judgments" (Louden and McCauliffe, "The 'Authentic Candidate': Extending Candidate Image Assessment," in Hacker, ed., *Presidential Candidate Images*, p. 89). See also Kenneth Hacker's quantitative analysis of message reception in which Hacker argued that voters receive campaign messages through a dual-processing model — issue positions and traits. Both tracts of reception result in the formation of candidate image (Hacker, ed., *Presidential Candidate Images*, p. 89).

10. Richard W. Boyd, "Presidential Elections: An Explanation of Voting Defection," *American Political Science Review* 63 (June 1969): 498–515.

11. Nimmo and Savage, *Candidates and Their Images: Concepts, Methods and Findings* (Reading: Scott Foresman, 1976).

12. For major research on the importance of image between 1976 and 1990, see James Campbell, "Jimmy Carter and the Rhetoric of Charisma," *Central States Speech Journal* 30: 174–186. See also Barry Brummet, "Gastronomic References, Synecdoche, and Political Images," *Quarterly Journal of Speech* 67: 138–145.

13. Kathleen Kendall and Scott Paine, "Political Images and Voting Decisions," in *Candidate Images in Presidential Elections*, ed. Kenneth Hacker (Westport, CT: Praeger, 1995).

14. William L. Benoit and John P. McHale, "Presidential Candidates' Personal Qualities: Computer Content Analysis," in Hacker, ed., *Presidential Candidate Images*, p. 51.

15. William L. Benoit and John P. McHale, "Presidential Candidates' Personal Qualities: Computer Content Analysis," in Hacker, ed., *Presidential Candidate Images*, p. 51.

16. Kendall and Paine, "Political Images and Voting Decisions," in Hacker, ed., *Candidate Images in Presidential Elections*.

17. Dan Nimmo, "The Formation of Candidate Images during Presidential Campaigns," in Hacker, ed., *Candidate Images in Presidential Elections*.

18. Dan Nimmo, "Political Image Makers and the Mass Media," *Annals of the American Academy*

of Political and Social Science 427, no. 33–44: 36.

19. Dwight Davis, "Issues Information and Connotation in Candidate Imagery: Evidence from a Laboratory Experiment," *International Political Science Review* 2: 461–479.

20. Alan Louden, "Image in the 1992 Presidential Campaign," in Denton, ed., *The 1992 Presidential Campaign*, p. 170.

21. Louden and McCauliffe, "The 'Authentic Candidate': Extending Candidate Image Assessment," in Hacker, ed., *Presidential Candidate Images*, p. 86.

Note on Sources

1. While I give equal time to the assumed publics of particular campaign messages as I do to the messages themselves, this book offers a woefully inadequate representation of the ways in which different publics may have received different messages differently. I do examine the polysemy of particular campaign media, but largely without regard for diverse communities of viewership. That is, alas, a topic for another project.

2. Several studies have examined the importance of campaign messaging on voters' evaluations of candidates' personalities. Extensive examination of the correlation between media expenditure and voting behavior has shown the effectiveness of campaign advertisements. See, for example, Wanat, "Political Broadcast Advertising and Primary Election Voting," *Journal of Broadcasting* 18 (1974); and Patterson and McClure, "Television News and Political Advertising: The Impact of Exposure on Voter Beliefs," *Communication Research* 1 (1974).

3. In *Media Messages in American Presidential Elections*, Diana Owen offered a model for analyzing voters' responses to and perceptions of candidate images and messages using analysis of multiple sources.

4. "Man-on-the-street" interviews conducted for television and print news are not wholly reliable, but do give a glimpse into voters' sentiments about candidates. To be sure, parsing these sources is difficult, as voters tended to highlight issues during these interviews, as tangible evidence to justify their more nuanced feelings about candidates. Nonetheless, increasingly throughout this period, voters did identify intangibles, for example "he represents me" and even invoked the vocabulary of authenticity to describe their voting patterns.

5. The post–1980 Deaver, Hannaford, and Nofziger files are closed.

6. Although Al Gore did not invent it, the Internet existed prior to the 1996 election. Nonetheless, it was not until 2000 that a significant number of voters began to interact with the medium on a regular basis as part of their daily consumption of information. In many ways, however, the 2000 election exists as a threshold cycle, where younger voters used the Internet as their primary medium,

while older voters continued to rely primarily on traditional sources of information. Internet platforms and web-based media did not yet precipitate campaign dialogue. By 2004, however, web-based media not only commanded voters' attention, but also began to drive mainstream news discourse. Internet rumors, blogs, and web-based videos became so viral as to consume mainstream print and television news sources. Take, for example, two conflicted and conflict-based issues in the 2004 campaign: George Bush's draft record and John Kerry's antiwar record. Both of these gained traction first on the Internet, before becoming major topics in the established press. As the Internet became the major source of information, it also became a forum for democratic dialogue, where voters could interact with one another and with their candidates. By 2008, campaign advertisements, fundraising, and networking were all Internet-based. More importantly, voters came to expect that campaigns would solicit their questions, comments, advice, and money via the Internet.

7. "December 2007 Political Communications Study," Interviewing Dates: Dec. 19, 2007–Jan. 2, 2008. Pew Research Center for the People and the Press.

8. These numbers divide dramatically along generational lines. In 2008, 42 percent of voters under the age of 30 reported that the Internet was their primary source of information about presidential campaigns. Older voters, who are historically more likely to vote, used the Internet as their primary source of information less often. In 2008, 26 percent of those aged 30–49 used the Internet regularly for political information, compared to 15 percent of respondents over the age of 50 ("December 2007 Political Communications Study," Interviewing Dates: Dec. 19, 2007–Jan. 2, 2008. Pew Research Center for the People and the Press).

9. In 2000, 48 percent of respondents reported regularly learning about the campaigns from local news, 45 percent from network news, and 40 percent from daily newspapers. Those numbers decreased proportional to the increase in Internet access. In 2004, 42 percent relied on local TV news, 35 percent on network news, and 31 percent on daily newspapers. By 2008, 40 percent of respondents reported that the local TV news was a regular source of information about campaigns, 35 percent relied on network news, and 31 percent still depended on daily newspapers for information about presidential campaigns ("December 2007 Political Communications Study," Interviewing Dates: Dec. 19, 2007–Jan. 2, 2008. Pew Research Center for the People and the Press).

Introduction

1. Maureen Dowd, "Can Hillary Cry Her Way Back to the White House?" *New York Times*, Jan. 9, 2008.

2. Ibid., p. 34.

3. In 1984, Kathleen Kendall and June Yum found that homophily was the most accurate predictor of blue-collar voters' candidate selections. See, in particular, Kathleen Kendall and J.O. Yum, "Persuading the Blue-Collar Voter: Issues, Images, and Homophily," *Communication Yearbook* 8 (1984); and Alan Louden and Kristen McCauliffe, "The 'Authentic Candidate': Extending Candidate Image Assessment," in *Presidential Candidate Images*, ed. Kenneth L. Hacker (Lanham, MD: Rowman & Littlefield, 2004), p. 88.

4. Drew Westen, *The Political Brain* (New York: PublicAffairs, 2007), p. 192.

5. It is important to note that this definition of authenticity is the result of a historical process. As Americans' lifestyles, habits, hobbies, and preferences changed, so too did their definition of "authenticity." To be sure, there are particular mythotypes that serve as representations of American values. Nonetheless, the contexts we apply to these cultural texts necessarily adjust their meaning and potency. Further, even as folk hero symbols bind Americans to a mythologized national past, the meaning of "American" is constantly contested. In 2008, for example, Sarah Palin's "real America" was small town, rural, and conservative. Joe Biden's "real America," by contrast, was working class and exurban. In both of these examples, and indeed in most of our examples, "authentic" typically means poor or working class, often white, and frequently male.

6. Richard Joslyn, "Political Advertising and the Meaning of Elections," in *New Perspectives on Political Advertising*, ed. Lynda Kaid and Dan Nimmo (Carbondale: Southern Illinois University, 1986), p. 183.

7. Toni Morrison, "Clinton as the First Black President," *New Yorker*, Oct. 1998.

8. Drew Westen studied partisanship and found that partisans' emotional connections to a political party trump their ideological investment in a party's platform or policies. See Drew Westen, *The Political Brain: The Role of Emotion in Deciding the Fate of the Nation* (New York: PublicAffairs, 2007).

9. This "just like me" construction of authenticity is not unexplored in the literature, although most studies of its effectiveness examined it as an ancillary value. Nonetheless, the power of "just like me" politics is potent. In *The New Politics of Old Values*, John Kenneth White observed that this construction of authenticity might be the most valuable candidate trait in American politics. "I believe that those who succeed politically — from the president to the county sheriff — somehow convince voters that they are 'like us.'" See John Kenneth White, *The New Politics of Old Values* (Lanham, MD: University Press of America, 1998), p. 4.

10. Christopher Lehmann-Haupt, "Why Me Can't Be Happy," *New York Times*, Jan. 6, 1977, p. 26.

11. W. Lance Bennett, "The Clueless Public," in *The Clinton Presidency*, ed. Stanley Renshon (Oxford: Westview Press, 1994), p. 94.

12. Samuel L. Popkin, *The Reasoning Voter: Communication and Persuasion in Presidential Campaigns* (Chicago: University of Chicago Press, 1994), p. 78.

13. Popkin, *The Reasoning Voter*, p. 111.

14. Ibid.

15. Doug Rossinow, *The Politics of Authenticity* (New York: Columbia University Press, 1998), p. 104.

16. Rossinow, *The Politics of Authenticity*, p. 4.

17. Bruce Schulman, *The Seventies: The Great Shift in American Culture, Society, and Politics* (New York: Free Press, 2001), p. 79.

18. Rossinow, *The Politics of Authenticity*, p. 5.

19. Alice Echols, *Daring to Be Bad*, p. 17.

20. Amy Abugo Ongiri, "Spectacular Blackness: The Cultural Politics of the Black Power Movement and the Search for a Black Aesthetic," p. 14.

21. Amy Abugo Ongiri, "Spectacular Blackness: The Cultural Politics of the Black Power Movement and the Search for a Black Aesthetic," p. 36.

22. Woody Allen is included here because his depictions of American life incorporated endlessly neurotic monologues by characters who were self-probing, self-disclosive, and constantly negotiating the lines between real realities and manufactured realities. In *The Seventies*, Bruce Schulman turned to *The Godfather* to explain the quest for authenticity as it appeared in the ethnic revival of the 1970s. In *The Godfather*, a thoroughly Anglicized Michael Corleone was only authenticated after he returned to his ethnic roots and his family business. In this way, the assimilated Corleone was an inauthentic charade. Only when he rediscovered his true self, his Italian mobster self, was he revealed and redeemed. See Bruce Schulman, *The Seventies*. See also Christopher Lasch, *The Culture of Narcissism: American Life in an Age of Diminishing Expectations*, rev. ed. (New York: W.W. Norton, 1991).

23. Tom Wolfe, "The 'Me' Decade and the Third Great Awakening," *New York*, Aug. 23, 1976.

24. Editors, "Introducing ... " *People*, Mar. 4, 1974.

25. Data compiled by Media Management Center, Northwestern University, Kellogg School of Management, and Medill School. Statistics available online: http://www.mediainfocenter.org/compare/penetration.

26. Data compiled by Media Management Center, Northwestern University, Kellogg School of Management, and Medill School. Statistics available online: http://www.mediainfocenter.org/compare/penetration.

27. For the Ford Campaign's analysis of the importance of television in 1976, see Campaign Strategy Plan, August 1976, p. 100; folder "Presidential Campaign — Campaign Strategy Program (1)-(3)," box 1, Dorothy E. Downton Files, Gerald R. Ford Presidential Library.

28. Jonathan Moore, in Harvard University, Institute of Politics, *Campaign for President: The Managers Look at '84* (New York: Auburn House, 1986), p. xvii.

29. Barbara Walters, "The Real Bob Dole," *20/20*, Sept. 13, 1996, 9:00 p.m. ET, ABC News Transcripts.

30. Jonathan Moore, in *Campaign for President: The Managers Look at '84*, p. xvii.

31. "Interactive" television began with live call-in programs. In political television, interactive programming was introduced in 1968 by the Nixon campaign.

32. Roderick P. Hart, *Seducing America: How Television Charms the Modern Voter* (Thousand Oaks, CA: Sage Publications, 1998), p. 24.

33. Quoted in Richard Jackson Harris, *A Cognitive Psychology of Mass Communication* (New York: Routledge, 2009), p. 169.

34. Ibid.

35. Kathleen Hall Jamieson, *Eloquence in an Electronic Age: The Transformation of Political Speechmaking* (New York: Oxford University Press, 1990), p. 81.

36. Shawn Parry-Giles and Trevor Parry-Giles, *Constructing Clinton: Hyperreality and Presidential Image-Making in Postmodern Politics* (New York: Peter Lang, 2002), p. 198.

37. Parry-Giles and Parry-Giles, *Constructing Clinton*, p. 198.

38. Ibid., p. 28.

39. Shawn Parry-Giles and Trevor Parry-Giles, "Political Scopophilia, Presidential Campaigning, and the Intimacy of American Politics," *Communication Studies* 47: 191–205.

40. We see this transition most clearly when we compare the language of the collective. When John F. Kennedy and Lyndon B. Johnson used collectivist language, they did so in relatively detached ways. Compare, for example, Lyndon B. Johnson's "the oath I have taken is not mine but ours together" with Jimmy Carter's promise to be "a President who is not isolated from the people but who feels your pain and shares your dreams." While this might seem like an odd and convenient parallel, Roderick Hart investigated the use of personal pronouns and the first and second person singular in presidential speech patterns. He found that as television matured, and as audiences came to expect emotional connections to television characters (including politicians), the structural language of political speech became more intimate.

41. Hart, *Seducing America*, p. ix.

42. Kathleen Hall Jamieson, *Eloquence in an Electronic Age*, p. 82.

43. John L. Sullivan, et al., "Candidate Appraisal and Human Nature: Man and Superman in the 1984 Election," *Political Psychology* 11, no. 3 (1990).

44. Judith A. Carter, "1972 Democratic Con-

vention Reforms and Party Democracy," *Political Science Quarterly* 89, no. 2 (June 1974): 325–350.

45. Jeffrey S. Walz and John Comer, "State Responses to National Democratic Party Reform," *Political Research Quarterly* 52, no. 1 (Mar. 1999): 189–208.

46. Ibid.

47. Ibid.

48. Watergate shifted voters' evaluations of candidates from policy issues toward character issues. For a few examples of this thesis elaborated, see Kathleen Hall Jamieson, *Packaging the Presidency* (New York: Oxford University Press, 1996), p. 329; Troy, *See How They Ran*, p. 233; E.D. Dover, *Presidential Elections in the Television Age: 1960–1992* (Westport, CT: Praeger, 1994), p. 128. Most broadly, candidates' personalities, backgrounds, and decision-making capabilities became increasingly important. This laid the groundwork for emphasis on personality, but not necessarily authenticity. During the same period, however, the internal machinery of campaigns and the mechanisms of electioneering became visible to voters. For evidence of this, see Troy, p. 246. During the period covered in this study, campaign advisors, managers, and consultants acquired new standing in the public eye, which is significant to this study. American voters also became aware of multiple changes in executive structure. First, even as the Executive Branch gained more power over the course of the twentieth century, the job of the president had also become symbolic, as the growth of the Executive branch increased the importance and influence of technocrats and experts. See Arthur Schlesinger, *The Imperial Presidency* (New York: Popular Library, 1973). Voters therefore based decisions not merely on a potential president's ability to craft policy, but also on his ability to represent them in a growing bureaucracy. For this, and the expectations of modern presidents, see Theodore Lowi, *The Personal President* (Ithaca, NY: Cornell University Press, 1986).

49. The 1976 Supreme Court decision in *Buckley v. Valeo 424 U.S. 1 (1976)* required amendments to the FECA, striking down mandatory limits on overall campaign expenditures.

50. Hacker, ed., *Presidential Candidate Images*, p. 5. For this argument, see also James Pfiffner, *The Modern Presidency* (Belmont, CA: Wadsworth, 2007), and Stephen Wayne, *The Road to the White House 1996* (New York: St. Martin's, 1997).

51. Troy, *See How They Ran*, p. 246.

52. Parry-Giles and Parry-Giles, *Constructing Clinton*, p. 192.

53. Ibid.

54. Kathleen Hall Jamieson and Paul Waldman, *The Press Effect: Politicians, Journalists, and the Stories That Shape the Political World* (New York: Oxford University Press, 2004), p. 27.

55. Ibid., p. 26.

56. The growing independence of voters is evident in the American National Election Studies survey data. Beginning in 1968, the first election year in which baby boomers could register to vote, the percentage of self-identified Independents climbed from 24 percent to 31 percent. Thereafter, the percentage of self-identified independents continued to rise. In 2000, Independents outnumbered both Democrats and Republicans (Source: ANES Guide to Public Opinion and Electoral Behavior, Party Identification 7-Point Scale 1952–2004). This apparent shift in voting behavior has been disputed by some political scientists who continue to analyze voting preferences within the framework laid out by Angus Campbell, et al., in *The American Voter* (Chicago: University of Chicago Press, 1980). These scholars argued that party affiliation is the only, or at least most important, criterion by which to effectively predict election outcomes. By contrast, other scholars have recognized the growth of independent voters relative to the decline in long-standing party identification. In previous generations, voters maintained strong and long-term ties (personal, cultural, and political) to particular political parties through ethnic organizations, labor unions, and social groups. In 1976, Norman Nie, Sidney Verba, and John Petrocik began to document a new trend in political affiliation. In their work, *The Changing American Voter*, Nie, et al. observed that there had been a "weakening of partisanship" in the years following World War II. "Fewer citizens have steady and strong psychological identification with a party," making partisanship "less of a guide to electoral choice." Instead, their study found that voters increasingly looked to other factors to make their candidate selections. See Norman Nie, et al., *The Changing American Voter* (Cambridge, MA: Harvard University Press, 1979). More recently, Thomas Holbrook conceded, "Party identification is less important to the electorate today than it used to be." See Thomas Holbrook, *Do Campaigns Matter?* (Thousand Oaks, CA: Sage Publications, 1996). As W. Lance Bennett found, "A growing body of evidence shows ... [that] voters increasingly shun party affiliation.... Not only has party identification declined in the electorate from peak levels recorded in the 1950s and 1960s, but something resembling a culture of political independence" has come to dominate voting behavior (W. Lance Bennett, "The Clueless Public," in *The Clinton Presidency* by Stanley Renshon [Oxford: Westview Press, 1994], p. 95). Bennett's conclusion is not the only interpretation of self-identification in the ANES data. Other scholars, including Michael Lewis-Beck, Helmut Norpoth, William G. Jacoby, and Herbert Weisburg argued that despite flaws in interpretive assumptions, Angus Campbell, Warren E. Miller, and Donald Stokes's original 1960 interpretation of ANES data remained valid. See Michael Lewis-Beck, et al., *The American Voter Revisited* (Ann Arbor: University of Michigan Press, 2008). See also Paul Lazarsfeld, *The People's Choice,*

3d ed (New York: Columbia University Press, 1968). For a more recent argument against campaign effects, see Thomas Holbrook, *Do Campaigns Matter?* My own analysis of polls and ANES data led me to conclude that party affiliation cannot solely account for election outcomes. According to Reagan campaign internal survey data, voters had become increasingly independent in their candidate preferences (importantly, unlike the ANES data, these data were taken prior to voters' Election Day decisions). In June 1980, 51 percent of the population identified as Democrats, 30 percent self-identified as Republicans, and 19 percent considered themselves Independent. Although a majority of voters considered themselves to be Democrats in June 1980, Reagan won almost 51 percent of the popular vote on Election Day in November. (See DMI June 1980 Survey for the Reagan for President Campaign, Richard Wirthlin: Political Strategy, Subseries B: DMI Polling Books, Ronald Reagan Presidential Library.)

57. See Charles Lindholm, *Culture and Authenticity* (Malden: Wiley-Blackwell), pp. 57–58, and pp. 65–74. Lindholm, p. 65. See also Mark Poster, ed., *Jean Baudrillard: Selected Writings* (Cambridge: Polity Press, 2001), p. 174.

58. See Charles Lindholm, *Culture and Authenticity* (Malden: Wiley-Backwell), pp. 57–58, and pp. 65–74. Lindholm, p. 65. See also Mark Poster, ed., *Jean Baudrillard: Selected Writings*, p. 174.

59. Low-information rationality is "the kind of practical thinking about government and politics in which people actually engage. It is a method of combining, in an economical way, learning and information from past experiences, daily life, the media, and political campaigns" (Popkin, *The Reasoning Voter*, p. 7).

60. Popkin called this "informational shortcuts." *The Reasoning Voter*, pp. 15–17.

61. Popkin, *The Reasoning Voter*, p. 73. The words "new" and "old" were omitted from this quote because Popkin went on to write that personal information is so compelling that voters give more weight to old personal information than new impersonal information; thus, the words "new" and "old" have no bearing on the content of Popkin's thesis.

62. Alan Louden, "Image in the 1992 Presidential Campaign," in *The 1992 Presidential Campaign*, ed. Robert E. Denton (Westport, CT: Praeger, 1996), p. 178.

63. Popkin, *The Reasoning Voter*, p. 65.

64. Ibid.

65. Ibid., p. 3.

66. Ibid., p. 64.

67. For a full account of the Eisenhower campaign's use of spot advertising in 1952, see Robert J. Donovan and Raymond Sherer, *Unsilent Revolution* (New York: Cambridge University Press, 1992), pp. 222–225.

68. While the "Eisenhower Answers America" spots offered the first example of television mini-

mizing the distance between president and people, they also provided an example of the kind of scripted inauthenticity that voters and viewers would later rebel against. The questions were written by Madison Avenue advertising experts, and read by tourists plucked from the streets of New York. Eisenhower's responses had been prerecorded in a television studio in Manhattan. For the spots and their history, see Museum of the Moving Image, *The Living Room Candidate: Presidential Campaign Commercials 1952–2008*: http://www.livingroomcandidate.org.

69. "High Prices," Citizens for Eisenhower. Maker: Rosser Reeves for Ted Bates and Co. Video courtesy of the John F. Kennedy Presidential Library. From Museum of the Moving Image, *The Living Room Candidate: Presidential Campaign Commercials 1952–2008*: http://www.livingroomcandidate.org.

70. For a full account of the Eisenhower campaign's use of spot advertising in 1952, see Robert J. Donovan and Ray Sherer, *Unsilent Revolution*, pp. 222–225.

71. For a full account of the Eisenhower campaign's use of spot advertising in 1952, see Robert J. Donovan and Ray Sherer, *Unsilent Revolution*, pp. 222–225.

72. For text and analysis of Nixon's "Checkers" speech, see Joseph S. Tuman, *Political Communication in American Campaigns* (Los Angeles: Sage Publications, 2008), pp. 82–92. See also Robert J. Donovan and Ray Scherer, *Unsilent Revolution*, pp. 38–40.

73. See Maurine Hoffman Beasley, *First Ladies and the Press: The Unfinished Partnership of the Media Age* (Chicago: Northwestern University Press, 2005), p. 112.

74. For more on Nixon's 1968 campaign, see Joseph McGinniss, *The Selling of the President 1968* (New York: Penguin Books, 1969). See also Robert J. Donovan and Ray Scherer, *Unsilent Revolution*, pp. 229–231.

75. For their analysis of this transformation, see Edwin Diamond and Robert Silverman, *White House to Your House* (London: MIT Press, 1997), pp. 25–27.

Chapter 1

1. Quoted in "Stampede to Carter," *Time*, June 21, 1976.

2. Spiro Agnew pled no contest to allegations of tax fraud. He settled the bribery suit with the state of Maryland out of court.

3. Campaign Strategy Plan, August 1976, p. 12; folder "Presidential Campaign — Campaign Strategy Program (1)–(3)," box 1, Dorothy E. Downton Files, Gerald R. Ford Presidential Library. Watergate shifted voters' evaluations of can-

didates from policy issues toward character issues. For a few examples of this thesis elaborated, see Jamieson, *Packaging the Presidency*, p. 329; Troy, *See How They Ran*, p. 233; and Dover, *Presidential Elections*, p. 128.

4. See Troy, *See How They Ran*, p. 246.

5. For analysis of the impact of Watergate on the 1976 election, see especially Jamieson, *Packaging the Presidency*, chapter 8, "Integrity, Incumbency, and the Impact of Watergate."

6. In *The Age of Reagan*, Sean Wilentz noted the phenomenon of the anti-politician in the 1976 election. Writing of Carter advisor Pat Caddell's new political philosophy, which favored the outsider, "'malaise' was causing Americans to yearn not just for new leaders but for" an "entirely new kind of" leader. These leaders would be "straight-shooting antipoliticians who ... spoke candidly, and won over voters by earning their trust." See Sean Wilentz, *The Age of Reagan* (New York: Harper-Collins, 2008), p. 77.

7. See Michael Malbin, "Many Races for Congress Are Contests in Morality," *New York Times*, Oct. 31, 1976, p. E3; R.W. Apple, "Campaign '76: Barren and Petty," *New York Times*, Oct. 20, 1976, p. 93; and Joseph Lelyveld, "So Far Carter and Ford Have Pushed the 'Trust' Issue," *New York Times*, Oct. 3, 1976, p. 146.

8. As a result of Watergate, American voters became aware of multiple changes in executive structure, which had been taking place at least since the 1930s. First, even as the office of the president had gained more power over the course of the twentieth century (see Schlesinger, *The Imperial Presidency*), the job of the president had become somewhat symbolic, as the growth of the Executive Branch meant also the increased importance and influence of technocrats and experts. Voters, therefore, based decisions not merely on a potential president's ability to craft policy, but also on his ability to represent them within a larger executive institution. On this, and the expectations of modern presidents, see also Theodore Lowi, *The Personal President*.

9. Campaign Strategy Plan, August 1976, pp. 12–26; folder "Presidential Campaign — Campaign Strategy Program (1)–(3)," box 1, Dorothy E. Downton Files, Gerald R. Ford Presidential Library.

10. Preliminary Media Plan, 8/21/76, p. 3; folder "Presidential Campaign — Preliminary Media Plan," box 1, Dorothy E. Downton Files, Gerald R. Ford Presidential Library.

11. Campaign Strategy Plan, August 1976, p. 111; folder "Presidential Campaign — Campaign Strategy Program (1)–(3)," box 1, Dorothy E. Downton Files, Gerald R. Ford Presidential Library.

12. Other scholars have also made the argument that Watergate provoked a shift toward more "image campaigns" and away from issue-centric campaigns and traditional appeals to partisanship.

For a few examples of this thesis elaborated, see Jamieson, *Packaging the Presidency*, p. 329; Troy, *See How They Ran*, p. 233; and Dover *Presidential Elections*, p. 128.

13. Jody Powell Interview, Miller Center, University of Virginia, Carter Presidential Oral History Project, Dec. 17–18, 1981, p. 15.

14. Presidential campaigns and the selection of presidents provide an opportunity for the country to construct and re-construct national identity. This was never more true than in 1976, as the country attempted to relocate its political culture in the first post–Watergate election.

15. Rex Granam Interview, Dec. 17, 1981. Carter Presidency Project, Final Edited Transcript, from The Miller Center of Public Affairs Presidential Oral History Program.

16. To be sure, this was not an "old-fashioned" or "traditional" campaign style in any sense. First, the Carter team's strategy was to gain national attention by winning state party primaries and caucuses. Carter did not start at the top with state party insiders in order to win convention delegates, a more traditional strategy that might have blocked him previously. Second, Carter was an active candidate who did not use surrogates to campaign for him, as he might have in a much older "tradition." On the sense that the 1976 campaign was "old-fashioned," see Jamieson, *Packaging the Presidency*, p. 329.

17. Douglas Brinkley argued that "he offered a biography of what we wanted to hear; a farmer, Main Street values, Plains — and he carried that message through, it was the right message at the right time" (Transcript, *Jimmy Carter: The American Experience*, www.pbs.org).

18. On the message of the Carter campaign, see Jody Powell Interview, Miller Center, University of Virginia, Carter Presidential Oral History Project, Dec. 17–18, 1981, p. 15. See also Rex Granum's comments from the same interview.

19. According to Joanne Morreale, still photographs and home videos from a candidate's pre-political past lend authenticity to a candidate's depiction of himself as a person. Morreale wrote, "Graphics and black-and-white footage serve as illustrative 'proof' of the events to which the narrator alludes.... Authenticity is also signaled by the use of still photographs," which were not originally taken to service as campaign materials. See Morreale, *A New Beginning* (Albany: State University of New York Press, 1991), p. 17.

20. "Rose," 1976 Democratic Presidential Campaign Committee, Inc., 1976. Maker: Gerald Rafshoon, from Museum of the Moving Image, *The Living Room Candidate: Presidential Campaign Commercials 1952–2008*: http://www.livingroom-candidate.org.

21. "Bio," 1976 Democratic Presidential Campaign Committee, Inc., 1976. Maker: Gerald Rafshoon, from Museum of the Moving Image, *The Living Room Candidate: Presidential Campaign*

Commercials 1952–2008: http://www.livingroom-candidate.org.

22. For analysis of cinéma vérité and Rafshoon's use of the technique, see especially Jamieson, *Packaging the Presidency*, pp. 329–330. Jamieson made the argument that "highly polished ads ... could not be central in a year in which the prime message of both campaigns was that their candidate was a person of integrity, dependability, leadership, and competence" (p. 329). While this was true, I have offered a different interpretation. The use of cinema vérité advertising was meant to invoke honesty and authenticity, but did not necessarily bolster a candidate's image of competence, dependability, or leadership.

23. "Selling 'Em Jimmy and Jerry," *Time*, Oct. 11, 1976.

24. Gerald Rafshoon Interview, Miller Center, University of Virginia, Carter Presidential Oral History Project, Apr. 8, 1983, p. 48.

25. See Michael Malbin, "Many Races for Congress Are Contests in Morality," *New York Times*, Oct. 31, 1976, p. E3.

26. This brand of celebrity-obsession is a trend that continues today. It is telling to compare Kennedy's campaign book about famous senators with Obama's recent campaign autobiography, in which he uncovered an often unappealing past of poverty and poor choices.

27. Ibid.

28. Ibid., p. 9.

29. Ibid., p. 12.

30. Ibid., p. 10.

31. Quoting Walter Mondale. Linda Charlton, "Daley Welcomes Mondale at End of Whistle-Stopping Train Trip," *New York Times*, Sept. 21, 1976, p. 24.

32. Peter Goldman, "Sizing Up Carter," *Newsweek*, Sept. 13, 1976.

33. "Carter Up Close," *Newsweek*, July 19, 1976.

34. Quoted in "Marching through Manhattan," *Time*, July 26, 1976.

35. Ibid.

36. Joyce Leviton, "This Is Carter Country," *People* 6, no. 3 (July 19, 1976).

37. Barry G. Golson, "When Carter and *Playboy* Spoke in Plains," *New York Times*, Sept. 30, 1976, p. 41. Golson explained that Carter's controversial comments — his remarks about lust and former president Lyndon Johnson — were made as the reporters were on the way out the door, and were, indeed, offhand comments. On the topic of lust, as noted, Carter admitted to having "lust" in his "heart." On former president Lyndon Johnson, Carter commented that religion had given him the moral grounding to avoid the mistakes of presidents Nixon and Johnson.

38. "Jimmy, We Hardly Knew Y'All," *Playboy*, November 1976, p. 136.

39. Ibid.

40. Segments of the interview ultimately reached a much larger audience than the expected

five million regular consumers of *Playboy*. In *The Age of Reagan*, Sean Wilentz reached the same conclusion about the *Playboy* interviews, noting that Carter did his best to "sound like an up-to-date regular guy" (p. 73).

41. See Edward Pessen, *The Log Cabin Myth* (New Haven, CT: Yale University Press, 1986) for this theme in presidential mythology. While previous candidates had spun their own yarns about hardships and bootstraps, it is interesting to note the relative absence of such themes in presidential campaigns. Harry Truman, for example, added a middle initial to give the appearance of status. Both Lyndon Johnson and Richard Nixon might have campaigned on childhood poverty, but both preferred to emphasize experience and earned status.

42. "Rose," 1976 Democratic Presidential Campaign Committee, Inc., 1976. Maker: Gerald Rafshoon, from Museum of the Moving Image, *The Living Room Candidate: Presidential Campaign Commercials 1952–2008*: http://www.livingroom-candidate.org.

43. Walter Mondale, quoted in *New York Times*, "Mondale Shows Wit in Accepting Supporting Role in the Campaign," *New York Times*, Sept. 16, 1976, p. 32.

44. Ibid.

45. "Jimmy's Mixed Signals," *Time*, Oct. 4, 1976.

46. Peter Goldman, "Sizing Up Carter," *Newsweek*, Sept. 13, 1976.

47. Charles Mohr, "Moments of Spontaneity Reveal Character of Carter's Campaign," *New York Times*, Sept. 13, 1976, p. 21.

48. "What's behind the Carter Magic?" *Economist*, Apr. 17, 1976, p. 31.

49. "Lawyer," 1976 Democratic Presidential Campaign Committee, Inc., 1976. Maker: Gerald Rafshoon.

50. Jody Powell Interview, Miller Center, University of Virginia, Carter Presidential Oral History Project, Dec. 17–18, 1981, p. 14.

51. *CBS News/New York Times* Election Survey, 1976. Part 7: Debate One Survey, from The Interuniversity Consortium for Political and Social Research. www.icpsr.umich.edu.

52. *CBS News/New York Times* Election Survey, 1976. Part 8: Debate Two Survey, from The Interuniversity Consortium for Political and Social Research. www.icpsr.umich.edu. 873 respondents selected Carter compared to 398 for Ford.

53. Campaign Strategy Plan, August 1976, p. 112; folder "Presidential Campaign — Campaign Strategy Program (1)–(3)," box 1, Dorothy E. Downton Files, Gerald R. Ford Presidential Library.

54. "Support with Serious Reservations," *Time*, Oct. 25, 1976.

55. Ibid. After the third debate, the CBS/*New York Times* poll showed that 984 respondents believed that "new ideas" were more important than experience, compared to 821 respondents selecting

"experience." Further in the September 1976 *New York Times*/CBS survey, 702 respondents graded Ford A or B for experience compared to about half that number for Carter (CBS/*New York Times* Election Survey, 1976. Part 6: September Survey). More telling was respondents' assessment of the candidates' "knowledge about how government works," a question asked during the Debate One survey. By a margin of nearly three to one, respondents believed that Ford had the advantage over Carter. The question, then, was whether voters preferred a candidate who was inside the system or out (*CBS News*/*New York Times* Election Survey, 1976. Part 7: Debate One Survey, from The Interuniversity Consortium for Political and Social Research. www.icpsr.umich.edu.)

56. Quoted in *Time*, "How Southern Is He?" *Time*, Sept. 27, 1976.

57. Quoted in William E. Leuchtenburg, *The White House Looks South: Franklin D. Roosevelt, Harry S. Truman, Lyndon B. Johnson* (Baton Rouge: Louisiana State University Press, 2007), p. 387. See also the campaign's regionally targeted television commercial, "South," 1976 Democratic Presidential Campaign Committee, Inc., 1976. Maker: Gerald Rafshoon, from Museum of the Moving Image, *The Living Room Candidate: Presidential Campaign Commercials 1952–2008*: http://www. livingroomcandidate.org.

58. Gerald Rafshoon Interview, Miller Center, University of Virginia, Carter Presidential Oral History Project, Apr. 8, 1983, p. 47.

59. On Carter's luggage-carrying skills, see James Wooten, "Carter Seeking to Regain Flavor of the Early Days of Campaign," *New York Times*, Oct. 2, 1976, p. 1.

60. "Mondale Shows Wit in Accepting Supporting Role in the Campaign," *New York Times*, Sept. 16, 1976, p. 32.

61. Russell Baker, "Jimmies for All Occasions," *New York Times*, Oct. 12, 1976, p. 28.

62. Eli Evans, "All the Candidates' Clothes: Costume Is Key in the Song and Dance of Politics," *New York Times*, Sept. 19, 1976, p. 238.

63. Ibid.

64. On youth and the quest for authenticity, see especially Rossinow, *The Politics of Authenticity.*

65. Eli Evans, "All the Candidates' Clothes: Costume Is Key in the Song and Dance of Politics," *New York Times*, Sept. 19, 1976, p. 238.

66. Ibid.

67. See, in particular, 1976 Carter campaign commercial, "Bio," 1976 Democratic Presidential Campaign Committee, Inc., 1976. Maker: Gerald Rafshoon, from Museum of the Moving Image, *The Living Room Candidate: Presidential Campaign Commercials 1952–2008*: http://www.livingroom-candidate.org.

68. "Daley Welcomes Mondale at End of Whistle-Stopping Train Trip," *New York Times*, Sept. 21, 1976, p. 24.

69. "Election," 1976 Democratic Presidential Campaign Committee, Inc., 1976. Maker: Gerald Rafshoon.

70. Quoted in Leuchtenburg, *The White House Looks South*, p. 387.

71. "Washington," 1976 Democratic Presidential Campaign Committee, Inc., 1976. Maker: Gerald Rafshoon.

72. "Bio," 1976 Democratic Presidential Campaign Committee, Inc., 1976. Maker: Gerald Rafshoon, from Museum of the Moving Image, *The Living Room Candidate: Presidential Campaign Commercials 1952–2008*: http://www.livingroom-candidate.org.

73. Rex Granum in Jody Powell Interview, Miller Center, University of Virginia, Carter Presidential Oral History Project, Dec. 17–18, 1981, p. 16.

74. Campaign Strategy Plan, August 1976, p. 14; folder "Presidential Campaign — Campaign Strategy Program (1)–(3)," box 1, Dorothy E. Downton Files, Gerald R. Ford Presidential Library.

75. Walter Mondale, Chicago, IL, Sept. 21, 1976. Quoted in "Daley Welcomes Mondale at End of Whistle-Stopping Train Trip," *New York Times*, Sept. 21, 1976, p. 24.

76. Tom Wolfe, "The 'Me' Decade and the Third Great Awakening," *New York*, Aug. 23, 1976, p. 30.

77. "Carter!" *Time*, Nov. 15, 1976.

78. "Carter!" *Time*, Nov. 15, 1976. It should be noted, however, that Carter's victory over Ford measured in at a wider popular vote margin than in any presidential race (except for 1964) since Eisenhower's reelection in 1956.

79. Memo, Dorrance Smith to Doug Blaser, 7/26/76; folder "Press Office Improvement Sessions — 8/6–7/76 — Press Advance (2)," box 24, Ron Nessen Papers, Gerald R. Ford Presidential Library.

80. Ibid.

81. Ibid.

82. Campaign Strategy Plan, August 1976, p. 31; folder "Presidential Campaign — Campaign Strategy Program (1)–(3)," box 1, Dorothy E. Downton Files, Gerald R. Ford Presidential Library.

83. Preliminary Media Plan, 8/21/76; folder "Presidential Campaign — Preliminary Media Plan," box 1, Dorothy E. Downton Files, Gerald R. Ford Presidential Library.

84. Campaign Strategy Plan, August 1976, p. 18; folder "Presidential Campaign — Campaign Strategy Program (1)–(3)," box 1, Dorothy E. Downton Files, Gerald R. Ford Presidential Library.

85. Ibid.

86. Ibid.

87. Preliminary Media Plan, 8/21/76, p. 5; folder "Presidential Campaign — Preliminary Media Plan," box 1, Dorothy E. Downton Files, Gerald R. Ford Presidential Library.

88. Campaign Strategy Plan, August 1976, p. 70; folder "Presidential Campaign — Campaign Strategy Program (1)–(3)," box 1, Dorothy E. Downton Files, Gerald R. Ford Presidential Library.

89. Ibid.

90. Preliminary Media Plan, 8/21/76, p. 8; folder "Presidential Campaign — Preliminary Media Plan," box 1, Dorothy E. Downton Files, Gerald R. Ford Presidential Library.

91. Campaign Strategy Plan, August 1976, p. 56; folder "Presidential Campaign — Campaign Strategy Program (1)–(3)," box 1, Dorothy E. Downton Files, Gerald R. Ford Presidential Library.

92. Ibid.

93. Gerald Rafshoon Interview, Miller Center, University of Virginia, Carter Presidential Oral History Project, Apr. 8, 1983, p. 48.

94. James Wooten, "Carter Seeking to Regain Flavor of the Early Days of Campaign," New York Times, Oct. 2, 1976, p. 1.

95. Gerald Rafshoon Interview, Miller Center, University of Virginia, Carter Presidential Oral History Project, Apr. 8, 1983, p. 48.

96. Campaign Strategy Plan, August 1976, p. 47; folder "Presidential Campaign — Campaign Strategy Program (1)–(3)," box 1, Dorothy E. Downton Files, Gerald R. Ford Presidential Library.

97. Preliminary Media Plan, 8/21/76, p. 10; folder "Presidential Campaign — Preliminary Media Plan," box 1, Dorothy E. Downton Files, Gerald R. Ford Presidential Library.

98. Ibid.

99. Campaign Strategy Plan, August 1976, p. 71; folder "Presidential Campaign — Campaign Strategy Program (1)–(3)," box 1, Dorothy E. Downton Files, Gerald R. Ford Presidential Library.

100. Preliminary Media Plan, 8/21/76, pp. 8–9; folder "Presidential Campaign — Preliminary Media Plan," box 1, Dorothy E. Downton Files, Gerald R. Ford Presidential Library.

101. "Family," President Ford Committee, 1976. Video courtesy of the Gerald R. Ford Presidential Library. From Museum of the Moving Image, The Living Room Candidate: Presidential Campaign Commercials 1952–2008: http://www.livingroomcandidate.org.

102. Ibid.

103. Preliminary Media Plan, 8/21/76, p. 9; folder "Presidential Campaign — Preliminary Media Plan," box 1, Dorothy E. Downton Files, Gerald R. Ford Presidential Library.

104. "Biography," President Ford Committee, 1976, original air date Oct. 7, 1976. Video courtesy of the Gerald R. Ford Presidential Library. From Museum of the Moving Image, The Living Room Candidate: Presidential Campaign Commercials 1952–2008: http://www.livingroomcandidate.org.

105. In The Reasoning Voter, Samuel Popkin re-told a story of President Ford's clumsy inauthenticity while campaigning in Texas in 1976. At a "San Antonio rally for President Ford ... the President of the United States was served his first tamale, a food not common in Grand Rapids, Michigan.... Ford proceeded with gusto to bite into the tamale, corn husk and all.... This gastronomic gaffe" became national news. Even the New York Times printed the story and accompanying photograph on the front page, reporting that "President Ford start[ed] to eat a hot tamale.... The snack was interrupted ... so that his hosts could remove the corn shucks which serve as a wrapper and are not supposed to be consumed." (See Popkin, The Reasoning Voter, p. 1).

106. This campaign strategy depended on voters to condense real information about Ford's geographic roots into symbolic understanding of the candidate as a neighbor. As Popkin noted, the "friends and neighbors" strategy is an essential tool used by voters to evaluate a candidate's sincerity and to project his future behavior. "When a candidate is in some sense a neighbor, the voter at least has a better chance of knowing whether he or she is a blatant crook or an obvious fool" (Popkin, The Reasoning Voter, p. 64).

107. On the importance of mastering regional and ethnic culture, in order to fit in with and relate to voters, Samuel Popkin observed (regarding food ways), "Showing familiarity with a voter's culture is an obvious and easy test of ability to relate to the problems and sensibilities" of particular types of voters. "Incidents involving such tests illustrate the kinds of cues that voters use to make judgments ... that need to be taken seriously in order to understand voters and campaigns" (Popkin, The Reasoning Voter, p. 3).

108. Memo, Jack Marsh to the President, 11/1/76; folder "States — Michigan," box 19, Richard Cheney Files, Gerald R. Ford Presidential Library.

109. Ibid.

110. Ibid.

111. Ibid.

112. Ibid.

113. Jody Powell Interview, Miller Center, University of Virginia, Carter Presidential Oral History Project, Dec. 17–18, 1981, p. 33.

114. Memo, Jack Marsh to the President, 11/1/76; folder "States — Michigan," box 19, Richard Cheney Files, Gerald R. Ford Presidential Library.

115. Ibid.

116. Gerald Rafshoon Interview, Miller Center, University of Virginia, Carter Presidential Oral History Project, Apr. 8, 1983, p. 50.

117. President Ford Committee Newsletter, no. 32 (Oct. 19, 1976): 2. President Ford Committee Newsletter, Oct. 19, 1976, box 1, Dorothy E. Downton Files, Gerald R. Ford Presidential Library.

118. Gerald Ford interview with Jim Lehrer in Debating Our Destiny. Transcript from pbs.org.

119. The major exception here was on questions

about the economy, where most voters favored Jimmy Carter.

120. *CBS News/New York Times* 1976 Post-Election poll, from The Interuniversity Consortium for Political and Social Research. www.icpsr.umich.edu.

121. Called "The Blooper Heard Round the World" by *Time* magazine, during the second debate, Gerald Ford aggressively and erroneously declared, "There is no Soviet domination of Eastern Europe, and there never will be under a Ford Administration" (*Time*, Oct. 18, 1976). To those watching on television, even those unversed in the state of Soviet relations with Eastern Europe, it was clear that Ford had made a grand gaffe as questioner Max Frankel repeated the question in disbelief. Nonetheless, Ford reasserted his claim, more aggressively and specifically. To those who did not watch the debate on television, the incident became well known, as the story was reprinted by the popular media and replayed on television news programs.

122. James Wooten, "Carter Seeking to Regain Flavor of the Early Days of Campaign," *New York Times*, Oct. 2, 1976, p. 1. There are other logical explanations for this, which have been thoroughly investigated in the existing scholarship. The most common argument is that Carter was an unknown. As voters came to know Carter better, opposition to his candidacy grew. It has been argued as well that as Carter articulated specific policy initiatives, he defined himself more clearly, thus circumscribing his potential constituency by positioning himself more definitively in opposition to many voters' beliefs and desires. While this certainly accounts for some of Carter's drop in the polls, it is not obvious that Carter did define his positions more clearly — voters increasingly saw Carter as "wishy-washy."

123. James Wooten, "Carter Seeking to Regain Flavor of the Early Days of Campaign," *New York Times*, Oct. 2, 1976, p. 1.

124. See especially *CBS News/New York Times* 1976 election polls 7–9, from The Interuniversity Consortium for Political and Social Research. www.icpsr.umich.edu).

Chapter 2

1. For a few such interpretations, see Andrew E. Busch, *Reagan's Victory: The Presidential Election of 1980 and the Rise of the Right (American Presidential Elections)* (Lawrence: University Press of Kansas, 2005); Schulman, *The Seventies*; McGirr, *Suburban Warriors;* Wilentz, *The Age of Reagan*; and Lassiter, "Inventing Family Values" in Schulman and Zelizer, *Rightward Bound: Making America Conservative in the 1970s* (Cambridge, MA: Harvard University Press, 2008).

2. "Reagan for President Campaign Plan,"

6/29/80, (Draft) folder, "Wirthlin — Reagan for President Campaign Plan (2/4)," box 177, Richard Wirthlin Files, Ronald Reagan Presidential Library.

3. Gerald Rafshoon Interview, Miller Center, University of Virginia, Carter Presidential Oral History Project, Apr. 8, 1983, p. 60.

4. Quoted in Editorial, *Washington Post*, June 6, 2004, p. B06.

5. John Kenneth White described this phenomenon whereby Reagan the actor was transformed into Reagan the average American on the campaign trail. White wrote, "Ronald Reagan's tender depiction of his upbringing is one many Americans can identify with." See John Kenneth White, *The New Politics of Old Values* (Lanham, MD: University Press of America, 1998), p. 5.

6. Michael Novak, *Choosing Presidents* (New Brunswick, NJ: Transaction Publishers, 1991), p. xix.

7. Lyn Nofziger Interview, Miller Center, University of Virginia, Carter Presidential Oral History Project, Mar. 6, 2003, p. 26.

8. Joanne Morreale made an interesting observation on this very point in "American Self Images and Presidential Campaign Film, 1964–1992," in *Presidential Campaigns and American Self Images*, ed. Arthur Miller and Bruce Gronbeck (London: Westview, 1994).

9. In 1976, Ford bested Carter by a 3:1 margin on "He seems to have a more detailed knowledge about how government works," where Carter scored higher by margins of 1.5:1, and 2:1 on questions about empathy and personal characteristics. For evidence of this, see *CBS News/New York Times* Election Surveys, 1976, Part 7 Q 9B–9H. In 1980, however, a Reagan campaign-sponsored DMI national survey revealed that Jimmy Carter's best assets in 1980 were experience and "second term will improve." (Reagan Bush/National Panel/8201/September 1980, DMI poll book, p. 261. In folder "National Panel Survey of Voter Attitudes," vol. 3, box 206, Richard Wirthlin: Political Strategy, Subseries B: DMI Polling Books, Ronald Reagan Presidential Library).

10. Gerald Rafshoon Interview, Miller Center, University of Virginia, Carter Presidential Oral History Project, Apr. 8, 1983, p. 54.

11. As Gil Troy noted in *See How They Ran*, "The man who had promised never to lie turned out to be as political as anyone else.... His twenty-two-month campaign for purity looked like a sham" by 1980 (Troy, *See How They Ran*, p. 240).

12. Rex Granum in Jody Powell Interview, Miller Center, University of Virginia, Carter Presidential Oral History Project, Dec. 17–18, 1981, p. 75.

13. Jody Powell Interview, Miller Center, University of Virginia, Carter Presidential Oral History Project, Dec. 17–18, 1981, p. 75.

14. See "Family," Carter/Mondale Reelection Committee, Inc. Maker: Rafshoon Communica-

tions, from Museum of the Moving Image, *The Living Room Candidate: Presidential Campaign Commercials 1952–2008*: http://www.livingroomcandidate.org. For focus group responses to Carter's advertisements, see DMI Focus Groups Conducted for the Reagan/Bush Committee, September 1980, box 207, Richard Wirthlin Files: DMI Polling Files, Ronald Reagan Presidential Library.

15. DMI Focus Groups Conducted for the Reagan/Bush Committee, September 1980, box 207, Richard Wirthlin Files: DMI Polling Files, Ronald Reagan Presidential Library.

16. Troy, *See How They Ran*, p. 240.

17. Martin Schram, *The Pursuit of the Presidency 1980* (New York: Putnam, 1980), p. 114.

18. DMI Focus Groups Conducted for the Reagan/Bush Committee, September 1980, box 207, Richard Wirthlin Files: DMI Polling Files, Ronald Reagan Presidential Library.

19. "Light," Carter/Mondale Reelection Committee, Inc. Maker: Rafshoon Communications, from Museum of the Moving Image, *The Living Room Candidate: Presidential Campaign Commercials 1952–2008*: http://www.livingroomcandidate.org.

20. DMI Focus Groups Conducted for the Reagan/Bush Committee, September 1980, box 207, Richard Wirthlin Files: DMI Polling Files, Ronald Reagan Presidential Library.

21. Ibid.

22. Bertram Lance Interview, Miller Center, University of Virginia, Carter Presidential Oral History Project, May 12, 1982, p. 57.

23. In fairness to Carter, he started his presidency by rejecting the limousine. After his inauguration, Carter left the capitol and walked back to the White House.

24. "Blueprint/Ford," folder "Meese, Ed — Campaign Planning — Tactics (2/4)," box 104, Reagan, Ronald: 1980 Campaign Papers, Series III: Ed Meese Files: Campaign Planning.

25. Stuart Spencer Interview, Miller Center, University of Virginia, Carter Presidential Oral History Project, Nov. 15–16, 2001, p. 75.

26. Memo, Ed Gray to Marty Anderson, 10/28/1980, folder "Meese, Ed — Campaign Operations — Debate Reactions, Thursday 10/30/1980," box 105, Ed Meese Files: Campaign Operations, Ronald Reagan 1980 Campaign Papers, Ronald Reagan Presidential Library.

27. Gerald Rafshoon Interview, Miller Center, University of Virginia, Carter Presidential Oral History Project, Apr. 8, 1983, p. 60.

28. Quoted in Troy, *See How They Ran*, p. 241.

29. Bertram Lance Interview, Miller Center, University of Virginia, Carter Presidential Oral History Project, May 12, 1982, p. 66.

30. Burton Kaufman in *Jimmy Carter: American Experience*. Transcript at: http://www.pbs.org/wgbh/amex/carter/peopleevents/p_bcarter.html.

31. Gerald Rafshoon Interview, Miller Center, University of Virginia, Carter Presidential Oral History Project, Apr. 8, 1983, p. 62.

32. Memo, Betty Southard Murphy to William J. Casey, June 18, 1980, folder "Meese, Ed — Campaign Planning — Tactics (4/4)," box 104, Reagan, Ronald: 1980 Campaign Papers, Series III: Ed Meese Files: Campaign Planning.

33. According to historian Gil Troy, the Democratic primary had "wrecked [Carter's] choirboy image" (Troy, *See How They Ran*, p. 241).

34. "Carter's Campaign Tone," The Monitor's View; Editorial, *Christian Science Monitor*, Sept. 22, 1980, Monday Midwestern Edition, p. 24.

35. Sam Donaldson, *ABC World News Tonight*, Oct. 7, 1980, ABC News Transcripts.

36. Memo, Elaine Donnelly to Ed Meese, Oct. 16, 1980, folder, "Meese Files — Camp Ops — Miscellaneous (3/3)," box 108, Ed Meese Files: Campaign Operations, Ronald Reagan Presidential Library.

37. Gerald Rafshoon Interview, Miller Center, University of Virginia, Carter Presidential Oral History Project, Apr. 8, 1983, p. 22.

38. Ibid., p. 21.

39. Lyn Nofziger Interview, Miller Center, University of Virginia, Carter Presidential Oral History Project, Mar. 6, 2003, p. 34.

40. Gerald Rafshoon Interview, Miller Center, University of Virginia, Carter Presidential Oral History Project, Apr. 8, 1983, p. 23. Emphasis in original.

41. Charles Kirbo Interview, Miller Center, University of Virginia, Carter Presidential Oral History Project, Jan. 5, 1983, p. 30.

42. Gerald Rafshoon Interview, Miller Center, University of Virginia, Carter Presidential Oral History Project, Apr. 8, 1983, p. 55.

43. Jimmy Carter, "Crisis of Confidence" Speech, July 15, 1979. Transcript from Scripps Library, Miller Center, University of Virginia.

44. News Release, Excerpts from Remarks of Ambassador George Bush, Oct. 21, 1980, folder "Press Material, Releases Book IV, 10/1/80–11/6/80," box 45: Hannaford/California Headquarters: General Campaign Files, Ronald Reagan Presidential Library.

45. As Gil Troy noted, "Most Americans disapproved of Carter's decision. Once again he had politicized his image" (Troy, *See How They Ran*, p. 242).

46. Jimmy Carter, in PBS Transcripts, Jim Lehrer, *Debating Our Destiny*, "Jimmy Carter Interview," Apr. 28, 1989: http://www.pbs.org/newshour/debatingourdestiny/interviews/carter.html#1980.

47. Ibid.

48. Gil Troy analyzed the debate this way: "The Carter-Reagan debate marked a clash between two styles, between ... a politics of issues and a politics of images. Carter played Nixon to Reagan's Kennedy ... Carter, tight-lipped, flashing forced

smiles at inappropriate moments" (Troy, *See How They Ran*, p. 244).

49. Carter-Reagan Debate, Oct. 28, 1980. Transcript from the Commission on Presidential Debates: http://www.debates.org/index.php?page=debate-transcripts.

50. Sean Wilentz analyzed the transaction in this way: "Carter ... made the error of ... trying to come across as a warm family man," which "sounded odd, as if he would trivialize his job" by discussing "weighty affairs of state" with his daughter (Wilentz, *The Age of Reagan*, p. 124).

51. Transcript, Presidential Debate in Cleveland, OH, Oct. 28, 1980. John T. Woolley and Gerhard Peters, *The American Presidency Project* [online]. Santa Barbara, CA: University of California (hosted), Gerhard Peters (database).

52. See Troy, *See How They Ran*, p. 250.

53. DMI Focus Groups Conducted for the Reagan/Bush Committee, September 1980, box 207, Richard Wirthlin Files: DMI Polling Files, Ronald Reagan Presidential Library.

54. "Reagan for President Campaign Plan," 6/29/80 (Draft) folder, "Wirthlin — Reagan for President Campaign Plan (2/4)," box 177, Richard Wirthlin Files, Ronald Reagan Presidential Library.

55. As the political scientist John Kenneth White wrote of Reagan, "Reagan has usually managed to present himself to voters as 'one of us.' Reagan's ... success rests in his ability to convey a sense of *shared values* ... that transform him into 'one of us'" (White, *The New Politics of Old Values*, p. 4).

56. This quote recalled the early days of Reagan's governorship in California, but was adopted by his 1980 campaign managers. See "The Creative Management of Ronald Reagan," Meese, Ed — Campaign Planning — Meetings, April 1980, Reagan, Ronald: 1980 Campaign Papers, Series III: Ed Meese Files: Campaign Planning, RFP Planning 1, Box 103.

57. Dolon Draft, "Vision" speech, Oct. 27, 1980, folder "Meese, Ed — Debate — Cleveland, OH, 10/28/80 (Reagan-Carter) (3/3)," box 140, Ed Meese Files: Debate Files, Ronald Reagan Presidential Library.

58. Stuart Spencer Interview, Miller Center, University of Virginia, Carter Presidential Oral History Project, Nov. 15–16, 2001.

59. "Governor Reagan's Visit to Detroit, Michigan," Briefing Documents, Copy #5, Policy Coordination, California Headquarters-Briefing Documents from Policy Coordination Office, 9/1–2/80, Reagan, Ronald: 1980 Campaign Papers, Series I: Hannaford/California Headquarters: Briefing Files, Ronald Reagan Presidential Library. As illustrated in this particular example, Reagan appealed to an older western typography. He famously signed his first bill into law on his California ranch, decked out in cowboy hat and blue jeans. It was not a style he acquired upon entering the office; he employed this look frequently on the campaign trail, at the advice of his advisors. They found that this image appealed not only on the Pacific Coast, Mountain West, and Midwest, but also on Jimmy Carter's home turf where "the key to changing votes" in the western Southeast was "the frontier spirit of this last-settled and most economically dynamic part of the South. This spirit is similar to the Western one, so Reagan has a natural appeal" (Memo, Dr. Donald J. Devine to Mr. William J. Casey and Dr. Richard B. Wirthlin, June 19, 1980, box 103, Reagan, Ronald: 1980 Campaign Papers, Series III: Ed Meese Files: Campaign Planning, RFP Planning 10).

60. Memo, Reagan Advisory Committee, June 26, 1980, Meese, Ed — Campaign Planning — Meetings, June 1980, Reagan, Ronald: 1980 Campaign Papers, Series III: Ed Meese Files: Campaign Planning, RFP Planning 1, Box 103.

61. DMI Focus Groups Conducted for the Reagan/Bush Committee, September 1980, box 207, Richard Wirthlin Files: DMI Polling Files, Ronald Reagan Presidential Library.

62. "The Reagan Kids: A Look at What Could Be the Nation's Next First Family: Patti, Ron, Maureen and Mike," *People* 14, no. 3 (July 21, 1980).

63. Memo, Richard Wirthlin to Ed Meese, Sept. 10, 1980, Re: Nancy Reagan's Stump Speech, folder, "Meese, Ed — Campaign Planning — Speech Planning," box 104, Reagan, Ronald: 1980 Campaign Papers, Series III: Ed Meese Files: Campaign Planning.

64. Ibid.

65. Ibid.

66. Ibid.

67. Ibid.

68. Ibid.

69. Memo, Jim Munn and Jeff Davis to Ed Meese, Oct. 20, 1980, folder, "Meese Files — Camp Ops — Miscellaneous (2/3)," box 108, Ed Meese Files: Campaign Operations, Ronald Reagan Presidential Library.

70. "Nancy Reagan," Reagan Bush Committee, 1980, made by Campaign '80, from Museum of the Moving Image, *The Living Room Candidate: Presidential Campaign Commercials 1952–2008*: http://www.livingroomcandidate.org.

71. Ronald Reagan, "Farewell Address to the Nation," Jan. 11, 1989, *Public Papers of the Presidents*, 1721. For audio, see UCSB's "Presidency Project" digital archive: http://www.presidency.ucsb.edu.

72. "Suggested Introduction of Ronald Reagan," folder "Intros for R. Reagan (for speaking engagements)," box 44: Hannaford/California Headquarters: General Campaign Files, Ronald Reagan Presidential Library.

73. Ibid.

74. "Reagan for President Campaign Plan" 6/29/80 (Draft) folder, "Wirthlin — Reagan for President Campaign Plan (2/4)," box 177, Richard Wirthlin Files, Ronald Reagan Presidential Library.

75. Ibid.

76. Memo, Rich Williamson to Bill Casey, Ed

Meese, Jim Baker, Oct. 21, 1980, folder "Meese, Ed — Debate — Cleveland, OH, 10/28/80 (Reagan-Carter) (2/3)," box 140, Ed Meese Files: Debate Files, Ronald Reagan Presidential Library.

77. "A Strategy of Peace for the 80s, draft," folder "Press Material, Releases Book IV, 10/1/80–11/6/80," box 45: Hannaford/California Headquarters: General Campaign Files, Ronald Reagan Presidential Library.

78. "Reagan for President Campaign Plan," 6/29/80 (Draft) folder, "Wirthlin — Reagan for President Campaign Plan (2/4)," box 177, Richard Wirthlin Files, Ronald Reagan Presidential Library.

79. Ibid. As Samuel Popkin explained, when making judgments in a low-information environment (where the ideology or policy positions of favored candidates were relatively unknown) voters often believed that candidates shared their views and opinions, despite evidence to the contrary.

80. Stuart Spencer Interview, Miller Center, University of Virginia, Carter Presidential Oral History Project, Nov. 15–16, 2001, p. 55.

81. "Draft of Strategy for First Debate," folder "Meese, Ed — Debate — Baltimore, 9/21/80, undated (1/7)," box 139, Ed Meese Files: Convention, Debate Files.

82. "Reagan Press Conference and the Debates," folder "Meese, Ed — Debate — Baltimore, 9/21/80, undated (4/7)," box 140, Ed Meese Files: Debate Files, Ronald Reagan Presidential Library.

83. In *The Age of Reagan*, Sean Wilentz argued that Reagan's casual comebacks presented a "calm, friendly, attractive man" (p. 124).

84. Lyn Nofziger Interview, Miller Center, University of Virginia, Carter Presidential Oral History Project, Mar. 6, 2003, p. 35.

85. Jimmy Carter in Jim Lehrer, Jimmy Carter "Debating Our Destiny" Interview, Apr. 28, 1989. Transcript from www.pbs.org. Gil Troy analyzed Reagan's style in this way: "Reagan was friendly and paternal, blocking Carter's jabs with a smile and a nod.... The sunny Californian chided the uptight Georgian" (Troy, *See How They Ran*, p. 244).

86. Jimmy Carter in Jim Lehrer, Jimmy Carter "Debating Our Destiny" Interview, Apr. 28, 1989. Transcript from www.pbs.org.

87. Memo, Anthony Dolan to Ed Meese (undated), folder "Meese, Ed — Debate — Baltimore, 9/21/80, undated (1/7)," box 139, Ed Meese Files: Convention, Debate Files.

88. Memo, Jim Munn and Jeff Davis to Ed Meese, Oct. 20, 1980, folder, "Meese Files — Camp Ops — Miscellaneous (2/3)," box 108, Ed Meese Files: Campaign Operations, Ronald Reagan Presidential Library.

89. Memo, Rich Williamson to Bill Casey, Ed Meese, Jim Baker, Oct. 21, 1980, folder "Meese, Ed — Debate — Cleveland, OH, 10/28/80 (Reagan-Carter) (2/3)," box 140, Ed Meese Files: Debate Files, Ronald Reagan Presidential Library.

90. Memo, Andy Carter to Ronald Reagan and

Nancy Reagan, May 5, 1980, folder, "Meese Files — Camp Ops — Political Memos," box 108, Ed Meese Files: Campaign Operations, Ronald Reagan Presidential Library.

91. Memo, Rich Williamson to Bill Casey, Ed Meese, Jim Baker, Oct. 21, 1980, folder "Meese, Ed — Debate — Cleveland, OH, 10/28/80 (Reagan-Carter) (2/3)," box 140, Ed Meese Files: Debate Files, Ronald Reagan Presidential Library.

92. Memo, Rich Williamson to Bill Casey, Ed Meese, Jim Baker, Oct. 21, 1980, folder "Meese, Ed — Debate — Cleveland, OH, 10/28/80 (Reagan-Carter) (2/3)," box 140, Ed Meese Files: Debate Files, Ronald Reagan Presidential Library.

93. Memo, Rich Williamson to Bill Casey, Ed Meese, Jim Baker, Oct. 21, 1980, folder "Meese, Ed — Debate — Cleveland, OH, 10/28/80 (Reagan-Carter) (2/3)," box 140, Ed Meese Files: Debate Files, Ronald Reagan Presidential Library.

94. Ibid.

95. Stuart Spencer Interview, Miller Center, University of Virginia, Carter Presidential Oral History Project, Nov. 15–16, 2001, p. 59.

96. Memo, Anthony Dolan to Ed Meese (undated), folder "Meese, Ed — Debate — Baltimore, 9/21/80, undated (1/7)," box 139, Ed Meese Files: Convention, Debate Files.

97. Jody Powell Exit Interview, Dec. 2, 1980, Washington, DC. Final Edited Transcript, Jimmy Carter Library and Museum.

98. Free Congress Research and Education Foundation National Poll, folder, "Meese Files — Camp Ops — Miscellaneous (2/3)," box 108, Ed Meese Files: Campaign Operations, Ronald Reagan Presidential Library.

99. Free Congress Research and Education Foundation National Poll, folder, "Meese Files — Camp Ops — Miscellaneous (2/3)," box 108, Ed Meese Files: Campaign Operations, Ronald Reagan Presidential Library.

100. As Gary Wills explained, "A visit to" Reagan's mythical American past "is always a pleasant experience. Visiting Reaganland is very much like taking children to Disneyland.... It is a safe past, with no sharp edges to stumble against." If Reagan's America "cannot be rooted in the real past it works to obliterate, then it will invent ... a substitute history to lull us" into his nostalgic version of a better America. See Gary Wills, *Reagan's America: Innocents at Home* (Boston: Penguin, 2000), pp. 459–460.

101. Memo, Bill Gavin to Bill Casey, Dick Allen, Dick Wirthlin, Ed Meese, Martin Anderson, Peter Hannaford, Mar. 20, 1980, folder "Speech Strategy — Community of Values (1980) — Bill Gavin," box 50, Reagan, Ronald: 1980 Campaign Papers 1965–80, Series I: Hannaford/California Headquarters: General Campaign Files, Ronald Reagan Presidential Library.

102. Stan Greenberg (and others) have argued that the America to which Reagan hoped to return was a pre–civil rights, pre–1960s America. The undertones of the blue-collar Reagan vote were clearly

racist. What follows is not an effort to romanticize Reagan's nostalgic vision for America, but rather capture what the majority of Reagan voters saw and felt when they interacted with their candidate.

103. Memo, Richard Wirthlin to Ed Meese and Bill Casey, May 12, 1980, folder "Meese, Ed— Campaign Planning— Political Memos, May 1980," box 103, Reagan, Ronald: 1980 Campaign Papers, Series III: Ed Meese Files: Campaign Planning, RFP Planning 1.

104. Stuart Spencer Interview, Miller Center, University of Virginia, Carter Presidential Oral History Project, Nov. 15–16, 2001, p. 66.

105. As Michael Novak noted, a presidential candidate must be an "authentic folk hero ... a symbol of some virtue or dream especially dear to Americans" (Novak, *Choosing Presidents*, p. 1).

106. Memo, Richard Wirthlin to Ed Meese and Bill Casey, May 12, 1980, folder "Meese, Ed— Campaign Planning— Political Memos, May 1980," box 103, Reagan, Ronald: 1980 Campaign Papers, Series III: Ed Meese Files: Campaign Planning, RFP Planning 1.

107. Memo, Bill Gavin to Bill Casey, Dick Allen, Dick Wirthlin, Ed Meese, Martin Anderson, Peter Hannaford, Mar. 20, 1980, folder "Speech Strategy— Community of Values (1980)— Bill Gavin," box 50, Reagan, Ronald: 1980 Campaign Papers 1965–80, Series I: Hannaford/California Headquarters: General Campaign Files, Ronald Reagan Presidential Library.

108. DMI Focus Groups Conducted for the Reagan/Bush Committee, September 1980, box 207, Richard Wirthlin Files: DMI Polling Files, Ronald Reagan Presidential Library.

109. Media Campaign, folder, "Campaign '80, 10/8/80 Meeting," box 207, Richard Wirthlin Files: DMI Polling Files, Ronald Reagan Presidential Library.

110. Memo, Jim Munn and Jeff Davis to Ed Meese, Oct. 20, 1980, folder, "Meese Files— Camp Ops— Miscellaneous (2/3)," box 108, Ed Meese Files: Campaign Operations, Ronald Reagan Presidential Library.

111. This bears out in political theory. Voters instinctively do not trust politicians. They rely on word-of-mouth recommendations from sources of authority they already know— trusted neighbors, friends, community leaders, and so forth.

112. Report on the 1980 Elections, Nov. 11, 1980, folder "Election Report, 11/11/1980," box 43: Hannaford/California Headquarters: General Campaign Files, Ronald Reagan Presidential Library.

Chapter 3

1. For Gil Troy's account of Reagan and patriotism and Olympic spirit, see *Morning in America: How Ronald Reagan Invented the 1980s* (Prince-

ton, NJ: Princeton University Press, 2007), pp. 150–155.

2. Howell Raines, "A Contrast on TV," *New York Times*, Sept. 5, 1984, Wednesday Late City Final Edition, Sect. A, p. 20.

3. Laurence Barrett, Evan Thomas, and Sam Allis, "Smelling the Big Kill," *Time*, Sept. 17, 1984. This "aw, shucks" quality was integral to Reagan's projection of presidentiality. He constantly seemed humbled by the experience, always with a particular remove between himself and the institution of the Executive Branch. This is why it was believable when Reagan professed no knowledge of Iran-Contra; it is also why voters were able to think of Reagan as a person rather than an actor or a president. Even when Reagan confessed (tongue-in-cheek) that "president" was the best role he ever played, he did not come across as a liar, but as a man who understood himself to be separate from the title.

4. It was in 1984 that the Democratic nominating process was first governed by the Hunt Commission rules. As a result, while Gary Hart garnered more support in primaries and caucuses, Mondale was able to secure the nomination through the support of superdelegates. Nonetheless, Hart continued to challenge Mondale through the early summer months of 1984, risking the potential for a divided convention.

5. Laurence Barrett, Evan Thomas, and Sam Allis, "Smelling the Big Kill," *Time*, Sept. 17, 1984.

6. Howell Raines, "A Contrast on TV," *New York Times*, Sept. 5, 1984, Wednesday Late City Final Edition, Sect. A, p. 20.

7. James Reston, "Washington: Debating the Debates," *New York Times*, Oct. 7, 1984, Late City Final Edition.

8. Ibid. I take issue with Reston's binary depiction of issues versus images in campaigns. Voters use personal images to interpret messages, calculate risk, and evaluate trust. Images, it is clear, are not only essential to voters' assimilation of information, but also constitutive to their assessment of issues.

9. Jonathan Moore, in *Campaign for President: The Managers Look at '84*, p. xvii.

10. Mike Shanahan, "Future Demo Candidates Must Look Good on TV," Associated Press, Nov. 8, 1984, Thursday BC cycle.

11. Jonathan Moore, in *Campaign for President: The Managers Look at '84*, p. xvii.

12. Howell Raines, "A Contrast on TV," *New York Times*, Sept. 5, 1984, Late City Final Edition. As Jonathan Moore observed at the conclusion of the campaign, "Television ... is prone to the entertainment side of" candidate "personality and to symbols and images which can be portrayed visually. Thus, candidates are encouraged to be more" visually expressive "in response to television's opportunities and requirements" (Jonathan Moore, in *Campaign for President: The Managers Look at '84*, pp. xvi–xvii). While Jonathan Moore might

have given the media too much credit, and voters too little credit, his comments challenged the assertion that the 1984 election reflected the ascension of conservatism and permanent party realignment.

13. As Elliott Roosevelt wrote in his foreword to Keith Blume's *The Presidential Election Show*, television privileges the ability to "be more natural" and "deliver ... lines in the most convincing manner.... The harsh reality is, to be a successful political leader today means little more than being a great television actor." See Keith Blume, *The Presidential Election Show* (Westport, CT: Bergin & Garvey Publishers, Inc., 1985), p. ix. While I have some fundamental disagreements with this assertion — presidentiality is about more than acting, it is about connecting — Roosevelt's argument offers an important insight into the public's reception of Reagan and Mondale in 1984.

14. Sidney Kraus, "Presidential Debates: Images and Issues," *Christian Science Monitor*, Oct. 4, 1984, Opinion, p. 15. It is interesting to note the media's interest in reporting backroom details. Rather than reporting voters' reactions to speeches, broadcast and print outlets were increasingly attuned to reporting the process of voting and viewership. Further, by deconstructing the medium, the campaign strategy, and the audience, media outlets engaged in reporting not just the campaign, but also the campaign about the campaign.

15. "To Finish What Is Well Started," *Newsweek*, Feb. 6, 1984, p. 18.

16. Interview transcript, Phil Dusenberry, with *PBS News Hour Media Unit*. Transcript from PBS: www.pbs.org/newshour/media/biofilms/dusenberry.html.

17. See American National Election Studies: Strength of Party Identification Table. While the number of self-identified Republicans climbed in 1984, the surge was both small and ephemeral. By 1992, the number of self-identified Republicans had decreased to the 1968 levels.

18. Troy, *Morning in America*, p. 148.

19. Ibid., p. 149.

20. Bob Teeter, in *Campaign for President: The Managers Look at '84*, p. 229.

21. Bob Teeter, in *Campaign for President: The Managers Look at '84*, p. 229. In fairness to Bob Teeter, immediately following the election he also noted that "we are in the midst of a major political realignment in this country." For the second comment, see James L. Sundquist, "The 1984 Election: How Much Realignment?" *Brookings Review* 3, no. 2, Special Election Issue (Winter 1985): 8–15.

22. James L. Sundquist, "The 1984 Election: How Much Realignment?" *Brookings Review* 3, no. 2, Special Election Issue (Winter 1985): 8–15. To be sure, Sundquist was writing from a very narrow vantage point. Realignment is measured over time and requires a more permanent shift in voting trends. It is therefore useful to turn to long-range measures of party identification. In the American

National Election Survey data, it is clear that party identification began to destabilize around 1968. While more voters identified with the Republican Party, and while key base groups of the New Deal–era Democratic Party (ethnic Catholics, Dixicrats, low-income and rural voters) began to identify as Republicans, this identification appears to have been ephemeral and dependent on individual candidates. Thus, we find that the percentage of self-identified "Strong Republicans" was significantly lower in 1984 than it had been in 1960. Instead, the trend indicates growth in self-identified Independent voters, resulting in de-alignment, or destabilization. The destabilization, which might have led some to confirm realignment and revolution, did upset the traditional base of the Democratic Party more than the historic base of the Republican Party. The reason for this is simple: the Democratic Party enjoyed a much larger coalition than the Republican Party. When voters abandoned political parties, the Democrats simply had more to lose. Thus, we ought to consider 1984 as part of a long-term destabilization in party identification. There are several likely causes for this destabilization. As de-alignment began in 1968, we can point to several contextual causes for de-alignment. In addition to the Vietnam War, the implosion of the Democratic Party, and the end of the postwar economic boom, 1968 was the first election year in which baby boomers could vote. The percentage of self-identified Independents continued to increase relatively steadily until 2004. This is reflected in American voting behavior since 1976. The same voters who turned out for Ronald Reagan also turned out for Bill Clinton and George W. Bush. Their identification appears to be decreasingly based in party loyalty and increasingly based on individual candidate measures.

23. Ibid.

24. See Gerald Pomper, *The Election of 1984* (New York: Chatham House, 1985), p. 79.

25. "Personalities Overpower Parties, Anderson Says," *New York Times*, Sept. 30, 1984, p. 28.

26. As historian Gil Troy noted, "Walter Mondale mounted a slow, plodding, honest, substantive campaign, in keeping with his slow, plodding, honest character.... Mondale was earnest, with a perpetual, burdened, bags-under-the-eyes look" (Troy, *Morning in America*, pp. 163–164).

27. In his introduction to Keith Blume's *The Presidential Election Show*, Elliott Roosevelt argued that Reagan's victory was not inevitable. "A good performance by Mondale ... could have overcome" voters' satisfaction with the economy in 1984. "Mondale could have exploited Reagan's foot-in-mouth remarks and he could have capitalized on the administration's obviously weak foreign policy record." Nonetheless, Mondale was disadvantaged by a news media that cared only about images, symbols, and the soft sell. See Keith Blume, *The Presidential Election Show* (Westport, CT: Bergin & Garvey, 1985), p. x. I take issue with this asser-

tion. Again, the public is not a passive entity duped by an image-obsessed media. Instead, voters and viewers (for good reason) look for nonverbal cues from candidates. While some do vote merely on which candidate they "like better" most use this as an efficient way to discover the candidate with whom they feel more comfortable. In the post–Watergate era, voters understand that campaign promises often mean very little. Therefore, Mondale's substantive promises, even if they had been taken more seriously by the news media, were of little use to many voters who were selecting a candidate on the basis of representation.

28. For a discussion of the networks' decisions to air (or not air) Reagan's and Mondale's convention films, see Martin Schram, "Reagan Introduced on Screen," *Washington Post*, Aug. 24, 1984, Friday Final Edition, p. A9.

29. Although Mondale's personal narrative was not established in this film, it is both interesting and important that display of hobbies had become sine qua non by 1984. See "A Lifetime of Leadership," Consultants '84 for Mondale/Ferraro Committee, Inc.

30. Transcript from *Vital Speeches of the Day*, Aug. 15, 1984, vol. 15, no. 21, pp. 642–644.

31. *San José Mercury*, Sept. 5, 1984, p. G3.

32. Maxine Isaacs, in *Campaign for President: The Managers Look at '84*, p. 172.

33. John Dillin, "'84 Campaign Follows Classic Script," *Christian Science Monitor*, Sept. 10, 1984.

34. Richard Leone, in *Campaign for President: The Managers Look at '84*, p. 188.

35. Ibid., p. 154.

36. Laurence Barrett, Evan Thomas, and Sam Allis, "The Goal: A Landslide," *Time*, Nov. 5, 1984.

37. Dick West, quoting Alan Lichtman, "Election Year Tremors," *Lodi News-Sentinel*, Aug. 13, 1984, p. 4.

38. Dick Wirthlin, in *Campaign for President: The Managers Look at '84*, p. 168.

39. As Dick Wirthlin told Mondale's key advisors, "With your strategy, you might as well have sat in Washington, D.C., in a studio and cut your spots every day. From our perspective you made it possible for us to go in on visits" (Dick Wirthlin, in *Campaign for President: The Managers Look at '84*, p. 173).

40. Brit Hume, *ABC World News Tonight*, Aug. 31, 1984. ABC News Transcripts.

41. Garry Clifford, "Welcome to Elmore, Home of Fritz Mondale," *People* 22, no. 4 (July 23, 1984).

42. It was well known, and often repeated, that Mondale had a terrific sense of humor in private settings. Known as a cut-up among friends and colleagues, this side of Mondale was rarely, if ever, seen by a majority of American voters.

43. Howell Raines, "A Chance to Change Psychology of Election," *New York Times*, Oct. 7, 1984, Sunday Late City Final Edition.

44. Meg Greenfield, "Mondale: Why He's

Falling Short," *Washington Post*, Sept. 12, 1984, Final Edition.

45. Mike Shanahan, "The Public Mondale: Quiet Dignity and Subtle Humor," Associated Press, Oct. 28, 1984, Sunday BC cycle. In early October 1984, Sidney Kraus highlighted the disparity in an Op-Ed in the *Christian Science Monitor*: "Thus far in the campaign Mr. Reagan's strategy has been image oriented, while Mr. Mondale's emphasis has been on issues. Reagan has been called the 'Teflon President': Though voters hold him accountable for certain negative events (issues), his popularity (image) ratings continue to be high." See Sidney Kraus, "Presidential Debates: Images and Issues," *Christian Science Monitor*, Oct. 4, 1984, Opinion, p. 15.

46. As Ron Phillips of UPI noted, "Despite his humorous and lively private personality, Mondale seems unable to translate it into a public personality" (Ron Phillips, United Press International, July 24, 1984, Tuesday a.m. cycle).

47. David Broder, "Forgive and Forget," *Washington Post*, Sept. 9, 1984, Sunday Final Edition.

48. Ibid.

49. "Geraldine Ferraro: A Break with Tradition," *Time*, July 23, 1984.

50. Lee Atwater, in *Campaign for President: The Managers Look at '84*, p. 162.

51. Bernard Weinraub, "Mondale's New Campaign Themes: Patriotism and Hard Work," *New York Times*, Aug. 3, 1984, Late City Final Edition.

52. Maureen Dowd, "Whaddaya Mean Accent? She Talks Queens!" *New York Times*, Oct. 1, 1984, Monday Late City Final Edition, Section A; Page 1.

53. Ibid.

54. See Margaret Shapiro, "Patronage Still King in Queens," *Washington Post*, Aug. 29, 1984, Wednesday Final Edition, p. A1.

55. Kathleen Hall Jamieson, *Eloquence in an Electronic Age*, p. 87.

56. See Margaret Shapiro, "Patronage Still King in Queens," *Washington Post*, Aug. 29, 1984, Wednesday Final Edition, p. A1.

57. Lee Atwater, in *Campaign for President: The Managers Look at '84*, p. 162.

58. Dick Wirthlin, in *Campaign for President: The Managers Look at '84*, p. 214.

59. Lee Atwater, in *Campaign for President: The Managers Look at '84*, p. 162.

60. "Walter Mondale: Getting a Second Look," *Time*, Oct. 22, 1984.

61. Ibid.

62. Ibid.

63. *The MacNeil/Lehrer News Hour* Transcript. Robert MacNeil, Jim Lehrer, "Too Old to Serve? Issue and Debate: The Character of the Court," *The MacNeil/Lehrer News Hour*, Oct. 9, 1984.

64. Source: Nielsen Media Research Report, "Highest Rated Presidential Debates: 1960–2008."

65. Ibid.

66. Gerald Pomper wrote at length about Rea-

gan's advantage in the second debate in *The Election of 1984*. Pomper wrote, "The overall effect of the debates was to assure Reagan's victory ... by the time of the second debate, expectations had changed. Mondale ... needed a spectacular second performance ... Reagan no longer had to meet high standards. He needed only to reassure the electorate that he was of sound mind." See Pomper, *The Election of 1984*, p. 77.

67. Jim Johnson, in *Campaign for President: The Managers Look at '84*, p. 216.

68. Ibid.

69. "When he appeared tentative and somewhat confused in the first debate, his age suddenly became an issue in the campaign. When he seemed in command in the second debate, the issue just as quickly receded" (Laurence Barrett, Evan Thomas, and Sam Allis, "The Goal: A Landslide," *Time*, Nov. 5, 1984).

70. "A Tie Goes to the Gipper," *Time*, Oct. 29, 1984.

71. Ed Rollins, in *Campaign for President: The Managers Look at '84*, p. 205.

72. Jim Johnson, in *Campaign for President: The Managers Look at '84*, p. 217.

73. "Pollsters Talking about Reagan Landslide," Associated Press, Sept. 21, 1984, Friday a.m. cycle.

74. Frank Newport, Jeffrey M. Jones, and Lydia Saad, "Ronald Reagan from the People's Perspective," Gallup News Service, June 2004.

75. Frank Newport, Jeffrey M. Jones, and Lydia Saad, "Ronald Reagan from the People's Perspective," Gallup News Service, June 2004. On aggregate, throughout the fall of 1984, Reagan's personal approval ratings stabilized around 66 percent. (See *Los Angeles Times* poll, Oct. 11, 1984; *CBS News/New York Times* poll, Oct. 23–25, 1984.)

76. In studies of Congressional approval ratings versus individual representatives' approval ratings, Americans consistently privilege the individual over the institution. When Democrats ran against a party (the Republicans) and an institution (the presidency) in 1982, they fared better than when they ran against a popular person (Ronald Reagan) in 1984.

77. Even political scientist Gerald Pomper, who has argued that economic conditions provide the best predictive model for the outcome of the 1984 election wrote, "Reagan was at a special advantage because of his great personal popularity. The President's ability to project an image of warmth and sincerity while also exuding strength and fortitude as the nation's chief of state was a potent combination" (Pomper, *The Election of 1984*, p. 91).

78. Stuart Spencer Interview, Miller Center, University of Virginia, Carter Presidential Oral History Project, Nov. 15–16, 2001, p. 100.

79. Ronald Reagan, "Remarks at a Reagan-Bush Rally in Fountain View, California, Sept. 3, 1984. The Public Papers of President Ronald W. Reagan. Ronald Reagan Presidential Library.

80. When *People* ran an informal survey of Rea-

gan voters across the country, they found that average citizens loved Reagan because he made them feel comfortable and because they felt that they could relate to him. One voter from Ohio, claiming to be "a Reagan girl through and through" said that she loved the president because "we have a lot in common — we're both as Irish as Paddy's pig" ("Once More, with Feeling" *People* 22, no. 21 [Nov. 19, 1984]).

81. Martin Schram, "Reagan's Cynical Campaign," *Washington Post*, Sept. 23, 1984, Sunday Final Edition, p. C1.

82. Robert Donovan and Ray Schrer, *Unsilent Revolution*, p. 237.

83. Martin Schram, "Reagan's Cynical Campaign," *Washington Post*, Sept. 23, 1984, Sunday Final Edition, p. C1.

84. *New York Times*, Sept. 14, 1984, p. 12.

85. John L. Sullivan, et al., "Candidate Appraisal and Human Nature: Man and Superman in the 1984 Election," *Political Psychology* 11, no. 3 (1990).

86. Stuart Spencer Interview, Miller Center, University of Virginia, Carter Presidential Oral History Project, Nov. 15–16, 2001, p. 75.

87. Editorial, "And Still Champion," *New York Times*, Nov. 7, 1984, Wednesday Late City Final Edition, p. A26.

88. "Many people have an innate distrust of politicians, but we expected that many voters would see Reagan as more trustworthy than Mondale." Even "when [Reagan] failed, he seemed to have tried his best.... He could be trusted politically and, it seemed, personally. Mondale had no such track record." For a cognitive psychology study of Reagan's image and reputation, see John L. Sullivan, et al., "Candidate Appraisal and Human Nature: Man and Superman in the 1984 Election," *Political Psychology* 11, no. 3 (1990).

89. John Edward Brown, "Letters: Nov. 12, 1984," *Time*, Nov. 12, 1984.

90. "To Finish What Is Well Started," *Newsweek*, Feb. 6, 1984, p. 18.

91. Roger Rosenblatt, "Reagan Country," *Time*, Nov. 19, 1984.

92. "Once More, with Feeling," *People* 22, no. 21 (Nov. 19, 1984).

93. Meg Greenfield, "Mondale: Why He's Falling Short," *Washington Post*, Sept. 12, 1984, Final Edition.

94. Ron Phillips, "Reagan and Mondale Bring Their Own Debate Styles to Louisville," United Press International, Oct. 7, 1984, BC cycle.

95. "Once More, with Feeling," *People* 22, no. 21 (Nov. 19, 1984).

96. Laurence Barrett, Evan Thomas, and Sam Allis, "The Goal: A Landslide," *Time*, Nov. 5, 1984.

97. Ibid.

98. Reagan also used incumbency to his advantage. While modern incumbents do not enjoy many of the advantages of their predecessors (for

in being authentic, they must also be anti–Washington), they do enjoy one distinct advantage. Challengers must convince voters that they require a change in leadership. In order to do so, challengers often resort to bleak and sad portraits of American life. Ronald Reagan was able to make people "feel good" where Mondale was required to make people feel that they could (and should) do better.

99. "Once More, with Feeling," *People* 22, no. 21 (Nov. 19, 1984).

100. Following the first debate, Reagan's campaign team decided to launch a foray into attack politics. The negative campaign lasted less than a week, with Reagan suffering his worst poll numbers in the period between October 7 and October 14. See *Campaign for President: The Managers Look at '84*, pp. 205–207.

101. Martin Schram, "Reagan's Cynical Campaign," *Washington Post*, Sept. 23, 1984, Sunday Final Edition, p. C1.

102. Ed Rollins, in *Campaign for President: The Managers Look at '84*, p. 42. For post-debate poll numbers, see also United Press International, Oct. 11, 1984, Thursday p.m. cycle.

103. Twenty years after the 1984 election, historian Gil Troy was still in awe of the feat. According to Troy, Reagan's reelection "remains one of the great American political mysteries … if blacks and women and intellectuals felt so marginalized — which they did; if the economy wavered and the poll ratings sagged, how did Reagan win reelection by a landslide? How did this president … succeed?" (Troy, *Morning in America*, p. 147). Troy surmised that Reagan won because he "made it clear that he preferred to be the Wizard of America's Id than lead a new revolution. Reagan wanted Americans to feel good, not think too hard." For more on this, see Gil Troy, *Morning in America*, pp. 148–149.

104. See Lyn Ragsdale, "Presidential Speechmaking and the Public Audience: Individual Presidents and Group Attitudes," *Journal of Politics* 49, no. 3 (1987: 704–736.

105. Michigan had 14 percent unemployment in 1984, but Reagan won that state by a margin of 59.23 percent to 40.24 percent.

106. Editorial, *Grand Rapids Press*, Sept. 19, 1984.

107. In addition to rust belt union workers, Mondale also won the support of women. Despite Geraldine Ferraro's position on the Democratic ticket, and despite the fact that women were historically more likely to support Democrats, women favored Reagan by a margin of 58–42 percent (Source: *CBS News/New York Times* Election Day Survey, Nov. 6, 1984). Reagan did not, however, win the traditionally Democratic black vote. African American voters overwhelmingly favored Mondale — 91 percent, Mondale; 9 percent, Reagan (Source: *CBS News/New York Times* Election Day Survey, Nov. 6, 1984).

108. David Broder, "Election '84; Overriding the Issues; Mondale Finds Message Obscured,"

Washington Post, Sept. 23, 1984, Sunday Final Edition.

109. "Ohio Economic Indicators Quarterly Report," record number S6260–1, Ohio Department of Development, 1984; "Employment, Hours, and Earnings in Ohio," record number S6270–1, Ohio Bureau of Employment Services, 1983.

110. Roger Stone, in *Campaign for President: The Managers Look at '84*, p. 174.

111. David Broder, "Election '84; Overriding the Issues; Mondale Finds Message Obscured," *Washington Post*, Sept. 23, 1984, Sunday Final Edition.

112. Phil Dusenberry, with *PBS News Hour Media Unit*. Transcript at: www.pbs.org/newshour/media/biofilms/dusenberry.html.

113. Reagan's most political commercial, "Bear," offered a wholly symbolic approach to the topic of national defense. The spot featured video footage of a bear wandering on a deserted mountain. An ominous-sounding narrator advised, "There is a bear in the woods. For some people, the bear is easy to see. Others don't see it at all. Some people say the bear is tame. Others say it's vicious and dangerous. Since no one can really be sure who's right, isn't it smart to be as strong as the bear? If there is a bear?" At the conclusion of the short spot, the bear encountered a human. The commercial ended without resolution, but it was clear that the Reagan campaign wanted to remind voters that the Cold War was not over. Although Reagan projected himself as a candidate of strength and peace, strength was always a part of the Reagan program. Nonetheless, rather than offering facts about the Strategic Defense Initiative, this spot offered an ambiguous riddle about a bear. What was important about this spot was that it was by far the most political advertising message produced by the Tuesday Team during the 1984 campaign, and yet even this commercial offered symbols in lieu of specifics.

114. Perhaps this is the magic of Reagan — he could connect Americans to a world in which they did not live, for which they felt nostalgic. The fantasy of the 1980s — seen in increased attendance at Walt Disney theme parks, offered on television dramas, and portrayed in Ronald Reagan's reelection campaign — in many ways became the reality of the 1980s. The historian Lizabeth Cohen (*Consumer's Republic*) examined some of this fantastical phenomenon through American commercial habits and architectural trends. The Mall — an icon of the 1980s — offered Americans a faux main street in a protected environment. The main streets of Reagan's iconic commercials were, in fact, long gone. Instead, they were replaced by private spaces such as shopping malls, enclosed sidewalks, and gated neighborhoods. It is possible that Reagan reconnected Americans to something that they experienced (or heard tell of) from a mythic past, even as Reagan represented these images as present-day realities.

115. The Tuesday Team, the group officially credited in Reagan's 1984 advertisements, included Phil Dusenberry, Sig Rogich, and Hal Riney, all of whom were advertising professionals. In a *PBS News Hour* interview, Phil Dusenberry informed Jim Lehrer that the team was put together because no one advertising firm would handle Reagan's re-election campaign media.

116. To illustrate, the use of crack cocaine reached epidemic proportions in Los Angeles in 1984. Associated rates of violent crime climbed in major cities as the crack epidemic expanded nationwide. It is clear that the Reagans were aware of problems related to drug abuse, trafficking, and crime, as Nancy Reagan adopted the anti-drugs campaign as her project during the first term in the Reagan administration. More importantly, Americans were not unaware of increases in urban decline, drug abuse, and violent crime. Nonetheless, even as they watched local news reports about kidnappings and crack, they bought Reagan's patriotic, idealistic, and nostalgic portrayal of America as he wanted it to be.

117. "Train," Reagan-Bush '84, 1984. Maker: Tuesday Team. Video courtesy of Ronald and Nancy Reagan/Ronald Reagan Presidential Library. From Museum of the Moving Image, *The Living Room Candidate: Presidential Campaign Commercials 1952–2008*: http://www.livingroomcandidate.org.

118. Although it is difficult to distinguish at first, the two commercials used the same background music, set in two separate octaves.

119. "Prouder, Stronger, Better," Reagan-Bush '84, 1984. Maker: Hal Riney, Tuesday Team. Original air date Sept. 17, 1984. Video courtesy of Ronald and Nancy Reagan/Ronald Reagan Presidential Library. From Museum of the Moving Image, *The Living Room Candidate: Presidential Campaign Commercials 1952–2008*: http://www.livingroomcandidate.org.

120. For an in-depth textual analysis of Reagan's 1984 convention film, see Morreale, *A New Beginning*.

121. Tom Brokaw, with reports and analysis from Andrea Mitchell, Roger Mudd, and John Chancellor, *NBC News Special Coverage*, Republican National Convention, Aug. 23, 1984, 8:00 p.m.

122. To be fair, NBC (in conjunction with the Reagan campaign) lent legitimacy to Reagan's image by offering viewers entrée into the backstage. Prior to its airing of *A New Beginning*, Reagan aired a live interview with Nancy Reagan and pre-taped footage of interviews with the film's producers, Philip Dusenberry and Doug Watts. On the one hand, Reagan's convention film might have been slick. On the other hand, to the postmodern sensibility, the full disclosure of production nullifies the negative effects of alienation in viewership (Tom Brokaw, with reports and analysis from Andrea Mitchell, Roger Mudd, and John Chancellor,

NBC News Special Coverage, Republican National Convention, Aug. 23, 1984, 8:02:30–8:07:50 p.m.).

123. *A New Beginning*, Phil Dusenberry, Tuesday Team, Reagan-Bush '84, 1984, from Museum of the Moving Image, *The Living Room Candidate: Presidential Campaign Commercials 1952–2008*: http://www.livingroomcandidate.org.

124. In her analysis, Joanne Morreale argued that *A New Beginning* offered its viewers security. Its "interpretive frame posited a reality that was familiar, intelligible, and reassuring." See Morreale, *A New Beginning*, p. 88.

125. Even the political scientist Gerald Pomper, who has argued that economic conditions offer the best predictive model for election outcomes, noted that the Reagan campaign emphasized personality over substance. Of *A New Beginning*, Pomper wrote, "Reagan's ... film biography ... pictured him ... representing the nation.... Almost nothing in the film dealt with specific programs and objectives" (Pomper, *The Election of 1984*, p. 79).

126. Martin Schram, "Reagan's Cynical Campaign," *Washington Post*, Sept. 23, 1984, Sunday Final Edition, p. C1.

127. Trevor Parry-Giles and Shawn Parry-Giles, "Political Scopophilia, Presidential Campaigning, and the Intimacy of American Politics," *Communication Studies* 47 (1996): 195.

Chapter 4

1. See *CBS News/New York Times* Poll, from The Interuniversity Consortium for Political and Social Research: www.icpsr.umich.edu. Quote from E.J. Dionne, "Voters Say They're at Fault as Well as the Candidates," *New York Times*, p. 6, Nov. 22, 1988, Tuesday Late City Final Edition.

2. In 1996, voter turnout dipped below 50 percent. In 1988, turnout was about 50.1 percent. The comparison, however, is misleading. By all measures, 1988 was a more competitive election year, featured no incumbent, and witnessed vast swings in pre-election polling results. By contrast, Bill Clinton's 1996 victory was relatively secure throughout the process leading to some natural voter apathy.

3. George H.W. Bush was allegedly connected to the Iran-Contra scandal, in which Reagan administration bypassed Congress, selling arms to Iran, securing the release of hostages, and using the funds to bolster the Contras in Nicaragua. The HUD scandal involved graft in the Department of Housing and Urban Development among top administration officials. The S&L crisis, resulting from bank deregulation in the 1980s, allowed hundreds of insolvent Savings and Loans banks to remain unchecked and insolvent through much of the 1980s.

4. David Broder, "California's Swing Voters Proving Hard to Please," *Washington Post*, June 5, 1988, Sunday Final Edition, p. A1.

5. Judy Mann, "Nicer Guys Finish First," *Washington Post*, July 20, 1988, Wednesday Final Edition, p. B3.

6. Ibid.

7. Lynda Lee Kaid, "Political Advertising in the 1992 Campaign," in Denton, ed., *The 1992 Presidential Campaign*, p. 113.

8. See Harvard University, Institute of Politics, *Campaign for President: The Managers Look at '88* (New York: Auburn House, 1989), p. 263.

9. Walter Shapiro, "Bush Scores a Warm Win," *Time*, Oct. 24, 1988.

10. Roger Ailes, in *Campaign for President, the Managers Look at '88*.

11. Roger Ailes, quoted in Stephen Diamond and Edwin Bates, *The Spot: The Rise of Political Advertising on Television* (London: MIT Press, 1992), p. 387.

12. Kathleen Hall Jamieson quoted in Richard Stengel, "The Likability Sweepstakes," *Time*, Oct. 24, 1988.

13. Judy Mann, "Nicer Guys Finish First," *Washington Post*, July 20, 1988, Wednesday Final Edition, p. B3.

14. Lynda Lee Kaid, "Political Advertising in the 1992 Campaign," in Denton, ed., *The 1992 Presidential Campaign*, p. 113.

15. Walter Shapiro, "It's the Year of the Handlers," *Time*, Oct. 3, 1988.

16. Ibid.

17. Ibid.

18. Lance Morrow, "Of Myth and Memory," *Time*, Oct. 24, 1988.

19. Walter Shapiro, "It's the Year of the Handlers," *Time*, Oct. 3, 1988.

20. Melvin Maddocks, "Cool Candidates — Hot Summer," *Christian Science Monitor*, July 1, 1988, p. 17.

21. George H.W. Bush had been employed in government service since 1967. He served in the House of Representatives, as chairman of the Republican National Committee, as ambassador to the United Nations, as chief of the US Liaison Office in the People's Republic of China, as director of the CIA, and as vice president to Ronald Reagan.

22. David Broder, "Bush KO'd 'Doonesbury' — and Himself," *Washington Post*, Aug. 21, 1988, p. A1.

23. Marjorie Randon Hershey, "The Campaign and the Media," in *The Election of 1988*, ed. Gerald Pomper (London: Chatham House, 1989), p. 77.

24. Richard Stengel, "A Dose of Old-Time Populism," *Time*, Nov. 7, 1988.

25. Stuart Spencer Interview, Miller Center, University of Virginia, Carter Presidential Oral History Project, Nov. 15–16, 2001, p. 101.

26. Margaret Carlson, "Shoot-Out at Gender Gap," *Time*, Aug. 8, 1988.

27. Lloyd Grove, "Simplicity Credited in Bush Surge," *Washington Post*, Oct. 15, 1988, p. A1.

28. John Harris, "A VP for Average Folks," *Washington Post*, Oct. 14, 1988, Friday Final Edition, p. C6.

29. Ibid.

30. Marc Nuttle, in *Campaign for President: The Managers Look at '88*, pp. 237–238.

31. Ibid.

32. *Campaign for President: The Managers Look at '88*, p. 215.

33. See *Newsweek* cover, October 17, 1987, headlined "Fighting the Wimp Factor." The issue appeared during the week that George Bush announced his candidacy. It featured a photograph (supplied by the campaign) of Bush driving a speed boat. *Newsweek*'s editors had requested a photograph of the vice president playing golf. The campaign, however, realized that such an image would dangerously legitimize existing impressions of the candidate and instead opted for a more macho picture. The "wimp factor" included not only Bush's patrician background, but also his supposed inability to stand up to Ronald Reagan on Iran-Contra and other scandals, for which Bush refused to be held responsible during the 1988 election.

34. Richard Stengel, "The Man behind the Message," *Time*, Aug. 22, 1988.

35. Robin Toner, "Political Memo; Dukakis Works at Warmth, Yet Tries to Keep His Cool," *New York Times*, Aug. 8, 1988, Monday Late City Final Edition, p. A1.

36. "Topics of the Times: Blue Blood," *New York Times*, June 12, 1988, p. 26.

37. Lee Walczak, "Pork Politics," *Business Week*, Aug. 15, 1988, p. 53.

38. Lance Morrow, "Of Myth and Memory," *Time*, Oct. 24, 1988.

39. Walter Shapiro, "Bush Scores a Warm Win," *Time*, Oct. 24, 1988.

40. On this strategy of the Bush campaign, see comments by Roger Ailes, in *Campaign for President: The Managers Look at '88*, p. 219.

41. See, in particular, *Campaign for President: The Managers Look at '88*, p. 151.

42. Richard Stengel, "The Man behind the Message," *Time*, Aug. 22, 1988.

43. Richard Stengel, "The Likability Sweepstakes," *Time*, Oct. 24, 1988.

44. Roger Ailes, in *Campaign for President: The Managers Look at '88*, p. 155.

45. Ibid.

46. "Family/Children," Bush-Quayle '88, 1988. Video courtesy of the George Bush Presidential Library. From Museum of the Moving Image, *The Living Room Candidate: Presidential Campaign Commercials 1952–2008*: http://www.livingroom-candidate.org.

47. Ibid.

48. Ibid.

49. Gerald Boyd, "Bush and Dukakis Fight On,

with Gap Closing a Bit," *New York Times*, Nov. 6, 1988, Late City Final Edition, p. 1.

50. Joseph C. Harsch, "Bush's Prospects," *Christian Science Monitor*, Aug. 16, 1988, p. 11.

51. Gerald Boyd, "Bush and Dukakis Fight On, with Gap Closing a Bit," *New York Times*, Nov. 6, 1988, Late City Final Edition, p. 1.

52. Richard Stengel, "The Likability Sweepstakes," *Time*, Oct. 24, 1988.

53. David Gergen interviewing Roger Ailes, in *Campaign for President: The Managers Look at '88*, p. 205.

54. "Gov. Dukakis: Trapped," *Washington Post*, Oct. 16, 1988, Opinion Editorial, p. C6.

55. In the October 13, 1988, debate, Michael Dukakis was asked whether he would support the death penalty for a rapist if his wife were the victim. Michael Dukakis had taken a firm position against the death penalty. In response, Dukakis coldly and calmly discussed his opposition to the death penalty. Rather than expressing appropriate emotional horror at the thought of his wife being raped, Dukakis opted to focus on his issue position. To many, Dukakis appeared to be a robot, unable to produce human emotion at the thought of an obviously horrible proposition. More importantly, this became the story of the debate. Rather than emphasizing Dukakis's ability to remain composed and true to his beliefs in spite of what might have been an unfair line of questioning, the reports focused instead on Dukakis's inability to project human qualities during the debate.

56. Walter Shapiro, "Bush Scores a Warm Win," *Time*, Oct. 24, 1988.

57. Ibid. Note that these reports were also notable for the backstaginess of the commentary: "spoon-fed one-liners" and "handlers" had become central to political reporting in 1988. Readers did not merely want to know what candidates said, but also how they said it, who told them to say it, and how the words were constructed. This postmodernist desire for authenticity became very clear in 1988 and is now sine qua non in political reporting.

58. David Nyhan, "'Nice' VP, Dull Duke," *Boston Globe*, Op-Ed, Oct. 14, 1988, p. 15.

59. Tom Wicker, "In the Nation: A Balance for Bush," *New York Times*, July 29, 1988, p. A27.

60. Margaret Carlson, "Shoot-Out at Gender Gap," *Time*, Aug. 8, 1988.

61. Ibid.

62. Lance Morrow, "Of Myth and Memory," *Time*, Oct. 24, 1988.

63. Roger Ailes, in *Campaign for President: The Managers Look at '88*, p. 64.

64. Richard Stengel, "A Dose of Old-Time Populism," *Time*, Nov. 7, 1988.

65. Susan Estrich, in *Campaign for President: The Managers Look at '88*.

66. "The Packaging of George Bush" (10/6/1988). Michael S. Dukakis Presidential Campaign Records, 1962–1989, M32 Box 1/71, Folder

17, Administrative Files: Advertising; Television. Northeastern University.

67. Transcript: "Crazy" QDML-0143 QDML-0144 01–6–88. Michael S. Dukakis Presidential Campaign Records, 1962–1989, M32 Box 1/71, Folder 17, Administrative Files: Advertising; Television. Northeastern University.

68. Margaret Carlson, "A Tale of Two Childhoods," *Time*, June 20, 1988.

69. Roger Stone, quoted in *Frontline*, "Boogie Man: The Lee Atwater Story," transcripts from www.pbs.org.

70. Mary Matalin, quoted in *American Experience*, "George H.W. Bush, Part I," transcripts from www.pbs.org.

71. George H.W. Bush quoted in *American Experience*, "George H.W. Bush, Part I," transcripts from www.pbs.org.

72. Lee Atwater, quoted in *Frontline*, "Boogie Man: The Lee Atwater Story," transcripts from www.pbs.org.

73. Henry Eichel, quoted in *Frontline*, "Boogie Man: The Lee Atwater Story," transcripts from www.pbs.org.

74. George H.W. Bush, quoted in *Frontline*, "Boogie Man: The Lee Atwater Story," transcripts from www.pbs.org.

75. Michael Dukakis, quoted in *Frontline*, "Boogie Man: The Lee Atwater Story," transcripts from www.pbs.org.

76. Susan Estrich, in *Campaign for President: The Managers Look at '88*, p. 149.

77. Ibid., p. 8.

78. Paul Brountas, in *Campaign for President: The Managers Look at '88*, p. 255.

79. Robin Toner, "Political Memo; Dukakis Works at Warmth, Yet Tries to Keep His Cool," *New York Times*, Aug. 8, 1988, Monday Late City Final Edition, p. A1.

80. Ibid.

81. Ibid.

82. Ibid.

83. Ibid.

84. Richard Stengel, "The Likability Sweepstakes," *Time*, Oct. 24, 1988.

85. Ibid.

86. Larry Marz, et al., "Dukakis by the People Who Know Him Best," *Newsweek*, July 25, 1988, p. 25.

87. Jane Grandolfo, clip from *Houston Post* in Michael S. Dukakis Presidential Campaign Records, 1962–1989, M32 Box 27, Folder 1387, Northeastern University.

88. Robin Toner, "Political Memo; Dukakis Works at Warmth, Yet Tries to Keep His Cool," *New York Times*, Aug. 8, 1988, Monday Late City Final Edition, p. A1.

89. Cover, *People* 30, no. 4 (July 25, 1988).

90. Alan Richman and Cable Neuhouse, "Up from Olympus," in *People* 30, no. 4 (July 25, 1988).

91. George Will, *ABC News Candidates Televi-*

sion Forum, June 8, 1988, and reported by Maureen Dowd, "Bush and Dukakis Spar Over Issue of Who Is the Better Conservative," *New York Times*, June 8, 1988, p. A24.

92. In their Paramus, New Jersey, focus group, Lee Atwater and Roger Ailes found that both gun ownership and the Pledge of Allegiance could be winning hot-button issues for the Republican campaign in 1988.

93. *Campaign for President: The Managers Look at '88*, pp. 113–115, 254–255, 289.

94. Printed in "Bush Draws Contrasts with Rival," *Washington Post* Wednesday Final Edition, Nov. 2, 1988, p. A1.

95. Gerald Boyd, "Bush and Dukakis Fight On, with Gap Closing a Bit," *New York Times*, Nov. 6, 1988, Late City Final Edition, p. 1.

96. Walter Robinson, "Campaign '88: To Envision Presidency to Come, Analysts Look beyond the Rhetoric," *Boston Globe*, Oct. 30, 1988, Sunday City Edition, p. 1.

97. The "Willie Horton" ad, formally titled "Weekend Passes," was produced by Americans for Bush, the campaign arm of the National Security Political Action Committee.

98. "Revolving Door," Bush-Quayle '88, 1988. Original air date: 10/03/88. Maker: Dennis Frankenberry and Roger Ailes. Video courtesy of the George Bush Presidential Library. From Museum of the Moving Image, *The Living Room Candidate: Presidential Campaign Commercials 1952–2008*: http://www.livingroomcandidate.org.

99. "Credibility," Bush-Quayle '88, 1988. Maker: Ailes Communications. Video courtesy of the George Bush Presidential Library. From Museum of the Moving Image, *The Living Room Candidate: Presidential Campaign Commercials 1952–2008*: http://www.livingroomcandidate.org.

100. Richard Stengel, "A Dose of Old-Time Populism," *Time*, Nov. 7, 1988.

101. Garry Wills, "The Power Populist," *Time*, Nov. 21, 1988.

102. Ibid.

103. Richard Stengel, "A Dose of Old-Time Populism," *Time*, Nov. 7, 1988.

104. David Nyhan, "'Nice' VP, Dull Duke," *Boston Globe*, Op-Ed, Oct. 14, 1988, p. 15.

105. "Tank Ride," Bush-Quayle '88, 1988. Original air date: 10/17/88. Maker: Dennis Frankenberry. Video courtesy of the George Bush Presidential Library. From Museum of the Moving Image, *The Living Room Candidate: Presidential Campaign Commercials 1952–2008*: http://www.livingroomcandidate.org.

106. Richard Hofstadter, *Anti-intellectualism in American Life* (New York: Alfred A. Knopf, 1963), p. 22.

107. Walter Shapiro, "It's the Year of the Handlers," *Time*, Oct. 3, 1988.

108. Edward Rollins, in *Campaign for President: The Managers Look at '88*, p. 258.

109. On "issues" broadly, as a waste of resources

and drain on campaign, see *Campaign for President: The Managers Look at '88*, pp. 136–137. Roger Ailes responded that running a campaign on issues was "suicide." See also *Campaign for President: The Managers Look at '88*, p. 160. Because earned media became such an important aspect of the 1988 campaign, as news programs spent the little time they devoted to the campaign largely reporting on advertisements and blockbuster events, issues speeches and advertisements did not sell to the nightly news programs. As Susan Estrich explained, "The only time we got coverage talking about issues is when we had major policy proposals." By comparison, Roger Ailes of the Bush Campaign laid out the major differences between winners and losers in a campaign when the choice is between "vision ... themes ... issues ... slogans ... [and] sound bites."

110. Richard Stengel, "A Dose of Old-Time Populism," *Time*, Nov. 7, 1988.

111. Richard Stengel, "The Likability Sweepstakes," *Time*, Oct. 24, 1988.

112. Richard Vernaci, "Delegates See Dukakis as Dependable, Honest, Dull, Short," Associated Press, July 16, 1988, Saturday a.m. cycle.

113. John Corrigan, quoted in *Campaign for President: The Managers Look at '88*, p. 230.

114. For the campaign managers' insights into the goals of the convention, use of free media, and impact of Jesse Jackson, see John Corrigan, Susan Estrich, Paul Brountas, and Ronald Brown's comments in *Campaign for President: The Managers Look at '88*, pp. 225–233.

115. John Corrigan, quoted in *Campaign for President: The Managers Look at '88*, p. 230.

116. D. Costello, "Cartoonists Lament Over the Presidential Bore and Wimp," *Courier-Mail*, July 16, 1988.

117. Ibid.

118. Mary McGrory, "Sharpening the Focus," *Washington Post*, Oct. 27, 1988, p. A2.

119. Ted Koppel, "Ted Koppel Recalls *Nightline* Politics," Nov. 20, 2005, ABC News Transcripts.

120. Garry Wills, "The Power Populist," *Time*, Nov. 21, 1988.

121. Walter Shapiro, "Bush Scores a Warm Win," *Time*, Oct. 24, 1988.

122. Edward Rollins, in *Campaign for President: The Managers Look at '88*, p. 257.

123. William Safire, "Salome Tactics," *New York Times*, Nov. 3, 1988, Late City Final Edition, Sec. A, p. 31.

124. Janet Hook, "Skeptical Voters Foster the Tell-All Candidate," *Congressional Quarterly Weekly Report* 50, no. 31 (Aug. 1, 1992).

125. Editorial, "Sure Loser in the Debate: The Format," *New York Times*, Oct. 15, 1988, Late City Final Edition, Sec. 1, p. 30.

126. "Gov. Dukakis: Trapped," *Washington Post*, Oct. 16, 1988, Opinion Editorial, p. C6.

127. Walter Shapiro, "Bush Scores a Warm Win," *Time*, Oct. 24, 1988.

128. Oct. 21–24, *CBS News/New York Times* Survey. The Interuniversity Consortium for Political and Social Research. www.icpsr.umich.edu.

129. E.J. Dionne, "New Poll Shows Attacks by Bush Are Building Lead," *New York Times*, Oct. 26, 1988, Wednesday Late City Final Edition, p. 2.

130. Ibid.

131. Richard Benedetto, "Who's More Likable, Bush or Kerry?" *USA Today*, Sept. 17, 2004.

Chapter 5

1. We now know that the economy was actually improving throughout the summer and fall of 1992. Whether its effects had yet to reach most voters is debatable. Further, the actual economic realities of individuals do not impact their opinions about the overall economic health of the country, nor their personal projected finances (optimism) immediately as the economy begins to improve. Nonetheless, even by the Clinton campaign's own admission, the focus on the economy was more symbolic than representative of real conditions on the ground for most voters.

2. Due to the popularity of the brief Gulf War, through the early stages of the campaign, the Bush camp emphasized the president's foreign policy credentials. As many historians — most notably David Halberstam — have argued, Americans were less interested in foreign policy in 1992. See David Halberstam, *War in a Time of Peace: Bush, Clinton, and the Generals* (New York: Scribner, 2002). At the end of the Cold War, American voters began looking inward — free of major foreign threats, and suffering a recessionary economy at home, foreign policy was not top of mind for voters in 1992.

3. Shawn and Trevor Parry-Giles examined the new campaign media as a trend in "political scopophilia." In both *Constructing Clinton* and "Political Scopophilia, Presidential Campaigning, and the Intimacy of American Politics," Parry-Giles and Parry-Giles argued that viewers are lured by the exercise of viewing candidates — in 1992, talk shows increased standard levels of personal and intimate display among candidates. Not only did such programs offer a platform for candidates to discuss their personal lives, but they helped to foster and encourage new and personal questions. Candidates, Clinton in particular, enjoyed mixed relationships with these media. On the one hand, Clinton was able to take advantage of the media to speak directly to people. On the other hand, direct communication, and communication through talk show host intermediaries, required Clinton to answer increasingly personal questions, resulting in his final standoff with Phil Donahue.

4. W. Lance Bennett, "The Clueless Public," in Renshon, ed., *The Clinton Presidency*, p. 92.

5. Not only did Clinton appear first, he also appeared most often on television talk shows, according to a tally compiled by Dirk Smillie, in "Breakfast with Bill, George, and Ross," published in Martha FitzSimon, *The Finish Line: Covering the Campaign's Final Days* (Nashville, TN: Freedom Forum Media Studies, 1993). Bill Clinton appeared on forty-seven talk format programs, compared to thirty-three for Perot and sixteen for Bush.

6. Bennett's graph appeared in Stanley Renshon, *The Clinton Presidency*, p. 107.

7. Trevor Parry-Giles and Shawn Parry-Giles, "Political Scopophilia, Presidential Campaigning, and the Intimacy of American Politics," *Communication Studies* 47 (1996): 191.

8. Richard Harris, *A Cognitive Psychology of Mass Communication* (New York: Routledge, 2009), p. 179.

9. Janet Hook, "Skeptical Voters Foster the Tell-All Candidate," *Congressional Quarterly Weekly Report* 50, no. 31 (Aug. 1, 1992).

10. Ibid.

11. Joe Klein, "The Year of the Voter," *Newsweek*, Nov. 1992, Special Election Issue, p. 14.

12. John Aloysius Farrell, "Candidates Compete to Satisfy Voter Craving for Authenticity; Campaign '92," *Boston Globe*, Aug. 24, 1992, Monday City Edition, p. 1.

13. Jerrold M. Post, "The Political Psychology of the Perot Phenomenon," in Renshon, ed., *The Clinton Presidency*, pp. 41–42.

14. Ibid., p. 42.

15. John Mintz, "Nobody Here but Us Country Boys? Yeah, Right," *Washington Post National Weekly Edition*, June 1–7, 1992, p. 13.

16. "Best Person Independent," The Reform Party, 1992, from Museum of the Moving Image, *The Living Room Candidate: Presidential Campaign Commercials 1952–2008*: http://www.livingroom-candidate.org.

17. Pew Research Center Report, Aug. 7, 1992: "The People, the Press and Politics Campaign '92: The Clinton Converts Survey X." Available at: people-press.org/reports/?year=1992.

18. "The People, the Press and Politics, Campaign '92 Survey XI." Released Sept. 17, 1992, Times Mirror Center for the People and the Press. Available at: people-press.org/reports/?year=1992.

19. Meg Greenfield, "Rediscovering 'Real People,'" *Newsweek*, Jan. 20, 1992, p. 62.

20. Maureen Dowd, "White House Memo: Adrift in Bush's Circle Seeking the Common Man," *New York Times*, Dec. 1, 1991, Sunday Late Edition — Final, p. 28.

21. Jonathan Alter, "Searching for Authenticity," *Newsweek*, Mar. 2, 1992, p. 31.

22. Paul Bedard, "Bubba-Courting Bush Invades Gore Country," *Washington Times*, Sept. 30, 1992, p. A3.

23. Maureen Dowd, "White House Memo: Adrift in Bush's Circle Seeking the Common Man," *New York Times*, Dec. 1, 1991, Sunday Late Edition, p. 28.

24. Linda Ellerbee, "How Will Texas Politics Influence This Year's Election?" *CNN News*, Democratic National Convention Coverage transcript, July 16, 1992.

25. David Von Drehle, "Bush Puts a New Spin on the Snob Compass: Privileged President Paints Rival as 'Elite,'" *Washington Post*, Sept. 25, 1992, p. A21.

26. Ibid.

27. Stuart Spencer Interview, Miller Center, University of Virginia, Carter Presidential Oral History Project, Nov. 15–16, 2001, p. 100.

28. The "Texan" was journalist and humorist Molly Ivins. For transcripts, see Molly Ivins, "Texan Molly Ivins on Democratic Convention," *CBS This Morning*, July 16, 1992. CBS News Transcripts Archive.

29. Jean Harmon, Letter to the Editor, "Bush's Gamble," *New York Times* Magazine Desk, Nov. 8, 1992, Late Sunday Final Edition, p. 12.

30. Betty Glad, "How George Bush Lost the Election," in Renshon, ed., *The Clinton Presidency*, p. 23.

31. Ann Devroy, "Bush Seeks to Dispel 'Crazy Rumors,'" *Washington Post*, July 23, 1992, Thursday Final Edition, p. A1.

32. Andrew Rosenthal, "Bush Encounters the Supermarket, Amazed," *New York Times*, Feb. 5, 1992, p. A1.

33. For an analysis of the reasons why the Bush campaign ran an "Oval Office" strategy, see Betty Glad, "How George Bush Lost the Election," in Renshon, ed., *The Clinton Presidency*, p. 12.

34. Betty Glad, "How George Bush Lost the Election," in Renshon, ed., *The Clinton Presidency*, p. 12.

35. "Maine," Clinton/Gore '92 Committee, 1992. Maker: Clinton-Gore Creative Team, from Museum of the Moving Image, *The Living Room Candidate: Presidential Campaign Commercials 1952–2008*: http://www.livingroomcandidate. org.

36. In *War in a Time of Peace*, David Halberstam effectively argued that George Bush lost the 1992 election in large part because he ran on his foreign policy record in an era when Americans began to care less and less about problems abroad. While this advertisement could be analyzed in that context, using the framework of candidate image and authenticity, we can give a different reading to this spot.

37. "What I Am Fighting For," Original air date: 09/12/92. Bush-Quayle '92 General Committee, Inc., 1992. Maker: The November Company, James Weller. Video courtesy of the George Bush Presidential Library, College Station, Texas.

38. Judith Miller, "But Can You Dance to It?: MTV Turns to News," *New York Times*, Oct. 11, 1992.

39. Unofficial Transcript, Oct. 15, 1992: The Second Clinton-Bush-Perot Presidential Debate, from the Commission on Presidential Debates: http://www.debates.org/index.php?page=debate-transcripts. Emphasis added.

40. Orson Swindle, in Harvard University, Institute of Politics, *Campaign for President: The Managers Look at '92* (Boston: Puritan, 1994), p. 266.

41. "Presidency: Plain Talk," Original airdate: 10/26/92, Bush-Quayle '92 General Committee, Inc., 1992. Maker: The November Company. The George Bush Presidential Library, College Station, Texas.

42. It is clear that the November Company was attempting to create an aura of authority by seating the president above his audience. Nonetheless, as president of the United States, Bush's authority was not a major question in the election.

43. Janet Hook, "Skeptical Voters Foster the Tell-All Candidate," *Congressional Quarterly Weekly Report* 50, no. 31 (Aug. 1, 1992).

44. Patrick J. Buchanan, 1992 Republican National Convention Speech, Aug. 17, 1992.

45. "The War Room Drill," *Newsweek*, Special Election Edition Nov./Dec. 1992, p. 78.

46. Ibid.

47. Landon Jones, "Road Warriors: At Home in Arkansas, the Clintons Talk about Friends, Family, Faith — and Pierced Ears," *People* 38, no. 3 (July 20, 1992).

48. "The War Room Drill," *Newsweek*, Special Election Edition Nov./Dec. 1992, p. 78.

49. Mary Matalin, in *Campaign for President: The Managers Look at '92*, p. 270.

50. Charlie Black, in *Campaign for President: The Managers Look at '92*, p. 271.

51. Stan Greenberg, in *Campaign for President: The Managers Look at '92*, p. 267.

52. Bennett's graph appeared in Stanley Renshon, ed., *The Clinton Presidency*, p. 107.

53. Ibid.

54. Stan Greenberg, in *Campaign for President: The Managers Look at '92*, p. 185.

55. W. Lance Bennett, "The Clueless Public: Bill Clinton Meets the New American Voter in Campaign '92," in Renshon, ed. *The Clinton Presidency*, p. 108.

56. "The Long Road," *Time*, Nov. 2, 1992.

57. Janet Hook, "Skeptical Voters Foster the Tell-All Candidate," *Congressional Quarterly Weekly Report* 50, no. 31 (Aug. 1, 1992).

58. "The Long Road," *Time*, Nov. 2, 1992.

59. Shawn Parry-Giles and Trevor Parry-Giles, *Constructing Clinton*, p. 10.

60. "The Price Is Right for Clinton," *USA Today*, Oct. 27, 1992, p. 7A.

61. Nancy Benac, "At 'Town Hall,' Undecided Voters Give Clinton Another Look," Associated Press, June 13, 1992, Saturday p.m. cycle.

62. Stan Greenberg, in *Campaign for President: The Managers Look at '92*, p. 258.

63. James Carville, in *Campaign for President: The Managers Look at '92*, p. 259.

64. Ronald Taylor, "Bubba Boys Campaign

with New Age Outlook," *Washington Times*, July 14, 1992, Tuesday Final Edition, p. A5.

65. David Wilhelm, in *Campaign for President: The Managers Look at '92*, p. 203.

66. "The Long Road," *Time*, Nov. 2, 1992.

67. John Aloysius Farrell, "Candidates Compete to Satisfy Voter Craving for Authenticity," *Boston Globe*, Aug. 24, 1992, Monday City Edition, p. 1.

68. Lynda Lee Kaid, "Political Advertising in the 1992 Campaign," in Denton, ed., *The 1992 Presidential Campaign*, p. 169.

69. Patricia O'Brien, quoted in Janet Hook, "Skeptical Voters Foster the Tell-All Candidate," *Congressional Quarterly Weekly Report* 50, no. 31 (Aug. 1, 1992).

70. *The Man from Hope* was also formatted for VHS and distributed to supporters, who were encouraged to share the tape with friends and neighbors. See *The Man from Hope* (with a special personal message from Bill Clinton).

71. Stan Greenberg, in *Campaign for President: The Managers Look at '92*, p. 185.

72. Shawn Parry-Giles and Trevor Parry-Giles, *Constructing Clinton*, p. 10.

73. David Von Drehle, "Bush Puts a New Spin on the Snob Compass: Privileged President Paints Rival as 'Elite,'" *Washington Post*, Sept. 25, 1992, p. A21.

74. Shawn Parry-Giles and Trevor Parry-Giles, *Constructing Clinton*, p. 31. See also Roderick Hart, *Seducing America: How Television Charms the Modern Voter.*

75. "The Long Road," *Time*, Nov. 2, 1992.

76. Harry Thomason and Linda Bloodworth-Thomason, *The Man from Hope*, Clinton-Gore 1992.

77. "The War Room Drill," *Newsweek*, Special Election Edition Nov./Dec. 1992, p. 78.

78. Stan Greenberg, in *Campaign for President: The Managers Look at '92*, p. 193.

79. "Journey," Clinton-Gore Creative Team (Linda Kaplan Thaler, Harry Thomason, Linda Bloodworth-Thomason), Clinton/Gore '92 Committee, 1992, from Museum of the Moving Image, *The Living Room Candidate: Presidential Campaign Commercials 1952–2008*: http://www.livingroom-candidate.org.

80. Bill Clinton, CNN interview, New York, July 13, 1992, transcripts from Lexis-Nexis.

81. Thomason and Bloodworth-Thomason, *The Man from Hope*, Clinton-Gore 1992.

82. Landon Jones, "Road Warriors: At Home in Arkansas, the Clintons Talk about Friends, Family, Faith — and Pierced Ears," *People* 38, no. 3 (July 20, 1992).

83. Ibid.

84. Joe Klein, "The Year of the Voter," *Newsweek*, November 1992, Special Election Issue, p. 14.

85. Lynda Lee Kaid, "Political Advertising in the 1992 Campaign," in Denton, ed., *The 1992 Presidential Campaign*, p. 118.

86. Ibid., p. 123.

87. "Leaders 2," Clinton-Gore Creative Team (Linda Kaplan Thaler, Harry Thomason, Linda Bloodworth-Thomason), Clinton/Gore '92 Committee, 1992, from Museum of the Moving Image, *The Living Room Candidate: Presidential Campaign Commercials 1952–2008*: http://www.livingroom-candidate.org.

88. Pew Research Center Report, "The People, the Press and Politics Campaign '92: The Clinton Converts Survey X," Aug. 7, 1992.

89. Pew Research Center Report, "The People, the Press and Politics Campaign '92: Survey XI," Sept. 17, 1992, p. 5.

90. Times Mirror Center for the People and the Press, "The People, the Press and Politics Campaign '92: Survey XI," Sept. 17, 1992.

91. Ibid.

92. Pew Research Center Report, "The People, the Press and Politics Campaign '92: The Clinton Converts Survey X," Aug. 7, 1992.

93. Dave Carney, in *Campaign for President: The Managers Look at '92*, p. 243.

94. Times Mirror Center for the People and the Press, "The People, the Press and Politics Campaign '92: Survey XI," Sept. 17, 1992.

Chapter 6

1. Bob Dole, Announcement upon resigning from the Senate, May 15, 1996. Transcript from CNN: http://www.cgi.cnn.com/ALLPOLI-TICS/1996/elections/president/timeline/index3.shtml.

2. Elizabeth Kolbert, "Politics: The Personalities — A Political Life," *New York Times*, Oct. 11, 1996, Friday Late Edition, Final, p. A27.

3. Ibid.

4. Clinton campaign chairman Peter Knight, quoted in Harvard University, Institute of Politics, *Campaign for President: The Managers Look at '96* (Hollis, NH: Hollis Publishing Company, 1997), p. xv. Peter Knight was not the only participant who found the 1996 election less than eventful. As journalist David Broder admitted in his introduction to *Campaign for President*, the 1996 election was "not one of high drama."

5. "Dole Can't Cash in on Mixed View of Clinton," National Survey Report, Pew Research Center for the People and the Press, Oct. 4, 1996.

6. "Solid Clinton Lead, Small Gain for Congressional Democrats," National Survey Report, Pew Research Center for the People and the Press, Sept. 13, 1996.

7. Ibid.

8. "Dole Can't Cash in on Mixed View of Clinton," National Survey Report, Pew Research Center for the People and the Press, Oct. 4, 1996.

9. Ibid.

10. Frank Fahrenkopf, in *Campaign for President: The Managers Look at '96*, p. 125.

11. Sarah Lee Smith, "Elect Elizabeth," Letter to the Editors of *St. Petersburg Times*, July 24, 1996, South Pinellas Edition, p. 13A.

12. Peter Grier, "Kindler, Gentler Conventions Target Key Swing Vote," *Christian Science Monitor*, Aug. 30, 1996, p. 1.

13. Ibid.

14. Peter Knight, quoting Ann Lewis, in *Campaign for President: The Managers Look at '96*, p. 15.

15. The American National Election Studies, Guide to Public Opinion and Electoral Behavior: Strength of Partisanship 1952–2004, Table 2A.3.

16. Peter Grier, "Kindler, Gentler Conventions Target Key Swing Vote," *Christian Science Monitor*, Aug. 30, 1996, p. 1.

17. The American National Election Studies Guide to Public Opinion and Electoral Behavior, Party Identification Scale 1952–2004: Strength of Party Affiliation.

18. *Wall Street Journal/NBC News* Poll, June 20–26, 1996.

19. Ibid.

20. Ibid.

21. Robert Lovey, *The Manipulated Path to the White House 1996* (Lanham, MD: University Press of America, 2002), pp. 264–265.

22. Stephen Seplow, "Crafting a Winning Message: Both Parties Skip Politics for Touchy, Feely Images," *Philadelphia Inquirer*, Sept. 1, 1996, p. E01.

23. Ibid.

24. Ellen Goodman, "Are Politics Getting Too Personal?" *Washington Post*, Aug. 31, 1996, Saturday Final Edition, Op-Ed, p. A31.

25. Ibid.

26. It should be noted that there are many reasons why Bob Dole lost the election in 1996. Aside from whatever assets Clinton may have brought to the table, the Dole campaign faltered on many fronts, not all of which centered on its dull standard-bearer. As with most unsuccessful campaigns, the Dole campaign was criticized for its lack of coherence, cohesiveness, and strategy. Many within the Dole campaign argued that the disparity in campaign funding prevented them from launching a successful general election campaign before public funds became available. Although I will argue that Bob Dole's relative absence from Americans' main street diners, high school gymnasiums, and living room television sets prevented people from getting to know "the real Bob Dole," it should be noted that the campaign had few funds to indulge such appearances. Nonetheless, Bob Dole did very little campaigning between his early victory in the Republican primaries and the Republican National Convention. As a result, by the time Bob Dole was prepared to "introduce" himself at the Convention in San Diego, most Americans had turned off or tuned out or, more likely, been introduced to the unflattering portraits of him on late-night television.

27. Tony Fabrizio and Scott Reed, Bob Dole's pollster and campaign manager, respectively, argued that they were at a disadvantage because they came out of the primaries with very little money to spend before the conventions, when public funds became available. For their analysis, see *Campaign for President: The Managers Look at '96*, pp. 116–117.

28. I do not presume to argue that Bob Dole won the Republican nomination because of his seniority alone. Nevertheless, leading the field of eight going into the early primaries, Bob Dole was able to win the Iowa caucuses and every state beginning with North Dakota on February 27, 1996. It has been argued that the frontloaded schedule advantages frontrunners and fundraisers. See Doug Sosnik's comment in *Campaign for President: The Managers Look at '96*, p. 117.

29. The frontloaded primaries afforded Dole a victory earlier than any cycle in the modern era (wherein party nominees are selected by primaries and caucuses rather than party leaders).

30. Richard Berke, "You Have Now Entered the Black Hole of American Politics," *New York Times*, Apr. 7, 1996, p. SM26.

31. Richard Lacayo, James Carney, Michael Duffy, and Eric Pooley, "Campaign '96: The Big Funk," *Time*, May 6, 1996.

32. James Brady, "One Pundit's Advice," *Advertising Age*, Nov. 4, 1996, p. 32.

33. *Campaign for President: The Managers Look at '96*, pp. 116–117.

34. Bob Dole, Announcement upon resigning from the Senate, May 15, 1996. Transcript from CNN: http://www.cgi.cnn.com/ALLPOLITICS/1996/elections/president/timeline/index3.shtml.

35. Adam Pertman, "A Democratic Beachhead amid Vast GOP Ocean," *Boston Globe*, Aug. 13, 1996, Tuesday City Edition, p. A15.

36. Adam Nagourney and Elizabeth Kolbert, "After the Election: Anatomy of a Loss," *New York Times*, Nov. 8, 1996, Friday Late Edition, Final, p. A1.

37. John Hohenberg, *Reelecting Bill Clinton* (Syracuse, NY: Syracuse University Press, 1998), p. 88.

38. Ibid.

39. Ibid.

40. "Bob Dole Beats President Clinton in Race for Laughs," Associated Press Worldstream, Sept. 13, 1996, 20:17 ET.

41. David Letterman, *CBS Late Show with David Letterman*, July 10, 1996.

42. Transcript, NBC *Saturday Night Live, Weekend Update*, Oct. 19, 1996.

43. Dick Polman, "Tonight, a Chance for Dole to Fill in Gaps," *Philadelphia Inquirer*, Aug. 15, 1996, p. A01.

44. Scott Reed, in *Campaign for President: The Managers Look at '96*, p. 12.

45. Mickey Edwards, "Commentator Advises Dole to Focus on Clear Message," *NPR News All Things Considered*, June 7, 1996, NPR 4:30 p.m.

ET, Journal Graphics Transcription. Equally interesting here was the persistent campaign about the campaign. Americans wanted to know, understand, and analyze the terms on which the election was being waged.

46. Haley Barbour, "Citizen Dole of Russell, Kansas," Republican National Committee, 1996 Presidential Campaign Press Materials, Aug. 14, 1996.

47. Dick Polman, "Tonight, a Chance for Dole to Fill in Gaps," *Philadelphia Inquirer*, Aug. 15, 1996, p. A01.

48. See Russ Mitchell, "Acceptance Speech by Bob Dole gives him a chance to reach out to voters and let them see the real Bob Dole," *CBS Morning News* 6:30 a.m. ET, Aug. 15, 1996. CBS News Transcripts. See also Ceci Connolly, "Tonight's Show Is All about Bob Dole," *St. Petersburg Times*, Aug. 15, 1996, South Pinellas Edition, p. 1A; Terrence Hunt, "A Personal Look at Dole as He Lays Claim to the GOP Nomination," Associated Press, Aug. 14, 1996, Wednesday p.m. cycle; Karen Ball, "Just Bob, in Grand Ole Style," *Daily News*, Aug. 11, 1996; Curt Anderson, "Roaming like Oprah, Elizabeth Dole Stresses Husband's Human Side," Associated Press, Aug. 14, 1996, Wednesday p.m. cycle; Noah Adams, "Biographer Sees Dole Striding Confidently into the Fall," *NPR News*, Aug. 16, 1996.

49. Stephen Seplow, "Crafting a Winning Message: Both Parties Skip Politics for Touchy, Feely Images," *Philadelphia Inquirer*, Sept. 1, 1996, p. E01.

50. Ibid.

51. Bob Dole, Acceptance Speech, Aug. 15, 1996. Transcript from PBS: www.pbs.org/convention96.

52. Peter S. Canellos, "Dole's Imagery, Values Ring True for Local Vets," *Boston Globe*, Aug. 16, 1996, Friday City Edition.

53. William Safire, Republican National Convention commentary, *PBS News Hour* special coverage, Aug. 15, 1996. Transcript from PBS: www.pbs.org/convention96.

54. Frederic Biddle, "Dole Forgot to Save the Best for Last," *Boston Globe*, Aug. 16, 1996, Friday City Edition, p. A27.

55. Frank Rich, "The Man from Russell," *New York Times*, July 27, 1996, Saturday Late Final Edition, Editorial, Sec. 1, p. 23.

56. Bob Dole, Acceptance Speech, Aug. 15, 1996. Transcript from PBS: www.pbs.org/convention96.

57. John Buckley, in *Campaign for President: The Managers Look at '96*, p. 127.

58. This seemed to be especially true in Bob Dole's anti-crime and anti-drugs advertisements. His two anti-drug spots featured a boy in his early teens. In the first, the child experimented with marijuana. The second substituted the joint with a crack pipe. This was not the bleak America that most viewers would recognize, nonetheless, Bob Dole asked them to return with him to Russell, Kansas, of the 1930s.

59. The dual narrative structure of *Unlimited Partners: Our American Story* (New York: Simon & Schuster, 1996) centered around the geography of Russell, Kansas, and Salisbury, North Carolina. Mixing metaphors and platitudes, Dole informed readers that, like Dorothy, he could go home again because his home was Russell, Kansas. While Dole effectively portrayed himself as a man with deep roots in his hometown, thus proving his authenticity, for the most part, the childhood stories were not tales to which average voters in 1996 could relate. Like the grandmother who asserts that things were much harder, much simpler, and much better during her childhood, Bob Dole projected a Russell, Kansas, that made the candidate unforgiving in his work ethic and expectations.

60. Suzanne Fields, "'Uncle' Bob Dole," *Washington Times*, July 8, 1996, Monday Final Edition, p. A19.

61. Royal Ford, "New Hampshire Seems Cool to Dole's Latest Try," *Boston Globe*, Oct. 20, 1996, Sunday First Edition, p. B5.

62. Pew Survey Center Report, Aug. 2, 1996: "A Dull Campaign, Clinton Will Win Say More than 70% of Voters."

63. Frank Lombardi, "Bob's Got Authority in N.Y.," *Daily News*, July 2, 1996, p. 13.

64. Richard Benedetto, "Dole Missing a Beat in GOP Heartland," *USA Today*, Sept. 20, 1996, Friday Final Edition, p. 6A.

65. Richard S. Dunham, with Jessica McCann and Elizabeth Roberts, "Bob's Doleful Demographics," *Business Week*, Oct. 14, 1996, p. 128.

66. David Nyhan, "For Dole, a Week that Went Up in Smoke," *Boston Globe*, July 14, 1996, Sunday City Edition, p. 40.

67. Elizabeth Kolbert, "Politics: The Personalities — Public Figure, Private Person," *New York Times*, Aug. 16, 1996, Friday Late Edition, Final, p. A27.

68. Ibid.

69. Ibid.

70. R.W. Apple, "A Muted Dole Persona," *New York Times*, Sept. 26, 1996, Thursday Late Final Edition, p. A1.

71. Anonymous, *In the Kitchen with Bill: 50 Recipes for Chowing Down with the Chief* (Kansas City: Andrews McMeel, 1996). For Chelsea's curly fries, made with frozen Ore-Ida French fries and southern spices, see p. 36. For Mello Jell-O Pineapple 7-Up Salad, see p. 106. For fast food, see p. xv.

72. Elizabeth Kolbert, "Politics: The Personalities — A Political Life," *New York Times*, Oct. 11, 1996, Friday Late Edition, Final, p. A27.

73. Richard Heller, "Junking the President for Votes on a Plate," *Mail on Sunday*, June 16, 1996, p. 33.

74. Elizabeth Kolbert, "Politics: The Personalities — A Political Life," *New York Times*, Oct. 11, 1996, Friday Late Edition, Final, p. A27.

75. John Harris, "Clinton Starts, Finishes with the Middle Class," *Washington Post*, Oct. 28, 1996, Monday Final Edition, p. A01.

76. Eric Hobsbawm, *The Invention of Tradition* (New York: Cambridge University Press, 1992), p. 1.

77. Jodi Enda, "Back in Hot Springs, Old Pals Remember a Presidential Boy," *Philadelphia Inquirer*, Sept. 24, 1996, Tuesday SF Edition, p. F01.

78. Barbara Walters and Hugh Downs, "The Clintons Up Close," *20/20*, Sept. 20, 1996, 9:00 p.m. ET, ABC News Transcripts.

79. Shawn Parry-Giles and Trevor Parry-Giles, *Constructing Clinton*, p. 97.

80. Ibid.

81. *Untitled (A Place Called America)*, Linda Bloodworth-Thomason and Harry Thomason, 1996.

82. Peter Knight, in *Campaign for President: The Managers Look at '96*, p. 17.

83. David S. Broder, "Campaign Is Wary of Garden Path," *Washington Post*, Sept. 1, 1996, Sunday Final Edition, p. A1.

84. George Stephanopoulos, in *Campaign for President: The Managers Look at '96*, p. 109.

85. José Diaz-Balart and Troy Roberts, "Small Towns Greet President Clinton on His Cross-Country Trip," *CBS This Morning*, Aug. 27, 1996, 7:00 a.m. ET, CBS News Transcripts.

86. David S. Broder, "Campaign Is Wary of Garden Path," *Washington Post*, Sept. 1, 1996, Sunday Final Edition, p. A1.

87. John F. Harris, "Next Stop, Campaign Heaven," *Washington Post*, Aug. 27, 1996, Final Edition, p. A1.

88. Todd S. Purdum, "Politics: The Democrat," *New York Times*, Nov. 1, 1996, Friday Late Final Edition, p. A1.

89. Al Gore in *Untitled (A Place Called America)*, Linda Bloodworth-Thomason and Harry Thomason, 1996.

90. Daniel Schorr, "Empathy Emerges as Main Theme in Presidential Race," *NPR News All Things Considered*, July 24, 1996, 4:30 p.m. ET.

91. John F. Harris, "Next Stop, Campaign Heaven," *Washington Post*, Aug. 27, 1996, Final Edition, p. A1.

92. Pew Research Center Survey, Sept. 5–8, 1996. http://people-press.org/reports/?year=1996.

93. *Wall Street Journal/NBC News* Poll, June 20–26, 1996.

Chapter 7

1. "Hanging chads" were the result of an error in the *Votomatic* punch card ballot system employed in many Florida counties during the 2000 election. As the election remained very close, and hinged on the state of Florida, a national debate about whether to count ambiguous ballots tied up the cable news networks, Florida election officials, and the Bush and Gore legal experts.

2. Some angry Democrats blamed Al Gore's defeat on Ralph Nader's Green Party candidacy. This historian will not tango with the counterfactual, but it is worth noting the Nader-Hater movement. Nader-haters made their argument based on the close tally in several states. In New Hampshire, for example, Al Gore lost by a margin of 7200 votes. Ralph Nader won 22,198 votes. New Hampshire's mere four electoral votes would have been more than enough to have tipped the electoral scales. Nonetheless, these arguments assume that all or many Nader votes would have gone to Al Gore, absent a Nader candidacy. As will be explained later, Nader votes did not merely reflect "green" votes, but also the voice of dissent — dissent from the two-party system, dissatisfaction with the two candidates, and protest against the system itself.

3. Some have attempted to compare 2000 with the controversial election of 1876, in which Samuel Tilden and the Democrats exchanged their popular vote margin, and ultimately the presidency, for an end to reconstruction, resulting in the victory of Rutherford B. Hayes. Despite the obvious similarities, such comparisons are dubious at best.

4. Despite the obvious similarities, there were several important differences between the two election cycles. First, by the end of his second term, Bill Clinton was considered a liability to Al Gore's candidacy. Clinton's inability to achieve a successful working relationship with the opposition Congress, combined with countless personal indiscretions, complicated Al Gore's relationship with the outgoing administration. By contrast, George H.W. Bush's candidacy in 1988 was structured around highlighting his association with the still popular Ronald Reagan. While Bush only slowly established a distinct identity, Al Gore's campaign managers believed that contradistinction needed to be their first task. Thus, Al Gore was doubly disadvantaged. Among loyal Democrats, Bill Clinton was still a popular personality and something of a martyr. Too much contradistinction could result in disaffection and low voter turnout among Democrats.

5. Karl Rove, in Harvard University, Institute of Politics, *Campaign for President: The Managers Look at 2000* (Hollis, NH: Hollis, 2003), p. 107.

6. George H.W. Bush was connected to the Iran-Contra scandal. Although he absolved himself of wrong-doing, his part in the Reagan administration became an issue during the 1988 election.

7. Diane Holloway, "Bush and Gore Hit the Talk-Show Trail to Show a Softer, Funnier Side," Cox News Service, Nov. 5, 2000.

8. "Who Would You Rather Sit Down and Have a Beer With?" *Business Wire*, Oct. 17, 2000.

9. I contend that the Beer Poll accurately condensed several traditional survey questions: Which candidate is more likable? Which candidate un-

derstands people like you? Which candidate cares about people like you? Which candidate is more honest?

10. Bob Shrum, in *Campaign for President: The Managers Look at 2000*, p. 192.

11. "Presidential Polls Glance," Associated Press Online, Oct. 14, 2000.

12. Matt Dowd, in *Campaign for President: The Managers Look at 2000*, p. 181.

13. For analysis of these and other "soft" television appearances, see "Pop Culture: Campaign Back to 'What America Really Watches,'" *Hotline*, Oct. 20, 2000. See also Kevin Sack, "Oprah Show Lets Gore Reach Out to Women," *New York Times*, Sept. 12, 2000; Diane Holloway, "Bush and Gore Hit the Talk-Show Trail to Show a Softer, Funnier Side," Cox News Service, Nov. 5, 2000; *CBS News*, "Bush and Gore Do New York," CBS Worldwide, Inc., Oct. 20, 2000; and Howard Fineman, "The Talk Show Primary," *Newsweek*, Oct. 2, 2000.

14. Gore informed Oprah and her audience that his favorite book was *The Red and the Black* by Robert Stendahl. His favorite film was *Local Hero*.

15. Diane Holloway, "Bush and Gore Hit the Talk-Show Trail to Show a Softer, Funnier Side," Cox News Service, Nov. 5, 2000.

16. Ibid.

17. Viewership numbers from Nielsen Media Research 2004 report, "Political Debates: Presidential Debates 1960–2004." See also the Commission on Presidential Debates, 2000 Debates, Oct. 3, 2000; Oct. 11, 2000; Oct. 17, 2000.

18. For these figures, see the report from the Museum of the Moving Image, "Television: The Great Equalizer?" at stable web address: http://www.museum.tv/debateweb/html/equalizer/stats_t vratings.htm. For *The Simpsons*, see "Prime Time Nielsen Ratings," from Nielsen Media Research. Numbers for Letterman and Leno were measured by Nielsen Media Research and reported by *Daily Variety* on Mar. 3, 2000. Numbers for *Saturday Night Live* are from the 1998 season, according to Nielsen Media Research (reported by *USA Today*, Sept. 23, 1999).

19. *Saturday Night Live*, Season 26, Episode 1, Oct. 7, 2000.

20. Brian Williams, "*SNL* Becomes Player in Campaign 2000," *The News with Brian Williams*, Oct. 13, 2000, 21:00. MSNBC, Transcribed by FDCHeMedia, Inc.

21. For an analysis of George Bush's relationship with the press corps, see Kathleen Hall Jamieson, *The Press Effect*.

22. Karl Rove, in *Campaign for President: The Managers Look at 2000*, p. 219.

23. John Hughes, "Gore's Friends Out to Dispel His Wooden Image," Associated Press, Aug. 17, Thursday BC cycle.

24. Ibid.

25. Ibid.

26. Between the conclusion of the Democratic National Convention, Thursday, August 17, 2000, and Monday, August 22, 2000, Al Gore and his surrogates appeared on five morning talk shows. On CBS's *The Early Show*, Jane Clayson quizzed Al Gore about the convention kiss. In her post-convention interview with Al Gore, it was the first subject raised by Diane Sawyer. On the *Today Show*, Matt Lauer grilled Gore about the kiss's authenticity, spontaneity, and appropriateness. See Martin Kasindorf, "Gore, under Questioning, Insists the Kiss Was Just a Kiss," *USA Today*, Aug. 22, 2000, Tuesday Final Edition, p. A1; "Gore: Convention Kiss Was Impromptu," Associated Press Online, Aug. 21, 2000.

27. Karl Rove, in *Campaign for President: The Managers Look at 2000*, p. 190.

28. Cable News Network Transcripts: Linda Stouffer, Skip Loescher, "Democratic National Convention: Gore Delivers Opening Statement in His Case to Be President," *Ahead of the Curve*, Aug. 18, 2000, 5 a.m. ET.

29. For the Rove quote, see Karl Rove, in *Campaign for President: The Managers Look at 2000*, p. 190. For Al Gore's post-convention bounce, see David Moore, "Gore 'Bounce' in Presidential Race Due to Overall Positive Reassessment of Vice President," Gallup News Service, Aug. 23, 2000. See also Will Lester, "Delegates Upbeat Despite Polls," Associated Press Online, Aug. 17, 2000. See also Leon Harris, "Gallup Poll: Gore Emerges Winner of Convention Season," *CNN News*, Aug. 29, 2000.

30. David Moore, "Gore 'Bounce' in Presidential Race Due to Overall Positive Reassessment of Vice President," Gallup News Service, Aug. 23, 2000. According to Gallup, a typical post-convention "bounce" is five points. See Jeffrey M. Jones, "Conventions Typically Result in Five-Point Bounce," Gallup News Service, Aug. 20, 2008.

31. A candidate's strong attributes can create "drag" for his weaker attributes (if voters begin to agree with a candidate's position on issues, typically they will also begin to see him as more likable and vice versa). In 2000, however, among independent and undecided voters, Bush and Gore's poll numbers in issue and image categories changed relatively independent of one another, suggesting that weak partisan, independent, and nonpartisan voters saw the candidates' personal images and issue positions as completely separate. For the most dramatic illustration of this, see polls following the second debate.

32. David Moore, "Gore 'Bounce' in Presidential Race Due to Overall Positive Reassessment of Vice President," Gallup News Service, Aug. 23, 2000.

33. Ibid.

34. Susan Schindehette, "Warming to the Task," *People* 54, no. 8 (Aug. 21, 2000).

35. Doug Hattaway, in *Campaign for President: The Managers Look at 2000*, p. 212.

36. Although Al Gore took the "real people"

method of speech-making to its extreme, Bill Clinton popularized the format on the national stage in 1992. Frequently citing the examples of people he had met, Clinton would describe their stories, share their names, and exude empathy for their plight. Although this style of political oratory has become commonplace, it is important to note that it was an invention of this era in American political culture.

37. Doug Hattaway, in *Campaign for President: The Managers Look at 2000*, p. 213.

38. Bob Shrum, in *Campaign for President: The Managers Look at 2000*, p. 183.

39. *Saturday Night Live*, Season 26, Episode 1, Oct. 7, 2000.

40. Bob Herbert, "In America; Defining Al Gore," *New York Times*, Aug. 17, 2000, Thursday Late Final Edition, p. A29.

41. Michael Powell, "The Sons of Their Fathers," *Washington Post*, Aug. 10, 2000, Final Edition, p. C01.

42. Bob Herbert, "In America; Defining Al Gore," *New York Times*, Aug. 17, 2000, Thursday Late Final Edition, p. A29.

43. Bill Adair, "Down the Stretch He Comes: The Real Gore," *St. Petersburg Times*, Nov. 1, 2000, Wednesday South Pinellas Edition, p. 1A.

44. Ibid.

45. Pew Survey Center Report, Oct. 25, 2000: "Voter Opinions Stalled."

46. Ibid.

47. Viewership numbers from Nielsen Media Research 2004 report, "Political Debates: Presidential Debates 1960–2004." See also The Commission on Presidential Debates report, 2000 Debates, Oct. 3, 2000; Oct. 11, 2000; Oct. 17, 2000.

48. Karl Rove, in *Campaign for President: The Managers Look at 2000*, p. 185.

49. See *Campaign for President: The Managers Look at 2000*, pp. 179–195. In the third debate, Al Gore came across as snobbish and aloof. In the final debate, the best of the three, Gore was nonetheless mocked for invading George Bush's personal space in a way that seemed scripted and stilted.

50. Pew Survey Center Report, Oct. 25, 2000: "Voter Opinions Stalled."

51. Pew Survey Center Report, Oct. 10, 2000: "Presidential Debate Clouds Voters' Choice."

52. Bob Shrum, in *Campaign for President: The Managers Look at 2000*, p. 164.

53. Rick Berke, in *Campaign for President: The Managers Look at 2000*, p. 179.

54. Howard Rosenberg, "Lessons of First Meeting Provide Candidates with Strategy," *Los Angeles Times*, Oct. 12, 2000.

55. *Saturday Night Live* program transcripts, Season 26, Episode 1, Oct. 7, 2000. *Saturday Night Live* program transcripts, Season 26, Episode 2, Oct. 14, 2000. *Saturday Night Live* program transcripts, Season 26, Episode 3, Oct. 21, 2000.

56. Tucker Eskew, in *Campaign for President: The Managers Look at 2000*, p. 213.

57. Pew Survey Center Report, Oct. 25, 2000: "Voter Opinions Stalled."

58. Karl Rove, in *Campaign for President: The Managers Look at 2000*, p. 159.

59. The "Love Canal" story began during a primary season campaign event in New Hampshire. Gore told an audience that he had called for a congressional hearing into water pollution in the 1970s saying, "That was the one that started it all." As for the Texas FEMA case, in the first debate Gore claimed that he was in Texas during the Parker County fires with "James Lee Witt ... when those fires broke out." The story proved untrue. The Internet story stemmed from a primary season interview with Wolf Blitzer on CNN's *Late Edition* in which Gore said, "During my service in the United States Congress, I took the initiative in creating the Internet" (Source: Cable News Network Transcript, "Vice President Gore on CNN's *Late Edition*," Mar. 9, 1999).

60. Bob Shrum, in *Campaign for President: The Managers Look at 2000*, p. 164.

61. Robert Parry, "He's No Pinocchio," *Washington Monthly*, April 2000.

62. Karl Rove, in *Campaign for President: The Managers Look at 2000*, p. 198.

63. Bill Adair, "Down the Stretch He Comes: The Real Gore," *St. Petersburg Times*, Nov. 1, 2000, Wednesday South Pinellas Edition, p. 1A.

64. Tom Raum, "Bush Campaigns in Gore Country," Associated Press, Oct. 10, 2000, Tuesday BC cycle.

65. Ibid.

66. "Governor George W. Bush (R-TX) Delivers Remarks at Campaign Rally," CNN Transcripts, "Special Event: Bush Holds Campaign Rally in Naperville, Illinois," Sept. 4, 2000, 10:15 a.m. ET. Cable News Network, 2000, FDCH Political Transcripts.

67. "Governor George W. Bush (R-TX) Delivers Remarks at Campaign Rally," CNN Transcripts, "Special Event: Bush Holds Campaign Rally in Naperville, Illinois," Sept. 4, 2000, 10:15 a.m. ET. Cable News Network, 2000, FDCH Political Transcripts.

68. Bob Shrum, in *Campaign for President: The Managers Look at 2000*, p. 208.

69. Ibid.

70. Matthew Dowd, in *Campaign for President: The Managers Look at 2000*, p. 20.

71. Krya Phillips, "Bush's Chief Strategist Karl Rove Previews Tonight's Debate," CNN's *Early Edition*, Oct. 3, 2000, 7:00 a.m. ET, CNN Transcripts.

72. See Karl Rove, in *Campaign for President: The Managers Look at 2000*, p. 215. It was not exactly this easy, however. In order to make a plausible case for his presidency, George Bush first had to pass the threshold test. Most candidates clear this hurdle through the party primary process. For

George Bush, however, it remained an issue. Aside from voters' satisfaction with the Clinton economy, George Bush's biggest problem was the threshold question: Is this man ready to be president? As the governor of the second largest state, and as a man who had enough charisma to attract a first and second look from voters, Rove was confident that Bush could pass the threshold test. Indeed, the Bush campaign's internal polling showed that Bush scored well with voters on the most important basic questions. As Karl Rove commented after the election, "We not only led on the individual dimensions, do you see Gore as a strong leader, do you see Bush, but which one is the stronger leader. We were constantly leading on that dimension." In sum, voters could see George Bush as president. By contrast, they could not always imagine Al Gore as president, despite the fact that he had been serving as vice president for the previous eight years.

73. Michael Powell, "The Sons of Their Fathers," *Washington Post*, Aug. 10, 2000, Final Edition, p. A1.

74. Jim Lehrer and Terrence Smith, "Building the Image," *News Hour with Jim Lehrer*, Aug. 3, 2000. Transcripts from PBS: www.pbs.org.

75. *The Sky's the Limit*, by Stuart Stevens and Mark MacKinnon for Bush-Cheney 2000.

76. *The Sky's the Limit*, by Stuart Stevens and Mark MacKinnon for Bush-Cheney 2000. Barbara Bush's words were chosen carefully. Her son did not go "on" to public high school but "off" to an elite boarding school in Massachusetts.

77. *The Sky's the Limit*, by Stuart Stevens and Mark MacKinnon for Bush-Cheney 2000.

78. The *Washington Post* offered an excellent definition of "Bushism" on June 18, 2000: "A Bushism is not merely a Spoonerism ("the hirsute of pappiness") or a malapropism or a Freudian slip, and it certainly is not a politically blunt bon mot ("Give me liberty to give them death"). A Bushism is a magnificent pratfall of the cerebral cortex, in which a lifetime of experience and learning and intuition comes hurtling out upside down and backward, wearing its underpants on its head." (See "The Style Invitational," *Washington Post*, June 18, 2000, p. F02).

79. Wayne Slater, "Bush Campaign Focusing on Texan's Personality," *Dallas Morning News*, July 30, 2000.

80. Pew Survey Center Report, Oct. 25, 2000: "Voter Opinions Stalled."

81. Helen Kennedy, "I'm Very Gracious and Humbled," *Daily News*, July 30, 2000, p. 7.

82. Edited by Jacob Weisberg, "Bushisms of the Week," *Slate*, Aug. 28, 2000.

83. Ibid., Sept. 15, 2000.

84. See, for example, "The Style Invitational: Everyone's a Critic," *Washington Post*, June 18, 2000, Sunday Final Edition, p. F02.

85. Tom Raum, "Bush Pokes Fun at Self on Leno," Associated Press Online, Oct. 30, 2000.

86. For humorous analysis of Bush's interview with Letterman, see Todd Gitlin, "It's the Stupidity, Stupid." Salon.com, Oct. 24, 2000: http://www.salon.com/news/politics/feature/2000/10/24/bush.

87. Wayne Slater, "Bush Campaign Focusing on Texan's Personality," *Dallas Morning News*, July 30, 2000.

88. Ibid.

89. Peter Sisler, "Policy versus Personality to Decide US Election," *Deutsche Presse-Agentur*, Aug. 18, 2000, Friday BC cycle.

90. Wayne Slater, "Bush Campaign Focusing on Texan's Personality," *Dallas Morning News*, July 30, 2000.

91. Peter Sisler, "Policy versus Personality to Decide US Election," *Deutsche Presse-Agentur*, Aug. 18, 2000, Friday BC cycle.

92. Howard Fineman, "Talk Show Primary," *Newsweek*, Oct. 2, 2000, US Edition, p. 26.

93. Ibid.

94. David Royse, "George W. Bush Greets NASCAR Racers, Fans," Associated Press State and Local Wire, July 1, 2000, BC cycle.

95. David Rosenbaum, "The 2000 Campaign: The Voters. New Respect for Age in Florida," *New York Times*, Oct. 21, 2000, Saturday Late Final Edition, p. A12.

96. Ronald Brownstein, "Gore Takes Hits for His Elian Stand from Friend and Foe Alike," *Los Angeles Times*, Apr. 1, 2000.

97. E.J. Dionne, "The Fight for Florida," *Washington Post*, Oct. 10, 2000, Tuesday Final Edition, Op-Ed, p. A25.

98. Noah Adams, "Profile: Views of Working-Class Men on Who Should Succeed President Clinton," *NPR News All Things Considered*, Jan. 27, 2000.

99. Dana Wilkie, "With Farmer Families and Southern Drawl, Bush like Gore Aims to Be the 'People's' Candidate," Copley News Service, Sept. 26, 2000.

Chapter 8

1. Stan Greenberg and James Carville, "Solving the Paradox of 2004: Why America Wanted Change but Voted for Continuity," *Democracy Corps*, Nov. 9, 2004.

2. Ibid.

3. "Kerry Claims New Hampshire Primary," CNN, Jan. 28, 2004.

4. Nancy Gibbs, "As Kerry's Fortunes Rise, Primary Voters Say They Are Searching for Electability. But Their Quest Is Not That Simple," *Time*, Feb. 2, 2004.

5. William Saletan, "Kerried Away: The Myth and Math of Kerry's Electability," *Slate*, posted Feb. 11, 2004, 12:41 a.m. ET.

6. "Electability the Magic Factor for the De-

mocrats," *Choose or Lose*, MTV, Feb. 18, 2004, 9:26 p.m. EST.

7. Riverfront Media, "Heart," John Kerry for President, Inc., 2004; original air date May 3, 2004. Video courtesy of Devine Mulvey, from Museum of the Moving Image.

8. John O'Neill and Jerome R. Corsi, *Unfit for Command*, pp. 5–7.

9. John O'Neill and Jerome R. Corsi, *Unfit for Command*, pp. 5–7.

10. Richard Corliss, "That Old Feeling: Where's the Best of Him?" *Time*, June 16, 2004.

11. Dick Cheney, Speech at the Republican National Convention, Sept. 1, 2004. Video from *Washington Post*. http://www.washingtonpost.com-/wp-srv/politics/shoulders/rnc_fullschedule.html# wednesday.

12. Amy Pohler, "Weekend Update," *Saturday Night Live*, Oct. 2, 2004.

13. *Late Show with David Letterman*, CBS, Mar. 30, 2004.

14. Jay Leno, *Tonight Show*, NBC, March 19, 2004.

15. Amy Pohler, "Weekend Update," *Saturday Night Live*, Oct. 2, 2004.

16. Russell Leslie Peterson, *Strange Bedfellows: How Late-Night Comedy Turns Democracy into a Joke*, p. 10.

17. Maverick Media, "Windsurfing," Bush-Cheney '04, Inc., 2004; original air date Sept. 23, 2004. Video courtesy of Maverick Media, from Museum of the Moving Image.

18. Maureen Dowd, "Whence the Wince?" *New York Times*, March 11, 2004. www.nytimes. com/2004/03/11/opinion/whence-the-wince.

19. Pia Catton, "Orange Alert: A Fake Tan Is On the Campaign Trail," *New York Sun*, Sept. 29, 2004.

20. Democracy Corps Focus Group Verbatims, College-educated male voters, Milwaukee, WI, Oct. 6, 2004.

21. Democracy Corps Focus Group Verbatims, College-educated male voters, Milwaukee, WI, Oct. 6, 2004. Non-college educated female voters, Milwaukee, WI, Oct. 6, 2004.

22. Democracy Corps and Campaign for America's Future combined national surveys of 2,000 voters, November 2–3, 2004. Margin of error +/- 1.5 percentage points at 95 percent confidence.

23. Peter Beinhart, "If Howard Dean Were the Candidate," *Time*, Oct. 4, 2004.

24. Richard Benedetto, "Who's More Likeable, Bush or Kerry?" *USA Today*, Sept. 17, 2004.

25. Joseph Carroll, "Was U.S. Involvement in Iraq a Mistake?" Gallup News Service, Oct. 6, 2004.

26. Data from Gallup Presidential Job Approval Center. http://www.gallup.com/poll/124922/presi-dential-approval-center.aspx.

27. Data from Gallup Presidential Job Approval Center. http://www.gallup.com/poll/124922/presi-dential-approval-center.aspx.

28. "Presidency Undecided: All Eyes on Ohio." *Minnesota Daily*, Nov. 3, 2004. www.mndaily. com/2004/11/03/presidency-undecided-all-eyes-ohio?page=2.

29. Jennifer Frey, "Dr. Phil's Advice to Candidates: Come on My Show." *The Washington Post*, Wednesday, Sept. 29, 2004, p. C01.

30. Ibid.

31. Stephen M. Silverman, "President Bush Gets Cozy with Dr. Phil." *People.com*, www.peo-ple.com/people/article. (updated Sept. 29, 2004 at 3:25 EDT)

32. Pew Research Center for the People and the Press, September 2004 Political Survey, Sept. 8–13, 2004.

33. Pew Research Center for the People and the Press, September 2004 Political Survey, Sept. 8–13, 2004.

34. Pew Research Center for the People and the Press, September 2004 Political Survey, Sept. 8–13, 2004.

35. Gallup tracking, www.gallup.com.

36. Ibid.

37. Richard Benedetto, "Who's More Likeable, Bush or Kerry?" *USA Today*, Sept. 17, 2004.

38. Jon Stewart, "No Message," *The Daily Show*, Tuesday, May 4, 2004.

39 "December 2007 Political Communications Study," Interviewing Dates: Dec. 19, 2007–Jan. 2, 2008. Pew Research Center for the People and the Press.

40. These numbers divide dramatically along generational lines. In 2008, 42 percent of voters under the age of 30 reported that the Internet was their primary source of information about presidential campaigns. Older voters, who are historically more likely to vote, used the Internet as their primary source of information less often. In 2008, 26 percent of those aged 30–49 used the Internet regularly for political information, compared to 15 percent of respondents over the age of 50. "December 2007 Political Communications Study," Interviewing Dates: Dec. 19, 2007–Jan. 2, 2008. Pew Research Center for the People and the Press.

41. In 2000, 48 percent of respondents reported regularly learning about the campaigns from local news, 45 percent from network news, and 40 percent from daily newspapers. Those numbers decreased proportional to the increase in Internet access. In 2004, 42 percent relied on local TV news, 35 percent on network news, and 31 percent on daily newspapers. By 2008, 40 percent of respondents reported that the local TV news was a regular source of information about campaigns, 35 percent relied on network news, and 31 percent still depended on daily newspapers for information about presidential campaigns. "December 2007 Political Communications Study," Interviewing Dates: Dec. 19, 2007–Jan. 2, 2008. Pew Research Center for the People and the Press.

Conclusion

1. See Kathleen Hall Jamieson, *Eloquence in an Electronic Age*.

2. Maureen Dowd, "Can Hillary Cry Her Way Back to the White House?" *New York Times*, Jan. 9, 2008.

3. Bo Obama was the Obama family's dog. During his 2008 Election Day victory speech, Obama informed his daughters that they could finally get the dog they had been asking for. Struggling to find a suitably hypo-allergenic "shelter dog," the Internet provided a useful outlet for first pet citizen suggestions. The Obamas eventually adopted Bo. Reille Hunter was the mistress of former Democratic vice-presidential candidate John Edwards.

Bibliography

Manuscript Collections

Barbour, Haley. "Citizen Dole of Russell, Kansas." Republican National Committee. 1996 Presidential Campaign Press Materials, August 14, 1996.

Bertram Lance Interview. Miller Center, University of Virginia. Jimmy Carter Presidential Oral History Project, May 12, 1982.

"Blueprint/Ford." Folder, "Meese, Ed — Campaign Planning — Tactics (2/4)." Box 104, Reagan, Ronald: 1980 Campaign Papers, Series III: Ed Meese Files: Campaign Planning.

Campaign Strategy Plan, August 1976. Folder, "Presidential Campaign — Campaign Strategy Program (1)–(3)." Box 1, Dorothy E. Downton Files. Gerald R. Ford Presidential Library.

Carter-Reagan Debate, October 28, 1980. Transcript from the Commission on Presidential Debates.

Charles Kirbo Interview. Miller Center, University of Virginia. Jimmy Carter Presidential Oral History Project, January 5, 1983.

"The Creative Management of Ronald Reagan." Folder, "Meese, Ed — Campaign Planning — Meetings, April 1980. Reagan, Ronald: 1980 Campaign Papers, Series III: Ed Meese Files: Campaign Planning, RFP Planning 1, Box 103.

DMI Focus Groups Conducted for the Reagan/Bush Committee, September 1980. Box 207, Richard Wirthlin Files: DMI Polling Files. Ronald Reagan Presidential Library.

Dolon Draft, "Vision" Speech, October 27, 1980. Folder, "Meese, Ed — Debate — Cleveland, OH, 10/28/80 (Reagan-Carter) (3/3)." Box 140, Ed Meese Files: Debate Files. Ronald Reagan Presidential Library.

"Draft of Strategy for First Debate." Folder, "Meese, Ed — Debate — Baltimore, 9/21/80,

undated (1/7)." Box 139, Ed Meese Files: Convention, Debate Files.

Free Congress Research and Education Foundation National Poll. Folder, "Meese Files — Camp Ops — Miscellaneous (2/3)." Box 108, Ed Meese Files: Campaign Operations. Ronald Reagan Presidential Library.

Gerald Rafshoon Interview. Miller Center, University of Virginia. Jimmy Carter Presidential Oral History Project, April 8, 1983.

"Governor Reagan for President Creative Strategy and Copy Presentation." Folder, "Meese, Ed — Campaign Planning — Tactics (1/4)." Box 104, Reagan, Ronald: 1980 Campaign Papers, Series III: Ed Meese Files: Campaign Planning.

"Governor Reagan's Visit to Detroit, Michigan." Briefing Documents, Copy #5, Policy Coordination, California Headquarters- Briefing Documents from Policy Coordination Office, 9/1–2/80. Reagan, Ronald: 1980 Campaign Papers, Series I: Hannaford/California Headquarters: Briefing Files. Ronald Reagan Presidential Library.

Grandolfo, Jane. News clip from *Houston Post*. Michael S. Dukakis Presidential Campaign Records, 1962–1989. M32. Box 27. Folder 1387. Northeastern University.

Jody Powell Interview. Miller Center, University of Virginia. Ronald Reagan Presidential Oral History Project, December 17, 1981.

Lyn Nofziger Interview. Miller Center, University of Virginia. Ronald Reagan Presidential Oral History Project, March 6, 2003.

Media Campaign. Folder, "Campaign '80, 10/8/80 Meeting." Box 207, Richard Wirthlin Files: DMI Polling Files. Ronald Reagan Presidential Library.

Memo, Andy Carter to Ronald Reagan and Nancy Reagan, May 5, 1980. Folder, "Meese Files — Camp Ops — Political Memos." Box

108, Ed Meese Files: Campaign Operations. Ronald Reagan Presidential Library.

Memo, Anthony Dolan to Ed Meese (undated). Folder, "Meese, Ed — Debate — Baltimore, 9/21/80, undated (1/7)." Box 139, Ed Meese Files: Convention, Debate Files.

Memo, Betty Southard Murphy to William J. Casey, June 18, 1980. Folder, "Meese, Ed — Campaign Planning — Tactics (4/4)." Box 104, Reagan, Ronald: 1980 Campaign Papers, Series III: Ed Meese Files: Campaign Planning.

Memo, Bill Gavin to Bill Casey, Dick Allen, Dick Wirthlin, Ed Meese, Martin Anderson, Peter Hannaford, March 20, 1980. Folder, "Speech Strategy — Community of Values (1980) — Bill Gavin." Box 50, Reagan, Ronald: 1980 Campaign Papers 1965–80, Series I: Hannaford/California Headquarters: General Campaign Files. Ronald Reagan Presidential Library.

Memo, Dorrance Smith to Doug Blaser, July 26, 1976. Folder, "Press Office Improvement Sessions — 8/6–7/76 — Press Advance (2)." Box 24, Ron Nessen Papers. Gerald R. Ford Presidential Library.

Memo, Dr. Donald J. Devine to Mr. William J. Casey and Dr. Richard B. Wirthlin, June 19, 1980. Box 103, Reagan, Ronald: 1980 Campaign Papers, Series III: Ed Meese Files: Campaign Planning, RFP Planning 10.

Memo, Ed Gray to Marty Anderson, 10/28/1980. Folder, "Meese, Ed — Campaign Operations — Debate Reactions, Thursday 10/30/1980." Box 105, Ed Meese Files: Campaign Operations, Ronald Reagan 1980 Campaign Papers. Ronald Reagan Presidential Library.

Memo, Elaine Donnelly to Ed Meese, October 16, 1980. Folder, "Meese Files — Camp Ops — Miscellaneous (3/3)." Box 108, Ed Meese Files: Campaign Operations. Ronald Reagan Presidential Library.

Memo, Jack Marsh to the President, November 1, 1976. Folder, "States — Michigan." Box 19, Richard Cheney Files. Gerald R. Ford Presidential Library.

Memo, Jim Munn and Jeff Davis to Ed Meese, October 20, 1980. Folder, "Meese Files — Camp Ops — Miscellaneous (2/3)." Box 108, Ed Meese Files: Campaign Operations. Ronald Reagan Presidential Library.

Memo, Reagan Advisory Committee, June 26, 1980. Meese, Ed — Campaign Planning — Meetings, June 1980, Reagan, Ronald: 1980 Campaign Papers, Series III: Ed Meese Files: Campaign Planning, RFP Planning 1, Box 103.

Memo, Rich Williamson to Bill Casey, Ed

Meese, Jim Baker, October 21, 1980. Folder, "Meese, Ed — Debate — Cleveland, OH, 10/28/80 (Reagan-Carter) (2/3)." Box 140, Ed Meese Files: Debate Files. Ronald Reagan Presidential Library.

Memo, Richard B. Wirthlin to Reagan/Bush Campaign. Folder, "Meese, Ed — Debate — Cleveland, OH, 10/28/80 (Reagan-Carter) (2/3)." Box 140, Ed Meese Files: Debate Files. Ronald Reagan Presidential Library.

Memo, Richard Nixon to Ronald Reagan, October 21, 1980. Folder, "Meese, Ed — Debate — Cleveland, OH, 10/22/80 (Reagan-Carter) (2/3)." Box 140, Ed Meese Files: Debate Files. Ronald Reagan Presidential Library.

Memo, Richard Wirthlin to Ed Meese, September 10, 1980, Re: Nancy Reagan's Stump Speech. Folder, "Meese, Ed — Campaign Planning — Speech Planning." Box 104, Reagan, Ronald: 1980 Campaign Papers, Series III: Ed Meese Files: Campaign Planning.

Memo, Stef Halper to David Gergen, June 11, 1976. Folder, "Strategy/Planning." Box 5, James Reichley Files. Gerald R. Ford Presidential Library.

News Release, Excerpts from Remarks of Ambassador George Bush, October 21, 1980. Folder, "Press Material, Releases Book IV, 10/1/80–11/6/80." Box 45, Hannaford/California Headquarters: General Campaign Files. Ronald Reagan Presidential Library.

"The Packaging of George Bush," October 6, 1988. Michael S. Dukakis Presidential Campaign Records, 1962–1989. M32 Box 1/71 Folder 17 Administrative Files: Advertising; Television. Northeastern University.

Preliminary Media Plan, August 21, 1976. Folder, "Presidential Campaign — Preliminary Media Plan." Box 1, Dorothy E. Downton Files. Gerald R. Ford Presidential Library.

President Ford Committee Newsletter, October 19, 1976. Box 1, Dorothy E. Downton Files. Gerald R. Ford Presidential Library.

Rafshoon, Gerald. Exit Interview, September 12, 1979, Washington, DC. Final edited transcript. Jimmy Carter Library and Museum.

Reagan, Ronald. "Remarks at a Reagan-Bush Rally in Fountain View, California, September 3, 1984." The Public Papers of President Ronald W. Reagan. Ronald Reagan Presidential Library.

Reagan Bush/National Panel/8201/September 1980. DMI Poll Book. Folder, "National Panel Survey of Voter Attitudes." Vol. 3. Box 206, Richard Wirthlin: Political Strategy, Subseries B: DMI Polling Books. Ronald Reagan Presidential Library.

"Reagan for President Campaign Plan," June 29, 1980. (Draft) Folder, "Wirthlin — Reagan for President Campaign Plan (2/4)." Box 177, Richard Wirthlin Files. Ronald Reagan Presidential Library.

"Reagan Press Conference and the Debates." Folder, "Meese, Ed — Debate — Baltimore, 9/21/80, undated (4/7)." Box 140, Ed Meese Files: Debate Files. Ronald Reagan Presidential Library.

Report on the 1980 Elections, November 11, 1980. Folder, "Election Report, 11/11/1980." Box 43, Hannaford/California Headquarters: General Campaign Files. Ronald Reagan Presidential Library.

Rex Granum Interview. Miller Center, University of Virginia. Jimmy Carter Presidential Oral History Project, December 17, 1981.

"A Strategy of Peace for the '80s, Draft." Folder, "Press Material, Releases Book IV, 10/1/80–11/6/80." Box 45, Hannaford/California Headquarters: General Campaign Files. Ronald Reagan Presidential Library.

Stuart Spencer Interview. Miller Center, University of Virginia. Ronald Reagan Presidential Oral History Project, November 15–16, 2001.

"Suggested Introduction of Ronald Reagan." Folder, "Intros for R. Reagan (for speaking engagements)." Box 44, Hannaford/California Headquarters: General Campaign Files. Ronald Reagan Presidential Library.

Transcript: "Crazy." QDML-0143 QDML-0144 01-6-88. Michael S. Dukakis Presidential Campaign Records, 1962–1989. M32 Box 1/71. Folder 17. Administrative Files: Advertising; Television. Northeastern University.

Transcript: Presidential Debate in Cleveland, OH, October 28, 1980. John T. Woolley and Gerhard Peters, *The American Presidency Project* [online]. Santa Barbara, CA: University of California (hosted), Gerhard Peters (database).

Books and Journals

Abramson, Paul R., John H. Aldrich, and David W. Rohde. *Change and Continuity in the 1996 and 1998 Elections*. Washington, DC: Congressional Quarterly Books, 1999.

Adatto, Kiku. *Picture Perfect: Life in the Age of the Photo Op*. Princeton, NJ: Princeton University Press, 2008.

Adorno, Theodor. *Jargon of Authenticity*. Chicago: Northwestern University Press, 1973.

Altschuler, Glenn C., and Stuart M. Blumin.

Rude Republic: Americans and Their Politics in the Nineteenth Century. Princeton, NJ: Princeton University Press, 2001.

Anonymous. *In the Kitchen with Bill: 50 Recipes for Chowing Down with the Chief*. Kansas City: Andrews McMeel, 1996.

Anton, Corey. *Selfhood and Authenticity*. Albany: State University of New York Press, 2001.

Arterton, F. Christopher, and Gerald M. Pomper. *The Election of 1992: Reports and Interpretations*. New York: Chatham House, 1993.

Auer, Jeffery. "Contemporary American Political Speaking: The 1976 Presidential Primary." *Communication* 1: 34–47.

Baker, Tod A., Laurence W. Moreland, and Robert P. Steed. *The 1988 Presidential Election in the South: Continuity amidst Change in Southern Party Politics*. Westport, CT: Praeger, 1991.

Barber, James David. *The Pulse of Politics: Electing Presidents in the Media Age*. New Brunswick, NJ: Transaction, 1992.

Bates, Stephen, and Edwin Diamond. *The Spot—Third Edition: The Rise of Political Advertising on Television*. London: MIT Press, 1992.

Beasley, Maurine Hoffman. *First Ladies and the Press: The Unfinished Partnership of the Media Age*. Chicago: Northwestern University Press, 2005.

Becker, Jane S. *Selling Tradition: Appalachia and the Construction of an American Folk*. Chapel Hill: University of North Carolina Press, 1998.

Bennett, W. Lance. "The Ritualistic and Pragmatic Bases of Political Campaign Discourse." *Quarterly Journal of Speech* 63: 219–238.

Benoit, William L. *Seeing Spots: A Functional Analysis of Presidential Television Advertisements, 1952–1996*. Westport, CT: Praeger, 1999.

Benze, James. *Nancy Reagan: On the White House Stage*. Lawrence: University Press of Kansas, 2005.

Berlant, Lauren. *The Anatomy of National Fantasy: Hawthorne, Utopia, and Everyday Life*. Chicago: University of Chicago Press, 1991.

Berlet, Chip, and Matthew N. Lyons. *Right-Wing Populism in America: Too Close for Comfort*. New York: Guilford Press, 2000.

Bitzer, Lloyd F., and Ted Rueter. *Carter vs. Ford: The Counterfeit Debates of 1976*. Madison: University of Wisconsin Press, 1980.

Blume, Keith. *Presidential Election Show*. Westport, CT: Bergin & Garvey, 1985.

Blumenthal, Sidney. *The Permanent Campaign: Inside the World of Elite Political Operatives.* Boston: Beacon Press, 1980.

Boyd, Richard W. "Presidential Elections: An Explanation of Voting Defection." *American Political Science Review* 63: 498–515.

Branch, Taylor. *Wrestling History: White House Dialogues with President Clinton.* New York: Simon & Schuster, 2008.

Bronner, Simon J. *Folk Nation: Folklore in the Creation of American Tradition.* Wilmington, DE: SR Books, 2002.

Brummet, Barry. "Gastronomic References, Synecdoche, and Political Images." *Quarterly Journal of Speech* 67: 138–145.

Buchanan, James M., Charles Kershaw Rowley, and Gordon Tullock. *The Calculus of Consent: Logical Foundations of Constitutional Democracy.* Indianapolis, IN: Liberty Fund, 2004.

Busch, Andrew E. *Reagan's Victory: The Presidential Election of 1980 and the Rise of the Right (American Presidential Elections).* Lawrence: University Press of Kansas, 2005.

Bush, George H.W. *All the Best, George Bush: My Life in Letters and Other Writings.* New York: Scribner, 2000.

Campbell, Angus, Philip E. Converse, Warren E. Miller, and Donald E. Stokes. *The American Voter.* Chicago: University of Chicago Press, 1980.

Campbell, James. "Jimmy Carter and the Rhetoric of Charisma." *Central States Speech Journal* 30: 174–186.

Campbell, James E. *The American Campaign: U.S. Presidential Campaigns and the National Vote.* College Station: Texas A&M University Press, 2008.

Campbell, Karlyn Kohrs, and Kathleen Hall Jamieson. *Deeds Done in Words: Presidential Rhetoric and the Genres of Governance.* Chicago: University of Chicago Press, 1990.

_____. *The Interplay of Influence: News, Advertising, Politics, and the Internet.* Belmont, CA: Wadsworth, 2005.

Cannon, Lou. *President Reagan: The Role of a Lifetime.* New York: PublicAffairs, 2000.

Capella, Joseph N., and Kathleen Hall Jamieson. "Broadcast Adwatch Effects: A Field Experiment." *Communication Research* 21: 342–365.

Carlin, Diana B., and Mitchell McKinney. *The 1992 Presidential Debates in Focus.* Westport, CT: Praeger, 1994.

Carter, Jimmy. *An Hour before Daylight: Memoirs of a Rural Boyhood.* New York: Simon & Schuster, 2001.

Carter, Judith A. "1972 Democratic Convention

Reforms and Party Democracy." *Political Science Quarterly* 89: 325–350.

Chafee, Steven H., and Sun Yuel Choe. "Time of Decision and Media Use during the Ford-Carter Campaign." *Public Opinion Quarterly* 44: 53–69.

Chiu, Tony. *Ross Perot: In His Own Words.* New York: Warner Books, 1992.

Cohen, Lizabeth. *A Consumers' Republic: The Politics of Mass Consumption in Postwar America.* New York: Vintage, 2003.

Combs, Dan, and James E. Nimmo. *Mediated Political Realities.* 2d ed. New York: Longman, 1990.

Critchlow, Donald T. *The Conservative Ascendancy: How the GOP Right Made Political History.* Cambridge, MA: Harvard University Press, 2007.

Davis, Dwight. "Issues Information and Connotation in Candidate Imagery: Evidence from a Laboratory Experiment." *International Political Science Review* 2: 461–479.

Demause, Lloyd. *Jimmy Carter and American Fantasy.* New York: Two Continents/Psychohistory Press, 1977.

Dennis, Everette E. *The Homestretch: New Politics. New Media. New Voters?* Nashville, TN: The Freedom Forum Media Studies Center, 1992.

Denton, Robert E. *The 1992 Presidential Campaign: A Communication Perspective.* Westport, CT: Praeger, 1994.

_____. *The 1996 Presidential Campaign: A Communication Perspective.* Westport, CT: Praeger, 1998.

_____. *The Clinton Presidency: Images, Issues, and Communication Strategies.* Westport, CT: Praeger, 1996.

_____. *The Primetime Presidency of Ronald Reagan.* Westport, CT: Greenwood, 1988.

Denton, Robert E., and Gary C. Woodward. *Political Communication in America: Third Edition.* Westport, CT: Praeger, 1998.

Devlin, L. Patrick. "Contrasts in Presidential Campaign Commercials of 1976." *Central States Speech Journal* 24: 238–249.

_____. "Contrasts in Presidential Campaign Commercials of 1980." *Political Communications Review* 7: 1–38.

_____. "Reagan and Carter's Ad Men Review the 1980 Television Campaigns." *Communication Quarterly* 30: 3–12.

Diamond, Edwin, and Robert A. Silverman. *White House to Your House: Media and Politics in Virtual America.* London: MIT Press, 1997.

Diamond, Sara. *Not by Politics Alone: The Enduring *Influence of the Christian Right*. New York: Guilford Press, 2000.

Dole, Robert, and Elizabeth Dole. *Unlimited Partners: Our American Story*. New York: Simon & Schuster, 1996.

Donovan, Robert, and Raymond Scherer. *Unsilent Revolution: Television News and American Public Life, 1948–1991*. New York: Cambridge University Press, 1992.

Dorsey, Leroy G. *The Presidency and Rhetorical Leadership*. College Station: Texas A&M University Press, 2008.

Dover, E.D. *The Disputed Presidential Election of 2000: A History and Reference Guide*. New York: Greenwood Press, 2003.

_____. *Images, Issues, and Attacks: Television Advertising by Incumbents and Challengers in Presidential Elections*. New York: Lexington Books, 2006.

_____. *The Presidential Election of 1996: Clinton's Incumbency and Television*. Westport, CT: Praeger, 1998.

_____. *Presidential Elections in the Television Age: 1960–1992*. Westport, CT: Praeger, 1994.

Druckman, James, Lawrence R. Jacobs, and Eric Ostermeier. "Candidate Strategies on Prime Issues and Image." *Journal of Politics* 66: 1180–1202.

Dukakis, Kitty. *Now You Know*. New York: Simon & Schuster, 1990.

Dukakis, Michael S., and Rosabeth Moss Kanter. *Creating the Future: The Massachusetts Comeback and Its Promise for the Future*. New York: Summit Books, 1988.

Echols, Alice. *Daring to Be Bad*. Minneapolis: University of Minnesota Press, 1989.

Eisinger, Robert M. *The Evolution of Presidential Polling*. New York: Cambridge University Press, 2003.

Erlich, Howard S. "Populist Rhetoric Reassessed: A Paradox." *Quarterly Journal of Speech* 63: 140–151.

FitzSimon, Martha. *The Finish Line: Covering the Campaign's Final Days*. Nashville, TN: Freedom Forum Media Studies, 1993.

Ford, Gerald R. *A Time to Heal: The Autobiography of Gerald R. Ford*. Surry Hills: Harper & Row/Reader's Digest, 1979.

Frank, Thomas. *What's the Matter with Kansas?: How Conservatives Won the Heart of America*. New York: Owl Books, 2005.

Finkel, S.E. "Reexamining the 'Minimal Effects' Model in Recent Presidential Elections." *Journal of Politics* 55: 1–21.

Gaines, Richard, and Michael Segal. *Dukakis: The Man Who Would Be President*. New York: Avon Books, 1988.

Garramone, Gina M. "Issue versus Image Orientation and Effects of Political Advertising." *Communication Research* 10: 59–76.

Geertz, Clifford. *The Interpretation of Cultures: Selected Essays*. New York: Basic Books, 1977.

Germond, Jack W., and Jules Witcover. *Mad as Hell: Revolt at the Ballot Box, 1992*. New York: Warner Books, 1993.

Gilbert, Robert E. *Television and Presidential Politics*. Boston: Christopher Publishing House, 1972.

Gilmore, James H. *Authenticity: What Consumers Really Want*. Cambridge, MA: Harvard Business School Press, 2007.

Goldman, Peter, and Tony Fuller. *The Quest for the Presidency 1984*. New York: Bantam Books, 1984.

Greenberg, David. *Nixon's Shadow: The History of the Image*. New York: W.W. Norton, 2004.

Hacker, Kenneth L. *Candidate Images in Presidential Elections*. Westport, CT: Praeger, 1995.

_____. *Presidential Candidate Images*. Lanham, MD: Rowman & Littlefield Publishers, 2004.

Hacker, Kenneth L., Walter Zakahi, Maury J. Giles, and Shaun McQuitty. "Components of Candidate Images: Statistical Analysis of the Issue-Persona Dichotomy in the Presidential Campaign of 1966." *Communication Monographs* 67: 227–238.

Halberstam, David. *War in a Time of Peace: Bush, Clinton, and the Generals*. New York: Scribner, 2002.

Handley, William R., and Nathaniel Lewis, eds. *True West: Authenticity and the American West*. Toronto: Bison Books, 2007.

Harris, Richard. *A Cognitive Psychology of Mass Communication*. New York: Routledge, 2009.

Hart, Roderick P. *Seducing America: How Television Charms the Modern Voter*. Thousand Oaks, CA: Sage Publications, 1998.

Harvard University, Institute of Politics. *Campaign for President: The Managers Look at '76*. Cambridge: Ballinger, 1977.

_____. *Campaign for President: The Managers Look at '84*. New York: Auburn House, 1986.

_____. *Campaign for President: The Managers Look at '88*. New York: Auburn House, 1989.

_____. *Campaign for President: The Managers Look at '92*. Boston: Puritan, 1994.

_____. *Campaign for President: The Managers Look at '96*. Hollis, NH: Hollis, 1997.

_____. *Campaign for President: The Managers Look at 2000*. Hollis, NH: Hollis, 2003.

Hayward, Steven F. *The Age of Reagan: The Conservative Counterrevolution: 1980–1989*. New York: Crown Forum, 2009.

Heidegger, Martin. *Being and Time*. New York: Harper Perennial Modern Classics, 2008.

Henry, David, and Kurt Ritter. *Ronald Reagan: The Great Communicator*. New York: Greenwood Press, 1992.

Hillygus, D. Sunshine, and Todd G. Shields. *The Persuadable Voter: Wedge Issues in Presidential Campaigns*. Princeton, NJ: Princeton University Press, 2009.

Hobsbawm, Eric. *The Invention of Tradition*. New York: Cambridge University Press, 1992.

Hofstader, Richard. *Anti-intellectualism in American Life*. New York: Alfred A. Knopf, 1963.

Hohenberg, John. *Reelecting Bill Clinton: Why America Chose a "New" Democrat*. Syracuse, NY: Syracuse University Press, 1998.

Holbrook, Thomas M. *Do Campaigns Matter?* Thousand Oaks, CA: Sage Publications, 1996.

Hunt, Lynn, and Victoria E. Bonnell. *Beyond the Cultural Turn: New Directions in the Study of Society and Culture*. Berkeley: University of California Press, 1999.

Jacobs, Meg, Julian Zelizer, and William Novak. *The Democratic Experiment: New Directions in Political History*. Princeton, NJ: Princeton University Press, 2003.

Jacoby, Susan. *Age of American Unreason*. New York: Pantheon Books, 2008.

Jacoby, William G., Michael S. Lewis-Beck, Helmut Norpoth, and Herbert F. Weisberg. *The American Voter Revisited*. Ann Arbor: University of Michigan Press, 2008.

Jamieson, Kathleen Hall. *Dirty Politics: Deception, Distraction, and Democracy*. New York: Oxford University Press, 1993.

_____. *Eloquence in an Electronic Age: The Transformation of Political Speechmaking*. New York: Oxford University Press, 1990.

_____. *Packaging the Presidency: History and Criticism of Presidential Campaign Advertising*. 3d ed. New York: Oxford University Press, 1996.

Jamieson, Kathleen Hall, and Paul Waldman. *The Press Effect: Politicians, Journalists, and the Stories That Shape the Political World*. New York: Oxford University Press, 2004.

Johnson, Victoria E. *Heartland TV: Prime Time Television and the Struggle for U.S. Identity*. New York: New York University Press, 2008.

Johnston, Anne, and Lynda Lee Kaid. *Videostyle in Presidential Campaigns: Style and Content of Televised Political Advertising*. Westport, CT: Praeger, 2000.

Jones, Kevin T. *The Role of Televised Debates in the U.S. Presidential Election Process (1960–2004)*. New Orleans: University Press of the South, 2005.

Kaid, Lynda Lee, and Dianne G. Bystrom. *Electronic Election: Perspectives on the 1996 Campaign Communication*. Mahwah, NJ: Lawrence Erlbaum, 1999.

Kaid, Lynda Lee, and Anne Johnston. "Image Ads and Issue Ads in U.S. Presidential Advertising: Using Videostyle to Explore Stylistic Differences in Televised Political Ads from 1952–2000." *Journal of Communication* 52: 281–300.

Kaid, Lynda Lee, and Dan Nimmo. *New Perspectives on Political Advertising (Political Communication Yearbook)*. 1st ed. Carbondale: Southern Illinois University Press, 1986.

Kendall, Kathleen, and J.O. Yum. "Persuading the Blue-Collar Voter: Issues, Images, and Homophily." *Communication Yearbook 8:* 707–722.

Kern, Montague. *30-Second Politics: Political Advertising in the Eighties*. Westport, CT: Praeger Paperback, 1989.

Lakoff, George. *Moral Politics: How Liberals and Conservatives Think*. Chicago: University of Chicago Press, 2002.

_____. *The Political Mind: A Cognitive Scientist's Guide to Your Mind and Its Politics*. New York: The Penguin Group, 2008.

Lasch, Christopher. *The Culture of Narcissism: American Life in an Age of Diminishing Expectations*. New York: W.W. Norton, 1991.

Lazarsfeld, Paul. *The People's Choice*. 3d ed. New York: Columbia University Press, 1968.

Leuchtenburg, William E. *The White House Looks South: Franklin D. Roosevelt, Harry S. Truman, Lyndon B. Johnson*. Baton Rouge: Louisiana State University Press, 2007.

Lieven, Anatol. *America Right or Wrong: An Anatomy of American Nationalism*. New York: Oxford University Press, 2004.

Lindholm, Charles. *Culture and Authenticity*. Malden: Wiley-Blackwell, 2008.

Loevy, Robert D. *The Flawed Path to the Presidency 1992: Unfairness and Inequality in the Presidential Selection Process*. Albany: State University of New York Press, 1995.

_____. *The Manipulated Path to the White House—1996*. Lanham, MD: University Press of America, 2002.

Lowi, Theodore J. *The Personal President: Power Invested, Promised Unfulfilled*. Ithaca, NY: Cornell University Press, 1986.

Lucas, Peter. *Luke on Duke: Snapshots in Time: Collected Michael Dukakis Columns by the Boston Herald*. Boston: Quinlan Press, 1988.

McCombs, Maxwell, Donald Lewis Shaw, and David Weaver. *Communication and Democracy: Exploring the Intellectual Frontiers in Agenda-Setting Theory.* Mahwah, NJ: Lawrence Erlbaum, 1997.

McGinniss, Joseph. *The Selling of the President, 1968.* New York: Penguin Books, 1969.

McGirr, Lisa. *Suburban Warriors: The Origins of the New American Right.* Princeton, NJ: Princeton University Press, 2001.

Meyer, Peter. *James Earl Carter: The Man and the Myth.* New York: Andrews McMeel, 1978.

Mickelson, Sig. *The Electric Mirror: Politics in an Age of Television.* New York: Dodd/Mead, 1972.

Miles, William. *The Image Makers: A Bibliography of American Presidential Campaign Biographies.* Metuchen, NJ: Scarecrow Press, 1979.

Miller, Arthur, and Bruce Gronbeck. *Presidential Campaigns and American Self Images.* London: Westview, 1994.

Mondale, Walter F. *The Accountability of Power: Toward a Responsible Presidency.* New York: D. McKay, 1975.

Morreale, Joanne. *A New Beginning: A Textual Frame Analysis of the Political Campaign Film.* Albany: State University of New York Press, 1991.

Nichols, David K. *The Myth of the Modern Presidency.* University Park: Pennsylvania State University Press, 1994.

Nimmo, Dan. "Political Image Makers and the Mass Media." *Annals of the American Academy of Political and Social Science* 427: 33–44.

Nimmo, Dan D., and Robert L. Savage. *Candidates and Their Images: Concepts, Methods and Findings.* Reading: Scott Foresman, 1976.

_____. *Politics in Familiar Contexts: Projecting Politics through Popular Media.* Norwood: Ablex, 1990.

Nimmo, Dan, and Larry David Smith. *Cordial Concurrence: Orchestrating National Party Conventions in the Telepolitical Age.* Westport, CT: Praeger, 1991.

Noonan, Peggy. *What I Saw at the Revolution: A Political Life in the Reagan Era.* New York: Random House Trade Paperbacks, 2003.

_____. *When Character Was King: A Story of Ronald Reagan.* New York: Viking, 2002.

Norton, Anne. *Republic of Signs: Liberal Theory and American Popular Culture.* Chicago: University of Chicago Press, 1993.

Novak, Michael. *Choosing Presidents: Symbols of Political Leadership.* New Brunswick, NJ: Transaction, 1991.

Nunberg, Geoffrey. *Talking Right: How Conservatives Turned Liberalism into a Tax-Raising, Latte-Drinking, Sushi-Eating, Volvo-Driving, New York Times–Reading, Body-Piercing, Hollywood.* New York: Public Affairs, 2007.

Ongiri, Amy Abugo. *Spectacular Blackness: The Cultural Politics of the Black Power Movement and the Search for a Black Aesthetic.* Charlottesville: University of Virginia Press, 2009.

Ortner, Sherry. *The Fate of "Culture": Geertz and Beyond.* Berkeley: University of California Press, 1999.

Orvell, Miles. *The Real Thing: Imitation and Authenticity in American Culture, 1880–1940.* Chapel Hill: University of North Carolina Press, 1989.

Owen, Diana. *Media Messages in American Presidential Elections.* New York: Greenwood Press, 1991.

Palin, Sarah. *Going Rogue: An American Life.* New York: HarperCollins, 2009.

Parry-Giles, Shawn. "Mediating Hillary Rodham Clinton: Television News Practices and Image-Making in the Postmodern Age." *Critical Studies in Media Communication* 17: 205–226.

Parry-Giles, Shawn J., and Trevor Parry-Giles. *Constructing Clinton: Hyperreality and Presidential Image-Making in Postmodern Politics.* New York: Peter Lang, 2002.

Patterson, Thomas, and Robert D. McClure. "Television News and Political Advertising: The Impact of Exposure on Voter Beliefs." *Communication Research* 1: 3–31.

Patton, John H. "A Government as Good as Its People: Jimmy Carter and the Restoration of Transcendence to Politics." *Quarterly Journal of Speech* 63: 249–257.

Perot, Ross. *United We Stand.* New York: Hyperion, 1992.

Pessen, Edward. *The Log Cabin Myth: The Social Backgrounds of the Presidents.* New Haven, CT: Yale University Press, 1986.

Peterson, Russell Leslie. *Strange Bedfellows: How Late-Night Comedy Turns Democracy Into a Joke.* New Brunswick, NJ: Rutgers University Press, 2008.

Pfau, Susan A., Michael Brydon, and Steven R. Hellweg. *Televised Presidential Debates.* London: Greenwood, 1992.

Pfiffner, James P. *The Modern Presidency.* Belmont, CA: Wadsworth, 2007.

Phillips, Mark, and Gordon Schochet. *Questions of Tradition.* Toronto: University of Toronto Press, 2004.

Pinsky, Drew, and S. Mark Young. *The Mirror*

Effect: How Celebrity Narcissism Is Seducing America. New York: Harper, 2009.

Podhoretz, John. *Hell of a Ride: Backstage at the White House Follies 1989–1993.* New York: Simon & Schuster, 1993.

Pomper, Gerald M. *Election of 1976: Reports and Interpretations.* New York: Prentice Hall, 1978.

_____. *Election of 1980: Reports and Interpretations.* New York: Chatham House, 1981.

_____. *The Election of 1984.* New York: Chatham House, 1985.

_____. *The Election of 1988: Reports and Interpretations.* London: Chatham House, 1989.

_____. *Elections in America.* New York: Longman's, 1980.

_____. *Voters, Elections, and Parties.* New York: Transaction, 1992.

Popkin, Samuel L. *The Reasoning Voter: Communication and Persuasion in Presidential Campaigns.* Chicago: University of Chicago Press, 1994.

Poster, Mark. *Jean Baudrillard: Selected Writings.* Cambridge: Polity Press, 2001.

Ragsdale, Lyn. "Presidential Speechmaking and the Public Audience: Individual Presidents and Group Attitudes." *Journal of Politics* 49: 704–736.

Rarick, David, Mary Duncan, David Lee, and Laurinda Porter. "The Carter Persona: An Empirical Analysis of the Rhetorical Visions of Campaign '76." *Quarterly Journal of Speech* 63: 258–273.

Reagan, Ronald. *An American Life.* New York: Pocket, 1999.

_____. *The Reagan Diaries.* New York: Harper Perennial, 2009.

Reeves, Richard. *President Reagan: The Triumph of Imagination.* New York: Simon & Schuster, 2005.

Reinsch, J. Leonard. *Getting Elected: From Radio and Roosevelt to Television and Reagan.* New York: Hippocrene Books, 1990.

Renshon, Stanley. *The Clinton Presidency: Campaigning, Governing, and the Psychology of Leadership.* Oxford: Westview Press, 1994.

Rodriguez, Joseph A. *City against Suburb: The Culture Wars in an American Metropolis.* Westport, CT: Praeger, 1999.

Rossinow, Doug. *The Politics of Authenticity.* Columbia: Columbia University Press, 1998.

Rossiter, Clinton. *The American Presidency.* New York: New American Library, 1960.

Rudd, Robert. "Issues as Image in Political Campaign Commercials." *Western Journal of Speech Communication* 50: 102–118.

Sabato, J. Larry. *The Rise of Political Consultants.* New York: Basic Books, 1981.

Scammon, Richard M., and Ben J. Wattenberg. *The Real Majority.* New York: Plume, 1992.

Scheuer, Jeffrey. *The Sound Bite Society: How Television Helps the Right and Hurts the Left.* New York: Routledge, 2001.

Schlesinger, Arthur. *The Imperial Presidency.* New York: Popular Library, 1973.

Schoenwald, Jonathan. *A Time for Choosing: The Rise of Modern American Conservatism.* New York: Oxford University Press, 2002.

Schram, Martin. *The Pursuit of the Presidency 1980.* New York: Putnam, 1980.

Schroeder, Alan. *The Presidential Debates: Fifty Years of High Risk TV.* New York: Columbia University Press, 2008.

Schuessler, Alexander A. *A Logic of Expressive Choice.* Princeton, NJ: Princeton University Press, 2000.

Schulman, Bruce J. *The Seventies: The Great Shift in American Culture, Society, and Politics.* New York: Free Press, 2001.

Shafer, Byron, and Anthony Badger. *Contesting Democracy: Substance and Structure in American Political History, 1775–2000.* Lawrence: University Press of Kansas, 2001.

Sheehy, Gail. *Character: America's Search for Leadership.* New York: Random House Value Publishing, 1991.

Shogan, Colleen J. *The Moral Rhetoric of American Presidents.* College Station: Texas A&M University Press, 2006.

Silbey, Joel H. *Voters, Parties, and Elections.* Waltham, MA: Xerox College Publishers, 1972.

Skewes, Elizabeth A. *Message Control: How News Is Made on the Presidential Campaign.* Lanham, MD: Rowman & Littlefield Publishers, 2007.

Smoller, Fredric T. *The Six O'Clock Presidency: A Theory of Presidential Press Relations in the Age of Television.* Westport, CT: Praeger, 1990.

Spero, Robert. *The Duping of the American Voter: Dishonesty and Deception in Presidential Television.* New York: Lippincott & Crowell, 1980.

Steed, Robert, Laurence Moreland, and Tod Baker. *The 1992 Presidential Election in the South.* Westport, CT: Praeger, 1994.

Stroud, Kandy. *How Jimmy Won: The Victory Campaign from Plains to the White House.* New York: Morrow, 1977.

Sullivan, John L., et al., "Candidate Appraisal and Human Nature: Man and Superman in the 1984 Election." *Political Psychology* 11: 459–484.

Suny, Ronald Grigor. "Back and Beyond: Reversing the Cultural Turn?" *American Historical Review* 107: 1476–1499.

Taylor, Charles. *The Ethics of Authenticity.* Cambridge, MA: Harvard University Press, 1992.

Tenpas, Kathryn. *Presidents as Candidates: Inside the White House for the Presidential Campaign.* Routledge Reference Library of Social Science. New York: Routledge, 2003.

Trilling, Lionel. *Sincerity and Authenticity (The Charles Eliot Norton Lectures).* Cambridge, MA: Harvard University Press, 2006.

Troy, Gil. *Hillary Rodham Clinton: Polarizing First Lady.* Lawrence: University Press of Kansas, 2008.

_____. *Morning in America: How Ronald Reagan Invented the 1980s.* Princeton, NJ: Princeton University Press, 2007.

_____. *See How They Ran: The Changing Role of the Presidential Candidate.* Cambridge, MA: Harvard University Press, 1996.

Tulis, Jeffrey K. *The Rhetorical Presidency.* Princeton, NJ: Princeton University Press, 1988.

Tullock, Gordon. *The Economics of Politics.* Indianapolis, IN: Liberty Fund, 2005.

Tuman, Joseph S. *Political Communication in American Campaigns.* Los Angeles: Sage Publications, 2008.

Ungs, Thomas, and Dan Nimmo. *American Political Patterns Conflict and Consensus.* London: Little, Brown, 1973.

Verba, Sidney, Norman H. Nie, and John R. Petrocik. *The Changing American Voter.* Cambridge, MA: Harvard University Press, 1979.

Walton, Hanes. *The Native Son Presidential Candidate: The Carter Vote in Georgia.* Westport, CT: Praeger, 1992.

Walz, Jeffrey S., and John Comer. "State Responses to National Democratic Party Reform." *Political Research Quarterly* 52: 189–208.

Wanat, John. "Political Broadcast Advertising and Primary Election Voting." *Journal of Broadcasting* 18: 413–422.

Watterson, John Sayle. *The Games Presidents Play: Sports and the Presidency.* Baltimore: Johns Hopkins University Press, 2009.

Wayne, Stephen J. *The Road to the White House 1996: The Politics of Presidential Elections.* New York: St. Martin's, 1997.

Weaver, David H. *Media Agenda-Setting in a Presidential Election.* Westport, CT: Praeger, 1981.

West, Darrell M. *Air Wars: Television Advertising in Election Campaigns, 1952–2008.* Washington, DC: CQ Press, 2009.

Westen, Drew. *The Political Brain: The Role of Emotion in Deciding the Fate of the Nation.* New York: PublicAffairs, 2007.

_____. *Self and Society: Narcissism, Collectivism, and the Development of Morals.* New York: Cambridge University Press, 1985.

White, John Kenneth. *The New Politics of Old Values.* Lanham, MD: University Press of America, 1998.

Wicker, Tom. *One of Us.* New York: Random House, 1995.

Wilentz, Sean. *The Age of Reagan: A History, 1974–2008.* New York: HarperCollins, 2008.

Wills, Garry. *Reagan's America: Innocents at Home.* New York: Penguin, 2000.

Woodward, Bob. *The Choice.* New York: Simon & Schuster, 1997.

Zelizer, Julian, and Bruce Schulman, eds. *Rightward Bound: Making America Conservative in the 1970s.* Cambridge, MA: Harvard University Press, 2008.

Newspaper and Magazine Articles, Radio and Television Transcripts

Adair, Bill. "Down the Stretch He Comes: The Real Gore." *St. Petersburg Times,* November 1, 2000, South Pinellas Edition.

Adams, Noah. "Biographer Sees Dole Striding Confidently into the Fall." *NPR News,* August 16, 1996.

_____. "Profile: Views of Working-Class Men on Who Should Succeed President Clinton." *NPR All Things Considered,* January 27, 2000.

Alter, Jonathan. "Searching for Authenticity." *Newsweek,* March 2, 1992.

American National Election Studies Cumulative Data File, 1952–1992.

American National Election Studies, Guide to Public Opinion and Electoral Behavior, Party Identification Scale 1952–2004: Strength of Party Affiliation.

American National Election Studies, Guide to Public Opinion and Electoral Behavior: Strength of Partisanship 1952–2004.

Anderson, Curt. "Roaming like Oprah, Elizabeth Dole Stresses Husband's Human Side." Associated Press, August 14, 1996, Wednesday p.m. cycle.

Apple, R.W. "Campaign '76: Barren and Petty." *New York Times,* October 20, 1976.

_____. "A Muted Dole Persona." *New York Times,* September 26, 1996.

Baker, Russell. "Jimmies for All Occasions." *New York Times,* October 12, 1976.

Ball, Karen. "Just Bob, in Grand Ole Style." *Daily News*, August 11, 1996.

Barrett, Laurence, Evan Thomas, and Sam Allis. "The Goal: A Landslide." *Time*, November 5, 1984.

_____. "Smelling the Big Kill." *Time*, September 17, 1984.

Bedard, Paul. "Bubba-Courting Bush Invades Gore Country." *Washington Times*, September 30, 1992.

Benedetto, Richard. "Dole Missing a Beat in GOP Heartland." *USA Today*, September 20, 1996.

Berke, Richard. "You Have Now Entered the Black Hole of American Politics." *New York Times*, April 7, 1996.

Biddle, Frederic. "Dole Forgot to Save the Best for Last." *Boston Globe*, August 16, 1996, Friday City Edition.

"Bob Dole Beats President Clinton in Race for Laughs." Associated Press Worldstream, September 13, 1996.

Boyd, Gerald. "Bush and Dukakis Fight On, with Gap Closing a Bit." *New York Times*, November 6, 1988.

Brady, James. "One Pundit's Advice." *Advertising Age*, November 4, 1996.

Broder, David. "Bush KO'd 'Doonesbury'—and Himself." *Washington Post*, August 21, 1988.

_____. "California's Swing Voters Proving Hard to Please." *Washington Post*, June 5, 1988.

_____. "Campaign Is Wary of Garden Path." *Washington Post*, September 1, 1996.

_____. "Election '84; Overriding the Issues; Mondale Finds Message Obscured." *Washington Post*, September 23, 1984.

_____. "Forgive and Forget." *Washington Post*, September 9, 1984.

Brown, John Edward. "Letters: Nov. 12, 1984." *Time*, November 12, 1984.

Brownstein, Ronald. "Gore Takes Hits for His Elian Stand from Friend and Foe Alike." *Los Angeles Times,* April 1, 2000.

"Bush Draws Contrasts with Rival." *Washington Post*, November 2, 1988, Wednesday Final Edition.

Canellos, Peter S. "Dole's Imagery, Values Ring True for Local Vets." *Boston Globe*, August 16, 1996.

Carlson, Margaret. "Shoot-Out at Gender Gap." *Time*, August 8, 1988.

_____. "A Tale of Two Childhoods." *Time*, June 20, 1988.

"Carter!" *Time*, November 15, 1976.

"Carter's Campaign Tone." *Christian Science Monitor*, September 22, 1980, Midwestern Edition.

CBS News. "Bush and Gore Do New York." *CBS Worldwide,* October 20, 2000.

CBS News/New York Times 1976 Election Polls 1–9.

CBS News/New York Times Election Day Survey, November 6, 1984.

CBS News/New York Times Poll, October 23–25, 1984.

Connolly, Ceci. "Tonight's Show Is All about Bob Dole." *St. Petersburg Times*, August 15, 1996, South Pinellas Edition.

"Daley Welcomes Mondale at End of Whistle-Stopping Train Trip." *New York Times*, September 21, 1976.

"December 2007 Political Communications Study." Interviewing Dates: December 19, 2007–January 2, 2008. Pew Research Center for the People and the Press.

Diaz-Balart, José, and Troy Roberts. "Small Towns Greet President Clinton on His Cross-Country Trip." *CBS This Morning*, August 27, 1996.

Dillin, John. "'84 Campaign Follows Classic Script." *Christian Science Monitor*, September 10, 1984.

Dionne, E.J. "The Fight for Florida." *Washington Post*, October 10, 2000.

_____. "New Poll Shows Attacks by Bush Are Building Lead."*New York Times*, October 26, 1988, Late City Final Edition.

_____. "Voters Say They're at Fault as Well as the Candidates." *New York Times*, November 22, 1988, Late City Final Edition.

Dowd, Maureen. "Bush and Dukakis Spar Over Issue of Who Is the Better Conservative." *New York Times*, June 8, 1988.

_____. "Whaddaya Mean Accent? She Talks Queens!" *New York Times*, October 1, 1984, Late City Final Edition.

_____. "White House Memo; Adrift in Bush's Circle Seeking the Common Man." *New York Times*, December 1, 1991.

Dunham, Richard S., with Jessica McCann and Elizabeth Roberts. "Bob's Doleful Demographics." *Business Week*, October 14, 1996.

Editorial, *Grand Rapids Press*, September 19, 1984.

Editorial, "Sure Loser in the Debate: The Format." *New York Times*, October 15, 1988, Late City Final Edition.

Edwards, Mickey. "Commentator Advises Dole to Focus on Clear Message." *NPR All Things Considered*, June 7, 1996.

Enda, Jodi. "Back in Hot Springs, Old Pals Remember a Presidential Boy." *Philadelphia Inquirer*, September 24, 1996.

Evans, Eli. "All the Candidates' Clothes: Costume Is Key in the Song and Dance of Politics." *New York Times*, September 19, 1976.

Farrell, John Aloysius. "Candidates Compete to Satisfy Voter Craving for Authenticity: Campaign '92." *Boston Globe*, August 24, 1992.

Fields, Suzanne. "'Uncle' Bob Dole." *Washington Times*, July 8, 1996.

Fineman, Howard. "Talk Show Primary." *Newsweek*, October 2, 2000.

Ford, Royal. "New Hampshire Seems Cool to Dole's Latest Try." *Boston Globe*, October 20, 1996.

Garry, Clifford. "Welcome to Elmore, Home of Fritz Mondale." *People*, July 23, 1984.

"Geraldine Ferraro: A Break with Tradition." *Time*, July 23, 1984.

Goldman, Peter. "Sizing Up Carter." *Newsweek*, September 13, 1976.

Goodman, Ellen. "Are Politics Getting Too Personal?" *Washington Post*, August 31, 1996.

"Gore: Convention Kiss Was Impromptu." Associated Press Online, August 21, 2000.

"Gov. Dukakis: Trapped." *Washington Post*, October 16, 1988.

"Governor George W. Bush (R–TX) Delivers Remarks at Campaign Rally." FDCH Political Transcripts, September 4, 2000.

Greenfield, Meg. "Mondale: Why He's Falling Short." *Washington Post*, September 12, 1984.

_____. "Rediscovering 'Real People.'" *Newsweek*, January 20, 1992.

Grier, Peter. "Kindler, Gentler Conventions Target Key Swing Vote." *Christian Science Monitor*, August 30, 1996.

Grove, Lloyd. "Simplicity Credited in Bush Surge." *Washington Post*, October 15, 1988.

Harris, John. "Clinton Starts, Finishes with the Middle Class." *Washington Post*, October 28, 1996.

_____. "Next Stop, Campaign Heaven." *Washington Post*, August 27, 1996.

_____. "A VP for Average Folks." *Washington Post*, October 14, 1988.

Harris, Leon. "Gallup Poll: Gore Emerges Winner of Convention Season." *CNN News*, August 29, 2000.

Harsch, Joseph C. "Bush's Prospects." *Christian Science Monitor*, August 16, 1988.

Heller, Richard. "Junking the President for Votes on a Plate." *Mail on Sunday*, June 16, 1996.

Herbert, Bob. "In America; Defining Al Gore." *New York Times*, August 17, 2000.

Holloway, Diane. "Bush and Gore Hit the Talk-Show Trail to Show a Softer, Funnier Side." Cox News Service, November 5, 2000.

Hook, Janet. "Skeptical Voters Foster the Tell-All Candidate." *Congressional Quarterly Weekly Report*, August 1, 1992.

"How Southern Is He?" *Time*, September 27, 1976.

Hughes, John. "Gore's Friends Out to Dispel His Wooden Image." Associated Press, August 17, 2000.

Hume, Brit. *ABC World News Tonight*, August 31, 1984.

Hunt, Terrence. "A Personal Look at Dole as He Lays Claim to the GOP Nomination." Associated Press, August 14, 1996.

"Jimmy's Mixed Signals." *Time*, October 4, 1976.

Jones, Jeffrey M. "Conventions Typically Result in Five-Point Bounce." Gallup News Service, August 20, 2008.

Kasindorf, Martin. "Gore, under Questioning, Insists the Kiss Was Just a Kiss." *USA Today*, August 22, 2000.

Kennedy, Helen. "I'm Very Gracious and Humbled." *Daily News*, July 30, 2000.

Klein, Joe. "The Year of the Voter." *Newsweek*, November 1992, Special Election Issue.

Kolbert, Elizabeth. "Politics: The Personalities — Public Figure, Private Person." *New York Times*, August 16, 1996.

Koppel, Ted. "Ted Koppel Recalls *Nightline* Politics." *Nightline*, November 20, 2005.

Kraus, Sidney. "Presidential Debates: Images and Issues." *Christian Science Monitor*, October 4, 1984.

Lacayo, Richard, James Carney, Michael Duffy, and Eric Pooley. "Campaign '96: The Big Funk." *Time*, May 6, 1996.

Lehrer, Jim, and Terrence Smith. "Building the Image." *NewsHour with Jim Lehrer*, August 3, 2000.

Lelyveld, Joseph. "So Far Carter and Ford Have Pushed the 'Trust' Issue." *New York Times*, October 3, 1976.

Lester, Will. "Delegates Upbeat Despite Polls." Associated Press Online, August 17, 2000.

Letterman, David. *CBS Late Show with David Letterman*, July 10, 1996.

Lombardi, Frank. "Bob's Got Authority in N.Y." *Daily News*, July 2, 1996.

Los Angeles Times Poll, October 11, 1984.

MacDonald, Norm. "NBC *Saturday Night Live*, Weekend Update." October 19, 1996. http://snltranscripts.jt.org/96/96cupdate.phtml.

Maddocks, Melvin. "Cool Candidates — Hot Summer." *Christian Science Monitor*, July 1, 1988.

Malbin, Michael. "Many Races for Congress Are Contests in Morality." *New York Times*, October 31, 1976.

Mann, Judy. "Nicer Guys Finish First." *Washington Post,* July 20, 1988.

Marz, Larry. "Dukakis by the People Who Know Him Best." *Newsweek,* July 25, 1988.

McGrory, Mary. "Sharpening the Focus." *Washington Post,* October 27, 1988.

Mintz, John. "Nobody Here but Us Country Boys? Yeah, Right." *Washington Post National Weekly Edition,* June 1–7, 1992.

Mitchell, Andrea, Roger Mudd, and John Chancellor. "NBC News Special Coverage, Republican National Convention." *NBC News,* August 23, 1984.

Mohr, Charles. "Moments of Spontaneity Reveal Character of Carter's Campaign." *New York Times,* September 13, 1976.

"Mondale Shows Wit in Accepting Supporting Role in the Campaign." *New York Times,* September 16, 1976.

Moore, David. "Gore 'Bounce' in Presidential Race Due to Overall Positive Reassessment of Vice President." Gallup News Service, August 23, 2000.

Morrow, Lance. "Of Myth and Memory." *Time,* October 24, 1988.

Nagourney, Adam, and Elizabeth Kolbert. "After the Election: Anatomy of a Loss." *New York Times,* November 8, 1996.

Newport, Frank, Jeffrey M. Jones, and Lydia Saad. "Ronald Reagan from the People's Perspective." Gallup News Service, June 2004.

Nielsen Media Research Report. "Highest Rated Presidential Debates: 1960–2008."

Nielsen Media Research Report. "Political Debates: Presidential Debates 1960–2004."

Nyhan, David. "For Dole, a Week That Went Up in Smoke." *Boston Globe,* July 14, 1996.

_____. "'Nice' VP, Dull Duke." *Boston Globe,* October 14, 1988.

"Ohio Economic Indicators Quarterly Report." Record number S6260–1. Ohio Department of Development, 1984.

"Once More, with Feeling." *People,* November 19, 1984.

Parry, Robert. "He's No Pinocchio." *Washington Monthly,* April 2000.

"The People, the Press and Politics, Campaign '92 Survey XI." Times Mirror Center for the People and the Press, September 17, 1992.

"Personalities Overpower Parties, Anderson Says." *New York Times,* September 30, 1984.

Pertman, Ada. "A Democratic Beachhead amid Vast GOP Ocean." *Boston Globe,* August 13, 1996.

Pew Research Center Report. "The People, the Press and Politics Campaign '92: The Clinton Converts Survey X." Pew, August 7, 1992.

Pew Research Center Survey, September 5–8, 1996.

Pew Survey Center Report. "A Dull Campaign, Clinton Will Win Say More Than 70% of Voters." Pew, August 2, 1996.

Pew Survey Center Report. "Voter Opinions Stalled." Pew, October 25, 2000.

Phillips, Krya. "Bush's Chief Strategist Karl Rove Previews Tonight's Debate." *CNN Early Edition,* October 3, 2000.

Phillips, Ron. "Reagan and Mondale Bring Their Own Debate Styles to Louisville." United Press International, October 7, 1984, BC cycle.

_____. United Press International, July 24, 1984, Tuesday a.m. cycle.

"Pollsters Talking about Reagan Landslide." Associated Press, September 21, 1984, Friday a.m. cycle.

Polman, Dick. "Tonight, a Chance for Dole to Fill in Gaps." *Philadelphia Inquirer,* August 15, 1996.

"Pop Culture: Campaign Back to 'What America Really Watches.'" *Hotline,* October 20, 2000.

Powell, Michael. "The Sons of Their Fathers." *Washington Post,* August 10, 2000.

Purdum, Todd S. "Politics: The Democrat." *New York Times,* November 1, 1996.

Raines, Howell. "A Chance to Change Psychology of Election." *New York Times,* October 7, 1984, Late City Final Edition.

_____. "A Contrast on TV." *New York Times,* September 5, 1984, Late City Final Edition.

Raum, Tom. "Bush Campaigns in Gore Country." Associated Press, October 10, 2000, Tuesday BC cycle.

_____. "Bush Pokes Fun at Self on Leno." Associated Press Online, October 30, 2000.

"The Reagan Kids: A Look at What Could Be the Nation's Next First Family: Patti, Ron, Maureen and Mike." *People,* July 21, 1980.

Reston, James. "Washington; Debating the Debates." *New York Times,* October 7, 1984, Late City Final Edition.

Rich, Frank. "The Man from Russell." *New York Times,* July 27, 1996.

Richman, Alan, and Cable Neuhouse. "Up from Olympus." *People,* July 25, 1988.

Robinson, Walter. "Campaign '88." *Boston Globe,* October 30, 1988.

Rosenberg, Howard. "Lessons of First Meeting Provide Candidates with Strategy." *Los Angeles Times,* October 12, 2000.

Rosenblatt, Roger. "Reagan Country." *Time,* November 19, 1984.

Royse, David. "George W. Bush Greets NASCAR Racers, Fans." Associated Press State and Local Wire, Saturday, July 1, 2000, BC cycle.

Sack, Kevin. "Oprah Show Lets Gore Reach Out to Women." *New York Times*, September 12, 2000.

Safire, William. "Republican National Convention Commentary." *PBS News Hour* Special Coverage, August 15, 1996.

_____. "Salome Tactics." *New York Times*, November 3, 1988.

Schindehette, Susan. "Warming to the Task." *People*, August 21, 2000.

Schorr, Daniel. "Empathy Emerges as Main Theme in Presidential Race." *NPR News All Things Considered*, July 24, 1996.

Schram, Martin. "Reagan Introduced on Screen." *Washington Post*, August 24, 1984.

"Selling 'Em Jimmy and Jerry." *Time*, October 11, 1976.

Seplow, Stephen. "Crafting a Winning Message: Both Parties Skip Politics for Touchy, Feely Images." *Philadelphia Inquirer*, September 1, 1996.

Shanahan, Mike. "Future Demo Candidates Must Look Good on TV." Associated Press, November 8, 1984, Thursday BC cycle.

_____. "The Public Mondale: Quiet Dignity and Subtle Humor." Associated Press, October 28, 1984, Sunday BC cycle.

"The Shape of the Next Four Years." *Time*, November 8, 1976.

Shapiro, Margaret. "Patronage Still King in Queens." *Washington Post*, August 29, 1984.

Shapiro, Walter. "Bush Scores a Warm Win." *Time*, Monday, October 24, 1988.

_____. "It's the Year of the Handlers." *Time*, Monday, October 3, 1988.

Sisler, Peter. "Policy versus Personality to Decide US Election." *Deutsche Presse-Agentur*, August 18, 2000, BC cycle.

Slater, Wayne. "Bush Campaign Focusing on Texan's Personality." *Dallas Morning News*, July 30, 2000.

Stengel, Richard. "A Dose of Old-Time Populism." *Time*, November 7, 1988.

_____. "The Likability Sweepstakes." *Time*, October 24, 1988.

_____. "The Man behind the Message." *Time*, August 22, 1988.

Stouffer, Linda, and Skip Loescher. "Democratic National Convention: Gore Delivers Opening Statement in His Case to Be President." *Ahead of the Curve*, August 18, 2000.

Sundquist, James L. "The 1984 Election: How Much Realignment?" *Brookings Review* 3, no. 2, Special Election Issue (Winter 1985).

"Support with Serious Reservations." *Time*, October 25, 1976.

"A Tie Goes to the Gipper." *Time*, October 29, 1984.

"To Finish What Is Well Started." *Newsweek*, February 6, 1984.

Toner, Robin. "Political Memo; Dukakis Works at Warmth, Yet Tries to Keep His Cool." *New York Times*, August 8, 1988.

"Topics of the Times: Blue Blood." *New York Times*, June 12, 1988.

Vernaci, Richard. "Delegates See Dukakis as Dependable, Honest, Dull, Short." Associated Press, July 16, 1988, a.m. cycle.

"Vice President Gore on CNN's *Late Edition*." Cable News Network Transcript, March 9, 1999.

Walczak, Lee. "Pork Politics." *Business Week*, August 15, 1988.

Wall Street Journal/NBC News Poll, June 20–26, 1996.

"Walter Mondale: Getting a Second Look." *Time*, October 22, 1984.

Walters, Barbara, and Hugh Downs. "The Clintons Up Close." *20/20*, September 20, 1996.

Weinraub, Bernard. "Mondale's New Campaign Themes: Patriotism and Hard Work." *New York Times*, August 3, 1984.

Weisburg, Jacob. "Bushisms of the Week." *Slate*, August 28, 2000.

West, Dick. "Election Year Tremors." *Lodi News-Sentinel*, August 13, 1984.

"What's behind the Carter Magic?" *Economist*, April 17, 1976.

"Who Would You Rather Sit Down and Have a Beer With?" *Business Wire*, October 17, 2000.

Wicker, Tom. "In the Nation: A Balance for Bush." *New York Times*, July 29, 1988.

Wilkie, Dana. "With Farmer Families and Southern Drawl, Bush like Gore Aims to Be the 'People's' Candidate." Copley News Service, September 26, 2000.

Williams, Brian. "*SNL* Becomes Player in Campaign 2000." *The News with Brian Williams*, October 13, 2000.

Wills, Garry. "The Power Populist." *Time*, Monday, November 21, 1988.

Wooten, James. "Carter Seeking to Regain Flavor of the Early Days of Campaign." *New York Times*, October 2, 1976.

Campaign Commercials and Films

"Bio." 1976 Democratic Presidential Campaign Committee, Inc., 1976. Maker: Gerald Rafshoon. Museum of the Moving Image, *The*

Living Room Candidate: Presidential Campaign Commercials 1952–2008.

"Biography." President Ford Committee, 1976. Original air date October 7, 1976. Video courtesy of the Gerald R. Ford Presidential Library. Museum of the Moving Image, *The Living Room Candidate: Presidential Campaign Commercials 1952–2008.*

"Credibility." Bush-Quayle '88, 1988. Maker: Ailes Communications. Video courtesy of the George Bush Presidential Library. Museum of the Moving Image, *The Living Room Candidate: Presidential Campaign Commercials 1952–2008.*

"Election." 1976 Democratic Presidential Campaign Committee, Inc., 1976. Maker: Gerald Rafshoon. Museum of the Moving Image, *The Living Room Candidate: Presidential Campaign Commercials 1952–2008.*

"Family." Carter/Mondale Reelection Committee, Inc. Maker: Rafshoon Communications. Museum of the Moving Image, *The Living Room Candidate: Presidential Campaign Commercials 1952–2008.*

"Family/Children." Bush-Quayle '88, 1988. Video courtesy of the George Bush Presidential Library. Museum of the Moving Image, *The Living Room Candidate: Presidential Campaign Commercials 1952–2008.*

"Family." President Ford Committee, 1976. Video courtesy of the Gerald R. Ford Presidential Library. Museum of the Moving Image, *The Living Room Candidate: Presidential Campaign Commercials 1952–2008.*

Ford, Gerald, interviewed by Jim Lehrer. *Debating Our Destiny.* Transcript from pbs.org.

"Lawyer." 1976 Democratic Presidential Campaign Committee, Inc., 1976. Maker: Gerald Rafshoon. Museum of the Moving Image, *The Living Room Candidate: Presidential Campaign Commercials 1952–2008.*

"Light." Carter/Mondale Reelection Committee, Inc. Maker: Rafshoon Communications. Museum of the Moving Image, *The Living Room Candidate: Presidential Campaign Commercials 1952–2008.*

"Nancy Reagan." Reagan Bush Committee, 1980. Maker: Campaign '80. Museum of the Moving Image, *The Living Room Candidate: Presidential Campaign Commercials 1952–2008.*

A New Beginning. Maker: Phil Dusenberry, Tuesday Team, Reagan-Bush '84. Video courtesy of Ronald and Nancy Reagan/ Ronald Reagan Presidential Library.

"Prouder, Stronger, Better." Reagan-Bush '84, 1984. Maker: Hal Riney, Tuesday Team. Original air date September 17, 1984. Video courtesy of Ronald and Nancy Reagan/ Ronald Reagan Presidential Library. Museum of the Moving Image, *The Living Room Candidate: Presidential Campaign Commercials 1952–2008.*

"Revolving Door." Bush-Quayle '88, 1988. Original air date October 3, 1988. Maker: Dennis Frankenberry and Roger Ailes. Video courtesy of the George Bush Presidential Library. Museum of the Moving Image, *The Living Room Candidate: Presidential Campaign Commercials 1952–2008.*

"Rose." 1976 Democratic Presidential Campaign Committee, Inc., 1976. Maker: Gerald Rafshoon. Museum of the Moving Image, *The Living Room Candidate: Presidential Campaign Commercials 1952–2008.*

"South." 1976 Democratic Presidential Campaign Committee, Inc., 1976. Maker: Gerald Rafshoon. Museum of the Moving Image, *The Living Room Candidate: Presidential Campaign Commercials 1952–2008.*

The Sky's the Limit, Stuart Stevens and Mark MacKinnon for Bush-Cheney 2000.

"Tank Ride." Bush-Quayle '88, 1988. Original air date October 17, 1988. Maker: Dennis Frankenberry. Video courtesy of the George Bush Presidential Library. Museum of the Moving Image, *The Living Room Candidate: Presidential Campaign Commercials 1952– 2008.*

"Train." Reagan-Bush '84, 1984. Maker: Tuesday Team. Video courtesy of Ronald and Nancy Reagan/Ronald Reagan Presidential Library. Museum of the Moving Image, *The Living Room Candidate: Presidential Campaign Commercials 1952–2008.*

"Washington." 1976 Democratic Presidential Campaign Committee, Inc., 1976. Maker: Gerald Rafshoon. Video courtesy of Ronald and Nancy Reagan/Ronald Reagan Presidential Library. Museum of the Moving Image, *The Living Room Candidate: Presidential Campaign Commercials 1952–2008.*

Index